EFFIE
IN
VENICE

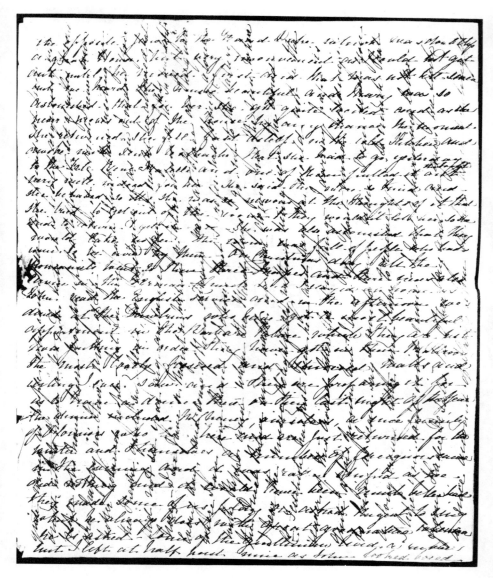

Effie Ruskin's letter of December 28, 1851

EFFIE
IN VENICE

᪜

Unpublished letters of Mrs. John Ruskin
written from Venice
between 1849 and 1852
edited by
MARY LUTYENS

PALLAS EDITIONS

If you would like further information
about titles published in the
Pallas Editions series,
please write to:
Dept. T,
Pallas Athene,
59 Linden Gardens,
London W2 4HJ
or visit our website at
WWW.PALLASATHENE.NET

Series editor: Alexander Fyjis-Walker
Series assistants: Jenny Wilson and Ava Li
Series designer: James Sutton

Special thanks to Peter Khoroche

This edition published by Pallas Editions
in conjunction with Ostara Publishing 2001
First published by John Murray 1965

ISBN 1 873429 33 9

Printed in Italy

CONTENTS

Preface to a new edition vii
Preface to the 1965 edition xiii

✺

PART ONE

Prelude to Venice   3
The Journey Out   41
Winter in Venice   63
Rawdon Brown   90
Paulizza   104
Dancing with the Military   130
The Journey Home   152
London Again   169

✺

PART TWO

The Second Journey   179
At Home in Venice   188
Arrival of the Russians   207
Kindness of the Austrians   226
Radetzky at Last   249
Shining in Society   261
End of Carnival   287
The Robbery   312
Challenge to a Duel   331

Books Consulted 345
List of illustrations 346
Index 347

Paulizza's balloon for bombarding Venice

PREFACE
TO A NEW EDITION

ↇ

I first went to Venice in November 1924 when I was sixteen. A party
of us, including my mother, Krishnamurti and his brother Nitya,
spent three nights there at the old Luna Hotel where the Crusaders had
stayed on the way to the Holy Land. From Venice we were taking a
Lloyd Triestino boat to Bombay which was much cheaper and nicer
in every way than the P&O Line which my father, as a Government
official, was obliged to travel by. I was miserably in love and in spite
of the terribly cold weather found Venice the most romantic place imaginable and this greatly increased my misery. No one should ever go to
Venice when they are unhappy.

The second time I went there was on a delayed honeymoon with my
second husband, Joe Links (his first time), in April 1946. We stayed
at the Hotel Danieli on the Riva degli Schiavoni because this is where
John and Effie Ruskin had stayed and Joe was already deeply interested
in Ruskin whereas I found him unreadable.

Venice was very run down after the war. There were beggars in the
streets, a few of them showing off deformed children; nevertheless we
were enchanted with it and usually went back there for our annual holi-
day for the next fifty years. We would drive out by different routes,
staying at different places on the way. As soon as the airport opened
we also went for short visits at other times of year, always staying at
the Danieli for as long as we could afford it. At one time we thought
of getting an apartment but came to our senses in time: to take on
another responsibility (we already had a large flat in London and a
house in the country) in exchange for dozens of house-maids and clean
sheets and towels every day would be sheer madness.

The last thing we ever wanted in Venice was a social life. Our friends that first year were the barman and the concierge of the hotel. The barman took us home to meet his father who produced very passable little Giacomo Guardis in gouache to sell to the tourists. Instead of being ashamed of his dishonest means of livelihood he was very proud of it, as well he might be, and since we were friends of his son he had no hesitation in telling us about it. As he had been painting and not selling during the war he had quite a stack of pictures and gave us two of them. When we got home we had them beautifully framed and I still treasure them. The genuine Giacomo Guardis acquired later we had framed in the same way but not hung together.

I cannot remember the order in which changes appeared year by year as Venice returned to normal and prices rose steadily. Not all the changes were pleasant. The greatest outrage was the new Danieli, a hideous modern building on that wonderful site. It was joined to the original building by a passage at bedroom level so that the original lift and staircase could still be used but it also had an entrance at street level and a new bar. I must say, though, that an early breakfast on the roof terrace was a delight. One could watch the boats coming in from the mainland and the day-workers pouring out.

One of the pleasantest happenings was the opening of Harry's Bar which had been started in Rome by the present Arrigo's father who came to Venice with his bar. By then we were for a short time allowed to take a ridiculously small amount of money out of England but one could make 'arrangements'. We paid for part of Arrigo's education in England. When his father died and he took over the bar we were already friends. The food was the best in Venice and if one stuck to the vegetarian dishes, which I myself preferred, one could afford to eat there occasionally and we often had our dry martinis there before dinner. Gradually it became a tradition that Arrigo gave us a free dinner on our last evening in Venice.

Joe published his abridgement of Ruskin's *Stones of Venice* in 1960. I read and enjoyed it and realised for the first time what a brilliant writer Ruskin was. Joe told me how easy his abridgement had been: he had simply left out all the religion. I also understood, as one must to understand Ruskin, that he detested the Renaissance. He considered

S. Giorgio a contemptible building.

By this time I was immersed in Effie, having been to New York to study the Bowerswell Papers and having read Effie's weekly letters home, translated for us in the way described in the original preface to this book. I think I was so attracted to Effie because she was everything that I was not. Her Venice had now become my Venice. I was miserable when I returned there on the second visit to find that Paulizza had died. Although he had invented the weapon that had brought Venice to submission, I couldn't help loving him. My favourite mental picture of him and Ruskin is of them running races around the old buildings at Torcello (p. 147).

Joe and I had done the sights once, such as the inside of the Doge's Palace, although we often returned to the Accademia to see the Bellinis and Carpaccios, but otherwise we lived the life Joe describes in *Venice for Pleasure* (1966, 6th edition 1999). The difficulty of such a life was meeting acquaintances from England who suggested joining up for dinner. It was impossible to say, 'Unfortunately we are engaged for dinner every evening you are here,' for the chances were they would find us alone at Harry's Bar or at one of the few decent restaurants. We solved the problem by finding a small, secluded restaurant frequented only by Italians who frowned on us when we first went in there but soon got used to us.

It was different with our friends, of course. The Venice in Peril Fund was set up in 1971 and the members were all our friends. We were at first members of the London Committee which decided what to preserve. I was no use on the Committee. It was the fabric of the city I loved. Had I dared I would have suggested the permanent removal of the rust stains on the back of palace walls rather than the restoration of some treasure inside a church.

The Danieli was at some time joined to an existing annexe at the other side from the new building, again joined by a corridor at bedroom level but without a street entrance so there was no outward sign of its existence. It was here that the largest and most luxurious bedrooms were situated, all looking on to the Riva.

When the Cipriani Hotel was built on the Giudecca it was intended as a second class priced hotel with first class food, and it was very pleasant going there in its private boat and having a delicious meal in the garden looking out at S. Giorgio (I remember the blue table cloths). Then they built the swimming pool at the back and everything changed. Lunch was served at the side of the pool in the smell of half-nude human bodies covered in sun-tan oil, and a pretentiously grand restaurant was devised which became so popular that one could not book a table there for dinner at a reasonable hour even if one were staying at the hotel, and prices increased to first class although the bedrooms remained second class. We stayed there twice, as guests in exchange for giving lectures, Joe on Ruskin and I on Effie. It might be thought that our bedroom was so small because it was free but I had a look into many of the other bedrooms and they were all the same.

The sad day came when we could no longer stay in the Danieli in spite of the generous discount they gave us as their longest clients. We considered moving to a cheaper hotel along the Riva but decided this was too far from the Piazza. Finally we decided to move to the Luna, the closest to the Piazza, long since rebuilt since I stayed there in 1924. We discovered one room, at the back, usually available, with a view over the water entrance and private garden (now public) of what had been the palace in Effie's day and which brought me much closer to her on her second visit. It was from the first floor windows of the palace that she had watched the arrival of the young Emperor Franz Josef.

I feel compelled to end this preface by quoting a letter I received referring to the first footnote on p. 198.

MRS CLINTON DAWKINS
THE ORANGERY,
OVER NORTON PARK,
6th October 1967   OXFORDSHIRE.

Dear Madam,

I am reading and very much enjoying your book 'Effie in Venice' – and am writing in case it would interest you that the cannon ball mentioned on p. 198 is now in this room! The Consul at Venice in 1848 was my husband's grandfather. He had the cannon ball mounted on an oak stand, with a description of the incredible incident engraved on a small silver plaque. This is in French, and was taken, I believe, from a newspaper. With it there is also the relevant page from the Consul's diary.

Thank you for your lively book!

Yours truly, V. S. Dawkins

I requested a copy of the page from the Consul's diary which confirmed the miracle.

Denmarkhill 30th Sept
1849.

My dear Mother

I received your kind note
on my arrival in Park St. last
night. we only arrived there. there was
Mr. Ruskin. met us at the station
we went. or rather came out here
and found. Mrs Ruskin looking very
well. Mr Ruskin very ill. but both
quite pleased to see us and to let
us go to Italy and quite delighted
that Charlotte was to go with us
next morning we had some talk
about our arrangements and
had some private conversation
with Mr Ruskin what an extraordinary man he is he was
quite delighted that I spoke to
him evidently and said he had

Effie's first letter after leaving Bowerswell

PREFACE
TO THE 1965 EDITION

⁊

The main source of this book is the collection of letters, known as the Bowerswell Papers, acquired by the Pierpont Morgan Library of New York from Effie's grandson, Sir Ralph Millais, Bt, in 1950. It consists of letters received by members of the Gray family (with a few acquired later), dating from Effie's childhood until after her marriage to Millais. My first acknowledgement must, therefore, be to the Trustees of that Library and to its Director, Mr F. B. Adams, Jr, for permission to use the letters and for the privilege of being allowed to work in their beautiful house; I must also thank Mr Herbert Cahoon, their Curator of Autograph Manuscripts, and Miss Mary M. Kenway, who presides over the Reading Room, for their courtesy.

The Bowerswell Papers have had the advantage of being studied by Dr Helen Gill Viljoen in the course of her researches for her forthcoming monumental biography of Ruskin and its preliminary volume, *Ruskin's Scottish Heritage*. Dr Viljoen's scholarship has been applied to the placing of many of the letters in chronological order and to adding a number of helpful notes on them. Apart from this, I am most grateful to Dr Viljoen for her graciousness in permitting the publication of this book before her own, far more important one, has been completed.

Next must come acknowledgement of my debt to Effie's granddaughter, the Hon. Clare Stuart Wortley – and here a word must be said about the history of the letters. The great majority of them went to Effie's brother (the 'George' so often mentioned in them) after their mother's death in 1894, and in 1910 he sent them to his niece, Mrs Stuart Wortley (later Lady Stuart of Wortley). Her only daughter, Clare, spent a great deal of time studying them with a view to publication until her death in 1945. She transcribed many of them and added invaluable notes on family matters, and I am indeed deeply grateful to her cousin, Sir Ralph Millais, for lending me these transcriptions, allowing me to quote from them, and giving his blessing to the publication of the letters themselves. Unfortunately she did not work on any of the letters written from Venice. For transcribing these, a most difficult task, as most of them are crossed, I have had the benefit of Miss G. Kemp's skill for which I tender my best thanks.

At the time of the Ruskin sale at Brantwood in 1932, some bundles of letters, not catalogued, turned up – among them Ruskin's engagement letters to Effie, which he had taken back from her. They were bought at the auction by a Mr Telford of Grasmere, an antique dealer in whose shop they were seen by a Ruskin enthusiast, Mr W. Sharp. Mr Sharp wrote to Effie's daughter, Mary Millais, to tell her of this find, and eventually she and her sister, Lady Stuart, bought them. Miss Clare Stuart Wortley also transcribed these letters, the originals of which are now in the Bowerswell Papers.

In 1947, Admiral Sir William James, G.C.B. (another of Effie's grandsons), made a selection from the Bowerswell Papers for his book *The Order of Release* (in U.S.A., *John Ruskin and Effie Gray*). Only some fifteen of Effie's seventy-five letters from Venice were used, and only about 3,000 words extracted from them, so virtually the whole of these Venice letters have remained hitherto unpublished; moreover those 3,000 words are now seen in their original context.

The tracing of names and places more than a hundred years after they were written about has, of course, involved much travel and importuning of many kind and patient people. In Venice, Prince Clary Aldringen, with his unrivalled knowledge of the great European families of the nineteenth century, has been unfailingly helpful, often knowing where to go for information on points too obscure to come within even his own vast sphere. In Perth, where the graveyards have yielded up otherwise forgotten dates and relationships, I have also turned repeatedly to the Staff of the Reference Department of the Sandeman Public Library, Perth, who have been to considerable trouble for me. I am also indebted to the Public Record Office, the

Metropolitan Museum of Art, New York, the Fogg Art Museum, Massachusetts, and the London Transport Museum as well as to the Lear School of Embalming, Marette Frères, and Beecham's Proprietary Medicines.

Others who have also been particularly helpful to me are: Mr Cecil Woolf, Mr Nigel Capel Cure, Mr Victor Cavendish-Bentink, Dr Paul Kaufman, Mr John Fleming, Major A. A. Flatow, Miss Elizabeth Davison of the Arts Council, Mr R. L. Arrowsmith of Charterhouse, Captain A. Viruly, Signora Rosita Necanati, Lord Bruce, Mr John Gage, and the managements of the Danieli and Gritti Palace Hotels. I would like to thank my excellent and patient typist, Miss Teresa Tanner.

Apart from the Pierpont Morgan Library, the great repositories of original source material on Ruskin are at Yale University Library and the Ruskin Galleries at Bembridge, Isle of Wight. Yale is in possession of many letters from Ruskin to his father, including those written on the second journey covered by this book (those written on the first journey have unaccountably disappeared). The letters written by John Ruskin from Venice, from September 2, 1851, until June 29, 1852, were published in 1955 by the Yale University Press under the editorship of John Lewis Bradley; I am grateful to the editor for his transcription and to the publisher and Library for permission to quote from it.

The Ruskin Galleries at Bembridge contain a large number of Ruskin's diaries and notebooks, and the account-books of his father, John James Ruskin, as well as the latter's illuminating letters to his son, extracts from many of which, as well as one important complete letter, are now published for the first time. Not only have I been allowed to make unreserved use of this material, for which I am grateful to the Educational Trust Ltd and its Chairman, Mr R. G. Lloyd, C.B.E., Q.C., but I have also had the benefit of the exceptional knowledge of the Gallery's Curator, Mr James Dearden, to whom I now express my deepest appreciation. I also wish to express my thanks to Messrs George Allen and Unwin, John Ruskin's Literary Trustees, for permission to quote from his published and unpublished writings.

As to the letters themselves, they have been printed in their entirety except for minor omissions, such as descriptions of scenery, and the

major omission of most of the Perth and family news which Effie usually
began her letters by discussing and often ended by commenting on
further. These matters, and the inevitable notes about the people
concerned in order to identify them, would have proved too burden-
some for the general reader. A full transcription of the letters, however,
including those written on the two journeys out and home, with
complete annotations, is available at the Pierpont Morgan Library, New
York, the Ruskin Galleries, Bembridge, the Sandeman Library, Perth,
and the London Library.

For the sake of clarity I have punctuated the letters, a convenience
Effie seldom adopted, but have retained her own emphasis, capitals,
exclamation marks and spelling (in French as well as English) except
for the spelling of proper names where I have followed common
usage. All passages deleted are indicated by dots.

I wish to acknowledge the gracious permission of Her Majesty the
Queen to publish an extract from Queen Victoria's journal, and to
accord my gratitude to Mr Robert Mackworth-Young, the Librarian
of the Royal Library at Windsor.

PART ONE

PRELUDE TO VENICE

൶

On April 10, 1848, two months after his twenty-ninth birthday, John Ruskin married a very pretty Scottish girl of nineteen, Euphemia Chalmers Gray, usually called Effie. Six years later she secretly left him to return to her parents, and three months afterwards procured an annulment. Ruskin prepared a written statement in his defence in which he denied the impotency with which Effie charged him and tried to explain why the marriage had never been consummated. He then decided not to defend the suit and the statement remained in the files at his lawyer's office until it was published almost a hundred years later.[1] On July 3, 1855, Effie married John Everett Millais, whom Ruskin had championed in 1851 at a time when the critics were venomously attacking the Pre-Raphaelites. In this second marriage, which produced eight children, Effie found fulfilment for all her talents. She died in 1897, the year after Millais, aged sixty-nine.

Ruskin's biographers have given little space to his marriage. Cook and Wedderburn in their giant edition of his *Works* give it a few lines and the annulment a footnote, while Millais's son in his *Life* of his father is reticent to the point of not even hinting that Mrs John Ruskin whom Millais met in the Highlands in Chapter V and the Miss Euphemia Gray whom he married three chapters later are the same person. Ruskin and Effie themselves did their best to expunge all memory of their incompatible union, and had it not been for the preservation of his letters to her during their engagement it would never have been known that there was once passionate love, at any rate on his side.[2]

Between 1849 and 1852 they had two long periods in Venice together. Effie wrote home every week describing their daily life there

[1] In *Vindication of Ruskin* by J. H. Whitehouse.
[2] These letters, with the exception of one, and the omission of a few paragraphs, are published in *The Order of Release* by Admiral Sir William James.

at a time when the Grand Tourists had long since departed and the
Cook's tourists had not yet arrived—consequently a time about
which very little has been written in English. Effie, when she left
Ruskin, declared that she had never known a moment's happiness
with him, yet these letters show beyond all doubt that they had many
moments of happiness together, of gaiety even, sympathy, fun and
affection, and that, whatever the underlying dissatisfactions, and
however little either of them was willing to make any real sacrifice
to hold their marriage together, they did unwittingly give each
other during those first years a great deal for which neither of them
afterwards showed the other the slightest gratitude. Ruskin was a man
who suffered abominably from the torments of frustrated love and
Effie was able to give him that emotional freedom so necessary for
his best work; while he, as well as giving her opportunities for
travel and education, opened to her, through his genius, worlds far
beyond her provincial circle.

    Effie's father was George Gray, a Writer to the Signet, with a
prosperous practice in Perth, and a substantial house, Bowerswell
(pronounced Bowers Well as originally spelt) on Kinnoull Hill just
across the River Tay. In 1827 he had married Sophia Jameson,
daughter of Andrew Jameson, Sheriff Substitute of Fife. Perth was
a link between the Grays and the Ruskins. John Ruskin's paternal
grandfather had lived at Bowerswell for some years before committing
suicide there in 1817, and his father's only sister, Jessie, married
to a Perth man, Patrick Richardson, lived close by at Bridgend
until her death in 1828. John's father, John James Ruskin, used to
visit Jessie from London, and thus kept up his old friendship with
Mr Gray, and although John James never returned to Perth after
Jessie's death, the Grays visited the Ruskins whenever they went to
London.
    Effie, born May 7, 1828, was the eldest of the Gray children. At
twelve she was sent to Avonbank, a school at Stratford-on-Avon. On
the way there at the end of August, 1840, she stayed for a few days
with the Ruskins at 28 Herne Hill, Dulwich, where they were then
living. This was her first meeting with John. His father, John James,
a successful, self-made sherry merchant, had married in 1818, after
nine years of painful waiting, his first cousin, Margaret Cock, a poor
relation who had been his mother's companion since at least 1804.

John was their only child and although they adored each other they both doted on him.

Effie was again at Herne Hill in the summer holidays of 1841 when John became sufficiently interested to write for her his only fairy story, *The King of the Golden River*. This was a tragic summer for the Grays. The eldest of Effie's three little sisters, aged six, had died of scarlet fever on July 2 and it was decided that Effie should leave school and return home to be a comfort to her parents, but before she arrived both the other little girls, of five and three, died within a week of each other of the same fever. Two sons had also died in infancy, so now, apart from Effie, there were only two boys left in the family—George, seventeen months younger than Effie to whom she remained devoted all her life, and Andrew who had been born in January, 1840. Andrew too was to die in November, 1844. The Grays, however, in the course of the next fourteen years, had four more boys and two more girls, the eldest of whom are constantly mentioned in Effie's letters from Venice.

At Bowerswell Effie had the benefit of an excellent governess, Miss Joanna Thomson, who had been engaged to teach her little sisters. All the same, Mrs Gray wanted to send her back to Avonbank for the companionship of other girls, but Mr Gray said no, the house would be too quiet without her. Nevertheless she did return there in January, 1844, but only until June when she left school for good. Her headmistress, Miss Ainsworth, reported that she had endeared herself by 'her artless affectionate disposition and her wish for improvement'. She was always very quick and very eager to learn. She won prizes for French and history and when a German girl came to the school she was the only pupil to make any effort to talk to her in her own language. Miss Ainsworth also wrote that she danced beautifully and had a 'very clear and beautiful-toned voice'. At Avonbank she studied the piano under a pupil of Aloys Schmitt of Frankfurt, and became a good player, finding joy in music all her life. One thing the school failed in, however, and that was in curing her of her Scottish accent, in spite of the fact that she was 'not allowed to go much together' with her Scottish friends 'for fear of speaking Scotch'. This accent must have been an integral part of her charm and personality. Miss Thomson had stayed on at Bowerswell as a companion to Mrs Gray so Effie was able to continue lessons with her when she returned there, and it was evidently with Miss Thomson

that she studied German, for there is no record of her learning it at
Avonbank.

In October, 1846, she again stayed with the Ruskins—at Denmark
Hill this time where they had moved in 1843 to a large pleasant Geor-
gian house in seven acres of ground, half a mile from Herne Hill on
the same ridge. It was during this visit that John fell in love with
her. His mother begged him to wait before taking any decisive step,
and this he sulkily agreed to do but only because he believed Effie
to be a year younger than she was. One can sympathise with his
parents' wish to temporise. With his gifts they had every reason to
hope for a brilliant marriage for him, yet they knew the devastating effect frustrated love could have on his nervous temperament.
At the age of sixteen he had fallen passionately in love with Adèle
Domecq,[1] the second of the five daughters of Peter Domecq, Mr
Ruskin's Spanish partner in the sherry business, who, with her three
younger sisters, had come on a long visit to the Ruskins in 1836.
Although it was afterwards made out to Effie that Adèle's Roman
Catholicism and her mother's bad character made it impossible for
her and John to marry, the truth was that she was quite indifferent
to him. He suffered appallingly for three years and, when he heard
in September, 1839, that she was engaged to be married he almost
went out of his mind; he certainly became physically ill and for a
time had to leave Oxford where he had gone in January, 1837. The
illness continued on and off for two years with threatenings of
consumption, and during a ten-month tour of the Continent with
his parents he had such bad haemorrhages that for some months his
condition was considered desperate.

Now, however, at the time of Effie's visit in October, 1846, John
was as fully recovered in health as he was ever to be, and already well
known. The first two volumes of *Modern Painters* had appeared in
1843 and 1846 and put him strikingly on the literary map. Mr
Ruskin was immensely proud of him—proud that he had had the
means to send him as a Gentleman Commoner to Christ Church
where he had won the Newdigate Prize for poetry, proud that he had
been asked to stay by the Duke of Leinster and was 'admitted to
Tables of Ministers, Ambassadors and Bishops'.

[1] Her full name was Adèle Clotilde. Her family always called her Clotilde
but Ruskin called her Adèle because when he wrote love poems to her he could
find no rhymes for Clotilde.

Effie and her father, who had come with her this time to stay at Denmark Hill, were treated coldly as soon as John's infatuation was suspected, and their visit cut short. Nevertheless, six months later, in April, 1847, shortly before her nineteenth birthday, when she came alone to England on a round of visits, she was invited to stay first at Denmark Hill. The Ruskins now believed this to be safe because John's affections and honour were pledged elsewhere, but to prevent any possibility of Effie's setting her cap at him, Mrs Ruskin told her on the very evening of her arrival that he was all but engaged to a young lady of fortune, 'elegant and high bred and in a higher rank of life' than their own. This young lady was Charlotte Lockhart, Sir Walter Scott's grand-daughter. Effie was not told her name but she sized up the situation in a postscript to a letter to her mother on May 14: ' … if he [John] marry the young Lady it is from prudence and a false notion of duty; he had only seen the young Lady six times at parties in his whole life and does not love her a bit, but believes they have each qualities to make the other happy were they married. Did you ever hear such philosophy? I think Mr and Mrs R are doing very wrong, at least they are wishing for their son's happiness and going the wrong way to work. He adores them and will sacrifice himself for them, as I see, too easily. Private!'

It soon became evident to the Ruskins that, in spite of John's commitment, he had fallen in love with Effie all over again and, worse still, that Effie, though fully aware of the situation, was flirting with him. Mr Ruskin, therefore, wrote off to Mr Gray on April 28 to inform him that John had met a young lady to whom he had made proposals the result of which were not yet known; but even if this were not so, though he himself laid no restraint nor prescribed any course to his son, Mrs Ruskin had such an 'insuperable dislike to Perth', having suffered such misery there, that she had a superstitious dread of her son connecting himself even in the most remote degree with the place. No sooner, however, had Mr Gray made arrangements for Effie to go to another friend than Mr Ruskin was writing again begging that she should be allowed to stay out her visit. Undoubtedly the reason for this change was a protest from John. There was a vital misunderstanding between John and his father at this time which was not cleared up until September. Mr Ruskin believed during the whole of Effie's long visit that John was still bound in honour to Charlotte Lockhart whereas in truth she had

refused him—when exactly is not known but certainly by the beginning of June. She was in love with another man, James Hope, a
barrister and grandson of the Earl of Hopetoun, whom she married
on August 19 of this same year, 1847.

Meanwhile Effie, whether fully aware of the undercurrents or not,
was enjoying herself exceedingly. She found Mr Ruskin 'as kind and
droll as ever' and got on admirably with Mrs Ruskin who 'graciously
approved' of her 'toilette' and told her she was 'well dressed without
being at all fine or extravagant'. Mr Ruskin was sixty-two at this time
and Mrs Ruskin sixty-six. She suffered from insomnia and bad
eyesight, and often dropped off in the evenings in her chair, but was
otherwise active. John was busy working most of the day and grum-
bled whenever he had to go out in the evening. He spent a lot of time
and destroyed 'a fortune in paper and paint' trying to draw Effie, and
wrote her a three-stanza poem for her birthday, addressing her as
'Sweet Sister'. She wrote to her mother that he was 'getting very celebrated in the literary world' and was 'much taken notice of'.

Effie was introduced to many artists whom John asked to dinner
especially to meet her, and many of his aristocratic friends and
acquaintances who came to Denmark Hill to see his collection of
Turners. Mr Ruskin took her to see the French players at the St
James's Theatre and to hear Jenny Lind at Her Majesty's. She visited
the new Houses of Parliament which she found 'gorgeous in the
extreme' (unlike Ruskin who found them 'vile') and saw the Duke
of Wellington on horseback in St James's Street touching his cap to
the people as he passed. She wrote home that Mrs Ruskin was very
extravagant in spite of her homilies on domestic economy, paying
6/- a dozen for eggs, 7/- for a pair of chickens, £20 a year to a cook
and £18 to the other women servants. Towards the end of her visit
Effie complained that her laundry cost her 12/- a week which nearly
ruined her, and that all her clothes were too warm and her feet hurt.
The heat gave her a daily headache—one morning she was obliged
to take a large dose of castor oil, and wrote in great discomfort to
her mother while waiting for it to take effect. She wrote to her father
that she had only £4 left. He made this up to £10 and she was able
to order a very pretty silk dress, which took twenty-two yards of
material, for only four guineas.

Apart from a week with some friends in Surrey, she stayed with the Ruskins until June 15 when she moved to the Gardners, old friends of the Grays, at 11 Sussex Gardens, Paddington. John let her go without saying anything definite although we know from a letter of his during their engagement that they were both sad when they said goodbye in her bedroom at Denmark Hill. In this same letter of November 30 of that year, 1847, he wrote: 'If I had known—or thought of—the truth [about her age] I wouldn't have waited an hour—and much suffering I should have saved to myself and a little perhaps to you...' but it is very doubtful all the same whether he would have proposed without his parents' blessing.

In spite of London gaieties Effie was not happy with the Gardners who were 'very kind but not so refined a class as the Ruskins'. 'I like the family here on the whole very well,' she wrote in another letter, 'but after being with the Ruskins it makes one rather particular.' Was she in love with John or merely with the ambience of genius—or was it impossible to separate the two? She was not feeling well and complained of sleeplessness. She was a bad sleeper all her life. This indisposition of hers, both at Sussex Gardens and Denmark Hill, should be noted in view of her later assertion that all her physical ills were due to the unnatural life she led with Ruskin. She begged her father to let her cut out her other visits and return straight home. This she did on July 1.

She knew that John was going to the Highlands to stay with his friend William Macdonald[1] at his shooting lodge, Crossmount, Pitlochrie, but this does not seem to have been her reason for wanting to go home for she had written to her mother on June 18, '... you need not expect to see him at Bowerswell. He cannot come for various reasons and as you know Mrs Ruskin would be miserable every moment he was in Perth or under our roof which would be much worse. It is extraordinary to me how a woman of her powers of mind and extreme clearness of understanding can be so superstitious.' Effie probably did not know that Mrs Ruskin had been living at Bowerswell when John James's father cut his throat there, the year

---

[1] The son of Mrs James Farquharson, one of John James Ruskin's oldest friends. In 1841 he had inherited St Martin's Abbey, near Perth, from his cousin, another William Macdonald, and had changed his name to Macdonald-Macdonald. Effie had met him on several occasions when she was staying at Denmark Hill and they were greatly taken with each other. He was to be John's best man.

before her marriage, in the very room, according to hearsay in the Gray family, in which Effie was born.

John left home for Oxford on June 22, but from there he sent his father such a bad account of his health that he was ordered to take a cure under Dr Henry Jephson at Leamington which he had done before when suffering from his passion for Adèle Domecq. After staying there for three weeks he went on to Edinburgh where he dined with the elder of Mrs Gray's brothers, Andrew Jameson, a lawyer; then, for the first time for twenty years, he passed through Perth. He did not call at Bowerswell, however, although he saw Mr Gray in his office at 14 South Street. From Perth he went by slow stages to Pitlochrie which he reached at the end of August. He was in a very depressed state. On September 1 he wrote to Mrs Gray apologising for not calling on her and explaining that 'the place and its neighbourhood have been to me so peculiarly & constantly unfortunate that I would not willingly associate any of my present pleasures with its hitherto ill-boding scenes'. (He had not been there since he was nine! As a child he had been very devoted to one of his Richardson cousins, Jessie, who was just his own age and had died in 1827.)

Mr and Mrs Ruskin, thoroughly alarmed by his state of mind, and fearing a recurrence of his illness, had evidently made up their minds by this time to accept his marriage to Effie with a good grace. We can only guess what John was writing to them but a few most illuminating letters from Mr Ruskin to him have survived.[1] On September 2 Mr Ruskin wrote: 'I have only time to thank you briefly for your very long & kind Letter to your Mother which I read to her & for your line to me. In regard to E. G. you have taken more objection out of my manner than I had in mind—Be sure of this that all *hesitation or pause* on my part is for fear of you—Vanity does mingle a little—but mortification I should have had double in the L union. I always knew this—but we had kept you to ourselves till marriage & I expected you might marry rather high from opportunities given & that then we must give you up—now with E. G. I gain much—but I escape also from painful communications even for a short time with people not of my sphere ... but for you I fear a little worldly trouble of affairs & I dread any future discovery of what you seem to fear—

[1] Now at the Ruskin Galleries, Bembridge and hitherto unpublished. Ruskin later attached a note to the letter of September 2: 'My Father to Crossmount. Extremely important and beautiful. Not for autobiog.'

motives of ambition more than Love—or of tutored affection or semblance of it, though I only do so from the knowledge of the desirability of the union to the Father not as you say from supposing you not lovable.... I cannot deliberate in an hour but in a moment I say—go on with E. G. but not precipitately—If her health is good (you suppose not)[1] watch her but do not *shew* her for 6, 8 or 12 months. I do not ask you to do this if you prefer to marry at once but as I want you to stand well with Lockhart & the Intellectuals I should be sorry to let him fancy that your affections were not at all concerned in your proposal to his Child.'

On the 8th Mr Ruskin wrote again, censuring Effie's behaviour at Denmark Hill. John's reply to this called forth the important and revealing letter below.

London 13/14 [Monday and Tuesday] Sept 1847

My dearest John

This is a blank morning to us for we can expect no Letters. ... I fear by your Satys Letter & asking if Mama sees my Letters that you are annoyed at my alluding to E's visit. I cannot help my opinions—they are often wrong—but I am glad to exhaust a subject & to get to the end of trouble because reserve, closeness—on either side—begets continued misunderstanding. It is I assure you no easy matter to draw you out & I am rather slow—what may be called thick headed—bullheaded—obstinately blind perhaps—Until I drew from you this last Letter—I could not see that you had been acting & I have been judging under entirely different Circumstances— You acted as if you had finally done with Miss L—& Miss G acted upon an idea *got from you* that you were not longer engaged. Now I judged you as pledged to another & likely to get another & I judged E as one knowing only this—Your argument would be right as of Miss G's leaving the House, even had you been engaged, being uncalled for, if you had been to her as to Miss Sydney[2] or any ordinary Visitor, but as all the world saw you were over head & Ears—& she was aware of our fears —it totally altered the case—When you saw me so angry under

---

[1] John's supposition about Effie's health should be particularly noted here.

[2] Step-daughter of Mr Ruskin's old friend Dr Grant.

false impressions—suffering almost agony in the French
Theatre [on June 12] for fear Lockhart or any of his party by
chance could see what no human Being could mistake—in
place of letting me alone & only thinking me unkind—I wish
you had done me the honour & justice or say flattered me so
far as to have reasoned thus

> "My Father has not been generally harsh
> "or unkind or non indulgent—what can be
> "the matter now? He must be under some
> "grievous error or delusion to be in such
> "a fury—I will enlighten him."

Had you openly & jocosely said "*Oh as to that affair L it is done
with—& E knows better than to suppose I am engaged*" for you tell
me for the first time in your last Letter—"Knowing as she did that
I had been refused by the other"—I see my dearest John
that I should have changed my tone & very interesting novels are
composed out of the misunderstandings that compose the web
or woof of Human Life—Why we might have gone on—
doubting, wondering—regretting, blaming—It is arguing about
the colours of the Cameleon—It is the White Shield & the
Black. Let us be done with it. I have your happiness at heart &
I think for me—you might have had French, Scotch or English
—but I daresay Mama judges best—Only trust to my Love,
give me your Love & pursue your Happiness & your duty. I
am even now assuming too much when I think that my opinion
would have been entirely changed had I known that E knew
your first affair was done with—She knew & was distressed at
knowing Mama & I had objections. I cannot persuade myself
that she should not have gone, but I have been too much with
Sir W Scott lately to make large allowances for human frailties.[1]
But let these matters past sleep—Mama has changed her objections into approval—I give mine & moreover add that I
deem it more likely to secure your happiness to be a married man
than a single, & that I know no young Lady I should my
self so much like for your wife *now* as Miss Gray.... Mama

---

[1] He was reading Lockhart's *Life* of Scott aloud to Mrs Ruskin, and thought
his character perfection.

sends affec. Love.... I am my dearest John your most affec.
Father

JJR.

On the 11th Mrs Ruskin had also written to him an extremely long
letter praising Effie and her parents and giving her full approval.[1]
Mrs Ruskin was very fond of Effie at this time and must have found
many compensations in the idea of having her for a daughter-
in-law. She could keep a much firmer hold on John through the
apparently docile, obliging, familiar Effie than through some strange
young lady of fashion who would overawe her (she always kept out
of the way when John's smart friends came to Denmark Hill); and
she also hoped, as Effie herself realised afterwards, to turn her into
another Mary Richardson, the phlegmatic niece they had adopted
at the age of thirteen who had been Mrs Ruskin's slavish companion
for nineteen years. This girl had recently married and Mrs Ruskin
was missing her dreadfully.

The belief that John would not have proposed without his parents'
consent, is borne out by the fact that on the 15th (by which time he
had certainly received his father's letter of the 2nd which he himself
afterwards called important, and probably his mother's of the 11th)
he was writing again to Mrs Gray asking if he might come to Bowerswell on his way south 'as I do not think my superstitions or painful
feelings will be so strong on a second visit as to compel me to run
away from my kindest friends'.

He arrived at Bowerswell on October 2. It is uncertain how long
he stayed and he does not seem to have proposed to Effie while he
was there. In his defence at the time of the annulment he states that
he offered marriage to her by letter and was accepted. All we know
for certain is that they were engaged by the beginning of November.
It is only from an unpublished letter of John's written to Mrs Gray
on December 9 that we have any hints of what took place at Bowerswell. ' ... it was my sense that her happiness must depend upon the
degree of her regard for me, and in the retired life which it may
perhaps be necessary for me to lead, there must be much that would
be irksome to her, unless rendered tolerable by strength of affection;

[1] One of six letters to John from Mrs Ruskin lent by the late Mr F. J.
Sharp to Effie's daughters to copy, and published in part in *The Order of
Release*.

which *in part* occasioned the singularity of my conduct at Bowerswell.
... I wished to be certain that I *could* be to her in some degree, at
least, the World that she will be to me.... And although you might
think that she gave me as much encouragement . . . as I had the
slightest right to hope for ... her manner had been so different (I cannot tell you how—but it was so), only four months before, that I felt
it severely.... I think, if she had not spoken a word or two to me, that
night, in her old way, I should have left Perth the following morning.'

The reason for Effie's coldness could have been because she was
hurt by his long silence, especially after Charlotte Lockhart's marriage, or because her father was in financial difficulties as a result
of speculating in railways. (Mrs Ruskin had informed John of this
in her letter of September 11, though evincing every confidence
that he would soon extricate himself.) Effie was very proud and may
well have needed extra persuasion from John in these circumstances.

The engagement lasted six months, and for the first few weeks was
kept secret from all but their closest relatives. This was probably in
deference to Mr Lockhart's feelings. They did not meet during this
time, but John sent her almost every day increasingly passionate letters. His mother shrewdly wrote to him on November 27 when he
had gone to Folkestone for a week on his own: '... as you say you
love her more the oftener you write to her may you not be in some
degree surrounding her with imaginary charms—take care of this'.
Their plan was to have a short honeymoon in the Lake District
and then go off on a tour abroad for three months with his parents,
all in one carriage. He longed to show her the places he loved so well,
particularly Chamonix and Venice, but was afraid to go with her
alone lest 'the double excitement of possession and marriage travelling' proved too much for her and she fell ill. When they returned
they were to have their own quarters at Denmark Hill until they
found a furnished house of their own. Mr Ruskin was very anxious
for them to have a house in a fashionable part of London where they
could entertain John's grand friends. John, however, told Effie over
and over again in his engagement letters how miserable he was in
society. In one letter he wrote: 'In our furnished house I am sure we
shall be very uncomfortable & I shall go all day to the British
Museum ... and when I want to etch or anything that requires light
I shall go out to Denmark Hill & get into my old room ... we shall

not be at all comfortable until we have a real *home* in the country and can make perennial arrangements and have our parlour painted with arabesques from Pompeii.' And in another letter he described in detail how Effie could help him with his work; while he was scrambling over a cathedral roof, drawing and measuring, she could sit in the aisle 'deciphering inscriptions' and examining the 'written traditions of the place'.

So Effie knew what John expected of her; nor does it seem impossible that she might have become interested in his work in the way he hoped. She could have helped him in so many other ways too. Instead of his servant, George,[1] it might have been she who copied out his manuscripts. He hinted at this when he wrote to her, 'It may be in your power to do me much great service by writing legibly.' And could she not also have learnt to take daguerreotypes for him? (Again it was George who did this.) Anyway, it was only by thus entering into his work and subserving her own personality that there could have been any chance of happiness for them. Unfortunately for John, Effie had a very strong personality and great gifts of her own which could be fulfilled only through the social life he so detested. As he said at the end of his statement: 'I married her, thinking her so young and affectionate that I might influence her as I chose, and make of her just such a wife as I wanted. It appeared that she married *me* thinking she could make me just the *husband* she wanted. I was grieved and disappointed at finding I could not change her, and she was humiliated and irritated at finding she could not change me.'

Nevertheless this ideal picture of their daily life together might have seemed attractive to her at the time, before she had experienced the cold reality of those Gothic cathedrals. Only three of her letters to John during their engagement have survived, written on three consecutive days—February 8th (his birthday), 9th and 10th. They were put by him into plain white envelopes and numbered 59, 60 and 61 so she must have written nearly every day. Although quite long and affectionate, and addressed to 'My dearest John', they have

[1] George's real name was John Hobbs but he was always called George so as to differentiate him from his master. He was the young brother of Mrs Ruskin's maid, and had first entered John's service in 1842 when he was eighteen. John described him in *Praeterita* as 'a sensible and merry-minded youth'. He is frequently mentioned in Effie's letters.

none of the 'weary yearnings' of his letters; moreover, Effie seems to have been more concerned with his love for her than with hers for him. She must have thought he was completely hers when he wrote on January 19, three months before their wedding: 'I don't profess to be in a good humour when I am away from you—A little thing puts me out now—but when I once get near you—Ah, what will become of me. I shall have no more independent existence than your shadow has— I feel as if I should faint away for love of you—and become a mist or a smoke, like the genie in the Arabian nights—and as if the best you could do with me would be to get me all folded & gathered into a little box—and put on your toilet table—and let me out a little now and then—when I wouldn't be troublesome.'

Then, in February, all their plans were upset. News reached London on the 26th that revolution had broken out in France, and a few days afterwards Louis Philippe and his Queen were smuggled into England. Thereafter, almost simultaneously in different parts of Europe, the forces of freedom which had been for so long fermenting underground burst through the crust of autocracy. Too late attempts were made to stuff the cracks with constitutions and reforms. The revolt in Vienna on March 13 and the flight of Metternich were soon followed by eruptions all over the Austrian province of Lombardo-Veneto. Panic seized the Austrian garrisons, and city after city surrendered to the rebels (or patriots, according to the point of view) with hardly a show of resistance until Verona and Mantua were the only strongholds left to Austria in the whole province. Charles Albert, whose kingdom comprised Sardinia, Piedmont and Savoy, saw his opportunity to unite Italy under his own crown and declared war on Austria.

Venice, under the leadership of Daniele Manin, had been one of the first cities to revolt. On March 22 of that year, 1848 (a never-to-be-forgotten day in Venetian history), the Arsenal was seized and a Republic declared. The Austrian Governors, civil and military, capitulated with an ease for which they were afterwards severely censured in Vienna; they and their troops were shipped off to Trieste, and the tricolor of free Italy flew in the Piazza.

As soon as John heard of the revolution in France, he foresaw that Sardinia and Lombardy would be involved too and that it would be impossible to get to Chamonix in Savoy, the place in Europe he loved best. The disappointment went very deep. He told himself how selfish and wrong it was to feel only for himself 'in so dark a time for thousands', but such a reflection seldom brings much comfort.

Effie went to Edinburgh at the beginning of March to stay with Lord Cockburn, the eminent judge, and his daughter Lizzie, 'a merry girl' who had been at school with her at Avonbank. She had a very gay time there, going to balls and dinners, until the 13th when she moved to her Uncle Andrew Jameson's house, 10 Blacket Place. There John joined her two days later. The day after this longed-for meeting Effie confessed to him that her father 'had lost immense sums by railroads'. He had been speculating in French as well as English and Scottish Railways and the disturbances abroad had had a disastrous effect on railway share values. The great railway boom had reached its peak in 1845, and like thousands of others who had been caught up in it, he was not able to meet his calls. John immediately wrote off a charming warm letter of sympathy to him, and after telling him that Effie had already given him the two happiest days of his whole life, assured him that he had known of his financial position before proposing to her.

Mr Ruskin on the other hand, who only became aware of the extent of Mr Gray's losses when, on drawing up a marriage settlement, he discovered that Mr Gray was not in a position to do anything for Effie, wrote to him with that characteristic and devastating outspokenness which was so often afterwards to cause offence to the Grays.

London, 22 Mch, 1848

My dear Sir

I have your kind letter of the 20 Inst & have consulted a person of very sound Judgement on Railroad Shares—He considers Boulogne as Mere Lottery Tickets as Total Blanks on prizes of perhaps £10 each—To Holders he says—if they have no other means of meeting Calls—sell—200 shares may give £1000—to those who can keep—keep. Everything depends on the Individual having power to hold Railroad property by settling all calls without selling—then at this period they should hold on for no doubt all Railroad property is below its value, but from the circumstances of your having bought 200 Shares in Boulogne in which I thought myself venturous to take 25 & from your saying you have heavy calls to meet I have no hope of your getting clear. My son seems to have gleaned as much at Edin^h—you desired me to keep your situation private—now—my dear Sir it may do good to tell you that six months ago when you were far better than you are now—you were publicly reported to me as a ruined man—We cannot mislead the World in these things long & it is ill natured enough to anticipate our fall—It knew your engagements which are publicly reported & you will I fear find its report true in the end—What distresses me is not your having nothing but your having to go to Bankruptcy & so losing confidence of the County of Perth & perhaps 2/3^ds of your Business.

I am sorely vexed at your just taking this time to disturb the young people who cannot pay your Calls—for John knows my Severity on money matters—and though I give where I can— were he to be Security for a Single hundred for the best friend he has—he should never see a shilling more of my money—I am so upset myself at hearing of any speculation that I would almost beg the great Kindness of you neither to tell me nor John &, if I dare presume, nor Phemy[1] anything about your affairs— I am as I told you made ill & my health is of some Consequence to John and Phemy yet. I should be greatly obliged if you could postpone any winding up—for a few months—after that I shall be prepared for the worst. I conclude your House is already as good as gone—I am happy to see my son's letter pleased you—He will write in a very different strain & feeling— but I am naturally annoyed at all this coming on the young people—Had you frankly told me in Octr or Novr it would surely have been better than just at the consummation— Excuse all this plain speaking or say writing—I had the same sort of thing with my Brother in Law [Patrick Richardson] whom I used to tell, when he boasted of his property, that I did not value any man in Perth at fifty shillings. I ought not with such opinions to show my face there—

Most kind regards to Mrs Gray & you from Mrs R & myself
I am My dear Sir Yrs very truly
John James Ruskin[2]

---

[1] The name Effie had been called as a child, and which her father and other members of the older generation were still in the habit of calling her.

[2] Unpublished letter from Bowerswell Papers.

Mr Ruskin in another letter owned that his disposition was to look on the worst side of things, and so it proved in this case. Mr Gray did not go bankrupt, nor lose his house. A banker friend came to his rescue with a loan at 3 1/2 per cent payable over three years and he eventually rode out the storm. But life at Bowerswell was for many months overshadowed by his dreadful anxiety, and his health suffered from it. It meant also that Effie went to John without a penny of her own[1] and became as dependent on Mr Ruskin's bounty as was John himself. This gave her father-in-law a right to criticise her conduct and expenditure in letters such as the one above. Mr Gray unwisely passed on to her the gist of these letters, thus stirring up great resentment.

There is no doubt that this financial trouble was a cause of much sadness and disquiet to the young people, just as Mr Ruskin had feared it would be, and, added to John's disappointment at not getting abroad, clouded their honeymoon. In his statement at the time of the annulment, he wrote that Mr Gray's 'distress appeared very great: and the fortnight or ten days preceding our marriage were passed in great suffering both by Miss Gray and myself'. He also stated, contrary to his letter to Mr Gray, that the situation had been concealed from him until Effie's revelation; he added, though, that no effort whatever was made to involve him in their embarrassment.

He went to Bowerswell on March 29, and at 4 p.m. on April 10 they were married according to Scottish custom in the drawing-room by the minister of Kinnoull. The old Ruskins were not at the wedding. This, however, had nothing to do with Mr Ruskin's annoyance; as early as February he had written to Mr Gray: 'It is just over 30 years this 1848 since I slept in a friend's house. I take my ease at an Inn continually & go on with my business pretty well—I have thought I might come to Perth but if I were unwell—I should only be in the way—a marplot & a nuisance.' Mrs Ruskin, of course, could not go for the old superstitious reasons, but that the two families were on very cordial terms is shown by this passage in a letter (now at Bembridge) from Mrs Gray to Mrs Ruskin written the day after the wedding: 'It is very gratifying to me that you already

---

[1] During her honeymoon she wrote to her father apologising for having to ask him to pay an old dressmaker's bill but assuring him that he would never have anything more to pay for her.

love her so much. I hope she will be to you all a Mother could
wish.'

The young couple spent their first night at Blair Athol, and then
after a short tour of the Highlands went on to Keswick. The reason
why John did not consummate the marriage can only be conjectured.
His statement offers an explanation: 'Miss Gray appeared in a very
weak and nervous state in consequence of this distress [her father's
financial worry] and I was at first afraid of subjecting her system to
any new trials. My own passion was also much subdued by anxiety;
and I had no difficulty in abstaining on the first night.' Nor does
he seem to have had any difficulty in abstaining on any other night.
Effie was a virgin at the time of the annulment as was testified by
two doctors—and this in spite of the fact that they shared a room
for the whole of their married life when they were together except
for a few days of illness. Later on in the statement he wrote: 'It may
be thought strange that I *could* abstain from a woman who to most
people was so attractive. But though her face was beautiful, her
person was not formed to excite passion. On the contrary there were
certain circumstances in her person which completely checked it.'

Effie's version of their honeymoon confirms this. In a letter to her
father written on March 7, 1854, six weeks before she left John for
good, in which she at last took him fully into her confidence, she
wrote: 'For days [during their honeymoon] John talked about his relation to me but avowed no intention of making me his Wife. He
alleged various reasons, Hatred to children, religious motives, a
desire to preserve my beauty, and finally this last year told me his true
reason (and that to me is as villainous as all the rest) that he had imagined women were quite different to what he saw I was and that the
reason why he did not make me his Wife was because he was disgusted
with my person the first evening 10th April. After I began to see things
better I argued with him and took the Bible but he soon silenced me
and I was not sufficiently awake to what position I was in—and then
he said after 6 years he would marry me when I was 25.'

John has a defence for this too in his statement: 'She sometimes
expressed doubts about it being *right* to live as we were living; but
always continuing to express her wish to live so. I gravely charged
her to tell me if she thought she would be happier in consummat-
ing marriage or healthier, I, being willing at any time to consummate

it; but I answered to her doubts of it being *right*, that many of the best characters in Church history had preserved virginity in marriage, and that it could not be wrong to do for a time what they had done through life.'

John must have been familiar with the female nude from his study of pictures. It is probable, though, that Effie was the only naked woman he ever saw. In what way could her body have been different from what he imagined? In only one particular, it seems: the female nudes he saw in galleries—statues as well as pictures—were either discreetly veiled or depicted as children. For a man as sensitive as he it may well have been a lasting shock to discover the adult reality. Had he seen other women he would have realised that the unattractive circumstances in Effie's person were common to them all; in his ignorance he believed her to be uniquely disfigured.

But even without such a shock one can imagine the condition he was in on their first night after those twelve days at Bowerswell in the gloom of Mr Gray's anxiety, subjected to the inquisitive scrutiny of the neighbours (he disliked even the most intellectual society) and suffering from a bad cold into the bargain; and then the strain of the wedding breakfast, followed by the long drive of thirty-four miles to Blair Athol which they did not reach until 10 p.m. All this, coupled with Effie's complete ignorance (she wrote in that same letter to her father, 'I had never been told the duties of married persons to each other and knew little or nothing about their relations in the closest union on earth')—all this might well have produced temporary impotency, and thus given him a chance to consider the drawbacks of burdening themselves with children. If they could have gone abroad immediately after their wedding they would have been home again before Effie's possible pregnancy incommoded her. Now, however, he was afraid that when conditions abroad became settled enough for travel, Effie's pregnancy might be a further hindrance to getting away.

Whatever Effie felt inwardly, she wrote very happy letters home during their short honeymoon, and after their return to Denmark Hill on April 27 all was outwardly as perfect as could be. It was the happiest time in her life with John. On the 29th she appeared in public for the first time as his wife at the Private View of the Old Water Colour Society (now the R.W.S.), a great social event in those days, and was introduced to so many people that she could

not remember them all, and John congratulated her afterwards on
her 'grand succès'. Mr Ruskin took her on his arm and was very 'notic-
ing' of her dress. A week later she went to a dinner party where she
met Lord and Lady Lansdowne, and the old Marquess, who took her
down to dinner, was charmed by her. When on June 1 they were asked
to *dine* at Lansdowne House, Effie could congratulate herself that she
had arrived socially. She justly took some credit to herself for the
invitation, for although John had known the Lansdownes for some
time he had never before been asked to dinner.

On May 3 she was writing home, 'I never saw anything like John,
he is just perfect!!!' and on the 24th: 'I am happier every day for he
really is the kindest creature in the world and he is so pleased with
me. He says he thinks we are a model couple ... we are really
always so happy to do what the other wants that I do not think we
shall ever quarrel.... Mr Ruskin is also I think very fond of me and
so is Mrs Ruskin.' In another letter she said that she had never
known anything so kind as Mr and Mrs Ruskin were to her, and in
another, 'Mrs Ruskin says he [Mr Ruskin] has a great deal of pride
about us, John and me. He is so anxious that we shall have a house
that we can receive anyone in that he says he will rather pay the rent
himself. For my part I am very happy here & do not care where we
go or stay.'

That John was not equally content is shown by a letter he wrote
to Mrs Gray on May 12: ' ... there is *nothing* here that I enjoy
except the society of your daughter in our home ... if I go into society at all, it is for *her* sake, and to my infinite annoyance—except
only as the pleasure I have in seeing her admired as *by* all she is—
and happy as *with* all she is—rewards me and more than rewards me
for my own discomforts and discomfitures.... I wish I had time to
tell you of the kind and honourable things that are said of her. I am
especially delighted to see how quietly and gracefully she receives
all marks of attention and admiration.' And at the end of May he
wrote to Mr Gray: 'I think it would please you to see Effie at
present—looking lovelier than ever—and—I think also—looking
very—very happy.... However—her beauty is her least gift.'[1]

Effie, being undoubtedly happy at this time, was probably looking her best. Mrs Gardner, with whom she had stayed in Sussex
Gardens, and who visited her in June, said she looked a hundred

[1] From unpublished letters in Bowerswell Papers.

times better and five or six years younger than the year before. Her hair was auburn and her rather heavy-lidded eyes grey-blue, but, according to John in one of his engagement letters, it was the 'sweet-kind half pensive depth of expression' that was the great charm of her face. She herself told her mother when she was sitting to Millais in March, 1853, as the model for the woman in *The Order of Release*: 'My head you would know anywhere. It is exactly like.' In this picture, however (now in the Tate Gallery), her hair is painted black in contrast to the fair hair of the child. Millais, in a letter to a friend written shortly before their wedding, stated that she was five foot six exactly because he had just measured her. Another detail we know of her appearance is that she still had some of her baby teeth, and from the regret she expressed to her mother that her teeth were not properly looked after when she was a child we can deduce that they were her worst feature.

F. J. Furnivall, who became Ruskin's disciple, described her when he met her for the first time at an evening party in 1849 as 'a handsome, tall woman, with a high colour, brown wavy hair, a Scotch woman evidently, dressed in a pink moiré silk dress'. (Pink was her favourite colour.) This description of her being tall does not tally with Millais's measurements, yet if she held herself well and had a good figure she would have looked taller than she was. She adored dancing, particularly the polka, and as her dancing was much admired, she must have been lithe and graceful. It was she who first invited Furnivall to meet Ruskin in their London house in Park Street, and he gives a vivid picture of John too at this time, as 'tall and slight, five foot ten or eleven, coming in from his study where he had been working wearing a buttoned-up frock coat with velvet collar and blue stock. He had rough light hair, red whiskers and deep blue eyes—fit to look through anything—a kindly genial manner and a winning smile. His only defect was his lower lip, bitten by a dog in early life, which had left an ugly protruding scar.'[1] A glove of his which has been preserved shows that he had very small hands, the size of a small woman's, so presumably he had small feet too.

On June 24, the young couple went to Dover and Folkestone

---

[1] These descriptions are taken from very scrappy shorthand notes of a lecture given by Furnivall in 1900 to the Ruskin Society of Birmingham and published by kind permission of Mr R. G. Lloyd.

(Folkestone was a favourite seaside resort of the Ruskins), and then on to Oxford for Commemoration, staying a night on the way at Reading and going over to see Miss Mitford, the author of *Our Village*, then 'a dear old lady' of sixty, as Effie described her, living very poorly in a little cottage 'with wee rooms'. (Miss Mitford was a great admirer of John's work and thought him the most charming person she had ever met, 'just what, if one had a son, one would have dreamt of his turning out, in mind, manner, conversation, every-thing', she wrote to a friend.) At Oxford they stayed with Dr Acland[1] and his wife, and after a fortnight of intense sociability went on to Salisbury where John wanted to start collecting material for his book *The Seven Lamps of Architecture*. They stayed at the White Hart Inn where Mr and Mrs Ruskin joined them. It was a disastrous visit. John, who had never completely recovered from the cold caught at Bowerswell, developed a very bad cough; Mrs Ruskin also had a bad cold and Mr Ruskin suffered more than usual from his stomach complaint. They were all in low spirits. Effie continued to get depressing news from home about her father's affairs and often cried at night from thinking of their troubles and her inability to help them. Moreover she fell out for the first time with her mother-in-law. Mrs Ruskin fussed terribly over John and this annoyed Effie who thought it only made him worse. In the morning his mother began, 'Don't sit near those towels, John, they are damp,' and in the forenoon, 'John you must not read these papers until they are dried,' and even though it was steamily hot, George, his servant, had to take all his clothes to the kitchen fire to air, and he was not allowed out after dinner, although dinner in those days was in the middle of the afternoon. Whenever his mother asked him how his cough was he began to cough, whereas when Effie was with him alone he did not cough at all. Eventually he went to bed for a week and Effie was moved out of his room. On one occasion when Mrs Ruskin wanted him to take a pill at bedtime Effie lost her temper and was rude to her, and John, instead of taking her part, rebuked her which hurt her dreadfully. Complete submission to a parent seemed natural to him. (He had written to her during their engagement 'I am always

---

[1] Henry Wentworth Acland had been a senior undergraduate at Christ Church when John was a freshman. They became life-long friends. He was Regius Professor of Medicine at Oxford from 1858 to 1894, and was knighted in 1884.

happiest when I am most dutiful'.) If Effie had been a little wiser and made more allowance for their anxiety over his health—an anxiety she never shared, not having seen him when he was really ill—she could easily have handled the situation, but unfortunately she became jealous of Mrs Ruskin during this illness of John's, and jealousy can never be wise. Whether Mrs Ruskin was ever really jealous of Effie is a matter of conjecture.

While they were at Salisbury they heard that Mr Ruskin's offer for a three-year lease of a furnished house, 31 Park Street, had been accepted. Effie wrote to her mother on July 30: 'Mr Ruskin kindly pays the ground rent which is £300[1] and John & I the rent which is £200 a year. I am sure you will think this a great deal and so do I as the house is not at all large but extremely suitable for us and elegantly furnished but is the most fashionable place in London ... and it was a great thing getting so small a house in that quarter.'

John recovered and they returned to Denmark Hill on August 2— only to be off again five days later—this time to France where the situation seemed fairly settled under a provisional government, although it was not until December that Louis Napoleon was elected President. They could not get into Park Street for six weeks and John was very anxious to continue in the French cathedrals his studies of the Gothic begun at Salisbury. They were away for over eleven weeks, touring Normandy. John was at first in raptures at getting abroad again but soon an unexplained depression settled on him. Nevertheless he worked fiercely all the daylight hours and Effie was left much alone. She does not seem to have minded this—at least she did not complain of it in her letters—and was able to help him with his notes, but his ideal picture of her sitting reading in the aisle of the cathedral while he scrambled about the roof never materialised. She stayed in the hotel sewing.

It was not a happy time for her, though. An undercurrent of ill-feeling between the Grays and the Ruskins, which had been in existence even during those first blissful weeks at Denmark Hill, came into the open while they were away. Mr Gray had hoped, ever since Effie's marriage, that she would use her influence with John to get her brother George into Mr Ruskin's business in London or into some other London House. George, who was nearly nineteen, had been at Charterhouse and was now working in his father's office in

[1] According to Mr Ruskin's account-book this £300 was a premium.

Perth. Mr Gray's business had fallen off since his financial difficulties and he did not consider there was enough in it to support George, especially as it had also to support his brother-in-law and partner, Melville Jameson, and *his* family. Moreover, as his own family had been augmented in the previous November by another son, he now had three sons and two daughters born since the death of the three little girls in 1841. Effie—and John too—were very willing to help, but it was a delicate situation for them and Effie particularly disliked the idea of Mr Ruskin thinking she was influencing John in favour of her own family.

While the young couple were in Normandy Mr Gray himself wrote to Mr Ruskin in August asking him if he could do something for George and received by return one of Mr Ruskin's offensively frank diatribes, expressing his disapproval of George giving up the law for commerce of any kind, deprecating his coming to London and refusing him any help at all if he did come, or any hospitality beyond an occasional Sunday dinner. (Mr Ruskin himself had suffered 'years of Toil and misery in a Colonial Broker's Office in London' which was his chief excuse for this lack of sympathy.)

Effie was shocked and indignant, and thought it 'very odd' that her father-in-law, Mr Gray's 'oldest friend in London, would not try to get George a situation'. Nevertheless she did her best to see Mr Ruskin's point of view and explain it to her father. The correspondence went on for weeks, and finally on October 17 she wrote from Gisors: ' ... I hope this will be the last said upon an unpleasant subject which corresponding upon has done no good.... I think you ought to excuse Mr Ruskin's suspicious character when you consider the claims he has upon him every day from his relations, most teasing for him who has given so much and makes him look on the worst side, but be sure no ill will was intended so there let the matter drop.' Before the end of the year Mr Gray had found a position for George in a lawyer's firm in Edinburgh, and in order that he might have comfortable lodgings, John and Effie, with Mr Ruskin's approval, contributed £2 a month out of their own allowance of £600 a year.[1]

They were in Rouen when news came on October 8 of the death

[1] This income was probably the interest on £10,000 which at John's request Mr Ruskin had made over to him on his marriage and which he

of Effie's Aunt Jessie, the wife of Mrs Gray's brother, Melville Jameson, Mr Gray's partner. The Melville Jamesons lived at Croft House near Bowerswell and Jessie had been Mrs Gray's best and only confidential friend. Coming on top of all the other family misfortunes Effie was overwhelmed with grief. Jessie had been 'one of those she loved most on earth', intimately connected with all her early years. She wrote that her head ached with crying, and she insisted on wearing mourning which John had a 'great dislike to'. It must have been difficult for John to understand such intensity of grief over the death of a mere aunt by marriage. Effie later told her mother that John had been made very unhappy by seeing her suffer so much at this time.[1]

They got home on October 24, and on their way heard that the Count and Countess Béthune had arrived to stay a month at Denmark Hill. Caroline Béthune was one of the five Domecq girls, a younger sister of the Adèle whom John had loved, and the only one of the family who came fairly frequently to stay with the Ruskins. Effie was dismayed to hear of their visit. She was in no mood for gaiety and only longed to be at home with her stricken family. She thought it very wrong of the Béthunes to leave their French tenantry.

On her return, Mr Ruskin gave her 'a beautiful black velvet dress'.[2] She had the impression that he regretted his letters to her father and this was his way of showing it. While she was still at Denmark Hill he wrote to Mr Gray on October 27: 'I am greatly delighted with Phemy. There is of course little change, but there is a touch of sorrow upon her from events at home & seriousness coming naturally from higher responsibilities, which makes her singularly interesting & which throw new charms around her to me ... something of a holy sweetness of character grown upon Phemy. It is a source of unfeigned & unbounded thankfulness to his Mother

---

had settled on Effie. It was returned to him after the annulment. As well as this £600 Mr Ruskin gave John frequent presents of money, paid all his travelling expenses and bought for him nearly all the pictures he asked for as well as other extras.

[1] Jessie had been ill for months. A stone in the old graveyard at Kinnoull tells us that she had an infant son, Melville, born August 20, died 21st. Effie does not mention this although she makes many references to Jessie's illness.

[2] There is a note in Mr Ruskin's account-book: 'Oct 1848 Effie velvet gown £18-10.'

& myself that our son has been led to chuse a Being of such promise
as your Daughter gives of a character at once strong & gentle & of
all that is right & graceful in woman.'[1]

After ten days at Denmark Hill she and John moved into Park
Street on November 2. (They had roast hare and apple tart for
their first dinner in their own house.) It was a little box of a place,
according to Effie, though six storeys high (she counted the base-
ment and ground floor as storeys) with only a couple of rooms on
each floor, but it had the great advantage of an excellent spring of
fine fresh water in the kitchen and looked over the gardens of
Grosvenor House belonging to the Marquess of Westminster. Mrs
Ruskin had procured servants for them and Mrs Gray supplied
linen from Scotland. Although John was intensely occupied in writing *The Seven Lamps*, Effie seemed happy enough in their new
home. She hired a brougham which they paid for themselves (though
Mr Ruskin very kindly gave them wine to the same amount, £45)
and this enabled her to get about and visit her friends. She saw a good
deal of Countess Béthune who was friendly, gay and vivacious and
whom she grew to like very much. Invitations came in from people
they had met in the spring, and they did a certain amount of enter-
taining themselves. In December, wearing the black velvet dress with
lace collar and cuffs, she sat for her portrait to Tom Richmond,
George Richmond's little known younger brother. He was a profes-
sional portrait painter and asked John to be allowed to paint her as
a favour. John also tried, though unsuccessfully, to draw her at this
time.

For Christmas they went to stay at Denmark Hill. There Effie most
unfortunately fell ill and lost her appetite completely. It is uncertain what was the matter with her; she may have had influenza
or she may have been just run down. The Ruskins evidently thought
at first that there was nothing wrong with her; they would not
allow her to stay in bed and blamed her for being dull. We learn from
a later letter from John to Mr Gray that Mrs Ruskin, finding her one
day in tears when she ought to have been dressing for dinner, gave
her 'a scold'. During this visit her relationship with the old couple
deteriorated beyond recovery. There was company every evening;
they did not dine until six—whereas she and John in their own
home dined at the exceptionally early hour of one, a habit they had

[1] From an unpublished letter in Bowerswell Papers.

copied from the Henry Aclands at Oxford—and they did not get to bed until after midnight. Mrs Ruskin insisted on dosing her with 'messes'—laudanum pills with spa water and ipecacuanha which she took only in order not to make a fuss. John was worried because she was getting so thin and wanted her to stay in bed, but he was over-ruled by his mother. When she was no better after a few days, two doctors were called in—Dr William Richardson, Mr Ruskin's nephew, and Dr Grant, a very old friend of Mr Ruskin's from Richmond—but they disagreed as to treatment and merely made her worse. She herself felt sure that once they returned to their own house and sensible way of life she would quickly recover.

While they were still at Denmark Hill, her Aunt Lexy died. She was the wife of Mrs Gray's other brother, Andrew Jameson of Edinburgh, at whose house Effie and John had met before their wedding. Effie had not loved this aunt as she had loved her Aunt Jessie, but all the same she was very depressed by the news of her death. The one thing she looked forward to now to cheer her was a visit from her mother for which she had been pressing ever since their return from France, and early in the new year, 1849, Mrs Gray came to stay at Park Street for a few weeks. There are no letters from Effie for this period, for although both she and Mrs Gray wrote to Perth, Mr Gray evidently did not keep their letters. We know, however, from a letter of his that Effie was still feeling ill and suffering very much from want of sleep.

At the beginning of February she returned with her mother to Bowerswell. They both stopped in Edinburgh on their way, and there Mrs Gray received a letter from her husband telling her that the four children had all been down with whooping cough for the last three weeks, a fact he had hitherto kept from her for fear of spoiling her visit to London. On March 1 their little boy, Robert, nearly seven years old, died as a result of complications following this illness. He was the seventh of their children to die young. Effie was with them, and one can imagine the grief of the household—this child's death following so soon after the deaths of the two sisters-in-law, with Mr Gray's affairs still causing grave anxiety, and Effie herself feeling far from well.

John had now finished *The Seven Lamps* and wanted to go abroad to collect material for the third volume of *Modern Painters*. It had been planned that Effie should go with him in the spring, together with the old couple—in fact the original plan of the year before. Peace had now been restored to most of Europe. On March 23, a month before they were to set out, Charles Albert of Sardinia was finally defeated by the Austrians under Field-Marshal Radetsky at the Battle of Novara. To save his kingdom from Austrian occupation Charles Albert abdicated in favour of his elder son, Victor Emmanuel (who twelve years later was to become the first king of united Italy), and the whole of Lombardo-Veneto, with the exception of Venice, was brought back under Austrian domination.

At some point Effie decided not to go with them after all. As there are no letters from her at this time we do not know whether she made up her mind to this before she went to Bowerswell or after she got there. It may be that she did not feel well enough to go, or that she could now no longer bear the idea of travelling with the old people. Mr Ruskin wrote to Mr Gray on March 4 in his letter of condolence, 'I hear she may remain with you a few months—whilst my son goes abroad—I should disapprove entirely of this, were my son going abroad for his pleasure—but it seems as much a matter of business as my travelling to Liverpool. I daresay Phemy had enough of this in Normandy—and since her illness at Xmas—I am sure she is not this year able for Swiss excursions.... They must however settle their comings and goings with each other.'[1] Judging by the date of this letter, three days after Robert's death, it does not appear that Effie's decision was influenced by her desire to stay at home with her heartbroken mother, though she may, of course, have made up her mind immediately he died.

No letters from her or John have been preserved during the period she was at Bowerswell before he went abroad, and no letters from *her* while he was away. He crossed with his parents to Boulogne on April 23 and wrote to her from Folkestone that his book would probably be out on her birthday, May 7th (in fact it did not come out until the 14th), and that she would find 'plenty of use made of the notes' she had helped him to write in Normandy. His first letters to her were lover-like, and in two of them there are passages which seem strongly to indicate that they had agreed to consummate their marriage on his return. On April 24 he wrote from Paris: 'Do you know, pet, it seems almost a dream to me that we have been married: I look forward to meeting you: and to your *next* bridal night:

[1] From an unpublished letter in Bowerswell Papers.

and to the time when I shall again draw your dress from your snowy shoulders: and lean my cheek upon them, as if you were my betrothed only: and I had never held you in my arms.' And from Dijon on April 27: 'I have your precious letter here: with the account so long and kind—of all your trial at Blair Athol—indeed it must have been cruel my dearest: I think it will be much nicer next time—we will neither of us be frightened.'[1]

At first he was solicitous for her, begging her not to run short of money but to apply to one of the clerks in his father's office for anything she needed, and encouraging her with her drawing—but quite soon a note of exasperation appeared; she was still ailing, he could not think what was the matter with her as she now had everything to which she was accustomed and 'a good deal of pleasant society and excitement'. Evidently people were gossiping about them at Perth. A friend of hers, Jane Boswell, was staying at Bowerswell and making remarks about his absence. 'Your friend Miss Boswell must be a nice clever creature,' he wrote from Geneva on May 10, 'but it seems to me that she has a great deal more cleverness than judgment or discretion, or she would understand the very simple truth that it was not *I* who had left *you* but *you* who had left *me*—Certainly I never wanted you to leave London, but you would not be happy unless you went to Perth: and away you went: much more to the astonishment of *my* friends in London than my departure for Switzerland can be to the surprise of yours in Scotland. I wonder whether you think that a husband is a kind of thing who is to be fastened to his wife's waist with her pincushion & to be taken about with her wherever she chooses to go.' After all, it was over two years since he had written that the best she could do with him was to get him all folded into a little box and put on her toilet-table.

Some time in May Effie went to Edinburgh to consult Dr Simpson, the gynaecologist who had introduced the use of chloroform in 1847 and who was now Professor of Midwifery at the University. He diagnosed that she was suffering from some nervous complaint of long standing. Mrs Gray wrote to Mrs Ruskin a 'didn't I tell you so' kind of letter which greatly provoked John. Mary Bolding, Mr

[1] Although part of this letter was quoted in *The Order of Release*, this important passage was left out and has never before been published. John and Effie had spent the first night of their honeymoon at Blair Athol, not at Aberfeldy as stated by Admiral James.

Ruskin's niece, who, as Mary Richardson, had lived with the Ruskins for so many years, was seriously ill at this time. Her brother, Dr Richardson, had made a mistake in his first diagnosis, thinking her less ill than she really was, whereas Mrs Ruskin had maintained all along that there was 'something very serious the matter'. 'Now that it has turned out so,' John wrote to Effie from Vevey on May 27, 'I think the delight of being right has quite consoled her for the moment for the illness [she died at the end of June]. In the same way your mother appears quite happy at discovering that you have a disease which may make you miserable for years. Your letter does not say a word of what Dr Simpson said was the cause of your complaint.'[1]

On June 24, however, he was writing a long, loving letter from Chamonix commenting on hers 'in which you tell me you are better —thank God: and that your father is so much happier and that Alice [the younger of her two little sisters] is so winning and that you would like a little Alice of our own—so should I: a little Effie at least. Only I wish they weren't so small at first that one hardly knows what one has got hold of.'[2]

The Ruskin parents were very puzzled and concerned about Effie's state of mind, and on June 13 Mr Ruskin was writing to Mr Gray from Chamonix to ask whether anything could be done on their part 'to bring about an amendment: It is evident to me that my son also suffers from not being able to make out what his wife's entire feelings and wishes are.' Apart from this anxiety, he had never seen John so well in his life. He confessed to disappointment and sorrow over Effie because 'the chief aim of our life when your daughter became ours was to make her and my son happy'. He felt a justified annoyance at all the expense of the London house which they had not lived in for three months, and stressed again and again

[1] From an unpublished letter in Bowerswell Papers.
[2] Effie's grand-daughter, Clare Stuart Wortley, made a note at the end of this letter, referring to this passage: 'This letter is one of the most important we possess; it supports what my mother [Effie's daughter, Alice, Lady Stuart of Wortley] always told me that Mrs Gray had told her, namely that Dr Simpson's opinion was that Effie ought to have children. No doubt he extracted from Effie the truth about her "Marriage", and disapproved of the practice of love-making without consummation which these letters of John's reveal.' If this was so, Effie does not seem to have told John except in this oblique way.

the fact that John was in Switzerland for work not pleasure. (He rather overstressed this point as if he were not quite sure himself whether John was not getting too much pleasure out of his work.) He felt that Effie was alienated from them, and believed that if only she could be completely frank with them, all misunderstandings would be cleared up. A good deal of criticism of her behaviour then followed and advice to her for the future, and a reiterated wish that she would state her grievances.

There is in the Bowerswell Papers an unpublished draft of Mr Gray's reply to this letter in which he wrote, '... that you both [Effie and Mr Ruskin] misunderstand each other's feelings and desires is apparent to me as the sun at noonday', yet he does not attempt to elucidate to either of them what those feelings and desires were. He went on to say that he had taken Effie for a walk in the garden and asked her why it was that she no longer received letters from her husband's parents, thus trying to draw her out as to the causes of alienation between them; he did not mean, however, to repeat a word of what passed between them, any more than he had told her a word of what was in Mr Ruskin's letter. He emphasised her reserve and doubted whether Mr Ruskin made enough allowance for her manner which was thoroughly Scotch, by which he meant that she made no display of feeling even to those to whom she was most attached and that she hated hypocrisy and would never be tempted to practise it. He ended by giving a piece of advice of his own: leave the young people alone.

One can see so clearly how these long letters from the parents, endeavouring with the best will in the world to heal the breach, merely succeeded in widening it. One can sympathise with both sides, but particularly perhaps with the old Ruskins at this time. They were evidently deeply hurt and puzzled, and completely ignorant of the fact, as were the Grays also, that Effie had any just cause for complaint against John.

And now, as was inevitable, John was embroiled. He was shown the correspondence and, stung by the injustice, as he thought, to his father, sprang to his defence. On July 5 he sent Mr Gray a letter which was evidently intended as a vindication of his father but turned into an attack on Effie. He wrote that he did not complain of Effie's conduct because of her state of health, but if she had not been seriously ill he *would* have had fault to find with her. The state of

her feelings he now ascribed 'simply to bodily weakness', that was
to say—and it was 'a serious and distressing admission—to a nervous
disease affecting the brain' under which she had long been labour-
ing. He did not know when the complaint first came upon her but
he first noticed it at Oxford the previous July when it showed itself,
as it still did, in tears and depression. When for the first time she
showed 'causeless petulance' to his mother while he was ill at Salisbury, merely because his mother wanted him to take a blue pill at
bedtime, he had not made due allowance for her state and had re-
proved her as soon as they were alone which she took in bad part,
never in her life before having heard herself blamed for anything,
and 'this effect upon her otherwise excited feelings was permanent—and disposed her—as I think—to look with jealousy upon my
mother's influence over me ever afterwards'.[1] He had his own opinion, he went on, as to the principal cause of the disease but it did
not bear on the matter in hand. He then continued: '... if Effie had
in *sound mind* been annoyed by the contemptible trifles that *have*
annoyed her: if she had cast back from her the kindness and the affection with which my parents received her, and refused to do her duty
to them, under any circumstances whatever but those of an illness
bordering on incipient insanity, I should not now have written you
this letter respecting her.' He only did so that Mr Gray might not
unwisely encourage her in those 'tones of feeling' that 'were so
likely to take a morbid form'. He continued by denying that his
parents had interfered in their lives—but even if they had, had they
not every right to do so? He concluded: 'With sincerest regards to
Mrs Gray—and dearest love to Effie if at any time you think proper
to show her this letter which for my part—you may show to the
whole world.' (The 'dearest' was inserted afterwards.) One wonders
whether Mr Gray had the tact not to show this letter to Effie.[2] The
harm done by both the old Ruskins and the Grays in showing letters
around, or, worse still, in passing on a mangled version of a letter as

[1] In his statement he alludes to this again: 'On one occasion, she having
been rude to my mother, I rebuked her firmly; and she never forgave either
my mother or me.'
[2] It was carefully preserved in a plain white envelope, evidently by Mrs Gray
for on it was written: 'Remarkable letter from J. Ruskin in which he artfully
puts down his then so-called *wife's* unhappiness to any thing but the cause
which he himself only knew. S. M. G.'

Mr Gray so often did, was undoubtedly responsible in part for the break up of the marriage.

What did John have in mind when he wrote that he had his own opinion of the principal cause of her disease? Evidently he did not put it down to their unnatural relationship for he maintained she had been suffering from her complaint, whatever it was, prior to their marriage. Possibly he attributed it to the fact that she had been so spoilt and indulged all her life that she was now incapable of submitting to the slightest discipline. He himself had been brought up with the utmost severity and beaten at the slightest provocation. Each of them blamed the other's parents for the worst faults in the other. John was quite capable of believing that wilfulness, uncurbed and unchecked, could lead to a diseased mind.

Then yet another grievance cropped up. John expected Effie to come to London with her father to meet him on his return, whereas she expected him to go to Perth to fetch her. There had been much unpleasant gossip in Perth about their long separation and it must have been very important to the Grays that the neighbours should see them together. Mr Ruskin as usual weighed in with one of his over-long explanatory letters, emphasising the fact that John always got ill in Scotland, but conceding that if they did not *mind* his catching cold, he would immediately on his arrival in England proceed to Perth. This merely confirmed Effie's suspicion that the idea of her meeting him in London had originated with his parents. This misunderstanding called forth the following important letter[1] from John which shows most painfully the irremediable injury their long separation and the interference of their parents had done to their relationship.

Champagnole, Jura

Sunday. 2nd September [1849]

My dearest Effie

I received about a fortnight ago at Chamouni a letter of yours—(from Viège [forwarded]), expressing your surprise at my having wished you to come to London with your father. There was much in the letter that would have displeased me, if I had not known that you were little used to weigh—or to consider, the true force of written phrases: and therefore—like

[1] In the Bowerswell Papers, and hitherto unpublished.

my cousin Andrew's[1] letters, yours sometimes take a tone and colour very different from that which you intended. However, putting the kindest interpretation I could upon it, there was still enough to cause me to delay my answer all this time, lest I should too hastily write what might give you pain: more especially your imputation of underhand dealing to me—as if I had expressed to you—as my own plan and wish, what was indeed a plan of my fathers. I never do anything of this kind—if it had been my fathers plan I should have told you so;—it was mine— and for the reasons which I gave you in my letter:[2] and you supposing it to be anyone else's was doubly foolish—first because it imputed to me an artful conduct towards you, of which you have never found, and shall never find, the slightest vestige in me: and secondly, because it supposed my father and mother either had less sense, or were less disposed to be kind to you, than I am: the *fact* being that they are continually pleading with me in your favour—begging me to write to you—and reminding me of my duty to you: and it is in fact only in obedience to their instances that I am coming home just now, instead of staying a month longer, and perhaps going to Venice. I am indeed not a little struck with the contrast between their acting and feeling towards you—and yours towards them; as both have appeared lately—*they* always doing all they can to increase my respect for you—dwelling on the best parts of your character—never speaking or thinking of you without affection, and often persuading me to write to you instead of to them [they had stayed in Geneva while John went to Zermatt for a week], while you are watching their every word with jealousy, and suspecting their every act, of unkindness: All this however is natural enough— it is on your side at least what you very properly express as the "Common feeling of Humanity"—and I am not going to blame you for it—you can hardly help it at present, and suffer from it, as people always do from ungenerous feelings, quite enough without any addition of pain from me. As for your wish that I should come to Scotland—that is also perfectly natural—nor

[1] Andrew Richardson, the youngest of the Perth Richardsons, was, according to Mr Ruskin, 'a drunkard & a fool'. He was constantly trying to borrow money from his uncle.
[2] This letter has not survived.

have I the smallest objection to come for you: only do not mistake womanly pride for womanly affection: You say that "you should have thought the first thing I should have done after eight months absence, would have been to come for you." Why, you foolish little puss, do not you see that part of my reason for wishing you to come to London was that I might get you a couple of days sooner; and do not you see also, that if love, instead of pride, had prompted your reply, you would never have thought of what I *ought* to do, or your *right* to ask, you would only have thought of being with me as soon as you could; and your answer would have been that of Imogen— "oh, for a horse with wings"—Look at the passage [*Cymbeline*. Act III, Scene II]. Her husband sends word he is to be at Milford on such a day—She does not "think he might have come nearer" or think that she is a princess and ought not to go travelling about the country with a single servant. She only thinks—only asks—how far is it to this same *blessed* Milford and how far she can ride a day: Your feeling on the other hand, is some more of the *common* feeling of humanity, which I am perfectly willing to indulge: though I should have been much more so if it had been more temperately and modestly expressed: I once wrote to you that you "would not have a *proud* husband" and on my word, you seem to have calculated thereupon to some extent; I have however at least so much pride that I do not intend to allow you to dictate to me what is right, nor even to take upon you the office of my mistress in knowledge of the world—If you knew a little more of it, you would be more cautious how you wrote impertinent letters to your Husband. The whole affair however is too trivial to occupy me longer—and I am not going to treat you like a child, and refuse you your cake because you don't kiss your hand for it properly: I shall come to Perth for you as soon as I get home: only have your calls and ceremonies over, as I shall not stay there: I hope to be at Dijon tomorrow and home in about a fortnight—I am keeping my father out as long as I can— (and but for his feeling that I ought to be with you—I could keep him longer), for fear of the cholera[1]—which I somewhat

[1] An epidemic of cholera from Asia had spread all over Europe at this time.

fear for *him*, as he is nervous and obliged to be in infected
neighbourhoods: for myself I would sleep in a cholera hospital as fearlessly as at Denmark Hill. Write Hotel Meurice, Paris.
I hope you have received my last letter from Chamouni as it
contains a curious story:[1] by the bye—did you ever write to
Thun: I sent to the postoffice there, but got no letter.

Evening. There are passages tonight in the journals about
cholera in France—which make our movements somewhat
doubtful—I am not sure whether we may not come direct
home: at all events, it is of no use risking letters to Paris: you
had better address anything you have now to say to Denmark
Hill—I will write you the day after tomorrow from Dijon,
D.V.—with more certain information—but at all events I
trust to be with you soon—and that we shall not be again so
long separated. I am ever your most aff^e Husband

J Ruskin.

If only we could know Effie's feelings when she received this letter
and her reply to it. At no time during this long separation, when
there were so many attacks upon her, do we hear a word of her own
in her defence. It must have been a very miserable time for her. We
know nothing of her activities except that she was having difficulty
with her drawing and taking exercise on horseback, recommended
by Dr Simpson. This she would have enjoyed, however, because
she loved riding and had ridden all her life. (Millais was later to write
to a friend that she looked beautiful in her riding habit.) We know
also that John had asked her to read Sismondi, the Swiss historian,
and note down in a little book kept for the purpose every word that
bore on the history of Venice as he wanted to get all the facts as
shortly as he could when he got home. This reading may well have
stimulated her wish to go to Venice. Venice was very much in the
news just then. After a year's respite, the Austrian counter-attack had
begun in April of this year, 1849, and for nearly five months Venice
had been bombarded from the mainland night and day without
cessation, and blockaded from the sea. (John had written to Effie on
April 25 from Paris: 'If they knock down Venice I shall give up all
architectural studies: and keep to the Alps: they can't knock down
the Matterhorn.') The most important of the defending Venetian

[1] See p. 49.

fortresses encircling the city was Malghera, close to Mestre, but even after the enforced evacuation of Malghera on May 26, 1849, and its occupation by the Austrians, the Venetians fought on with an heroic spirit of 'Resistance at all Cost' under the leadership of Manin as President of the Provisional Government and old General Pepé, a Neapolitan, as commander of the army. After every other Italian city had been reconquered, Venice held out, hoping for French or British aid. At length on July 29, the Austrians discovered a means of mounting their guns so as to give them a longer range, and their shells fell into the heart of the city, almost reaching the Piazza. Even so it was not until cholera broke out and food and ammunition were completely exhausted that Venice finally capitulated on August 22 while Ruskin was still in Switzerland.

We do not know the exact day on which John arrived in Perth but it must have been some time in the third week in September (he had been in Calais on the 16th). It had been planned that they were to spend the winter in Park Street where John was to write the next volume of *Modern Painters*, and in his last letter to Effie from Paris on September 8 he had written that he was afraid she would be very dull in London as he saw a 'vast quantity of work' in front of him and would be less with her than before, not more probably than if he went to business every day. His mother had suggested therefore that she should ask some friend to come and stay with her for the winter to keep her company during the day. He made his position uncompromisingly clear: 'I am more disinclined for society than ever. I will not see anybody when they call on me, nor call on anybody. I am going to do my own work in my own way, in my own room.' But as soon as he got to Perth Effie asked him to take her to Venice. It was a very wise and somehow touching move on her part, and the very best chance of a full reconciliation between them away from parental influence and interference.

John jumped at the idea; the continuation of *Modern Painters* was postponed (for ten years as it happened), and on their way south they went together to see Dr Simpson in Edinburgh and obtained his whole-hearted approval of the plan. John must also have written to ask his father's permission, for Mr Ruskin wrote to him to Carlisle on the 25th: 'I quite approve of your going to Venice.' He urged, however, that they should go first to Florence 'till a Bill of Health' came from Venice.

Effie had already asked a friend to spend the winter with her in London and now the invitation was extended to Venice. This friend was Charlotte Ker, a daughter of Robert Ker, a Perth neighbour living at 7 Athole Crescent, and Secretary of the Scottish National Railway. Charlotte had sung at the party after Effie's wedding and was said to write very good letters. Effie must have got to know her well while John was abroad because formerly she had been referred to as Miss Ker; now she was Charlotte.

At last, after all these months, we hear Effie's own voice, hopeful and excited at setting off on a new adventure with John.

THE JOURNEY OUT

એ

Denmarkhill, 30th Septr [1849]

My dear Mother,

I received your kind note on my arrival in Park St last night.
We only arrived there then. As Mr Ruskin met us at the
station [Euston Square] we went or rather came out here and
found Mrs Ruskin looking very well, Mr Ruskin very ill but
both quite pleased to see us and to let us go to Italy and quite
delighted that Charlotte was to go with us. Next morning we
had some talk about our arrangements and I had some private
conversation with Mr Ruskin; what an extraordinary man he
is; he was quite delighted that I spoke to him, evidently, and
said he had nothing to blame me for and thought I had behaved
beautifully. I begged him to tell me what he was not pleased
with. He said there was nothing but that he thought sometimes
John could not make me happy which was a new light certainly
on the subject. However we settled it all in the best possible
manner, but who can know what such a man thinks!!

John and I then drove into town to look for a carriage. We
concluded by fixing to take two, one for John, George [Hobbs],
stores & books, and an elegant *Pilentum* for Charlotte and me.
It is an open carriage but shuts very easily and large enough
to hold John when he wants to come and chat with us. It is
rather heavy but very handsome and will require three horses.[1]
We all think that a capital arrangement for we shall be able to
enjoy the country so much more but do not tell the gossips
in case they think that although John and I intend going abroad
we are not to travel together which would be a delightful catch

[1] The *Pilentum* was invented in about 1834 by David Davies, a famous
coachbuilder of Albany Street, London, who built Queen Victoria's first
railway carriage. John and Effie had not taken their own carriage on the
Normandy trip.

for not the *Birrel*[1] but some others. By the way, a capitle joke
Mr Ruskin heard when he came home that the report was that
I was so unhappy with John that proceedings were instituted
for a separation. He was fearfully angry and thinks less now
of what the Farquharsons said. By the bye, if I could only
collect my ideas I could give you some brilliant hints. What
do you think the great Philanthropist[2] gave my servants when
he went away, I suppose to do them good? A Volume of
Pilgrim's Progress.

We found the house in beautiful order and every thing just
as I left it, and the servants looking very well but very sorry
that we are not to remain at home. I was dreadfully tired. I
could not go on this way for many days longer and I was nearly
obliged to come out of Church this morning. I ought never
to have been there for the heat and closeness of the air here
is dreadful but Mr R wished us to be seen in Church and I
could make no objection. To-morrow will be another awful
today but Tuesday I hope we shall be off....

The things John brought from Paris are quite beautiful. The
bonnet crimson velvet with little feathers on one side and
white flowers on the inside, very open in the front.[3] The cloak
very thickly wadded and quilted in a broad pattern all round,
extremely warm and quite light. Two scarfs for evening, one a
white crape with blue, and the other rose and white checked
silk, very curious. He wants us to get an evening dress or so in

---

[1] Miss Ann Birrel was a neighbour living at Bellwood Cottage, Bridgend.
She was a great gossip.

[2] Nickname for William Macdonald. When Effie first met him while
staying at Denmark Hill in June, 1847, she wrote: 'I never met anyone so
good, in fact we all think he is too good to live.' He had been staying for a
time at Park Street. His parents, the Farquharsons, had evidently been
gossiping. There had been a coolness between them and John since John's
marriage.

[3] Effie had evidently asked John to get her a bonnet, for he had written to
her from Paris on September 8: ' ... do you not think the Louvre is enough
to find me employment, my Effie, without the grave responsibility of going
to choose bonnets to make my pretty wife proud?—I will fetch you one
certainly, my pet, as you ask me; but you know there is nobody here just
now—and there will most assuredly be nothing in the way of bonnets but
refuse of last winter and spring—and things intended for the bourgeoisie.'

Paris as we shall be visiting in Venice and Florence. John is in great spirits and quite delighted with the thought of going abroad and full of business. I hope you will all keep well and be very happy. I can hardly believe now that I have spent so many months in Perth and if I was not in a dreadful hustle I would send many messages....

Give my best love and kisses to the dear little ones and my dear Papa & George. I shall try and write to him on his birthday.[1]

Ever Yours most affectionately

Effie Ruskin

They did not get off until Wednesday, October 3. They drove down to Folkestone in their carriages which were then taken aboard the steam packet to Boulogne and lashed to the deck. Had they wished, they could have remained in the carriages during the crossing. (This Effie did on the way home.) The horses were left behind, for where there was no railway from one place to another they travelled post. Where there was a railway, as between Boulogne and Paris, the carriages were put on trucks at the back of the train, and here again passengers, if they liked, could stay in their carriages. The journey by rail took eight hours. The branch line between Calais and Boulogne was as yet unfinished, which was the reason why they went to Boulogne in spite of the longer Channel crossing.

There were still so many gaps in the network of railways at this time that public coaches as well as private carriages were used as much as ever. Murray's *Hand-Book for France* for 1847 tells us that 'on those routes upon which railways have been begun, the diligence [stage coach] pursues the line of the rail, the body of the vehicle being taken off from its wheels by a crane, and deposited, luggage, passengers and all, upon a truck attached to the train. On arriving at its destination it is taken off and placed upon a different set of wheels, and is instantly driven off.' The private carriage, on its own wheels, was, however, pushed on to the truck up a ramp over the end of the buffer stops. The truck was placed in a siding for this purpose and afterwards attached to the train; but it was only at first-class stations, where there was suitable accommodation and sufficient staff, that private carriages could be loaded on to the trains. Passengers who chose to remain in their carriages suffered the

[1] October 4, when he would be twenty.

discomfort of being hoisted over the buffer stops as well as the dirt from the engine. Nevertheless this practice continued right up to the 1870's.

Passports had to be carried, but could be obtained en route. A passport issued by the Foreign Office cost more than any other (47/-) and was not regarded as having any advantages. *Visas*, or signatures on the passport of representatives of every country to be entered, were also essential. In France, moreover, the signature of the Minister of the Interior was necessary to enable the traveller to leave the country. The passport had therefore to be handed over to the police on arrival, even though it may just have been issued, and collected again in Paris. Meanwhile, a *Passe Provisoire* was needed, and getting this could be a tedious business just after the arrival of a boat at a Channel port.

Passports were liable to be called for at any time by the police who could stop a traveller on the highway, enter the hotel dining-room or even a bedroom to demand a sight of 'the precious document'. Murray advised that it was 'needless to expatiate on this restraint, so inconsistent with the freedom which an Englishman enjoys at home. It is the custom of the country and the stranger must conform or has no business to set his foot into it.' Customs examination could be tiresome, especially for those travelling by public conveyance. Those posting, however, were advised to offer a 'fee' and could then be fairly confident that no examination would take place. Austrian customs officers were the exception to this rule: being persons of higher character it was more difficult to 'fee' them—and, says Murray, 'less necessary; for as they do not regularly look forward to being bribed they are less disposed to be vexatious'. The next edition of Murray's *Hand-Book for France* did not appear until 1853, and although by that time the railways had been extended a little, travelling conditions had not changed.

John and his father wrote to each other almost every day during this trip. Two of John's letters are published in the *Works* but none of the others have been traced. Many of Mr Ruskin's, however, have survived and throw a little light on and embellish some of Effie's.[1]

It was three days before Effie found a chance to write home from

[1] Mr Ruskin's letters covering this period are at the Ruskin Galleries, Bembridge, and the extracts quoted from them have never before been published.

Dijon. She told her mother that they had stayed the first two nights in Paris at the Hotel Meurice, and on the 5th had posted to Montbard, then a flourishing little town which was to be ruined two years later by the opening of the railroad from Paris to Dijon. She wrote also to George from Dijon telling him about the French postillions. 'Every hour or so we have a new one and their dress and the way they crack their long whips above their heads is most amusing. Their dress is generally a peaked hat, enormous moustache & beard, a blue Jacket with lots of buttons, scarlet waistcoat braided with gold, full blue Cotton trowsers and enormous long jackboots, always dirty, complete their attire.'

From Dijon they posted to Champagnole, a distance of seventy miles, and from Champagnole to Geneva, fifty-four miles. A post-stage varied between seven and twelve miles. The second day, although covering a shorter distance, would have taken longer because the road ran through the Jura mountains. Usually the Ruskins stayed a night at Morez, between Champagnole and Geneva, but this time John was pressing on to cross the Alps before the snow came, so they did not rest even on the Sunday which was almost unprecedented.

Effie's next letter was from Geneva.

Hotel des Bergues,[1] October [9th]

My dearest Papa

I have just received a nice letter from Mama enclosing a note to John with which he is much pleased.... I have not been at all well these last two days. Posting two whole days one after the other and no help for it has quite tired me out but we shall not have to do it again John says. I was as ill as ever yesterday and my throat in a very bad state. I think the cold winds striking on me amongst the Jura in a open carriage have hurt me and yet whenever we shut it I turned so sick that I was forced to open it again. I got better towards the end of the days and enjoyed passing through the Jura from Champagnole exceedingly. I was very much delighted with the Pine forests and as the day could not have been finer the Autumn tints on

[1] The façade of this hotel, opened in 1834 and still one of the best in Geneva, is almost unchanged. Murray's 1847 *Hand-Book for Switzerland* described it as 'comfortable and well-managed'.

the hills and the fall [*sic*] rushing torrents were exquisitely beautiful and the first view of the Alps, the plain of Geneva and the Lake seen from an elevation of 3,000 feet the most striking Panorama I ever beheld but curious to say I was not in the least surprised by the magnificence of the view as it was exactly like what I had always supposed it would be.[1] A very fine sunset illuminated Mont Blanc and the other hills to a great degree of beauty, the gardens full of grapes and flowers and the people with the large round straw hats adding greatly to the picture. John was excessively delighted to see how happy we were and went jumping about and executing *pas* that George and I agreed Taglioni would have stared her widest at.

This is a dull misty morning but I am greatly pleased with the aspect of Geneva and the beautiful river at our feet. If I could only feel better I should enjoy every thing far more. I am exceedingly happy but my want of strength keeps me from seeing a great deal that I ought to see. We leave tomorrow for St. Martin's and the next day to Chamouni. John is exceedingly thoughtful for my want of strength but we must cross the Simplon before the end of the month for fear of being stopped all together and every day is precious.... Charlotte keeps very well and is intensely delighted with every thing. Her want of French is much against her enjoying many things but it is good for me for I have to speak for both and then translate to her. Give little Sophie, Alice, John and Melville my best love.[2] Tell Mama I do not suffer from cold feet as George got a very nice fur foot bag before I left and we are always quite warm....

Chamouni,[3] October 14, 1849

Dearest George

... We left Geneva and posted to Bonville [Bonneville] a

[1] Effie was lucky to see this view at all; it appears eighteen miles north of Geneva, just past the Col de la Faucille. Forty years later Ruskin wrote in *Praeterita*, 'I have never seen that view perfectly but once—in this year 1835.'

[2] Sophie or Sophia was six, Alice four, John three and Melville not quite two.

[3] The Ruskins always stayed at the Hotel de l'Union at Chamouni (as it was then spelt) which can be seen in old prints. The car-park now occupies the site of this hotel.

village in Savoy at the foot of the Alps exquisitely situated and the hills extremely fine ... but the people in these exquisite vallies are without exception the most hideous creatures you can possibly conceive. The men are bad enough but the women are fearful, nay perfect hags, and the children wretched little distorted creatures, some without any arms and others half a hand. The women, every second one we saw, had a huge goitre which they appear to consider rather ornamental than other for they never cover them but hang necklaces upon them and crosses &c.[1] Their teeth for the most part fallen out and their skins dark brown, wrinkled & dirty, and horried expressions make them look perfect Harpies. Charlotte and I were perfectly horrified with the general appearance of them-selves, their children and their houses.... We left our carriages at St. Martin's and drove in char-a-bancs, or rather were shaken to pieces nearly, to Chamouni....[2]

It is most amusing to see the surprize and delight of the people at the return of John. They seem so fond of him and they pay me pretty little compliments. We are now going to walk to Couttet's[3] to the place where the *Ghost* is seen and try and see it. John declares neither Charlotte nor I are good enough to see it however. The story remains the same and I will not close my letter till we return. Mont Blanc is in the clouds and

[1] Goitres at that time were greatly prized as they secured exemption from military service, and as they were thought to be hereditary, a goitre to a woman was as good as a dowry. Goitre and cretinism, due to thyroid deficiency and lack of iodine in the drinking water, were then endemic in the Alps.

[2] A char-à-banc was rather like a sofa placed on wheels. The road from St Martin was so bad that there was no other means of reaching Chamonix except on foot or mule-back. In those days the old road from Maglan went along the right bank of the River Arve to St Martin, and thence over the lovely stone bridge of 1783 to Sallanches. Consequently St Martin was then a busy and important place. Now the road goes along the left bank direct to Sallanches, and St Martin is a forgotten hamlet. Ruskin always stayed there at the Hotel du Mont Blanc which is the title of Chapter XI, Part II, of *Praeterita*.

[3] Joseph Couttet had been Ruskin's guide since 1844. Ruskin called him his guide, philosopher, friend and doctor. He accompanied Ruskin on all his Alpine excursions up to the year before his death in 1877 aged eighty-four.

the snow is very low and the air so thick that it must be snowing thickly above but it is not very cold & the air is deliciously fresh and bracing.

We had a delightful walk as far as the wood which the Ghost haunts. After looking about for some time and seeing nothing we sat down whilst John went & brought some of the children who first saw it. They ran & looked quite naturally and came back saying it was not there. I questioned them, & Constance Balmat[1] said that it had not been seen by any one for three weeks, the last time was Sunday three weeks ago when all the village came to the spot and it was like a fete. The children saw it and when all the men & women with the Curé at their tail were looking for it in the little thicket of trees, one little child was following slowly when she cried out that they need not look in the wood, for it was behind her. I asked the children if they were not much afraid. "Yes," they said, "the first time and it stood by us at night in our sleep but now we have not fear because it come not near us but stands by the fence" (for the tree you know was dug up). The Curé has told the people not to mind it or look for it and he went and said some Christos over the place. The treasure seekers in the valley have tried the Hazel-wand at the place and find it works for thirteen feet square. I saw that done and John is going to get men to dig so far. The Hazel-wand is most curious and as it worked in my hands as well as in Judith Couttet's [Joseph Couttet's daughter] and would not stir with any one else I am no longer incredulous. I assure you I did not like feeling the piece of green stick moving round in my hands slowly upright without me stirring and them all staring to see if my hands moved in the least. I tried to see if it would do in several places but it remained quite still excepting at the place above mentioned. This custom is so universal in the valley with those who have the power that they constantly find water and minerals by it. The same is practised in Cornwall & in the Highlands (see Dousterswivel in the Antiquary[2]) and there is no quackery about it. It is a kind of

---

[1] The twelve-year-old daughter of Ruskin's other guide, Gideon Balmat.

[2] Herman Dousterswivel was the German mountebank in Scott's novel *The Antiquary* who claimed to be an 'adept' and to divine buried treasure by witchcraft.

natural magic and acts with persons in the same way that some have the power of mesmerizing and others not. As to the Ghost one cannot say anything about it, but should like to have the ground examined....[1] Write as often as you can till I tell you to stop, to Poste Restante, Venice, and do not pay the letters....[2]

Chamouni, 17th October [Wednesday]

My dear Mother

... We leave tomorrow crossing the Tête Noir and getting to Martigny next day. We ought to go in one day but eight hours on mule-back is too much for us and we are going to do half one day and do the next four hours next day. It saves us going round the way we came and the weather is so mild that John has no fear about our crossing the Simplon next week. John and I had a delightful walk this morning among the pine-woods on the Brevon picking cloud berries and throwing the huge blocks of stone down seven hundred feet and watching them bounding from rock to rock. When we came in he got Balmat and put Charlotte upon his mule under his charge and sent her away to see the source of the Arveron and the Glaciers des Bois. I was too tired to go as I have not been well for several days and was in bed yesterday till the evening but since my walk today I feel better and John was anxious that Charlotte should see as many of the sights of Chamouni as she could.

We are both learning Italian steadily. Every day John hears me my lesson and I hear Charlotte hers but when we get to Venice we shall have a regular master. Mons. Le Curé is

---

[1] The story about the ghost was evidently told in John's letter of September 2 from Chamonix. This letter has not come to light, but we know the story from a letter to his father written on August 26 and quoted in Volume 36 of Ruskin's *Works*. Several children had seen the figure of a woman in a black dress leaning with folded arms against a young pine tree within two hundred yards of Couttet's house.

[2] At that time full or part postage could be paid by the recipient without paying extra, but on November 1, 1851, a new rule came into force whereby letters which were not pre-paid were charged double the other end. Postage from the United Kingdom to the Austrian Dominions was 1/5 under 1/4 oz and 2/5 under 1/2 oz. A letter from Perth to Venice took from eight to ten days.

going to dine with us today. Couttet has been in and tells us
the men are getting on surely with the hole. They think it will
be finished on Friday night. They all think there is something
there but have come to nothing yet....[1]

Brieg [Brig], 21st October, 1849

My dear Brother

We have passed through some exquisite country since I last
wrote to you. After leaving Chamouni we passed the night at
Trient half way to Martigny in the mountains, a solitary
auberge and dirty enough. John & I escaped but poor Charlotte who had an obscure brown blanket covering her bed was
dreadfully bitten.[2] The guides and George slept amongst the
hay. We had a lovely ride across the mountains to Martigny.
The people in the slopes of the hills were busy gathering their
fruit harvest of Chesnuts, apples and making wine. Couttet &
the carriages met us at Martigny and we posted to Sion, a most
romantic town with two rocks in the middle and Castles on
them as high as Edinburgh Castle and as large. It was the
market day and all the women had on their little Valoisan hats
with a satin & gold ribbon crumpled round....

At Viège [Visp] we saw idiots and goitres in plenty and
could hardly get Postillions to bring us here a stage and a half.
The proper Postillion (for they are all German and John was
particularly delighted with the specimens I had for I was so
anxious to hear German and John hates them so much), well
the proper Postillion was rushing about as fast as his drunken-
ness would allow him in his Sunday clothes for he had just
buried his mother. John would not have him and the Postmaster took his place. We had not gone twenty yards before

[1] They left on Thursday before the hole was finished. Effie afterwards turned
sceptical and ten months later wrote: 'I had a good laugh against John who
spent some English coin in digging a great hole fourteen feet square ... and
was rewarded by only finding an old key.'
[2] The 1847 Murray tells us that a new room had been built as a *salle à manger*
on to the little auberge at Trient but that the dormitory was wretched. The
only inn there today still looks horribly uninviting. Effie does not complain
of discomfort at Brig so they were apparently not staying at the Poste which
Murray describes with the one word: 'bugs'. There were two other inns.

the Postmaster met one of his Postillions on the road and asked him to take his place. In dismounting he was so drunk that he pulled the saddle round and lay on the ground with one foot in the stirrup unable, so fat was he, to move till George assisted him. The drunken contentment with which he lay amused John excessively. But that was not all. The new Postillion was as tipsy as his master and on reaching his place executed the same feat with sounds in German and French of anything but a melodious character. Charlotte's and my Postillion nearly tumbled all our equipage into the Rhone, so that altogether it was perfectly dreadful.

This town is exceedingly picturesque at the foot of the Simplon which we cross tomorrow and hope D.V. to reach Domo d'Ossola for dinner. Couttet goes with us so far and is trying to persuade John to take him to Venice. John thinks of doing it as he is afraid of robbers. I think it would be a very useless expence as one can get a guard from one town to another whenever you like and we never travel in the dark as it is not healthy....[1]

Albergo Reale,[2] Milan, Octr. 27th, 1849

Dearest Papa

... We passed the Simplon most comfortably on Monday. There was no snow and as warm as June at the top. John was telling us about a monk, the Père Barras, who was sent to the Hospice there for a punishment as he was discovered dancing at a Ball at Geneva with a Lady, and just as we were speaking up came the very man himself with two splendid dogs. He had some conversation with us and wished us to come into the Hospice where he had now been eight years, but we declined. He was not very attractive, very red in the face with dirty hands and a beard a week old.[3]

[1] John had taken Couttet with him to Venice in 1845 'by way of pro-papa' because his father could not go with him. Couttet received 4 francs a day as well as his board and lodging. He did not go with them this time.

[2] This hotel was in the Contrada dei Tre Re and no longer exists. It was described in Murray's *Hand-Book for Northern Italy* as 'a house highly spoken of, and now reasonable as to charges; attendance good'.

[3] The Hospice of the Simplon, which had been founded by Napoleon but left unfinished for want of funds until 1840, was occupied by a few brothers

We passed through the celebrated Defile of Gondo.... We
posted on to Baveno, a most lovely place on the Lake Maggiore.
We took a boat and went to the Borromean Islands on it,
belonging to the Count Borromeo, one of the most influential noblemen in North Italy and fined £20,000 by the
Austrians. We visited his Palace on the Isola Bella and saw him
and his children. He is a fine looking fair man not like an Italian.[1] We are going today to see the tomb of his ancestor, the
great St. Carlo Borromeo, who was Archbishop of Milan in the
15th Century & from whom the immense estates descend.
They were given to him by Milan for his services during the
great plague.

[*Later.*] The saint is buried in a Chapel, the walls of which
are all of Silver with the Coffin in the middle of Rock crys-
tal. Through it all you see him dressed in his robes of cloth of
Gold with gems and on his breast an emerald cross worth
£5,000. The face is not disagreeable.[2]

This is a delightful place, still in a state of siege and therefore
melancholy, full of Austrians & Croat Soldiery, the best dressed
and finest looking men I ever saw in their white coats & tight
blue Italy trowsers. The people are very unhappy and complain
dreadfully of the way in which they were betrayed to Radetzky
by Charles Albert.[3] We were at the Opera the other night. It

---

of the Augustine order, the same community as that of the Grand St Bernard.
Père Barras had been sent from the Grand St Bernard where he had been
bursar for thirty years, but it could not have been much of a punishment,
for the Simplon Hospice was said by Murray to be much more comfortable
than the St Bernard and 'even warmed by a heating apparatus'. There was a
good post road over the pass.

[1] Count Vitaliano Borromeo (1792-1874) had married in 1826 Maria,
Marchesa d'Adda. Many of his descendants are alive and still own the great
Palazzo Borromeo in Milan and the lovely Isola Bella with its terraced
garden, laid out by an ancestor in 1671.

[2] The tomb of San Carlo, who died in 1584, is in the crypt of the Cathedral. The body is embalmed, but even in 1847, Murray tells us that 'The skill
of modern embalmers has not been able to preserve the body from decay. The
brown and shrivelled flesh of the mouldering countenance scarcely covers the
bone.' This face, which Effie did not find disagreeable, was covered in 1961
with a polished silver mask because, according to a verger, so many women
fainted in horror at the sight of it.

[3] The Milanese, who had driven out the Austrians in March, 1848, were

was full of Austrian Officers with a sprinkling of their wives and daughters but no Italian Ladies. The people here are not good-looking but wear the black veil very gracefully over their magnificent black hair. We are going to the City of Romeo & Juliet, Verona, on Monday by way of Monza to see the Iron crown & jewels there. I will write soon again but I am very tired but I think I have been better since I came into Italy the air is so delightful....

Albergo Reale, Milan, 28th October, 1849

My dearest Papa

... John saw part of the old Visconti Palace being in course of removal the other day and the only reason they gave was that the modern Italian Piazza [Palazzo] is much more comfortable to live in and that they were going to build one after their own mind instead. We are in great hopes of seeing Radetzky who is expected here every day from Vienna and we are determined to see him, as he is a *decided* Lion even if we should have to wait for him.[1] Charlotte and I have a very nice open carriage, and with a valet-de-place[2] on the box we drive out every forenoon and I assure you strike far more terror into the hearts of the Austrian Officers & Soldiers than Radetzky himself for such a thing as two Ladies has not been seen here for months, and with the exception of young Lady Otway[3] who is in the house here, Charlotte and I reign supreme and many are the cigars

---

prepared to fight to the death, but Charles Albert, on his defeat by Radetzky in July, signed an armistice which delivered Milan into his hands. The Milanese aristocracy were still refusing to mix socially with the Austrians at this time. The city had been under martial law since August 7, 1848.

[1] He was the Civil and Military Governor of Lombardo-Veneto with his headquarters in Verona.

[2] The valet or laquais-de-place was a guide who, as well as taking the traveller to places of historical interest, acted as interpreter, introduced him to shops and did his bargaining for him.

[3] Eliza, daughter of John Campbell of Burnham Grove, Bucks. In March, 1848, while still a minor, she had married Sir George Otway, Bt, born 1816. He was a captain in the Navy. They lived at Brighton and also had a house in London at 6 Portman Square. They had no children. He died in 1881.

that are taken out of the mouths as we pass and innumerable are the prancing of the horses trotting and galloping after us on the Corso, but they are all Austrians or Croats and I am a thorough Italian here & hate oppression, therefore wish them far enough.

Today we visited one of the galleries of art [the Biblioteca Ambrosiana] and saw amongst other curious things a letter from Lucrezia Borgia to Cardinal Bembo with a long lock of her hair which is very fair and fine tied with black [still on show], one splendid Fresco of Raphael and a great number of sketches of Leonardo da Vinci's. We went into the Refectory of a Monastery and saw his Fresco of the Last Supper which you know from prints. It is much faded and dimmed, but still the hand of the great master is visible throughout, and the centre figure, Our Lord, is full of dignity and sweetness but the whole place was very sad to see, on the Entrance door the Large black Austrian Eagle painted, showing it was a Barrack, with soldiers looking out of every window, the Cloister full of them smoking and playing at dice and the centre a receptacle for all the refuse from the cavalry stables on one side.[1]

This Milan is a most wonderful place for street organs and the Italians seem to do little else but sit at their doors, accompany the organs with their voices and eating hot chesnuts which are roasting in Bins on little wood fires in every part of the town and which are certainly very nice indeed for they roast them so well and they taste just like sweet Potatoes, but the Organs are delightful and we have a sort of continuous concert every evening. John is very busy drawing an old Pulpit in St. Ambrogio full of grotesque monsters and most elegant devices of every kind of 9th century work. He is immensely pleased both with the work and the pulpit.[2]

I hope Melville is quite well again. These teething attacks

[1] Napoleon had turned the military out of the refectory. The story has it that he sat on the ground in front of the picture and wrote in his pocket-book on his knee the order for their removal.

[2] This drawing, in water colour, reproduced in the *Works*, Volume 16, plate XIV, is now in the Victoria and Albert Museum. This is established by un-published entries in Ruskin's notebooks.

must keep Mama very anxious about him and he is such a pale little thing but I hope he will soon recover his lost strength and play about with the others....[1]

I think we shall enjoy our stay at Venice very much and as they are doing all they can to propitiate the Austrians we may go out a little. Lady Otway tells me, for she has just come from there, that numbers of the refugee French and others, nobles, Spaniards etc, the Duc de Bordeaux, Conde Montemolin and others are crowding there and going to make it very gay so that we may meet some curious characters....

The Count of Montemolin (1818-61) was the eldest of the three sons of Don Carlos, uncle of the young Queen Isabella and first claimant to the throne of Spain. In 1845 Don Carlos had renounced his rights to the throne in favour of Montemolin who was then recognised by the Carlists as Charles VI. The Duc de Bordeaux (1820-83) was better known as the Comte de Chambord. He was the Bourbon claimant to the throne of France, son of the last Duc de Berry who had been assassinated seven months before his birth. On the death of his grandfather, Charles X, in 1836, Chambord had been proclaimed King Henry V by his supporters. He had a palazzo in Venice as well as a castle in Austria.

Effie wrote next from Verona. They stayed there at the Due Torri Hotel, where John had always stayed, a converted palace in the Piazza S. Anastasia. The old palace originally belonged to the Scaligeri family, Lords of Verona, but at their fall it became an inn where the post-office was established. It remained an hotel until 1882 when it became a private house. In 1958 it was entirely rebuilt on the old site and opened again as an hotel, one of the best in Europe.

4th November

My dearest Mother

... We came in here from Brescia last night and are comfortably settled here for a week.... We have been rather in a state of excitement this evening, indeed Mama so excited that we jumped up in the middle of dinner and refused to return.

[1] Melville, who had been born during Effie's engagement, lived to be ninety-eight. In 1939, at the age of ninety-one, he married for the first time.

The reason was this, that we heard Radetzky, who is living in Verona, was coming to pay a visit to a Russian, next room to us, the Princess Samoilow at half past 5, and the people said they would let us know when he arrived and as our hotel is like all others here, a court in the centre [now covered in] with a Balcony running all round the square, when we heard his carriage arriving which was a handsome Brougham with two Jet black horses, we had only to go to our door to see him. The Princess, a tall fine looking dark woman in a black coat & pink kid shoes with a white dog in her arms, went to the top of the stairs to receive him and having paid her compliments went into her room till he took off his cloak.[1] We had then a very good look of him. He is much better looking than I expected and a perfect wonder for his age. To look at him he appears a hale stout old man of 70 with white hair and not tall, but he is 86 and he is as straight as any of us with a pleasant face.[2] He was attended by two splendid looking men in very fine uniforms, one of them General Kölun who is staying here, and dressed in white coats and cloaks lined & turned up with scarlet cloth and cocked hats. Radetzky had on a very beautiful surtout and trowsers of a very pale blue Italy cloth, a fine plume on his cocked hat, and his sword and gold orders &c. showed to great advantage.

After remaining half an hour we saw him depart in the same manner. The Princess seemed to have lost one of her pet dogs during the visit, a little thing very fat & stupid. It came and sat itself under my chair and nothing would move it. I was threatening to kick it out and did not know it was the dog for which her highness was rushing about the Balcony for. At last George comprehended her and fetched the dog and presented

---

[1] Julie, Countess (not Princess) Samoilow had been born in 1803, the daughter of Count Paul Pahlen of a very rich Baltic family. In 1825 she married Count Nicholas Alexander Samoilow, A.D.C. to the Tsar. He died in 1842, and in 1849 she married an Italian singer called Peri. She had lived a very gay life in Milan for over twenty years and was particularly well known there to the foreign residents. In 1863 she married Charles, Comte de Mornay. She died in Paris in 1875.

[2] He was only eighty-three. He had been in the army since he was fifteen. The last of his illegitimate children was born in Milan in 1846.

it to her. You would have thought it was a favourite child for she seized it in her arms and kissed it over & over again until I fairly laughed outright. I never saw a woman make such a fool of herself. She then entered her room to prepare for departing at seven.

Just at this time a Band of 60 men in all entered the Square and set themselves in order to play by arranging a kind of trellis work all in a circle, putting candles and music thereupon, and with the bandmaster in the Centre began to play. We imagined that it was a compliment of Radetzky's sending this magnificent band to serenade the Princess, but we found out that they were the Band of a Regiment from the Grand Duke of Baden, and hearing that their former General, General Kölun, was in the Hotel they had come to Serenade him. His sons were chatting with us for an hour, talking English perfectly. The eldest, I should think about my age, already a Captain of Cuirassiers at Milan and very handsome, accosted us on the Balcony with his brother, a very lovely boy of about 14 also in his Father's Regiment.[1] They informed us, taking off their hats and keeping them in their hands all the time they remained with us, that our servant had asked them some questions regarding the band and that they were afraid he had misunderstood them, which he had, and they had taken the liberty of answering them to us if they could be of any use. They gave us a great deal of information and appeared to reverence their Father extremely and I do not wonder for I never saw a finer man. They told us that no one could be a General with them unless he spoke five languages, and they both, I found out, spoke four. After the Princess left, their Father sent for them and they were off in a moment. Not to make us think them rude they returned again to make their adieus. The little one came first; I never saw such a face, so fine in features and so smooth a skin. He had talked with Charlotte and he came

---

[1] Effie had made a mistake here as transpires in the next letter. These brothers were the sons of Lt.-Field-Marshal Count François Wimpffen (1797-1870); and it was Wimpffen Effie had seen with Radetzky and for whom the band was playing. He had been Governor of Milan for a time after its reoccupation; Bologna had capitulated to him in May, 1849, and he was now commanding at Trieste.

to bid us goodbye & tell us he was going next day to Trieste
with his Father but he hoped we should come there and it
would *make him* & his Father & Mother *much happiness.* I said
we could not have that pleasure. Then the elder one came. He
said that he put himself entirely at our disposal whilst we remained and that he had only two field days with Radetzky to
interfere, and away he went cap in hands. Charlotte and I were
perfectly charmed with their conversation and manners, so
quiet & yet such high breeding. When we came into the room
we found John deep in his books. I asked him why he had not
come out to see the two Austrians. He said that he knew by
the voices who we had with us and he was afraid if he came
out that it would drive them away and he was very glad we had
somebody to talk to like ourselves....

> Le Due Torri, Verona, 8th November, 1849
... John says there is work for him here for at least six
months and we intend returning here after we leave Venice for
another week which will enable us to see three important
towns, Mantua, Modena & Parma, which we otherwise should
have missed, and being a new line of country it was well for
us to see as much as we can. John is engaged in some very elaborate and beautiful drawings from the Monuments of the
Scaliger family, formerly Lords of Verona in the middle ages.
They are very splendid and stand in a little court in the
middle of the town beside their former Palace so that as Charlotte and I breakfast alone, we do not see John till three when
he walks with us till dinner.
We occupy ourselves in Charlotte learning French & me
Italian, working and reading and taking exercise for the stone
floors make one's feet dreadfully cold and I dance and jump
about for an hour sometimes to make my blood circulate in a
manner that would edify you exceedingly. We are all extremely
happy and John is as kind and thoughtful for me as can be.
My throat troubles me exceedingly and the irritation in the
inside very stationary. I have none on my skin at all and although I am able to take more exercise, the pain in my stomach,
bowels & throat are as bad, the latter much worse in fact. I
never saw anything in my mouth when at Perth but now I see

all the back of the tongue covered with little blisters it appears to me, not in the least painful to the touch but on damp days very hoarse and uncomfortable and always worse after damp although I do not go out. There is no tickling of the throat or like cold, but like sore throat and so hoarse that my voice goes away entirely sometimes and I cannot speak. In other respects I am better, not languid or dull, and better excepting in this. I wish you would ask Dr. Scott if I could take anything or if you could write a few lines to Dr. Kirkmichael and he might tell Simpson.[1] I get mustard and try it as he ordered, and a Holloway's Pill[2] when I require such medicine, or a little magnesia.... Charlotte and John are very kind but know nothing about my complaint....[3]

How you would enjoy a few days sketching with John in this lovely weather, not too warm and yet so exquisite a sky & bright sun. John has written to England to Lady Davy[4] and others for some letters of introduction for us that Charlotte & I may go into a little Society at Venice & Florence, and as he is so busy he would like us to get acquainted with some English and amuse ourselves, and during the Carnival we may have some amusement without troubling him.

Our acquaintance of the other evening is likely to prove very

[1] Dr Kirkmichael presumably practised in Edinburgh as he could 'tell' Simpson, but there is no record of him in the postal directory. Dr David Scott was a surgeon druggist of 35 High Street, Perth. He had attended Jessie Jameson in her last illness.

[2] A laxative, on the market from 1837 for over a hundred years. Thomas Holloway built and gave to the nation the Holloway Sanatorium at Virginia Water and the Holloway College at Egham Hill.

[3] John had written on September 28 to Mrs Gray from York, after visiting Dr Simpson: 'I believe now that I understand what Effie needs—whether of care or of management—her complaint being one from which, in a somewhat different form, I long suffered myself.' (From an unpublished letter in Bowerswell Papers.)

[4] Née Jane Kerr, widow of Shuckburgh Ashby Apreece and of Sir Humphry Davy, Bt, the scientist, who had invented the Davy Safety Lamp. She was well known in both Roman and London society; was a great lion-hunter and a terrific talker. John introduced her to Effie soon after they returned from their honeymoon and Effie thought her 'perfect'. She gave 'a very select' dinner party for them. She lived at 26 Park Street. She died in 1855 aged seventy-five.

useful to us. We found out next day that his father for whom the
Band played was Field Marshall Wimpffen and a very distinguished officer. He & the other young son went to Trieste
near Venice and our friend is Count Albert or some such
name and lives with Radetzky, one of his Staff Majors I think.[1]
He came to us next day to call and on asking what we should
like to see I said I should like very much to see the inside of
the bombproof and fortified Towers outside the town over-
hanging the city on the line of Hills which kept the Veronese
in such terror that they never revolted. He said he would
have great pleasure and he would ask Radetzky to give him
three hours in the afternoon, for they never have any leisure
and are kept hard at work the whole day, at least those on the
staff, till tea-time [about 7 or 8 p.m.].

Next day the time came and no John appeared although a
very handsome carriage & pair was ready for us by his order.
He came into my room whilst I was dressing and I said, "Are
you not ready John to go with us?" "Oh! dear no," said he,
"what possible interest have I in lines of fortification? I never
intended to go and not having to walk with you today I shall
have such a famous drawing day. Count Wimpffen is exceedingly intelligent & modest, a very nice companion for you &
Charlotte, just the sort of person who it is good for you to be
with and I daresay it makes him very happy too. George shall
accompany you if you think proper." I said, "Well, John, I don't
think you would be understood by the world at all." "Oh, no,"
said he, "never. I think it very absurd that because I enjoy
myself, you & Charlotte should be kept moping in the house."
With this he took us down stairs and telling our companion
he gave us into his charge, and the young man laying
his hand on his heart and making a low bow, we went on our
drive, saw the fortifications, had them explained to us and
thought that if the Veronese ever did get up an emeute they
would all be blown in the air before they knew where they
were. The view was splendid and he pointed out to us the
different fields of Battle where they fought Charles Albert. I
asked him what sort of man their new emperor is.[2] He says, a

---

[1] He was Count Alphonse. The younger son was Count Victor.
[2] Franz Joseph, born August 18, 1830, had been Emperor for less than a year.

fine young man of 19, has been very carefully educated by his mother, the Archduchess Sophie. I said, "Have you seen him?" "Oh, yes I danced in the same Quadrille with him at a Court Ball in July, & in August I was fighting near him in a Battle." He told us that Radetzky was a very good old man and he was very happy with him, that he hated ceremony and never allowed any of his officers to remain standing. He is over- whelmed with business as he has both the civil & military affairs of the whole of Lombardy to look after. His Countess is an old Lady and has lived with him for two months very happily, not having been with him for 30 years before, a curi- ous couple they never quarelled but wrote to each other always, and were very good friends. The other day, Radetzky happened to pass through the town where she lived, called upon her and brought her here, and our friend thinks they will not separate again. They have one daughter married ten years ago, a very fine woman and her mother lived mostly with her.[1]

We had a deal of conversation of England, and Major Wim- pffen told us quantities about Ireland, Aberdeen, Perth, in short every thing about our manners and customs he knew as well as ourselves and is very anxious to visit England & America. He had been living at Coburg Gotha when the Queen [Victo- ria] and Prince were there. They made themselves exceedingly disagreeable by her caprices and him putting on airs to his former friends. One day the Queen would not come down to dinner at all because it was fixed that the Grand Duke Fred- erick was to conduct her & not Prince Albert and she could not bear to think that he was of higher rank than the Prince, and after keeping dinner waiting ever so long sent to say that she would dine in her own room. He read in the English Papers afterwards that the Queen wept there on seeing the Deer slain in such quantities, and he was by and said on the contrary that she was quite delighted and heard her say to the Grand

---

[1] As well as two sons, Radetzky had had three daughters, two of whom died young. The remaining daughter, Friederike, was very close to her father and they wrote to each other every day. In 1838 she had married Count Charles Wenckheim and they had four children. Radetzky's wife, born Countess Frances Strasoldo Grafenberg in 1779, had married him at the age of nine- teen. She died in 1854, four years before him.

Huntsman that she was extremely delighted with the sport,
and he wondered at her unfeminine taste for it was perfect
butchery....

It was in August, 1845, that Queen Victoria went with Prince
Albert for the first time since their marriage to visit his old home
at Coburg. The Queen's journal shows that she did not retire to her
room for dinner or miss any of the festivities during the three
nights they stayed there. She and Albert then moved on to Gotha
where Duke Ernest had another palace. Frederick, Grand Duke of
Saxe-Weimar (no doubt the Grand Duke Frederick mentioned by
Count Wimpffen) was a guest there, and although Albert had
warned her of his peculiarities, she did not take exception to him
in any way nor fail to come down to dinner while she was there. It
was from Gotha, on Saturday, August 30, that an excursion was made
to the Thuringian Forest for a drive of deer. The deer were driven
into an enclosure in the heart of the forest where the guns waited,
and thirty-one stags were shot between luncheon and a quarter to
four. The Queen wrote in her journal: 'I cannot say that the sport
is to my liking & it seems to me that it is hardly *real* sport....
Everything was so well managed, & quite in the old style, but even
the gentlemen, none of them, from a sportsman's point of view, care
for what really amounts to a kind of slaughter.'[1]

[1] Unpublished extract.

WINTER IN VENICE

❧

Effie's next letter is from Venice. They stayed during the whole of this visit at the Hotel Danieli on the Riva degli Schiavoni facing the lagoon where Ruskin had stayed on his four previous visits. A side canal gives access to the water entrance, and in *Praeterita* Ruskin tells us that 'The beginning of everything was in seeing the Gondola-beak come actually inside the door at Danieli's, when the tide was up, and the water two feet deep at the foot of the stairs.'

It was originally the Palazzo Dandolo, built in the fifteenth century. In 1822, a Swiss, Joseph dal Niel, opened part of it as an hotel and the name was contracted to Danieli. In 1845 the whole of it was taken over and improved. In one of Effie's later letters, with a little engraving of the hotel at the top, she marked with dots the two windows of their sitting-room: it was in front, on the first floor, at the far end on the Piazzetta side. A double bedroom with windows looking on to the Calle delle Rasse leads out of this large sitting-room (room No. 32 in the Danieli today), and what is now the adjoining bathroom was presumably John's dressing-room. We know from a letter of Mr Ruskin's that John could see the Campanile from his dressing-room but this view has now been blocked by the new Danieli building.

They paid 16/- a day for their rooms, including Charlotte's, and 7/6 a day each for meals. This John tells us in a letter to his father of September 18, 1851, in which he was comparing prices in Venice with those of 1849.

When they arrived, the railway bridge into Venice, inaugurated in January, 1846, was out of action, forty of its two hundred and twenty-two arches having been destroyed during the bombardment, five of them by the Venetians themselves when they were forced to evacuate Fort Malghera on May 26, 1849. It can be seen from a picture in the Correr Museum that normally carriages were brought

into the city by train, and Murray gives information about diligences
that left daily from Venice for Milan and Trieste. (At that time the
railway ran only between Venice and Verona.) Without the bridge,
it is probable that the Ruskins left their carriages at Mestre, though
they could have brought them into the city by boat.

Venice, 13th November [Tuesday], 1849

My dearest Mother

... I have so much to say and answer that I don't know where
to begin.... I think you will see from my Verona letters that I
do take much more exercise and I am able to take far more. John
is much delighted with my increased strength and if my throat
was only better I should think myself recovering fast. As to
food—I am very careful. Although the fruit here is so tempting I never touch either it, or vegetables or eggs. A little fish,
& generally roast fowl and sometimes a little pudding & boiled
rice constitute my fare, and coffee with bread and butter in the
morning. I one night took tea and was very ill after it, but that
was in Switzerland. I make tea for Charlotte & John every night,
but I never take anything after dinner myself and I find, & agree
with you, that the less I eat the better I am. We are going to
buy Battledors & Shuttlecocks here to play in the forenoon as
we find playing at *Teg* round the table takes away our breath
in a few minutes. You will hardly believe the change in me but
it shows how perfectly Simpson understood my state for I
find that the warmer it is and the hotter the sun, and the
hotter I can get, the better. The cold bracing air of Chamouni
was too strong and seemed to shut up my skin and made me
quite ill but here it is most delicious, always mild, never damp,
the skies and sunsets of the most heavenly colours, and the sea
and canals so fresh & calm & green with the streets of Palaces,
and no marks of the year-&-a-half blockade they are just
recovering from.[1] It is the most exquisite place I have ever

----

[1] Flagg wrote in his *Venice*, published in 1853: 'The façade of nearly every
mansion on the west side of the Grand Canal bears traces of balls, even to
this day.' The climate of Venice had then a much more salubrious reputation than it has today. There was thought to be a peculiar virtue in the salt
air and slime of the mud, so that doctors from all over the world sent their
chronic patients there.

seen and we shall not quit it in a hurry if I can help it, and
at any rate not till this time next month.

Your letters take exactly 8 days so that you can always count.
We are living in Danieli's Hotel, formerly a splendid Palace
with marble staircase and doors and Balconies looking out on
the sea covered with ships and churches and the Doge's Palace,
the finest building in the world, with St. Mark's Place &
Church 100 yards off. There, every night the Austrian Band
plays, the finest trained I ever heard, numbering about 60 men.
The whole of Venice seems to turn in there at that time. The
place is like a vast drawing room lighted enough by the gas
from the arcades all round the square under which sit all the
Ladies & gentlemen at their coffee, iced water and cigars
with a dense crowd in the centre of men, women, children,
soldiers, Turks, magnificent Greek costumes and sky above
studded with innumerable twinkling stars. I was walking there
with John last night till past eight without any bonnet but my
hair dressed—walking about like all the rest amongst the
crowd, taking our coffee under the Arcade and enjoying
ourselves extremely.[1] The women here have the most magnificent black hair I ever saw, so beautifully plaited and standing
in a complete circle of three to four inches in width all round
their heads but I can't draw it to give you the slightest idea,
but the consequence is that whenever a bonnet is put on over
such a mass they look the most extraordinary antics you ever
saw & any Ladies that do wear bonnets, they are the shape
worn some six years ago and look as if they had been brought
out of the ark. Charlotte and I intend getting the black veils
of the country and discarding our bonnets till the winter
begins as it is far too warm yet for velvet or satin.[2]

[1] It was not done for ladies to go inside the cafés in the Piazza. Florian's,
on the south side, was patronised by the Italians, and Quadri's, on the north,
by the Austrians.

[2] Mr Ruskin wrote to John on November 27: ' ... as I cannot bear to make
remarks here that I could not make in the presence of both of you—I
would just say that I hear from Perth that the Ladies walk in St Mark's
Place without their Bonnets—This in Scotland is only remarked on in
admiration of the climate. It strikes me unpleasantly—We were there in
warmer weather far than Nov^e—The amiable & beautiful Daughter of the
Emperor of Russia walked among the Crowds but she wore her Bonnet for

I cannot understand why Dr Macfarlane [of 1, Athole Place, Perth] had not enough exercise here. It must have been entirely his own fault because there is no better or more delightful exercise for every muscle than standing and rowing a Gondola and not easy either, and if he did not like that, there are most charming little streets intersecting the whole of Venice like a puzzle, none more than ten feet broad where you could run about and lose yourself in for a whole day as we did yesterday for a couple of hours, and it is so delicious to think that you can never be run over, no carriages, carts, horses, barrows or anything but people and gondolas. This last is the most luxurious conveyance in the world if you can fancy yourself moved through canals of oil. There is no more motion on the green canals and you lie all your length on soft cushions and pass other people in the same happy ease as yourself. I often wish you were all here for nothing could be more enjoyable.

We had a delightful sail across the Lagune [sic] from Mestre on Saturday having passed Vicenza and Padua in the railway. Formerly it brought you into Venice across the Lagune but parts of the Bridge were thrown down during the Bombardment and they are now repairing it. If I was Radetzky not one stone of it should be left on another. It completely destroys your first impressions of Venice and it cost the Italians £150,000, and no good has come of it so far & the everlasting shame besides of turning half their Churches into Mills because they can't be troubled to keep them in order, covered with invaluable Frescoes of Titian, Giorgione, the Bellinis & others and giving all that money for a Railway bridge, but they have been dreadfully punished already...[1]

I have told John that some of his notes to his Father would let you know oftener about us. I read most of them. They are on indifferent subjects and John has told Mr R. [Ruskin] who, with Mrs R., appear to be in a very amiable temper, to send them to you. He is much pleased just now, that the first wine

---

I well remember the simplicity & stuff of said Bonnet—now I do not want Effie to be otherwise in Venice than a princess.'

[1] Effie was most unfair to the Venetians here. The Austrians had heavily taxed them to pay for the bridge which greatly facilitated their own use of the valuable port of Venice.

the Prince of Wales & Princess ever tasted was some Paserete [Paxarete, a sweet sherry] he sent for their table at the Banquet the other day, and Prince Albert allowed them to taste that....

The banquet Effie refers to was at the new Coal Exchange opened on October 30, 1849, by Prince Albert in the Queen's absence, due to illness. Accompanied by the Prince of Wales (who had received his title when he was barely a month old) and the Princess Royal, then eight and nine respectively, the Prince had gone by water from Whitehall to Custom House Quay.

The old Ruskins were not in as amiable a temper as Effie supposed. In a letter of October 20 Mr Ruskin had told Mr Gray that he had received an anonymous letter, postmarked Bridge of Earn, warning him that Charlotte Ker was encouraging Effie to separate John from his parents. Mr Gray's advice that anonymous letters should be disregarded called forth another letter from Mr Ruskin in which all the old grievances were raked up.

At the beginning of November, Mrs Gray felt impelled to reply to this herself and a draft of her letter was kept. She defended Effie by stressing that not enough allowance had been made for her illness, and ended: 'I am afraid even although her health was completely restored that you would continue to be disappointed in the apparent coldness of her manner. She never had an endearing manner neither in words nor actions—she does not show it to her own parents & it would be too much to expect her in that case to shew it to you. I am sorry you feel the want of it so much—you have been accustomed to it from the Domecqs. I acknowledge it is very pleasing—but from the Countess's [Béthune] letters to Phemy I thought her terms of love & friendship very French—and it would be a decided improvement to Scotch manners if they had a little of it.'

Mr Ruskin was mollified by this letter and graciously acknowledged it on November 10. One passage of his letter reads: 'I am sorry you seem to consider your endeavour to restore peace between your daughter & me a hopeless task—I should only call it an unnecessary task, there actually being no dispeace betwixt us—witness the Letters I here enclose or may continue to enclose from the Travellers at Effie's suggestion—in case you may be longer in getting news. I have rather been combating with Mr Gray & you than with

Phemy—because you would have it that I required my Daughter in Law to be something she never had been—very frank & open in place of rather reserved—now I want nothing but that Mrs J Ruskin should be what Phemy Gray had been, very agreeable in our Society, and not after being so & apparently always happy with us before becoming our Daughter—become the very reverse when she was our Daughter both to ourselves & friends. You repeat we make no allowance for illness. We make every allowance except that allowing that sickness should quench Love & annihilate affection.' Further on in the letter he wrote: 'What you seem to fear Mrs Ruskin & I may consider coldness—is a part of Phemy's Character I quite admire—you are quite right in her superiority—to all the kissing & flattering nonsense of School Girls—I never saw so little pretention of affectation about any one—so little consciousness of her good looks. Her deportment & presence are admirable.'[1]

Knowledge of this correspondence was evidently kept from Effie at the time, but later Mrs Gray must have told her something about it, for on her way home she wrote to thank her mother for the perfect good sense with which she had acted towards Mr Ruskin.

Venice, 15th November

Dearest George,

I have been intending for some days to answer your kind note but I have got an Italian master and what with writing exercises and learning Dialogue I find all my spare time taken up as our afternoons and evenings are spent in the open air.... I find myself much better since I came here and the air seems to agree very well with me. John thinks, if his Father will allow him, of buying a little house here as he finds so much work before him, and I think if one lived years in Venice there would still be half of its treasures to explore....

Charlotte did not go out yesterday so John and the Gondolier rowed me over to Lido, one of the outer Islands between Venice and the Adriatic. I wished to see the open sea and we walked across the Island over the Jews' burying Ground, where they formerly were all obliged to be buried. All the tombstones

---

[1] From unpublished letter in the Bowerswell Papers.

were well sculptured and with Hebrew writing on them.[1] On the other side we ran down to the sea. The tide was coming in and the green waves crested with white foam were very splendid, and pretty shells striped in many colours were lying on the sand. When we returned the wind rose and it was quite stormy. A fleet of Venetian fishing boats literally flew past us with their beautiful sails spread. They are of a rich orange color with a cross and the world in black painted on them and when the sun shines on them you cannot conceive anything more vivid in colour or more elegant in form. John is very busy in the Doge's Palace all day and as yet he has only drawn one capital of one Pillar and there is something like hundreds on each side. He is going to return however for us today at two & take us through the picture Gallery inside....

Charlotte and I had a great deal of amusement yesterday. We went out to shop alone and as in most of the shops they can neither understand German, English or [French? word omitted] and only Italian which at present I only know about a dozen words of, you may fancy the signs on both sides to get what we want, and the difficulty is not a little increased by all the payments being made in Austrian zwanzigs,[2] something less than a Franc.... I was anxious to buy some of the pretty gold & coral necklaces with charms hanging at the end which I thought would suit Sophia, Alice & Eliza[3] very nicely but I found them so dreadfully dear that I was obliged to give up the idea entirely as they would be each above £3. When they were showing me all the different kinds of Venice chain I could not help thinking of your friend Mr Capes[4] with his bit of fine chain....

Many of the Italians here appear to have no homes at all and to be perfectly happy. At eight o'clock in the evening when we return from hearing the Band we see them all lying packed

[1] The Jews' burying ground is at the east end of the Lido near the church of San Nicolo. It covers several acres and is now surrounded by a high stone wall. The modern Jewish cemetery is an extension of it, and from here can be seen the beautiful graves of the old ground half smothered in brambles and undergrowth.

[2] This was the Austrian lira. There were 29 zwanzigers to £1.

[3] Melville Jameson's only daughter, aged six.

[4] A Perth neighbour often mentioned by Effie in a spirit of ridicule. He was droll, pushing and not quite a gentleman.

together at the edge of the bridges, wrapped in their immense brown cloaks and large hoods as warm as fires. Then in the morning there are little stands on all parts of the Quay where they can get hot fish, rice soup, hot elder wine, all kinds of fruit, cigars, and this eating al fresco goes on the whole day, with the occasional interruption of Punch or a Juggler or a storyteller when immediately an immense crowd is collected. Here also some of the Austrian Infantry are exercised and sometimes it is very merry and exciting. The other day an immense Fire and a large cauldron was put in the Square where they burned all the paper money issued by the Provisional Government here while it lasted. I saw the ashes of above 2,000,000 of notes. I must stop now....

Venice had been in desperate need of money during the revolution. A National Loan of three million lire had been raised in September, 1848, by Manin's government, and a paper issue of small notes from one to five lire printed. This paper was called *Moneta Patriottica* being guaranteed by rich and patriotic citizens. As coin became scarce the troops were paid in this paper money which could be changed at a discount for Napoleons at the National Bank. The loan was increased to five million in October. Another big paper issue was brought out in December, this time guaranteed by the government and raised by taxes—the *Moneta del Commune di Venezia* with notes up to 50 and 100 lire. This loan was continually increased until in June, 1849, it reached 24 million lire. During the siege the rich gave their jewels and the title deeds of their estates for the redemption of the *Moneta Patriottica*, but even the poorest citizen gave what he could, down to his bed and cooking utensils. Venice contributed more to the cause of united Italy during the 1848-9 revolution than all the other Italian cities put together. Under the terms of the surrender, Austria agreed to redeem the *Moneta del Commune* at half its value, which would have been generous if the sum for redemption had not been raised by a special tax on the Venetians, but of the patriotic money not a single lire was recognised. It was this worthless *Moneta Patriottica* that Effie saw being burnt and of which she enclosed in her letter a note for two lire.

Venice, 19th November, 1849

My dear Mama,

I have just received your letter dated 10th November which is extremely interesting and agreeable for us to receive as we have not heard from any one for some few days, although Charlotte had, I think, on Saturday long letters from Mrs Ker & Annie [one of Charlotte's sisters]. The latter writes such excellent chatty letters and tells us all that is said &c. The way that John's book [*The Seven Lamps*] is spoken of in Perth seems to disgust her very much. She says none of them understand it in the very least, but some praise it because they think they must & others do it in a condescending manner as if they thought their praise necessary to ensure its success....

I had a nice long letter from Mr Ruskin two days ago. It is too heavy or else I would send it to you. He appears to be getting fonder of England and to enjoy his drives in the country. I hope he now sends you some of John's Notes; he said at once he would. I am going to write to him in a day or two. We cannot be home any sooner than we fixed, John has so much to do. We shall spend Christmas week here which I am very glad of, but we have made no acquaintances as yet. We could easily amongst the Austrian Officers if we gave them the slightest encouragement, meeting them in scores every night at the Band or in the Cafés or Theatre, but as yet we have avoided them as George only being with us I do not like to make acquaintance with every man with a moustache and sword who may choose to be civil to us, at night especially. John would like us to walk about chattering with some half dozen and amusing ourselves but we have some ideas of English propriety remaining, and I tell him he must get us introduced in some other way as all our Austrian admirers might not turn out as well as Count Wimpffen. Accordingly he is going to ask his Banker to call on us, Mr Valentine, a young man & unfortunately unmarried.... All the English, with the exception of four gentlemen, have left Venice for the last year & have not yet returned and our letters of Introduction if Lady D. [Davy] sends us any, cannot be here for a week yet and, if she was not at home when John's note arrived, may be longer....

I have so much to do for my Italian Master who I like very

much now that I have little time for writing and sometimes
I feel inclined to adopt John's plan of never writing anywhere
but home. On Saturday he took us into the Doge's Palace and
showed us the suite of rooms.... I daresay Charlotte will send
a fine description of it, but she is apt to overflow not in the
least intending it, and if John wrote more fully of things as they
are and she less brilliantly you would have a truer idea of what
we see, so that if you add considerably to mine & take as much
from hers you will have a very correct idea of our doings. But
to return to Doge's Palace.... Its chief riches are in several pictures of enormous dimensions of Tintoretto's and Paul
Veronese, one of the former, the three circles of Paradise,
covering one entire end of a hall and of most wonderful
invention and the colouring wonderful....[1]

Several others of his, one I admired exceedingly, are in other
rooms, the Marriage of Bacchus & Adriadne,[2] the Bacchus
most lovely, crowned & girt with vine leaves & grapes and such
a face, and one can imagine exactly where he got his model,
for there is a Cigar boy on the Piazza below, the very creature
that I see every day I go out, and that is always the case here
showing you that the race is the same although much degraded
to what it was, for every where you see men, women, children
& dogs here that you think have stepped out of the canvasses
of Titian, Tintoretto, Veronese, Giorgione, the Bellinis, &c.
and so remarkably so, that we are perpetually turning in the
street and saying, "Oh, there is the boy in Tintoretto's Mercury
& the Graces," or, "There is the Europa of Paul Veronese."

Today John was occupied all the forenoon working at the
Casa D'Oro, one of the most beautiful houses on the Grand
Canal belonging to and now under repair for Mde. Taglioni....[3]

[1] Flagg wrote that to preclude the possibility of Austrian shells damaging
the pictures in the great hall of the Doge's Palace, they were taken down in
1848 'and, two years later, had not been replaced'. Yet Effie saw the *Para-
diso*, one of the pictures particularly mentioned by Flagg as having been
removed.

[2] Ruskin complained that every afternoon the sun blistered this picture.

[3] Marie Taglioni, the dancer, had owned the Ca' d'Oro since 1845. According to Ruskin in his *Venetian Index* she ruined it by her restorations. 'I saw
the beautiful slabs of red marble which formed the bases of its balconies,
and were carved into noble spiral mouldings of strange sections, half

John took us at three to the Scuola de St Rocco[1] entirely filled with the works of Tintoretto.... I find I can go through as much work as Charlotte now and we see everything together. We have got battledores & shuttlecocks, and famous fun & laughing we have over our games in the morning. I just take two meals a day, breakfast rather late and dinner at five. We have had the Piano tuned and bought some duettes....

I have just been out with Charlotte at the Band and I tried in one of the shops to get a view of St. Mark's Place & Ducal Palace but I could only get note sheets which however I will write upon next time. It would greatly help you in understanding what we see if you would accept from me Murray's Hand-Book of Northern Italy, last edition. Get Mrs Paton[2] to get it for you and add the price to what I already owe you. We use it constantly and when I want you to get a fuller description or more detailed of any particular Church than I have time to give you I will refer you to the particular page in Murray.... Murray is invaluable and we never turn a step without its being useful. Some of it on the Churches is written by John....[3] You may say anything you like in your letters for I destroy every one after it is answered....[4]

---

a foot deep, dashed to pieces when I was last in Venice [1851-2]; its glorious interior staircase, by far the most interesting Gothic monument of the kind in Venice, had been carried away, piece by piece, and sold for waste marble, two years before.'

[1] Ruskin regarded this as one of the three most precious buildings in Italy (with the Sistine Chapel and the Campo Santo of Pisa). 'Whatever the traveller may miss in Venice,' he wrote in his *Venetian Index*, 'he should give unembarrassed attention and unbroken time to the Scuola di San Rocco.' (He then devoted twenty-six pages, a third of the whole index, to describing its pictures.)

[2] Charles Paton was a bookseller and stationer of 32 St John Street, Perth.

[3] John's notes were on churches at Carrara, Lucca, Pisa and Florence, not Venice. They first appeared in the 3rd, 1847, edition of Murray's *Hand-Book for Northern Italy* which was evidently the one Effie was asking her mother to get because the next edition did not come out until 1852. The 1st edition had appeared in 1842. Murray preceded Baedeker as the popular travel guide.

[4] She had written to her mother from Rouen in 1848: 'John never wants to know more of your affairs than I like to tell him.'

Venice, 24th November

... I have written today a very long letter to Mr Ruskin
containing an account of the "Fete of the Madonna della
Salute" which has been held on the 22nd Novbr. every year since
1682 when a church on the other side of the Lagune was built
by the Senate as a thanksgiving from the plague which carried
off at that time 60,000 people in Venice.[1] The letter when you
get it from Mr R may amuse George so send it to him as I have
not time to write so long an account over again.... The weather
is now cold and misty and these last two evenings have been
too inclement for us to attend the Band in the Square and we
are very sorry that just after making such nice acquaintances
as Dr Birch & Dr Purvis we should lose them the same day as
they went to Vienna. You will see about them in Mr R's letter.[2]
It was a treat to meet Englishmen again and John, you know,
is the most extraordinary person, he does not mind us going
with anyone we like but till now we have not known any more
people than I had before mentioned to you.

Today, after we had heard the splendid mass for the dead in
St. Martin's [near the Arsenal] Charlotte & I, attended by our
Valet-de-Place and our Gondolier, who is a very handsome
fellow of the fine Giorgione red brown complexion, rowed us
fast home. On the Bridge above the Canal leading into Danieli's
were standing to see us land from our Gondola two Italian
gentleman who had sat beside us at St Martin's and knowing
the Gondola had walked quickly through the bye-streets and
reached the Hotel as we did. Having followed us into the
house and seen where our rooms were, and I suppose asked who
we were, they waited for a long time before the Hotel expecting
I suppose that we would either come down or send for them to
call on us. I tell you this as a specimen of foreign well-bred manners which I think would astonish us in the North not a little but

[1] This ceremony still takes place every year, but on November 21.

[2] Mr Ruskin in a letter to John of December 3 thanked Effie for 'her long
& interesting & amusing letter', but added, 'I think you should have gone
or provided a better escort than a scamp of a Valet de Place'. He does not
mention Dr Purvis, so all we know of Effie's meeting with him is from a
passage in a letter written to her mother from Park Street on August 1, 1850:
'I was also very sorry to miss Dr Purvis [who came to call], our handsome
friend who rescued us at Santa Maria della Salute at Venice.'

here we find it is quite common and I daresay they think us as much wanting in manners as we think they rather overdo the thing. Charlotte and I are quite used to it now, but the first night when we were followed into the Hotel, although George was with us, by some Austrian Officers, we thought it very funny, but now we are accustomed to it. I half expect we shall get letters from some of them next but this is joking and John thinks it most delightful and when he takes us to the Opera he is quite lively as long as the Lorgnettes are all turned to our box but when they are not during the Ballet, which is much patronized and a superior thing to our ballet, he says, "How tiresome," and goes to sleep in the back of the box to Charlotte's and my infinite amusement. We never saw any body like him, so perfectly devoid of jealousy, and I am sure Papa will wonder at him as he thought at one time quite differently....[1]

John is very hard at work and I think the Stones of Venice, if it is that work he is now preparing, will be worth something but it is not easy to find out for he finds that he has so many things to write about that have never been written about before that he requires to bring out one before another is able to be understood....

You with your kind sympathy will be very glad to hear we are so happy and that I am in such good spirits. My handsome acquaintance of the other day, Dr Purvis, said to me that he had never seen so perfectly happy looking a person as I was and he supposed I had never known a single grief or care. We could hardly keep from paying him compliments his face was so beautiful, and John did say to him that when he saw him one day in the Salle à Manger he could not think what handsome Greek he could be, but although he smiled at the compliment he did not seem to think himself handsome at all and was not in the least affected....

[1] John had written to Effie during their engagement on November 9, 1847: 'Indeed I *never* will be jealous of you—and I will keep that purer form of jealousy—that longing for more love—within proper limits.' And she had written to him on February 8, 1848: 'I told Papa the other day that you said you never would be really jealous without cause and he says unfortunately jealous people always *find cause* which I think quite true but I hope at heart you are really not a jealous being.'

Charlotte is just saying she thinks of writing a pamphlet on what a husband ought to be and giving John as a model, which he really is. I never saw any person so free from petty faults & narrow mindedness although peculiar in many ways. His gallantry of behaviour to us both is most charming and he is so considerate and thoughtful for me that I am sure Papa would be quite delighted if he saw how kind he is. And now goodbye....

Venice, 27th November, 1849

... John was looking at my throat for the first time yesterday since we came to Venice and he says it is decidedly better. Indeed Venice seems to agree with me admirably, and John is occupying himself actively in looking at all the houses which are to let in case we should return next winter. I have also got balls to play with as well as battledores and I find the former much better exercise....

Thank you very much for telling me about the Mannings. We were all much interested and had not heard of them since we read in the last Papers. Mr Ruskin sent their letters to each other.[1]

I am glad to hear such accounts of the children. I should think both Sophie and Alice would attract great attention even without their street dresses, they are a most perfect little pair. Sophia is I daresay like me in some things but both of them are much prettier I suppose than I was at their age. I am however also looking well just now and don't want admirers either, and as my acquaintances are of a lower rank they only express their sentiments to John and opinion of me before my face. The other day when I was rowing the Gondola in the Grand Canal[2] the

[1] Frederick Manning and his wife, Maria, had been publicly hanged together in London on November 13 for the murder of their lodger. A crowd of 30,000 collected to see such a unique spectacle. The Mannings had exchanged letters through the prison chaplain which were published in *The Times*.

[2] John had evidently already told his father that Effie rowed the gondola, for on November 27 Mr Ruskin wrote: 'It hurts me to have said a syllable bearing on the Rowing of Effie when you seem not only to derive pleasure from it, but she, health—I do not know—when out—so far as passage to Lido I should be startled by a lady's taking the oar except that the Exertion

Valet de Place started from his reverie and said to John in French, "Ah! Monsieur, comme votre femme est belle," continuing that he had seen a great many English but never any like me, and he supposed there were not ten more beautiful in England. John said that I was well enough and would do if I was as good as I was pretty. The valet said, "Ah! monsieur, Madame est aussi bonne comme une ange et elle a toutes les vertues." I roared and laughed & so did Charlotte and I rejoined that the reason he admired me was because there were no other Ladies to be seen at present, but he kept assuring John that Madame was "jolie comme une ange!" The Gondolier also pays me nice "piccolo complimento" in Italian which Charlotte thinks highly improper as she does not understand them....

After we left home today we went to St. Mark's where we found John near the high Altar stretched all his length on the ground drawing one of a series of exquisite Alabaster columns surrounded by an admiring audience of idlers.... John was not quite ready so Charlotte and I went to an old curiosity shop where we were buying some pieces of point lace which Charlotte was getting made into a collar and cuffs, and me a narrow berthe [a falling collar] about a fingers length broad for my velvet dress which I had not thought of buying at all but John was much struck with the richness of the pattern which is particularly fine and it is so cheap that I did not hesitate a moment. It was only 18/-.... We then returned for John who walked with us till dinner-time through an infinite number of narrow streets, past innumerable Palaces with ogee arched windows, the Venetian style all exactly the same, but if you look in Seven Lamps you will see, I think, some examples of this, at any rate you will find one beautiful Balcony from a Palace here and one of the capitles from the Ducal Palace with birds....[1]

---

to me is not feminine, but in the Grand Canal I cannot reconcile the notion at all to what is beautiful.' He wrote again on December 16 saying how sorry he was that his remarks had caused offence, and adding: 'I only do shrink a little, & ventured to say others would, from seeing the Loveliest part of Creation ever unsex itself.' The spectacle of a woman rowing a gondola is still one which few, if any, visitors to Venice can have seen.

[1] On the Piazzetta side, the second column from the Carta della Porta. According to Ruskin's own note he made his drawing from this Renaissance

I mentioned before that John was anxiously looking at the houses to be let. Mr Danieli is anxious we should take the half of this Palace which is one of the most perfect in Venice and he says he could make it easily into a private house with another entrance but I do not know whether John & he will be able to agree about terms, but the situation could not be improved and I should like it as well as any I have seen. I passed a fine orderly looking Palace on the Grand Canal yesterday and seeing a man in gay livery lounging at the door I found the house was inhabited by a young man, one of the Infantes of Spain.[1] I hope next month some of the Venetian families may return for Christmas when we may see something of the upper classes for there are none here at present and the shopmen complain sadly....

Venice, 3rd December, 1849

I have just received your note dated 23rd November.... I am very much obliged for Dr K's note and prescription. It is some water mixed with nitrate of silver. Caustic wouldn't suit me at all, but I hope this will, and as there is an English Chemist's here I will easily get it.[2] These last few days owing to the extreme cold & frost my throat has again been troubling me much. Such cold is quite unusual and at night no quantity of clothes or warm bottles appeared to have the slightest effect, but last night was a little milder, but we saw quantities of ice in our walks and the Italians say they do not remember such cold for years and attribute it to the very fine Autumn they have had....

---

copy of an earlier capital, the eleventh from the Vine Angle on the lagoon side. The other drawing is of a balcony of the Palazzo Pesaro in the Campo S. Benedetto.

  [1] Don Juan, second son of Don Carlos and younger brother of the Pretender, the Count of Montemolin. He owned the Palazzo Loredan at Campo San Vio. He was born in 1822 and married, in 1847, Beatrix d'Este, youngest sister of the Duke of Modena. Effie was to meet them in London in May, 1850, and be received by the Infanta during her second visit to Venice.

  [2] 'There is an excellent English dispensary near the post office in the Campo San-Luca, No. 3801, and which is in correspondence with Savory and Son, London' (Murray, *Hand-Book*, 1847). It no longer exists.

On Saturday we rowed to Murano, an island about 20 minutes sail from here.... It is now nearly deserted but the Cathedral is extremely interesting and the island for several centuries has been chiefly celebrated as being the seat of Manufactories for the famous Venice glass, which amongst other merits broke in pieces when poison was put into it. One Manufactory entirely for beads we went over.... All sizes and colours are made but always of the same form. They are cheap. I got an immense bunch of all colours for 2/6 but they were very small ones. I have ordered some red of a peculiar kind and extremely beautiful and much more expensive to make into necklaces for Sophie, Alice & Eliza [Jameson]. I will get pretty clasps for them at Genoa where they work gold so beautifully.

Although there are 50 people living in the house here they are nearly all Austrians, Officers who pay nothing for their rooms and always dine at a Restorateur's. They bring a line from the Governor saying they are to have such and such rooms and whoever is in them must turn out to make them comfortable. We were nearly turned out by a General at Verona but he *considerately* took some other rooms. The poor Innkeepers have had them in this way for the last 20 months and they are never paid a farthing. As long as the country is in a state of siege they say they can do this and Italy still remains so.

The last few days the Prince & Princess of Mecklenburg-Schwerin, married four weeks ago, have been here but they left yesterday for Milan. In bringing their carriages across the Lagune one very handsome one tumbled into the sea & was five hours under water and everything soaked as you might suppose. It looked very melancholy drying in the sun. The Prince, for we met them often walking about, was exactly like hundreds of other young men, fair & gentlemanly enough, about one & twenty. She was much taller and walked very badly, enormous long steps and about 27 I should think & fine looking, but her bonnet completely spoiled her face and was most extraordinary, being of cased blue velvet but the shape was truly frightful. It was exactly as if you had taken the centre of your bonnet & made it touch your forehead, in this way [a drawing] and the face very far back so you could hardly see it. Then a tight maroon velvet polka jacket with a deep border and collar of white fur, but so clumsily made, & a maroon & black glacé silk. Another day she had on a splendid black velvet cloak trimmed with fine sables reaching from her neck to her ancles; she looked much better in this but the same dreadful bonnet.[1]

We have not heard from Lady Davy yet, but Mr Murray has sent us a letter of introduction to the Marquis Carlo Torrigiani at Florence who he says is a nobleman of distinguished character and amiability & who John would be glad to know. He adds that the complete dispersion of English since the revolution has lessened the number of his friends but that when he can find out their present addresses, as a few have gone back, he will send us more which is very kind.[2]

Mr Ruskin says in his yesterday's letter that our not being presented at Court may make it difficult for us this winter to get into the highest foreign society but if John could suffer a six hours plague and to be dressed like a footman and a pretty dress for me would obviate the difficulty, so I suppose during the spring we shall be presented, but for my own part I would rather not unless for the above reason which makes it almost necessary, for every one says it is an immense bore and I don't think I have the slightest right to go, but I daresay Papa would like that I should as I remember him saying so, and Mr Ruskin wants me to go for he said to me before when I said I would never like to

[1] Augusta, daughter of Henry XXXIII, Prince of Reuss-Schleiz-Koestritz (it was customary for all male members of the Reuss family to be called Henry), was born in May, 1822. On November 3, 1849, she had married the Grand Duke Frederik Francis of Mecklenburg-Schwerin. He was older than Effie supposed, having been born in February, 1823. He had succeeded his father in 1842 and was head of a ruling house. His wife died in 1862 having borne him three sons and a daughter. He married again twice.

[2] John Murray (1808-92), who edited and published the *Hand-Books*, was son of John Murray (1778-1843), Byron's publisher. The Ruskins had met Mr and Mrs Murray soon after their return from Normandy in 1848. The Murrays called at Park Street and John and Effie went to Albemarle Street to return the call on November 14. Lady Davy failed to send any introductions and on December 9 Mr Ruskin wrote: 'I wonder if Lady Davy be ill or absent or punctilious of requiring you to go to Court or to know more of you both that she does not answer.' The Marchese Carlo Torrigiani was the youngest son of Pietro Guadagni and of the Marchesa Teresa Torrigiani. As she was the last of her line her children took her name.

go that he would give me the prettiest dress I could get if I would go.

We went today and looked over several Palaces but although the outsides are splendid Venetian Gothic I cannot fancy how the Italians live, for the insides although perfectly clean have such a want of comfort about them, and the people in them never appear to be doing anything and no fire places, even in this cold weather. Each member of the family carries about on their arm an earthen basket or pot with hot charcoal in it and this remains hot for a considerable time. Charlotte and I had it one day but I cannot fancy it healthy for we both got headaches while we used it. The people seem to be in great distress for money and wish to sell their houses immediately. We could get one cheap, as in Italy you give always considerably less than is asked, but there is a heavy tax to the Austrian Government and they do not know whether the war is ended or not, but they hope so. Another expense would be putting it in habitable order for us, for we could not live the way they do. The tesselated floors, although very smooth and glittering, are extremely cold and all their arrangements seem made for heat & not cold.

Our Commissionaire [valet-de-place] introduced an old woman to us this morning who wished to sell us some point lace. She was a poor, decent but careworn old woman and I did not expect to see any thing particular, but when she opened her old blue handkerchief after first kissing my hands which all the poor women do, she shewed us a most exquisite scarf of the finest point just like a gossomer web for which she asked the moderate sum of £20. In London it would have cost £40 at least. She then shewed us some very fine for handkerchiefs such as I never saw before, and other two complete pieces for the skirt of a dress, one nearly the width of this paper and the other about half, namely not quite a quarter of a yard, and the other nearly half a yard and most exquisite pattern. She asked a moderate price for them and John who was as much struck with them as me, and you know he is very fond of buying me Lace, said he was very sorry he had not enough money at present to give them to me and he wished he had very much as there was nothing he liked to see on me so much as point Lace. I said I had not spent my quarter's allowance and if he did not think giving 18 Napoleons

[£14.8.0] too much that I could easily give it.[1] He said he was very glad to find I had the money, and as it is in reality *his* money I was glad to spend some of it in a way to please him for he never asks how my money goes and I did not think it extravagent as if we should tire of it any day I could get at least double or three times what I paid for it in London.

I was more inclined to buy it as from the English not being here many poor people's living has been entirely cut off, for two years this poor woman amongst the number, and with these riches in her possession she has been actually starving. Her son who could have supported her was forced into the conscription and taken away, leaving his wife and two infants dependent on her. The Italians are very selfish and I suppose all were too miserable to give her any money on her lace. She supplicated us with tears in her eyes to take it, and she would give it us at any loss as she must have the money. We agreed for the sum given when we were all contented. She looked at John and pointing to me asked earnestly if he knew when any more of these "Benedette anime" (blessed souls) would come, for she continually prayed for them. She gave us a thousand blessings and it was most amusing to see her pantomime gestures when John said that the golden Napoleons which are 16/- were better than the paper money of Venice. Her gestures *so Italian* of disgust, and face of displeasure, were perfectly unequalled. Poor creature, it was a great pleasure to make her so happy and it is delightful to be able to make some of these miserable beings here happy by the power of money. Our Valet de Place, Gondolier and Italian master, with regular pay have, as Jane Boswell would have it, become since our arrival *new men*. The Signor Lempreshe at our first lesson was in a deplorably miserable condition, his beard unshaven and linen dirty; now every day he improves; he is as clean & merry as a lark, with nice Paletot and trim moustache. He pays us compliments and comes to tea sometimes to play chess with John. The latter has taught me

---

[1] John gave Effie £25 a quarter as her personal allowance. Before her marriage her dress allowance had been £30 a year. Miss Stuart Wortley noted: 'Effie had a great deal of extremely fine Venetian lace; she gave it— or some of it—to my mother, and I have it now.' This lace is still in the Millais family.

that game. He was quite astonished with the facility I took it up and as he has some of the Richardson ability for playing chess[1] he is astonished at the length of time he takes to beat me, but he always does. He says however that in time I will be a very good player which I am particularly surprised at for I thought it so difficult a game that I never could understand it in the least, but I find it very amusing on the contrary....

The man brought the red beads from Murano last night but I find in daylight that they are not nearly so pretty, therefore I must get the children something else and I do not know what has become of the things for I do not see a single thing worth bringing so far. I think on my way back that Paris is the best place and the only Place I have seen. I am so glad to hear you are all well, we are so too. Charlotte and I have a great deal of fun together one way or other but I wish we knew some people. Mr Valentine is still ill. We play most energetically at Ball and find it the best exercise for warming....

I am afraid it is too cold for Papa to play golf but I hope he enjoys his cigar. Tell him that it is perfect Elysium to think of him and his well flavoured weed but the thousands upon thousands of vile things smoked here daily, and the perfect ponds of spittle every where and before the Inn door by the Soldiers on Guard, is enough to make one sick, and the smoke is so bad in the smell John never goes to the band just because of that. Now Goodbye....

Danieli's Hotel, 10th Decbr.

My dear Papa,

... I was very unwell all yesterday till midnight with very severe nervous headache and pains through my bones. I am quite well today although a little weak from it. It began in the morning with a violent bleeding at the nose. When it stopped I felt the headache, and in the afternoon John thought the air would do me good but when we came in I found he had taken

---

[1] John was connected to two families of Richardson who were no relation to each other, and he was no blood relation of either. Mrs Ruskin's sister had married George Richardson of Croydon, and Mr Ruskin's sister Patrick Richardson of Perth. John described his cousin, Dr William Richardson of the Perth family, as the best chess player he had ever known.

me much too far, only it was quite with my own inclination
as he never makes me walk more than I like and takes great care
of me, and this made me worse, but I have lain in bed this forenoon till after dinner as I had so little sleep, and since I rose
John and I have been playing at ball for an hour and a half
which is the most famous exercise thanks to Mama's hint, and
the way we do it is this; we sit in a very large room, and
although we are at a dreadful expense for wood as each basket
costs 2/6 and there is no other kind of heat but charcoal which
is unhealthy, we cannot keep ourselves warm all these rainy days
but by exercise; John stands at one end of the room and I at
the other, we catch each others balls and it is so exciting and
warming that we do not tire until we are very hot. We have also
a kind of cricket, and a kind of shell-practice. This is extremely
difficult and we are hardly able to succeed as it is throwing the
ball in the air to strike a particular point in its descent.

Saturday forenoon being the Fete day of the Madonna Charlotte and I went in St Mark's where we saw a very fine Mass
performed.... On these occasions Charlotte & I get on much
better without John for as I have some of your talent for
making my way, and the people are very civil, and I can now
get myself understood and Charlotte follows always at my
back, we always get excellent places and I never find I get the
slightest harm from the people. John on the contrary finds them
so filthy that he cannot bear to touch them or be amongst them,
for which I laugh at him most heartily as during the whole time
I have been in Italy I have never been bit or seen a flea and in
Switzerland I was half eaten up. I also take my muff with me
and as we are obliged to stand all the time I always stand
upon it and I am extremely comfortable. Well, on Saturday we
got into an excellent place and saw very fine things. Above us,
were two splendid Organs accompanied by choristers and different Instruments besides, answering one another and playing
together a sort of running accompaniment to the Mass below,
hardly ever stopping. In front of us was the archbishop[1] seated

[1] Cardinal Jacopo Monico who had been Patriarch of Venice since 1826.
He was very unpopular at this time as he was thought to have had Austrian
sympathies during the revolution and favoured an earlier capitulation to
avoid the terrible suffering Venice was undergoing. A proclamation to this

on his Throne and surrounded by his Bishops and then a host
of inferior priests and assistants, the splendid silver candelabra
all lighted and the Altar and Throne and blaze of silver & gold
tissue, the splendor of the whole heightened by the solemn edifice with its glittering gold mosaic roof with gold plate and the
Archbishop's mitres set on stands. He was continually changing one & putting on the others at different parts of the mass
and when they were all on their stands the table put me very
much in mind of Miss Watson's table of Bonnets for sale....[1]

John has just gone out in the rain to call on Mr Blumenthal
[partner of Mr Valentine] who left his card for us on Saturday
as we were out which I hope will bring us some acquaintances.
John could & would make plenty if he had time. It will however
take all the time he has, & curtail our stay at Florence besides,
for him to get the materials for the Stones of Venice completed,
and nothing I see interrupts him so much as people coming in
& out and I can hardly press it unless it comes from himself for
the book being already advertised it would require to stand still
to be finished next year if he did not finish his notes just now,
and as his present work is of an extremely healthy kind, and I
never saw him so well, I should like him to finish it.[2] He lets
us go anywhere and do any thing we like and he takes us to the
Opera whenever I ask him. I like to go as a kind of Lesson for
pronunciation and dialogue which one hears purer there than
any where else, and to hear some music, which we never hear
in England, for they always play new Operas.

effect addressed to the Assembly and signed by him was read out in the Piazza
on August 3, causing such fury that his palace adjoining St Mark's was
broken into. He might have been lynched had not some of the Deputies
arrived in time to pacify the mob. He died in 1851 and is buried in the crypt
of St Mark's.

[1] Miss M. Watson was a milliner of 9 Charlotte Street, Perth.

[2] *The Stones of Venice* had been advertised in *The Seven Lamps of Architecture*. On December 11 Ruskin wrote to the Rev. Walter Brown, his tutor
at Christ Church: '... when I came home I found my wife better and very
desirous of some change of scene. She asked me to take her to Venice, and
as I had need of some notes for the sketch of Venetian Art which you
would perhaps see advertised by Smith and Elder, I was glad to take her there.'
Had Ruskin intended then to complete *The Stones* without returning to
Venice? It may well be that it was Effie's request which led to the projected
sketch becoming a major work.

I began this letter two days ago in hopes of having a little more news for you but it has rained ever since along with a kind of snow and cold wind so that this is the third day we have been in the house not able to stir out. You would be amazed at the delicacy of the Italians. Every one about us is coughing and complaining of cold. Our valet, gondolier and Italian master are all ill.... John's friend Mr Valentine is still laid up and young Mr Blumenthal, who John found at home, is to come and see us whenever he is better and I suppose the invalids are no longer ill from slight illnesses than we are, as their houses are so very uncomfortable. John is working today in the house of the Prefect of Police who he says is a very jolly old fellow who asked him to come and draw in his Palace[1] all day if he liked. He seems to sit judgeing cases between a double file of Austrian soldiers inside a couple of huge Iron doors which bye the bye in Venice are of the same age and form as that curious old door at Glamis, and when I pointed out to John the curious construction of it, he had never remarked them before and was much interested in it. All the old windows in Venice are made in the same way and are about 700 years old.

We understand that a number of Italians and Strangers are coming into Venice for Christmas when "The Fenice" is open for Operas, being shut all the rest of the year.[2] The only people we have heard of being here, and they are living in a Palace on the Grand Canal, are the famous Don Carlos, his wife & son, the Conde de Montemolin, but we have not seen them yet....[3]

John had a letter from his Father yesterday enclosing some notes and a very nice review of "7 Lamps" from the Architects Journal. They have returned to London and appear to be living

[1] Referred to in Ruskin's diary as the 'Police House', and in *The Stones* as the 'Madonetta House', one of the eight remaining Byzantine palaces. It is on the Grand Canal almost opposite the Ca' Grimani and is now the privately-owned Palazzo Dona.

[2] When the Fenice was shut operas were performed at the Teatro San Benedetto. The Fenice was burnt down in December, 1836, but re-built by May, 1837. It was, after the San Carlo in Naples and the Scala in Milan, the largest theatre in the world.

[3] They were staying at the Palazzo Loredan, belonging to Don Juan. When Effie met Don Juan in London in May she said she had seen his family in Venice and he told her they had been staying at his house.

quietly as ordered by the doctors.[1] He does write such curious
letters to John, sometimes so clever and at other times so
foolish and so contradictory. John reads them aloud to Charlotte and me and puts them into his pocket without making
much comment upon them. We hear that the frost has been
severe with you everywhere. The approaching winter seems to
have begun severly and in addition to the flannel drawers I got
before I left Scotland I have now added flannel chemises and
I do not think I shall find them a bit too warm....

Danieli's Hotel, 15 Decbr., 1849

My dear Mama
   ... Our minds this morning have been filled with horror at
George's account of a dreadful event which occured yesterday
in Venice. At the time the Austrians again took possession of the
town and were changing various situations and giving them to
their own inferiors, they turned out of the Arsenal a man, an
Italian, who had worked there for 26 years, promising that
when things were settled they would give him another situation,
but the time passed on and his family and himself were reduced
to extreme distress and then to absolute starvation notwithstanding his many demands for employment. Yesterday it
appears he left home saying that if he did not get something from
them today they would hear of him. He got admittance to the
Commandant of the Arsenal who was sitting in his room with
another officer at work. The Italian asked for the promised
work in such a peremptory tone that the Commandant said
unless he used more temperate language he should have none.
The Italian rushed at him with a Stiletto and stabbed him to the
heart. He died instantly. The other Officer cried out and ran to
the wall for a sabre that was hanging. In the meantime he received
a thrust which it is feared is mortal, at least they did not know
last night whether he was dead or alive, and then the man killed
himself. So ended the dreadful Tragedy. One dare not blame

---

[1] Mr Ruskin was not at all well at this time and later confessed that he had
a double rupture, caused by a fall from a mule, and had to wear a truss. He
and Mrs Ruskin had been at the end of November at Ipswich and Yarmouth.
On December 3 he had written: 'I enclose a review of 7 Lamps by an architect from the opposition Builder paper.'

the Italian, his provocation and distress and peculiar religious notions probably brought him to think his sin small. Perhaps the Commandant & his companion had never seen or heard of the man before & did not know he had suffered so deeply, but it is all very dreadful and I fear very Italian.

We read in the *Times* today a long account of the Queen Dowager, very interesting. What a good woman she appears to have been and I daresay will be deeply regretted by the poor who in her found a never failing friend....[1] Today we walked to the Post Office, or Grimani Palace, on the Grand Canal. I daresay you will remember it in Turner's large oil painting of Venice in the dining room at Denmark Hill where its square white marble form is a prominent feature. The grandfather of the present Count who dines almost every day in this Hotel gambled away the whole property and it is now the Post Office.[2] We went out to look at the view up & down and Charlotte dropped her handkerchief into the Canal. George & the Austrian Guard rushed to seize it before it disappeared, when George's fine new cap fell of[3] and he & Charlotte had the satisfaction of seeing their property sailing away comfortably together, the Austrian and I laughing very heartily.. The afternoon was fine although cold and immense numbers of people were walking about in all directions and many nice looking people, I suppose from the Country come in for Christmas. The Duchess of Berry had also arrived at her Palace.[4]

Yesterday after walking about till we were tired we came

---

[1] Queen Adelaide had died on December 2, aged fifty-seven.

[2] The Grimani was bought by the State in 1806 and occupied by the Post Office until 1872 when the Post Office moved to the Fondaco dei Tedeschi and the Grimani became the Court of Appeal. Turner's painting of the Grimani, under the title *The Grand Canal*, is now in the Huntington Gallery, San Marino, California.

[3] Effie nearly always spelt off with one 'f', as she no doubt pronounced it.

[4] The Vendramin Calergi on the Grand Canal which at that time was one of the few palaces occupied by one family and kept in perfect order. Caroline, Duchess of Berry, had bought it in 1844. She was the eldest sister of the King of Naples, Ferdinand II, and widow of the last Duc de Berry, a younger son of Charles X, assassinated in 1820. Her only son, the Comte de Chambord, claimant to the French throne, inherited the Palazzo Vendramin on her death in 1870. It is now the winter Casino.

back and got Carlo, who was in a state of great despair because the Gondola was not ready the minute we asked for it, to take us across to St. Giorgio Maggiore (vid. Murray) where after some difficulty occasioned by the tide's running so fast, we landed amongst a number of Soldiers and Cannon, the Austrians having placed a Battery just in front of the Church. This Edifice, of which you will read the account, is a style of which there are a great many in Venice, to my mind a very corrupt form of architecture and very ugly, half Greek Temple-ish and half anything else you like, the inside heavy and unimpressive but the inlaid flooring of different marbles nice & clean....[1]

18th. We have just received another letter of introduction from Mr Murray to a Mr Rawdon Brown who had been residing some time in Venice. I hope he will come and see us for both Mr Blumenthal & Mr Valentine continue ill and we have not seen them at all yet.... I got some of these gold stars the other day from a Turkish Merchant. They are Turkish and intended to scent one's clothes and I think the smell very agreeable. That about giving Mrs Manning the Sacrament was horrible.[2] I thought so at the time I read it, but she is only one woman in a century and the Italians here appear to me to be too degraded & ignorant to be so clever or so knowing as she. The Lower population here are exactly like animals in the way they live, and the fishermen's families live in rooms without an article of furniture and feed in the streets, but I must now conclude as I have had my Italian lesson this morning & feel rather tired. I asked for the wounded Officer this morning and hear that having had his arm amputated at the shoulder it is hoped he will recover....

[1] Effie was gradually coming to understand the purpose of Ruskin's studies in Venice, summarised in his introduction to *The Stones*: 'It is in Venice, and in Venice only, that effectual blows can be struck at this pestilent art of the Renaissance. Destroy its claims to admiration there and it can assert them nowhere else.'

[2] The Mannings had been given the Sacrament together by the chaplain just before their execution. Effie thought it horrible because Mrs Manning was a self-declared atheist. A Church of England clergyman expressed the same horror in a letter to *The Times*.

RAWDON BROWN

※

Rawdon Lubbock Brown, who is described in the next letter, became a life-long friend of both Effie and John, no small achievement after the annulment. He was born in London in 1806 (not 1803 as stated in the *Dictionary of National Biography*), the son of Hugh William Brown and Anne Elizabeth Lubbock, sister of Sir John Lubbock, Bt. He was a boarder at Charterhouse from January, 1820, until April, 1821. Thereafter nothing is known of him until he went to Venice at the age of twenty-seven. Falling in love with Venice, he stayed there until his death fifty years later and made deep and scrupulously accurate researches into the Venetian archives. He edited, as well as lesser works, the despatches of Sebastian Giustinian while he was Venetian Ambassador at the Court of Henry VIII from 1515 to 1519, which was published in 1854 by Ruskin's publisher, Smith, Elder. Ruskin himself cast his eye over it, but it was Effie who helped him to correct it and see it through the press (he called it her godchild), and who gave him much needed encouragement when it was but coolly received.

Brown hoped to be made Consul in Venice, for he was not at all well off, but never achieved this ambition. However, in 1862 he was commissioned by Lord Palmerston to calendar the Venetian State Papers that had some bearing on English affairs. He was proud to accept this assignment, and the accompanying salary enabled him to devote the rest of his life to the work he loved. The last of the eight volumes of the Calendar was not published until after his death.

Danieli's Hotel,[1] 22nd December

Dear Mama
   ... We have found a most agreeable acquaintance in Mr Rawdon Brown who is a most agreeable, clever literary person

[1] On the second double sheet of this letter there is a coloured engraving of the Danieli, at the side of which Effie has written: 'The two black dots under

and yet not at all grave. He knows and has seen everybody worth seeing of English [*sic*] and has lived in a beautiful Palace on the Grand Canal for the last 15 years. He is exceedingly energetic, something of a Mr Capes in telling stories and knowing about people, but he is not pushing and a gentleman.[1] He is between forty & fifty and suits me very well and also John. He has much influence here and has got John already some very precious books out of the Library of St Mark's regarding the old architecture of Venice which will be most useful to him, and is helping him in every possible way, and on the other hand he will take Charlotte & me into many places that we had no conception of before, and he knows and visits with all the best Society, but he says there will be no visiting this winter as the Italian families won't come back which he is very angry at, and we hear it is not on account of the Austrians at all, but they are kept in a sort of fear by what the Republican party would say in Venice and it is a want of moral courage on their part. The losses of the Venetian nobles has been much exaggerated and as they have all fine places in the country they prefer staying where they are. Radetzky told a person the other day, and this is quite true, that he should give dinners at Verona and if no one came his Officers should eat them. He should also give Balls and if the Italian Ladies would not come his Officers should waltz together.

We looked in vain amongst the staff the other day for our friend the Count [Wimpffen] but he must have been left behind at Verona. There is a rumour that Radetzky is going to remove his headquarters here which would benefit Venice much and

---

window those of our sitting room in front, *fine* carved stone Balconies, underneath crowds of people always passing.' The dots are on the balcony of the *piano nobile* on the extreme left.

[1] Millais, who met Rawdon Brown in May, 1854, wrote to Mrs Gray: 'Like yourself I was astonished to find Mr Brown such a youthful gentleman—I had conceived in my mind (I don't know why) that he was slightly infirm in appearance, and paternal in character, but I think Mr B will have a young wife yet. He is very nervous and quaint.' He lived in the Palazzo Businello, but between 1838 and 1842 had lived in the Palazzo Dario. M. J. H. Bunney, in his diary for 1871, records that Brown bought the Dario for £480 when it was almost a ruin. He restored it to something like its original condition but finding it inconvenient and expensive he sold it.

the people then perhaps would come back, but at present the town is certainly not pleasant for the soldiery who really behave extremely well. One man was stabbed the other day, his clothes stripped off and thrown into a canal. The next day at Lido a soldier who had charge of some money was found stabbed in the morning, and really such things are not pleasant to be happening every day.

I am very much delighted with Radetzky and all I hear of him is to his credit. I have quite set my heart on being presented to him and I am determined to do so if possible. John says he would like it very much too and that perhaps I may succeed but that he has not time to help but that I may do any thing I like. Now if I was a Mr Capes, I would ask Count Alphonse [Wimpffen] at Verona to do it, but that would be too much of a good thing, for in the first place he is too young and placed too immediately beside Radetzky and it would put him in an awkward position which I would be sorry to do, so my plan is this. I asked Mr Brown if he knew of any way and he said, "Oh! young Wimpffen could do it at once". I said is there no other way and he said none but through Austrians belonging to him, when I said I would not ask the Count, so my plan is this; there is a very pretty woman, the wife of an Austrian Artist, a Madame Nerly, herself Venetian, who lives in the Pisani Palace and Mr Brown knows them very well and is going to take us to see Mr Nerly's studio. I intend to get acquainted with Madame, who is past her first youth, about thirty, & the only handsomely dressed and Ladylike person I see here besides being very well conducted. She is always walking in the Square with her little Boy and her husband and always one or two Officers, who are glad to have an agreeable person to talk to, besides she and her husband being very high Austrians. I intend then to walk with her and get acquainted with some of the Staff and so find out if it cannot be done.[1]

---

[1] Mr Nerly (1807-78) had been born von Nerlich, a Prussian, but had Italianised his name to Federigo Nerly when he settled in Venice in 1837 after living some years in Rome. He had been a protégé of Baron Rumhor, a distinguished art historian, who enabled him to go to Italy and who remained his patron. Nerly had considerable success as a painter of Venetian scenes. In 1840 he had married the ward, and probably the illegitimate

Alas! I have just come in from my walk and all my hopes have fallen to the ground for the present for one of the Austrian Officers tells me that Radetzky went yesterday to Milan and they do not know when he returns which finishes me for the present. Mr Brown took us yesterday forenoon first to St Mark's Library where we saw several treasures which the public never see....[1] After we had looked through it Mr Brown took us to a place we had never heard of being in Venice, the Botanical Gardens close to where the Railway Bridge is. You will see the position from being so exposed to the Austrian Lines several shells fell in the Gardens and we saw one which had not exploded, 900 lbs. weight. The gardens are therefore not in good order at present, but the glass houses were in beautiful order and the collection of Cacti and their flowering plants extremely good and well worth seeing. Mr Brown used to go very often to this garden to view the seige operations and had a kind of seat made for himself in one of the high trees, and when the shot & shells were falling about, he took the best care of himself he could, but it must have been a very dangerous pastime but he seemed to have seen a great deal & got no harm.[2]

After we left the gardens we partly walked, then partly rowed, for it was a long way, and when we reached home we were very glad of a rest as we had been on our feet since twelve and it was then past four. We dressed and Mr Blumenthal came

---

daughter, of the enormously rich Marchese Constantino Maruzzi. She had been educated in Paris, had fallen in love with Nerly at one of his exhibitions in Venice and begged to become his pupil. They lived in part of the Palazzo Pisani, now the Academy of Music.

[1] The Marciana Library was then in the Great Council chamber of the Doge's Palace. It was transferred there in 1812 from the Sansovino Library, and moved back again in 1905.

[2] The Botanical Gardens were between the station and the Cannaregio, on the site of the convent of San Giobbe and the vineyard belonging to it which were appropriated by the state when the convent was suppressed by Napoleon. The gardens were laid out in 1812 and closed in 1870. Mr Brown would have been in great danger, for most of the Austrian shells fell in the Cannaregio district which was bombarded from Campalto on the mainland as well as from the island of San Giuliano. At a safer distance many Venetians built belvederes, cupolas or turrets on their rooftops in which they ate and slept in order the better to watch the bombardment like a display of fireworks.

to dinner, a nice young man, an Italian, speaking extremely good English and quite a business man.[1] We liked him very well and he spoke almost all in Italian to me and complimented me very much on knowing so much in a month's time. Poor Charlotte comes off very badly in cases where English is not the order of the day, for she hardly knows anything of French although she is now studying it every day, and here German, French and Italian are always in requisition and as I know F. quite well now, and enough of Italian and German to be very useful, poor Charlotte hears me chattering away with whoever I am talking with, languages of which she does not learn a word, but I am much more pushing than she is and she has a most peculiar difficulty in acquiring any new thing.... I often tell her, she should ask for things herself but she says she does not know a single word and so she never learns, but I am very vexed with John now for making me lose so much of my German since my marriage. He is sorry for it himself now that he sees to get into Austrian Society it is indispensable, but I tell him that I am not going to keep from it any longer & I am going to buy a Dictionary and revise what I can.[2]

I happened today to feel the want of it extremely. Hanoverian German I understand pretty well but Viennese, which these Officers speak, is very different and this afternoon, happening to have a tête à tête with an Officer for some quarter of an hour, we both looked particularly foolish. He was telling me something he wished particularly to make me understand. I could not, in his Vienna Tongue, and the aid of seeing the expression of his mouth, which would have been and always is a great help to one, was entirely lost in a pair of long moustaches, but

[1] Ruskin described Carlo Blumenthal to his father in 1851 as 'single—about my age, I fancy, my banker here, amiable but commonplace'. He was connected with the management of the lagoons and was therefore useful to Ruskin not only as a banker.

[2] During their second visit, when they had an apartment of their own, John complained to his father that he had to do more about organising the household than he should have done because Effie had learnt German instead of Italian. Yet during their engagement he had written to her that her knowledge of German would 'often and often be of use to' him. When she did eventually get into Austrian society she found that only French was spoken.

very nice ones, reaching to the bottom of his face on each side and I only saw the white teeth between occasionally....[1]

24th. I have just received your nice letter written upon the 14th.... Thank you for your remarks on my health. John is much grieved at the smallness of my appetite. I am now so little hungry that if I only eat a little meat and bread at dinner I am satisfied and my digestion seems feeble and not right. I shall try your plan of taking a cup of arrowroot at night. I sleep well but am dreadfully annoyed with dreams of an unpleasant description on all kinds of subjects and I work so hard in my dreams that I wake in the morning as exhausted as if I really had gone through what I have dreamt of. I think my mind is rather too active for my circulation. These last few nights I have dreamt of nothing but learning German and in my dream I am trying so hard to put sentences into proper Grammar that really it is quite a labour and one which I have no power to prevent, but don't let this trouble you for I am really able to walk so much every day. Yesterday for instance I went to the Greek Church and saw the impressive service there at ten o'clock....[2]

We then returned home, read our own English morning service which we always do on Sunday and afterwards we took a little soup and I went to St Mark's and read my Bible quietly for an hour. Then Charlotte came for me and we walked up and down the Square. The band was playing and we soon got warm. Presently we passed a very nice looking group of two well dressed Ladies, a little girl and two handsome young men in Uniform. I was puzzled but suddenly bowing again recognised Count Alphonse. After two more turns he came to us and said that he was walking with his mother, brother and cousin, and that he felt sure if we were still in Venice that he would see us there, and if not he was coming at any rate to Danieli's to ask

---

[1] This Austrian officer became Effie's most devoted friend in Venice, and if she had been ready to love anyone but John at this time she might well have lost her heart to him. According to his visiting card, which she enclosed in a later letter to her mother, he was Charles Paulizza, First Lieutenant of Artillery. At first Effie spelt the name Paulitzka as it was probably pronounced.

[2] San Giorgio dei Greci, on the Rio San Lorenzo, is an unmistakable landmark from its tower which has been leaning dangerously ever since it was built at the end of the sixteenth century.

for us. I said we had expected to see him on the Parade day.
He said he had made a little rubrique with Radetzky not to
come with him because if he had he could only have been
absent two days but now he has permission for a few weeks.
He had only arrived in Venice in the morning and was going
at night to Trieste to remain a fortnight with his Father, after
which he returns to Venice. He said he would if he had time
come and see John but I suppose his mother kept him with her
for he did not come.

This is a most lovely day for Christmas Eve. The whole
town near the Rialto is one mass of poultry with cock's feathers stuck in them for sale, all kinds of vegetables and lots of
things I can't describe. By the bye some one came the other
night and stole our Gondola. Poor Carlo has looked everywhere
for it and it is not to be found. The people here sometimes steal
Gondolas for smuggling purposes, returning them again at
night after they have got what they want and tying them up
in the same way they took them away....

I have not told you that Mr Brown put me in the plan of rub-
bing myself all over with hair gloves morning and night, which
I hope will promote circulation. They have not done so yet &
he has advised me to rub a little camphorated spirits of wine on
them and that will I daresay make them warmer. These two last
days we have really been doing nothing but walking and seeing
the Churches and customs of Venice. Yesterday was Christmas
Eve and as the Romanists eat no flesh all day, and not anything
till the evening when they have a fish dinner, and I suppose every
tenth family had a party of friends last night, and the massacre
of eels that went on all day was perfectly dreadful. Under our
windows there was a perfect pool of blood and they kill them
in such a savage way. They pin down the head and tail and then
cut slices in them all along, and after they have bled they weigh
them in scales so much the pound, but as they never kill them
till the moment of their sale every customer has to see this
process gone through and I fancy the length of eels killed in Italy
yesterday would go round the world.

Mr Brown came for us at six and took us into six or seven
churches.... We came home tired rather. The cold & frost were
bitter but the moon made it almost as bright as day. This

morning being Christmas every one saluted us with "Buona
Festa, Signora" to which I replied in the same strain, and
proceeded at ten to see Mass in St Mark's which continued for
two hours. The two Organs and band were very splendid and
played the whole time. The nave was crowded. I was much edi-
fied by the Austrian Soldiery who are very good Romanists,
giving thanks down upon their knees and saying their prayers
with their bayonets between their arms and Holly in all their
caps. Every shop was shut and all the world walking about, and
the front of the Doge's Palace and all the part looking towards
the sea and over the Bridges presented one unbroken line of
people walking.

Venice is such a capital place for playing hide & seek in; you
see an immense way of [off] and if you don't want to meet any
person who is looking for you, two turns down the cross lanes
which intersect every corner [two words effaced] at once from
observation. Charlotte & I had great fun today watching
Paulitzska. I don't know whether he is captain or major but he
took the important fortress of Malghera during the Blockade
with his Battery of Artillery and he is a very fine man, the officer before mentioned (you will think us fortunate in our
Military acquaintances), so we are, for he & the Count are the
most distinguished looking men we have seen, but this man is
the handsomest and about thirty. Well, today he knew we had
left Danieli's, and Charlotte and I went into fits of laughing
seeing him an immense distance of rushing madly over the
bridges, running down into off lanes, then out again, then all
round the Square and true German fashion never looking behind but always looking before him till at last he came, in the
course of an hour, by chance to the place where we had remained
the whole time amusing ourselves and thinking what capital exercise we were giving him. We took no notice of ever having seen
him at all and continued our promenade, which I think would
have amused you immensely. He speaks high Vienna German
and not a word of English but speaks Italian, Danish &
Spanish perfectly, but I find the German the best, and of it
I understand as much of his speaking as he does of mine and
the little I understand I translate to Charlotte, as it is very
stupid, for not speaking a word he always begins his speeches

to me with "Gnadige Dame" and assists the conversation by
Italian, but sometimes we come to a dead stop. John & he of
course speak Italian and get on nicely[1] and I think he will be
useful to us as he has been in Venice for three years stationed
and will be going to Verona about the same time as us, and
perhaps by the time I understand him a little better I may get
him to introduce us to Radetzky.

Mr Brown has also promised to present us to the young and
old Mesdames Mocenigo, one of the famous Italian families still
existing and who he is very intimate with and who have said
they would be delighted to know us. I am afraid we shall not
know the Countess Wimpffen. I think she must be a bad-
tempered person for her husband and she, says Mr B., quarrel
like cat & dog and I cannot fancy it is the Count's fault for he
looked so grand and had so much affection and respect shown
by his sons, but the fact is, she was an immense heiress, only
daughter of a Vienna Banker & she may have presumed there
[?] her wealth. Her house here is splendid and she has, owing
to the revolution, never been able to enjoy it till now and *her
Husband at Trieste*.[2] But the people here do things in a curious
way, especially as to matrimony, and I think a sprinkling of
English morals would not be amiss here, only they would not
be accepted by the Italians although they admire them in us.

We get plenty of admiration and attention, and the number
of our admirers increases daily and they are extremely polite and
don't make love to us which is a comfort. For instance, I had
real mince pies sent to me today for my Christmas dinner and
I astonished the waiter by setting fire to it with Brandy and as
it was very bad for me I only tasted it and John ate his & mine
too. Another person sent me the books of the Opera & Ballet

[1] John later wrote about him to his father that 'we never could get through
two consecutive sentences on any subject—he and I knowing equally little
of Italian'.

[2] She lived on the main floor of the Palazzo Fini, now the Grand Hotel,
where she had a fine collection of contemporary pictures. Effie wrote to her
mother on August 31, 1852, after returning from the second Venice trip. 'I
think sometimes I should like to do what Ctsse Marie Wimpffen does who
never leaves her bed unless the sun shines.' She was a daughter of Baron
Bernard Eskeles, Deputy-Governor of the Austrian National Bank, and
died in 1862, aged sixty.

for the Fenice tomorrow night and things of that sort. Men
are really great fools! and if you suppose that I ever forget my
duty for an instant to my husband, you are not at all wrong
in your remarks as to decorum! I hope I have inherited a
little of my Father's sense and your discretion to some purpose.
In fact John would require a wife who could take [care] of her
own character, for you know he is intensely occupied and
never with us but at meal times, so that we can do anything
we like and he does not care how much people are with us or
what attention they pay us. I understand him perfectly and he
is so kind & good when he is in the house that his gentle
manners are quite refreshing after the indolent Italian and the
calculating German, but we ladies like to see & know every
thing and I find I am much happier following my own plans
& pursuits and never troubling John, or he me....

I am so sorry I have not been able to send you a nice New
Year's present but don't you think you could order one for yourself? I have long wished to give you a black velvet cloak and
I think in this cold weather you would be much the better of
it. Name your own price to Miss Rutherford and if there is
anything the children require ask her to send it along with the
cloak....[1]

Our not being home till April is entirely on account of John's
accumulation of work and I believe after the London season is
over we shall very likely return again. My health in this matter
has not been at all consulted and I am astonished at your putting it on that head. John always says in his letters to his Father
that he thinks it right for him to follow out his profession and be
away from them. Mr Ruskin agrees and they never speak about
my health, but the truth is that it was exceedingly kind of them
to let us away in the sudden way they did and I assure you that
I am not at all insensible to their kindness in this, but our staying away now till April & for the future is entirely John's doing

---

[1] Miss Grace Rutherford, a very old friend of the Jameson family who had
first known her at Cupar, was in business as a dressmaker with her sister Janet
at 56 Pall Mall. She was able to make a dress without a fitting in a couple
of days as she did for Effie when she and John came up to London for the
night from Folkestone on June 29, 1848, to attend a great party at Lansdowne
House.

into which neither I nor his parents have in the least interfered....

                              Danieli's Hotel, Venice, 30th Decbr.
My dear Mother
    ... I have been much better these last few days. In addition to
the hair gloves, Mr Brown kindly sent me a hair strap which I
use morning and night and which excites the skin. The mustard
was losing its effect and I have given it up for a little time until
I can use it with advantage again. Although we have had a good
deal of snow here, before the forenoon is past every trace of it
disappears into the canals and the streets are so clean and dry that
we have been walking as much as usual. Mr Blumenthal often
walks with us after three o'clock when his business is over and
we are much the better of him for the Italians do not in the least
mind what they do or say to you for I suppose their own Ladies
are not over and above well conducted and they suppose us the
same. They pass me and say "dear creature" and lots of things
like that and throw bouquets at me. One gentleman came yesterday with a beautiful bouquet of carnations and Heliotrope
(flowers are now very expensive) and was advancing to throw it
at me as we passed when Mr Blumenthal joined us and he put
his bouquet into his coat pocket and walked away. Such marks
of attention make Charlotte and me exceedingly indignant for
we walk so exceedingly quietly, never pay the slightest attention
to any one or look behind. It is all the same when George is with
us; they follow us about and annoy us all the same. Such manners
are so different from ours at home and it just shows us how very
badly conducted the Italians, both Ladies & gentlemen, are. The
Austrians are never so rude nor do they annoy us so much. We
have not seen "Paulitzka" for nearly a week. I do not know
what he is about but I imagine he is learning English and the next
time we see him he will indulge us with what he has committed to memory.
    It is very nice for us Mr Blumenthal speaking English so per-
fectly for he takes great trouble in teaching me what Italian he
can in the course of conversation. His brother is coming from
England this week. He has been also in Scotland on business so
that we will hear what his impressions of Britain have been. The

other night he brought an Italian artist, a Signor Pividor, to tea with us. He is master of perspective in the Academy here and his drawings were most beautiful, perhaps rather finical but so exquisitely finished and so true. He had most perfect pen & ink sketches of every steeple in Venice and he seemed to have understood the Architecture thoroughly.[1] He was a nice clever little man and spoke sufficient French to be understood by me. He was talking of Phrenology and spoke by chance of two Italian Ladies of rank, young & beautiful, who had had their characters read so truly that they were extremely annoyed. They died about the same time, aged 25 and thirty, a year and a half ago only, from the effects of disippation. One night they were seen together walking in men's clothes and were put in the Guard house all night. In the morning it was discovered that they were the wives of the Marcheses so & so, two principal noblemen here. I suppose such conduct is not uncommon for he told it to John in Italian quite cooly as if there was nothing extraordinary about it....

I am translating Hans Andersen's *Poet's Bazaar* from German. I have not much time but I like German so very much that I try to do two or three pages a day although it gives me a good deal of trouble as I have forgotten it nearly all and now that Paulitzka has gone I am not obliged to try even the little I know excepting with my Italian Master who speaks it very well, but then when he is here all my time is taken up with Italian and I am going to translate with him "I Promessi Sposi" of Manzoni which is considered very good Italian reading for those who are beginning the Language.

I have always forgotten to tell you two things until my letters were away, the first was that John & I would like to give Mr & Mrs Ker the two volumes of *Modern Painters*.... The other thing was about Melina Genoud, Lady Otway's maid, who I half engaged at Milan. I have always had, like you, a great horror of French maids and I never intended that any foreigner should enter my service, but at the same time I intended having an English maid during next season as I shall be going out a good

---

[1] Giovanni Pividor's drawings of Venetian views were in good demand by the several publishers of albums of coloured lithographs flourishing at that time. He often lithographed his own work. See plate II.

deal and it will be indispensable that I have some one while
I am in town to take care of my things and alter them for me
&c, for before, every little thing that was to be done I had to
send backwards and forwards to Miss Rutherford.... Lady
O., who had had Melina before she was married and was very
fond of her, was much distressed to part with her and gave us
so nice an account of Melina's family, who she had visited at
Vevey, that John, who you know loves Vevey and liked the girl,
declared I must have her.... She is young & pretty but her chief
recommendation to me was her beautiful French accent which
will be very useful to me, for nowadays one must speak French
as well as English and it is very necessary for me both when
I am at home and here. She made all Lady Otway's clothes
which were particularly neat and took care of everything she
had.... She is older than me and small and very neat. I never
saw such a beautifully put on net cap as she had, or more taking
manners.... If I find however that she has got any French
trickery about her I will turn her off directly....[1]

   1st January.... Today is kept as a Fete but nothing particular
is going on. The shops are all shut and crowds of people are
pouring in and out of St. Mark's which is brilliantly illuminated.
I was there for an hour and heard some very pretty music, and
services seem to go on this week for the whole day. It is very
interesting to sit still and watch the faces as they pass, say their
prayers for a couple of moments and then depart. The men are
so very fine and for their class so superior to English or Scotch.
The nose particularly, half Greek half Roman, is so splendid and
the mouths finely cut. The fishermen are particularly Grand and
they carry their enormous brown hooded cloaks lined with
scarlet in a manner peculiarly their own. They are decidedly the
finest animals in Venice. When you go a little higher to the
young men with paletots & moustaches the type is still fine
and the features still more delicately formed, but all look sickly

---

[1] Melina did enter Effie's service and stayed with her for over a year. She
made all her clothes, including her Court dress in June which was greatly
admired and pleased Mr Ruskin so much that he presented Melina with a
guinea. She became discontented because Effie, instead of giving her all her
old dresses, sent some of them to her mother, and later Effie accused her
of being intriguing but we are never told exactly why she left.

& disippated and a general want of energy and mind is
desernable....

John is always busy and many many times he mourns over
his little time for work here. He once thought of giving up
Florence for this year, but I believe we shall still go but necessarily for a shorter time....

They decided not to go to Florence. Mr Ruskin was pleased about
this for not only would it save money but he felt it right that John
should stay in Venice to finish his book.

PAULIZZA

❧

My dear Papa,

I have just received your kind and most welcome letter on my return from St. Mark's where I have been since ten o'clock.... When I came out the snow was falling heavily and I ran home as quickly as possible arriving however covered with snow. The Gondoliers who always stand down stairs seemed greatly surprized to see me, for Italian Ladies never go out hardly in fine weather and in a day like this they would think it perfect madness, I suppose, to stir. Carlo rushed to me and beat all the snow off saying all the time, "Cattivo tempo Signora," to which I perfectly agreed.

I am most truly thankful to hear how fortunate your business has been this year and I trust you may yet have enough and to spare. When I see the misery and wickedness of this place, your quiet happiness in Perth, if you could only contrast the two, would notwithstanding your anxiety make you very contented that things are not worse. You seem sorry I write such long letters but you know it is the only pleasure I can give you when I am so far away and I have almost cut all my correspondents....

We have seen a good deal this last week, and tomorrow forenoon Captain Paulizza takes us over the Arsenal which as yet we had only seen the outside of. Paulizza in the absence of the young Count is a most useful friend for us to have notwithstanding that he does not know a word of English nor can speak French. Still I begin to understand his German exceedingly well and he mine. I became acquainted with him in a very curious way, which will be a nice story for me to tell you some day, and will interest you greatly, but I have not time now. [We never learn the circumstances of their meeting.] I am exceedingly proud of him for he is no common character, although you will not think this a proof of it when I tell you that it was he who directed all the bombs against Venice, but I suppose he cried about it every day but was obliged to obey. John took to him directly from his exquisite drawings, many of them engineering ones, plans of attack and plans of the Lagoons so finely finished that John, who you know is a first rate judge, was perfectly surprized with their delicacy and style, and he is very useful to John in getting him into Barracks & Guardrooms &c of Palaces which before were closed to him. He is a very brave man & was decorated by the Emperor with two crosses. He is besides a Poet, plays on the Piano, speaks five or six Languages, etches on steel, in short, as he himself simply says, God has given him talent enough to work at a great many things and as his father could not leave him much money, as he has nine brothers older than himself, he has always been very busy since he was a boy. He was greatly delighted with some of Turner's etchings[1] and his foreign manners greatly delighted us by their grace. When he saw them he seized John in his arms and said, "Now I must lay by my pencil, I never can draw any more after seeing such pieces of art." He is constantly acting and we understand as much by his actions as his words. He has besides great personal advantages. He is very fair, a very fine clear complexion & eyes without being effeminate and although 38, he looks not much above thirty. Charlotte and I agree that he is the handsomest man in Venice & his grey military cloak lined with scarlet, which bye the bye the Officers here do not wear but hang it upon them in a very becoming manner over the rest of their uniform, sets off his fine figure to great advantage.

I give you thus a long description of this person because we see a good deal of him and as I must frequently mention him you may like to know what sort of person he is. Like many men of mind, he has also something at times of childish simplicity about him which comes out occasionally very queerly from under his long curling moustaches, and when you think he has been 21 years in the army you wonder still more, for instance, we had not seen him last week for two or three days and we supposed, which was the case, that he was occupied with the

[1] John never travelled without a few of Turner's etchings.

Governor.[1] Charlotte and I were sitting in St. Mark's in the half
light—in the afternoon the organs play & it is very nice to sit
still and hear the sound—suddenly I heard the peculiar clank
of the Austrian sword on the marble floor. I turned and here
was Paulizza crossing himself very diligently and saying his
prayers. On raising himself he saw us and bowed gravely and
went out. I said to him next day, "Why did you look so surprized on seeing us in St. Mark's yesterday?" "Oh!" he said, "I
had just come from the Governor and I had not time to go to
Danieli's so I came in here to say some prayers for myself and
for you & the Fraulein and I prayed that you might be preserved
until I saw you again." So I said, "Thank you, we are much
obliged. We are just going back to St. Mark's again today to see
the Procession of the Host." "Then," said he, "may I ask you
to remember me in your prayers and as it is this day year since
my Father whom I loved so much died may I also ask you to
think of his soul?" John was greatly touched and said to me,
"Only fancy an English Officer making such request, how
perfectly ashamed most of our fashionable young men would
be to be suspected of any such feelings," to which I agreed.

He went to the Opera with us the other night. He amused
me with his conversation but I did not enjoy the Opera, it was
so dreadfully cold and the house was nearly empty. The music
was very pretty, Linda di Chamouni [by Donizetti], but you
know when one is shivering of cold one cannot enjoy themselves and I was very glad to get home. We passed the next
evening in playing chess which I like very much. I first played
two games after dinner with John, then my Italian master
came in and I played two games with him, then Paulizza came
in & I played other two new with him. I gained one with the
Italian & one with Austrian but John beat me both games.

The snow storm has continued all day, the ships in the
Lagoon quite white, and St. Giorgio Maggiore looking clean
& cold over the water. The wind is howling furiously and I should
rather stay here than go with the Fishermen who every midnight sail to Chioggia. I was looking down at the snow before
dinner and saw Paulizza wrapped in his cloak half covered with

---

[1] Count Anthony Pachner, who had become Governor of Venice in
November, replacing for a short time General Gorzkowski.

snow walking below. He came up & after unrobing himself in the [word omitted] walked in, and showed us a beautiful miniature he had painted of a little nephew of his about Alice's age. He asked permission to play at chess in the evening with me, but I said in England it was customary for people to spend Sunday evening alone. He said, "Do you read the Heilige Buch?" I said, "Yes!" "Ah!" he said, "we do not do so in Italy, we go to the Theatres, at least I don't but it is customary, ours is a bad religion, it's all for the eyes and not for the mind." I could not help thinking such a state of things very melancholy and wondering how, as both the Count and he had expressed exactly the same sentiments, that they could be so amiable & clever as they both are.

Mr Brown is also exceedingly kind to us. We went to see his House the other day and were quite delighted with it; it was furnished in such exquisite taste, and besides possessing a great many pictures illustrative of Venetian History or Costume which are most interesting, he has a very fine collection of manuscripts of the Doges[1] and many curiosities of great value which could only be got by a long residence in Venice and watching continually whenever any rarity or other fell in his way. He had a beautiful coal fire burning which I assure you was a treat and the first we have seen since we left Britain. He is a curious person Mr Brown, extremely clever, and greatly occupied in research. He continually talks of people who living 4 or 5 hundred years ago seem to have been his partic-ular friends or guests. "Here," he says, "are some letters from Worcester, a very fine fellow indeed, Ambassador from Henry VIII to Rome, came to Venice such a day of such a month, lived in that house over there," then he describes his dress & how many dinners were given him, what he said & how he looked. "And here are his letters to his friends in England telling them how he was enjoying himself etc," and the same way he talks of Doges, Bishops, every body. He showed me some very touching letters of a Doge Mocenigo to Mary Queen of Scots on the death of her first Husband the Dauphin.

When we go to Verona he is going to give us letters of intro-duction to some Italian families there which will be delightful

[1] Rawdon Brown bequeathed all his Venetian manuscripts to the Record Office in London as well as 126 volumes of valuable transcripts.

as although Verona is most interesting it is very dull indeed
and in bad weather exceedingly dirty. From Mr Brown's he took
us to the House of a friend of his, a Colonel Cheney, now at
his estates in England but he comes to his Venetian House once
a year. A nice Venetian Servant received us and we found the
Palace in most beautiful order for us to see. It was fitted up
so splendidly, a mixture of Italian taste & English comforts.
There were cabinets of gems, fine pictures, statues and I don't
know what all. The marble floors were all covered with fine
crimson cloth and nice coal fires blazing. I am quite astonished
he, Col. C., was not terrified to leave such valuable property
so open and the place so insecure but to see the cleanliness &
propriety of everything you would have thought that the
Master intended to be back to dinner.[1] These are the only two
English who are resident here. Mr Brown wants us to take the
two lower floors of his Palace which are unoccupied which
would be delightful and economical as we would both have the
same cook. The plan here is a curious one. The cooks are all
men and never take longer than two hours to prepare a dinner.
They do not stay in the house but, supposing we dined at five,
he comes at three and goes up to Mr Brown to prepare his
dinner for seven. I don't think the custom a bad one at all.

   9th January. Since writing the two previous sheets, we have
been almost entirely confined to the house from the snow
storm.... Mr Brown has taken a great interest in my health and
told me the other day that he saw the things I was persevering
in were not doing me the least good and he would advise me
to allow him to bring one of his friends, the Dominican Friars,
to see me. These men are extremely clever; they take care of the
hospitals here and come over from their island [San Servolo]
every morning for that purpose. Their Monastery is endowed
and every thing they do is for charity. They will not accept

[1] Colonel Cheney (1803-84) was the second of three brothers, Robert-Henry,
Edward and Ralph, who lived together at 4 Audley Square, London (now
the Leicester Galleries) and at Badger Hall near Shifnal, Shropshire. The
brothers were devoted to one another and never married. In Venice Edward
lived at the Palazzo Soranzo-Piovene on the Grand Canal, near the Palazzo
Vendramin Calergi. Before coming to Venice he had lived some years in Rome
and in 1838 had published a romantic novel *Malvagna or The Evil Eye*. He
was a great friend of Monckton Milnes and Lord Holland.

money in any shape. Mr B. said there were plenty of Doctors in Venice but these men are the only ones he has any faith in. They came together yesterday and the Padre looked at my throat. He was a very intelligent looking, melancholy-like person in the dress of his order and Mr Brown acted as interpreter. He so far agreed with Simpson in directly finding out that the disease was internal and the irritation & blisters in the throat symptomatic, but the Italian spoke much more decidedly of what he considered really the matter. Simpson always said it was an inflammation of the mucous membrane and that I never could be well until it went away. His prescriptions have kept me as I am, certainly stronger as to bodily strength, but the disease not the least removed, my throat showing always the presence of the internal derangement. The Dominican says that it is a slow inflammation of the intestines which will be the more difficult to remove as it has continued so many months without necessary treatment, that it is now absolutely necessary something were done, that I never can have any appetite as long as I have it, that I never can feel warm outside as long as I have fever inside and that if I was his patient he should put on 8 Leeches just inside the waist, after they come off apply Linseed & almond oil poultice and repeat this treatment three times perhaps until the inflammation is gone. John does not know what to think and I write for your opinion. I own, as I told him [the Padre], I had an objection of taking blood and I was afraid I had not strength to spare for such treatment. He says that with women who are in the habit naturally of losing a great deal of blood that I should find it not such severe treatment as I anticipate. I should like your advice as soon as possible. You can think over it & tell me as soon as you can. I am inclined to believe what the Padre says, as really with all I have tried my throat only seems to remain in the same state. I am obliged to finish....

Danieli's Hotel, Venice, 18[50][1]

My dearest George

I was extremely delighted to receive your long and interesting

[1] This letter is postmarked January 16 from Venice, but was probably begun a few days earlier.

letter.... Be sure and not let your knowledge of German sleep;
sometime or other it will come into play and you will be thankful you know it.[1] I am getting much practice from having a
German Femme de Chambre and being so much with "Paulizza".
He makes me read a piece of Andersen's Dichter's Bazaar and
then tell him the meaning of what I have been reading in
German over again. I return the compliment by trading him a
few English words. Amongst his many accomplishments he is
a Doctor and he is greatly taken up with the state of my health
and curious enough both he and the Padre Prosdocimo are of
the same opinion regarding my malady although they have not
seen each other. Both seem to agree that several leechings are
necessary, that a slow internal inflammation is going on and will
continue to go on until removed by this means. Paulizza brought
me a quantity of Linseed & almond oil for poultices and the
Padre a kind of treacle and almond oil to take, both of which
have much benefited me during the last few days. You would
be greatly amused to see me with my two Doctors, both such
different men from any I have ever seen before. The Friar with
his meek deportment and sparkling black eyes and long black
robe and cowl is perhaps the most interesting of the two. There
are 18 brothers in the order and only one Priest, all the rest are
doctors like this one. They call themselves the "Fate-Bene
Fratelli", the "do-good Brothers". They are immensely rich,
both here and the different Branches of the order throughout
Lombardy, most of them gentlemen who have received their
Doctor's degree at the University of Padua and have devoted their
lives to the sick and their fortunes to ammeliorate the distress
of the poor. They are extremely good & Radetzky, who saw the
good they did in the Milan Hospitals, has increased their priv-
ileges. They have their Monastery on an Island across the
Lagoon and each brother has his daily work in Venice in the
Hospitals & Madhouse which they have under their care.[2]

---

[1] George had been at school at Wiesbaden in 1841 before going to
Charterhouse.
[2] The lunatic asylum, for males only, was situated on the island of San
Servolo. The Fate Bene Fratelli had had charge of it since 1725, though
originally they looked after insane members of only rich or aristocratic
families. It was not until 1797 that lunatics of all classes were accepted. In

The Padre Prosdocimo was here today. I never saw any thing
so kind as he is. Mr Brown always comes too to act as interpreter and the Padre was explaining that I must take as much
milk food, rice, & other simple foods as possible. I said, and
Mr Brown assented, that the milk here was worse than London
milk, and the Padre immediately said he would bring me a little
Flagon of new milk from their Cows every day if George
would be waiting at the place where their Gondola lands to
receive it. The Padre recommended Jelly without any wine in
it and Mr Brown kindly made his cook make some which has
turned out extremely good. I may call Mr Brown my third
Doctor for he also comes every day, but, as they all say, no one
would know I was in the least ill for I look so uncommonly
well and I am able to enjoy myself so much more and to take
so much exercise; I have such a good colour and I am always
in good spirits and enjoying myself.

Paulizza, my second doctor, would also interest you. I have
described his appearance before, but he seems to know as much
of Physic as if he had lived in Hospitals & laboratories all his
Life. He either comes himself or sends his servant, a tall Croat
Soldier, with the enclosed card every day, and when he comes
he takes a spoon in a scientific way, examines my throat and feels
my pulse at the hand which he says is steady enough but he
pointed out to John that the pulse just under the ear told a different story and was much more excited. I always thought before
that all pulses were the same but on feeling at the Throat, the
motion was distinct and nervous and at the hand steady and
slow. The place is just under the jaw and must have sympathy
with the state of my throat. He next explained to us that we had
better allow him to come and put on the Leeches for me. I
thought surely my ears had deceived me but now I am astonished at nothing foreigners do, for their life & education is so
different from ours, and when he repeated his request, John &
I could hardly help smiling when we looked at our handsome
friend with his long curling moustaches and striking dress, and

---

Effie's day mad females were housed on the island of San Clemente. Both
sexes are now in the psychiatric hospital on San Servolo while the Fate Bene
Fratelli have moved to the Palazzo Benzi-Zecchini on the Fondamenta della
Madonna dell'Orto where they have a hospital.

I thought of the horror such a request would be listened to in
our country and I said to him that, with us, women did these
things and I could easily get a person here, but he said, "No!
No! I can't bear to think of you being in such women's hands.
I shall be as tender to you as any women. Do, my dear little
sick one, let me come and wait upon you." Nothing that I
could say seemed to have the slightest weight in making him
understand that it could not be done and John only laughed
& seemed highly delighted with the novelty of the thing. We
asked him where he had learnt so much about medicine and
the female constitution. He said from his mother, who had had
a Degree conferred on her for her knowledge in that science
and that as his Father had so many sons he had given him the
best education to be got and he has been studying all his Life
up to this time.

He took Charlotte & me through the Arsenal the other
day.... We were obliged to come back for an appointment we
had, to receive Mr Brown who with the Count & Countess
Minischalchi were to wait on us at three, but we return to see
the Artillery department on Tuesday. Our visitors arrived and
greatly pleased we were with them. They are a Veronese family
of great antiquity, the Count having the same estates possessed
by his ancestors in the 13th Century and living in the same
Palace at Verona which was occupied by the family contemporary with Romeo & Juliet. It is covered with frescoes (vid
Murray at Verona, Palazzo Minischalchi). Mr Brown was to
have given us a letter to them when we returned to Verona but
they have come here to get their passport to go to Paris &
England for the season. They are going to stay with Lord
Grenville[1] & the Duke of Northumberland so that we shall see
them probably when we return. They are very rich and curious enough. A large part of their income arises from the
cultivation of silk worms and the sale of silk. They are getting
much richer as silk is in greater demand than ever.[2]

The Count is celebrated as an Arabic scholar and he has

[1] The Grenville barony had become extinct in 1834, so Effie probably
meant Lord Granville.

[2] At that time the production of silk was the most important industry in
Lombardy.

promised to give John the means of getting into any Houses, Churches, or anything else at Verona. Charlotte and I could hardly take our eyes off the Count, he was so handsome. Although only thirty-eight his head is almost bald but half his face is covered with black beard & moustache, beautiful teeth and a very fine forehead & eyes. He speaks English with great elegance and understands it thoroughly. The Countess spoke in French. She has a very lovely complexion and eyes, but much too stout to be admired.[1] She was very pleasant and looked much handsomer on the following day when we went to the Palazzo Bembo to return their visit, which it is etiquette to do here on the following day. I was disappointed at not seeing the Countess Bembo,[2] who although only 18 has been some time married but when I was in the house she was with her Music Master, which sounded very odd to me. The House of the Bembo is a very ancient family of Venice. It was to Cardinal Bembo that Lucrezia Borgia wrote so many letters and sent a lock of her hair which we saw at Milan. Mr Brown possesses some very fine China plates and the ground of them is filled with portraits of Lucrezia made at that time. As they are coloured they give you a pretty good idea of what she was. I fancy she was more admired from being totally unlike all other Italian women than from any great beauty of her own, for her features are exceedingly sharp and the nose very long but with black eyes her skin was extremely fair and she had an immense quantity of fair hair with a natural wave all over it which was then, as now, esteemed a great beauty.

We have been able to go out today for a walk as they are most diligent here in clearing away the snow.... The Friar sent me a bottle of milk which was as good as any Scotch milk I ever tasted and as Mr Brown says he should quarrel with the Friar if he was the only person allowed to send me my breakfast, so he sent two pots of Keiller's Marmalade,[3] Dundee. You cannot

[1] She was the daughter of Count Guerrieri Gonzaga, a family very active in the Risorgimento.

[2] *Née* Alfonsina de Morando. She had married Count Pier Luigi Bembo Salamon in March, 1848. He was a writer on social and economic subjects, and became a Senator of the Kingdom of Italy.

[3] Then in the white stone jar now marketed for only special occasions.

think the pleasure it gave us to see the printed Characters so well known once again....

The next letter is from Rawdon Brown. He and Effie corresponded for many years. Her letters to him were returned to her after his death, and are now, together with his letters to her, in the Bowerswell Papers.

Casa Businello, Saturday 9.30. [January 12.]
Dear Mrs Ruskin,

I'm an impatient mortal and ill able to wait until 2 o'clock for the bulletin, so please let me know how you are this morning and believe that Prosdocimo & myself will never pout at the whole parish peering down your throat, or pinching your pulse, *provided* similar investigations can in the least accelerate your well being or indirectly contribute thereto.

I should never have much cared to know "why an apple fell", but since many a day I have cudgelled my brains for the "wherefore of the eye's glistening"; the Julian Alps [north of Trieste] of themselves merely show a stern but beautiful outline from the "fondamente nuove", the snow that covers them was indebted to its enemy the sun for that evanescent blush, the type of an Italian twilight even in the month of January, and why should this combination of mere color bring the tear to the eye? mine, *could* at certain moments (not when vexed or mortified) be moved even by those same rays falling on the front of St. Giorgio Maggiore, whereas you, would most fastidiously frown on them, because Palladio (who believe me must have devoted a good three months at least to the study of architecture) eschewed the pointed arch: you lose much enjoyment by this disdainful humor, to say nothing of injustice to the dead, of whom Montaigne said so feelingly the care of them: "*nous est en recommendation ... ils son trespasser ils ne s'aydent plus; ils en requerent d'autant plus mon ayde. La gratitude est la justement en son lustre*"—I consider myself not less indebted here to Sansovino and to Baldassar Longhena than to the unknown architect of the Ducal palace.

To turn from ancient architecture to ancient needle work I

send your initials and the book of patterns & paper, and
remain very sincerely yours

Rawdon Brown

Dear Mr Brown

The paper will do beautifully and I will begin directly to copy
the patterns that I may return your precious book which
believe me I will guard as the apple of my eye till it is safe in
your keeping again, but won't I give it to you when I see you
today? Indeed I don't think you require my friend "Paulizza's"
virtue at all. Your remarks so cutting upon my humble little
tastes are too unkind. Why should I leave my first love, the
Northern Gothic, for a set of lines crossing one another at
wrong places even worse than our English Tudor style and
admire figures of Moses & all the Prophets with long beards
and crabs put into niches and awkward corners to make the
building look even on both sides, the whole principal of beauty
being destroyed by the Pillars being cut in two by the windows
and the same in the Pediment, but here in Venice one has the
Northern Architecture softened and enriched by Eastern refinement and love of splendour, and nothing can be more glorious,
and I believe I only admire this one style here the more because
I find no sympathy in the other.[1] However I must not write any
more nonsense about what I don't understand, only I know what
I like and what I don't like. I am pretty brisk this morning and
although I fight with you I didn't with your bread, for I break-
fasted off it & the Marmalade and I inwardly thought how
good & kind you were and how much I liked you although I
wouldn't say it to you for the world, for I intend to fight my
own battles with you although the Austrian [Paulizza] last night
drew his sword and declared he intended to make short work of
it with you when he heard that after his telling me it was cold,
I had gone to see the Alps with you, but about the tears, you

---

[1] It was the Renaissance architects' attempts to fit the image of a Greek
temple to the requirements of churchgoers of their age which exasperated
Ruskin. Of San Giorgio Maggiore, after paying tribute to its unique position, he wrote: 'It is impossible to conceive a design more gross, more
barbarous, more childish in conception, more servile in plagiarism, more
insipid in result, more contemptible under every point of rational regard'
(*Stones of Venice, Venetian Index*).

didn't see any. So Goodbye. Come at two, and with best
thanks and an advice to you to clean and polish your Armour
& lance well, I am yours most sincerely,

                                                        Effie

                              Danieli's Hotel, January [18], 1850
My dear Mama
   I have only this one sheet of paper remaining in my best, and
as all the rest are out walking in this lovely day, for it is now
just like summer, and I am lying in bed with the windows open
and extremely comfortable upon the whole although I would
much rather be out too, but nothing besides my usual illness
keeps me here and I am very glad it has come as Padre Prosdocimo is anxious to put on the leeches and will now be able
in about a week's time. He thinks me much better. I took a dose
of Castor oil the other night and I take a small pot-full daily
of a preparation of Cassia & almond oil which has greatly
reduced the inflammation and keeps the tongue clean, but
the Padre says that although the medicine has answered remarkably well, the leeching is the only thing that will remove the
internal irritation completely which I am now quite willing to
try. I do not know what we shall do for him for I never saw a
man so kind and so good.
   I have had some delightful walks for the last few days with
Mr Brown. He devotes half his day to us, or rather to me, and
he sends me notes in the morning which I enclose. You will
see some of his cleverness in them. I also enclose one of
Paulizza's for George's edification. I generally answer Paulizza's
before I read them for it takes me about an hour to decipher
them and as they are generally moving enquiries about my health
I can't go far wrong. This one was about the Fenice last night
where we went to hear Donizetti's Opera "I Martire", (The
Martyrs), very beautiful music and well got up. The Ballet was
Esmeralda, the premier Danseuse, Augusta Maywood, an
Englishwoman, married, and a very good person.[1] I never saw

[1] Augusta Maywood was an American born 1825. She trained in Phila-
delphia and in 1838 was taken to Paris by her step-father, where she made
her debut a year later. She was the only nineteenth-century American
ballet dancer to achieve international fame. After a very successful season at

such dancing, it was really the poetry of motion and her acting was so beautiful that John, who to Paulizza's great amusement had been writing a Chapter on Chamfered edges all during the Opera, left his studies and got quite excited and said he had never seen such dancing excepting from Taglioni.[1] The House was full and the Venetian Ladies actually came; amongst them I saw Baroness Hessler, the mother of Thalberg the Pianist,[2] the Countess Mocenigo and several others that I begin to know, the Count Grimani &c. These last two I know by the kindness of Mr Brown & will describe more particularly afterwards. When we left the House, and got through the crowd, what between our two Cavaliers, we lost the way to where the Gondola was lying. We ran about the narrow canals and back into the Theatre. I never saw such a puzzling Place until at last we lighted upon the right alley and when we arrived at the Gondola we found a complete crowd assembled as our non-arrival had caused some astonishment and our servants with Lamps were searching all about the place for us in the greatest consternation....

21st. Today the Padre comes at twelve, Mr Brown at two, La Sposa, the Countess Mocenigo, to call, and the Nerlys, the German and his lovely wife, now a little old but once the prettiest girl in Venice, come to tea this evening. I am a good deal with her for she was brought up in Paris and speaks good French. The husband is an artist and much patronised by the King of Prussia. They visit with everybody in Venice and are very pleasant people.

---

the Scala in 1848 she organised her own independent touring company. She retired in 1862. Far from being 'a very good person', the gossip about her private life prevented her from ever returning to America where her love affairs were not condoned. *La Esmeralda* by Cesare Pugni, based on Victor Hugo's *Notre Dame de Paris*, was produced first in London in 1844 with Carlotta Grisi as Esmeralda.

[1] Ruskin had first seen Taglioni dance in Paris in 1834. In *Praeterita* he calls her 'A woman of faultless genius'. Towards the end of Vol. I of *The Stones* there are two pages on chamfers (a bevelled cutting of stone) and an appendix on varieties of chamfers.

[2] Sigismund Thalberg (1812-71) was the natural son of Count Maurice Dietrichstein, who had been tutor to the Duke of Reischstadt. His mother was Baroness Wetzlar, not Hessler as Effie writes.

The other day Mr Brown came to take me to the Palazzo Mocenigo. I went with him because when I go to pay visits Charlotte never goes because for one thing she cannot speak a word and John prefers my going alone & she likes better not to go. Well, we went and as my visit had been advertised both the Dama Lurietta, the senior Countess, and Mde Clementine, La Sposa, or The Bride, although she is not very young, to distinguish her from the old Lady, were at home. They live in separate Palaces but joined together. The family is still a powerful one and is one of the most illustrious in Venetian History. The walls of the rooms are covered with full length pictures of Doges of the family in their Ducal robes, Admirals and Statesmen. It was also in this Palace that Byron lived when in Venice, and as the Count was not then married he lived with his mother in the adjoining Palace which he now occupys with his wife.[1]

We were received by some well dressed servants and conducted through a number of cold, grand, marble & frescoed appartments, to some nice warm well furnished ones where sat the Lady on a small couch. She received us very kindly and considering her age, 80 years, she was extremely well looking and upright. She considers herself a sort of Queen in Venice as she is the last of the great Venetian Dames, and as she can no longer go out she receives visitors all day, or relations. Her manners were quite beautiful and took away from your first impressions caused by the absurdity of her dress which though excessively rich was not becoming for her age, and I could not help feeling thankful that in Britain old Ladies did not disfigure themselves. Generally speaking her features were marked and fine and still sparkling black eyes, her hair gray but false curls

[1] There are three Mocenigo Palaces in a row. Byron went to live there in 1818 for two years. First he leased the centre palace, but afterwards moved to the one nearest the Rialto which was joined to it. Four Doges came from this great family. The old Countess was Donna Lucia, born in Venice in 1770, daughter of the former Governor of Padua, Marchese Andrea Memmo, a friend of Casanova's. In 1787 she married Count Alvise Mocenigo (1760-1815). Her son, Count Alvise Francesco Mocenigo (1799-1884), was an Imperial Chamberlain. He had married in 1840 Clementine, born 1816, daughter of Count John Spaur zu Flavon (1777-1852), one time Governor of Venice.

of jet black at each side of her face, the hair surmounted by a
blonde cap with blue artificial flowers, a brown loose satin
Polka cloak lined with white, hanging open and showing her neck
very bare, pale yellow kid gloves and exquisite point lace collar
and handkerchief, a fan and dress of purple & green silk. A little
table stood beside her covered with Jars of flowers & two little
antique bells, one she rang when she wanted her women attendants and the other the men. After we were seated she rang for
the men servants and they entered instantly bearing on massive
silver, plate & cups, black coffee, cake, & iced Lemonade in
Tumblers. The latter I took & found delicious. She was very affectionate to me and kissed me on both cheeks, speaking French,
and presented me with a work written I suppose a century ago
by her Father, the Marquis Memmo.[1] Whilst we were sitting, two
young Ladies with their governess entered of the illustrious
family of Lynar, the eldest not yet 14 but could speak already three
Languages perfectly and a little English.

We took leave of the old Lady and walked through her sleeping apartment by her permission. Here I was much astonished
by the toilette table; I had never seen anything like it before;
there was the Mirror frame, two little other mirrors, essence pots,
rouge pots, perfume bottles and boxes of various kinds, everything in wrought silver. It was very beautiful. Passing through
some other apartments we found ourselves in the Luxurious
boudoir of La Sposa. We chatted and laughed with her for half
an hour. She is pleasant & plain but fashionable looking. She
is daughter of Count Spaur, the last Governor of Venice, an
Austrian.[2] Her house and servants were in very good order,
and you may believe I was much obliged to Mr Brown for
taking me to see so much that was new and interesting, and all
that I have yet seen of the Italians makes me come to this opinion that whatever their private morals may be, they respect
those who are well conducted, and are themselves extremely
goodnatured, amiable and well-bred and when they find English

[1] A book on architecture, published in 1786 and re-issued by his daughter
in 1833.
[2] He was not the last Governor. The last Military Governor had been Count
Zichy and the last Civil Governor Count Palffy. It was they who had been
censured in Vienna for capitulating to Manin.

who sympathize with their tastes and understand them, they
will do any thing for them.

We were afterwards walking on the Place with La Sposa
when we stopped and spoke to several interesting people.
The Duc de Bordeaux [Comte de Chambord] passed, a fair
stout young man, lame and uses a stick in walking.[1] After him
Marshall Marmont, made Duke of Dalmatia by Napoleon, and
whom I had thought dead long ago. He did not look at all old
and Mr Brown says he is very good company and full of anec-
dote.[2] We next stopped and spoke to Mlle Taglioni who was
walking to her Gondola with her two children. She only came
to Venice a few days ago and I was very glad to have the
opportunity of seeing her so near. The Palace Mr Brown lives
in is hers [the Businello] and as she stays above him I intend
to make him take me to call upon her. She is considered a very
good person here and is extremely wealthy. She is plain in the
face but her figure is very distinguished and she walks well. She
was dressed in a close black bonnet, handsome Indian Plaid
& beautiful green velvet dress. Her son, about seven, is one of
the handsomest boys I ever saw. The Daughter is extremely fair
and pretty, about thirteen. She was going with her the same
evening to Verona to be present at a Ball given by Radetzky. The
Father of the children, a Frenchman, Taglioni's husband, behaved so cruelly to her that after enduring for many years she
was obliged to separate from him. She went to Petersburg and
the Emperor was so enchanted with her dancing that he said he
would give her any thing she desired. She prayed for the pardon
of a Russian Prince and his family whom the Emperor had
sent into Siberia in a passion. He was loath to do it as they were
powerful people and popular, but he kept his word and when
they returned the son of the family, now Prince Troubetzkoi,
flew to thank Taglioni, whom he had never seen before, for the

[1] He limped because he had been born with one leg shorter than the other.
In 1846 he had married Maria Teresa, eldest sister of the Duke of Modena.
He kept a Court at Frohsdorf in southern Austria. He had no children, and
the present Pretender to the throne of France, the Comte de Paris, is of the
Bourbon-Orleans line descended from Louis-Philippe.

[2] Effie meant the Duke of Ragusa who was then seventy-six. It was
Marshal Soult whom Napoleon had created Duke of Dalmatia. She made
great friends with Marmont during her next visit to Venice.

release of his parents. When he saw her, he declared he would stay. She never thought the youth in earnest and after a few days she told him that she felt honored by his being her guest but that it was not right and she could not allow him to remain any longer, but he insisted and said he never intended to leave her any more—and that no power on earth should send him away, that perhaps she did not like him but that he did not care, stay he would, and so he did and has for six years stayed with her, and every where she goes he goes and he never leaves her. The people here when they call on Taglioni always leave a card for Prince Troubetzkoi and seem to think him an exceedingly good-natured, well-behaved person. He is about 36 but that is the way people here often live and their constancy to one another is truly surprizing.[1]

The other day Mr Blumenthal told John that a friend of his, a Monsieur Marzari, was going to give a Concert in his house and that Mr B had asked leave to bring us if we would like to go. John said it would depend upon how I was, and when the evening came I dressed and at eight o'clock our kind little friend came for us and Charlotte and I found ourselves soon in a house near the Rialto. John begged to be excused going as he was busy, and of course I did not wish him to lose an evening when we could go quite well here with Mr Blumenthal. We did not know what kind of party it was to be but we dressed for the evening. I had on my rose colored silk dress, velvet roses in my hair and Jacket of blue velvet trimmed with black lace which I wear always in the house and is very elegant & warm. It hangs

[1] Prince Alexander Troubetzkoi, born 1813, had, in 1846, bought the Ca' d'Oro as a present for Taglioni. He was a retired Colonel in the Russian Guards, now in the Austrian Army and had at one time been on the staff of Field-Marshal Haynau. (In the Risorgimento section of the Correr Museum in Venice there is a print of Haynau and his staff, including Troubetzkoi, watching the bombardment of Venice from Mestre.) Marie Taglioni was at this time forty-five. She had married in 1832 Count Gilbert de Voisins, and the same year danced *La Sylphide*, the ballet for which she was most famous, for the first time at the Paris opera. She had gone to Russia in 1837 for five years but had now retired on a fortune, and owned property on Lake Como as well as in Venice. She was very extravagant, however, and later went bankrupt and was forced to teach dancing in London. (Among her pupils were Ada Leverson and Max Beerbohm.) She lived at 14 Connaught Square during 1875 and 1876, and died in 1884.

open in front and I kept it on all the time as there was not any dancing.

When we entered the first Salon, where the music was to be, it was crowded with gentlemen but not a Lady to be seen, but on lifting a silk curtain at the end we found ourselves in a pretty little drawingroom with Ladies in full dress sitting all round in the stiffest manner, but good looking, well dressed people. Mr Blumenthal presented us to Madame Marzari and then brought his sister and mother to sit by us and then went out of the Ladies Sanctum. I spoke German to the mother and French to the sister & we soon got good friends. We soon afterwards moved into the music room. The Ladies sat in two long lines and the gentlemen stood behind and talked, and between the songs came inside and spoke to their acquaintance, but instead of thinking the Italians loose in their manners I never saw such good-breeding, almost amounting to severity & prudery. The singers did not mix either with the company but had a room to themselves and when they were much applauded they curtsied and retired. In short it was like a private Theatre. The performances were of the very best description, being all the principal artists from the Fenice, so that we almost knew them before hand. The Fenice is a private Theatre—that is, it is kept up by the Nobility in Venice and not by the public. M. Marzari is one of the Three Presidents. The Count Mocenigo the second. I don't know the third.[1]

Amongst the company, which was entirely Italian, were many Italian names I do not remember. Madame Mocenigo was not there but the Count was. It was the first time I have met him and I was not at all pleased with his appearance. He has been Ambassador to several places and is very talented, very like his old mother in appearance, but extremely dark. I believe he is a very unprincipled man and certainly to look at him you never could believe he was a descendant of the Doges who lie entombed in St. Giovanni e Paolo, each Mocenigo face finer & more beautiful than the other, even in old age.

The Prince Giovanelli & his amiable and handsome son were there. The former begged to be presented to me but I was leaving at the time and as he could not have any conversation with

[1] It was Cavaliere Torniello.

me he said it did not signify as Mr Brown had promised to
introduce us. He is an old man much respected in Venice
and the richest man here. His wife is a very sensible good
person and as they are allied with Austria and live here they
are popular with both parties and before the Revolution were
the principal people who gave Concerts, balls and entertainments to keep the two parties on as good terms as they could,
& will do so again whenever things are settled. Their only child
is this young man who is very well behaved. He wishes to know
us too, and Mr Brown will bring him. His name is Betta, why
so I don't know.[1] Is it not a pity that just when we are getting
acquainted we must leave this nice place? But to return to the
party—coffee, tea, cake & ices were the refreshments and we
returned home very much pleased with our evening.

The Padre has just been here and thinks my throat much better, but intends putting on the Leeches on Monday. I enclose
a note from Mr Brown & Paulizza; John declares they spoil &
pet me as much as Papa could possibly desire, but he sees Papa
was right, that I thrive best on that kind of treatment.[2] Every
morning they either come or write to me, sometimes both,
regarding my precious health. Really I ought and am very much
obliged to them.... In Mr Brown's note you will see that he
declares I cried one day on seeing the Alps one mass of snow
& rose colours: I didn't however....

Danieli's Hotel, 27th January
... Today I have been leeched for the first time, and although
I feel slightly weak nothing could have been better managed.
Mr Brown's housekeeper [Joan] came at ten in the morning and
waited on me till past two. The Padre came in at twelve in the
middle of it and said he did not think I should require to have

[1] His full name was Joseph. He had been born in 1824 the only son of Count
Andrea Giovanelli and his second wife Marie, Contessa Burri. She was
Dame de la Croix Etoilée and Dame du Palais to Franz Joseph's grandmother.
The Count, who had been born in 1783, had in 1847 been created an
Austrian prince by the Emperor Ferdinand I.
[2] Effie wrote to Rawdon Brown in February, 1855, seven months after
obtaining her annulment: 'It was hardly fair his [Prosdocimo] having me for
a patient as he could never, nor anyone else, have cured me till I was
amongst good people and my mind at ease.'

them again which I was thankful to hear as the part of the stomach they were on is so tender a place that the biting and sucking took away my colour at first and made me feel quite sick.[1] Joan, after they all came off, put one hot Linseed Poultice after another on till the two hours were expired and then she put a kind of powder and Leather on the wound. I got up and dressed and felt quite well. I never saw any one so clever as this good creature was. There was no mess and I was so amused with her Venetian dialect and her quiet and nice ways that I could not possibly have been less tired or better nursed. John was very anxious to make her a present but no persuasions would make her take a farthing. She said her whole desire was to see the Signora well and she was ready to wait upon me night or day whenever I was in need of a nurse.[2]

In the course of the day, Mr Brown came to inquire for me. I saw him, but was not dressed when Paulizza came an hour before for the same reason. He spent last evening with me. John always spends the evening in his own room and Charlotte learns French at the fire and Paulizza and I play at Chess and chatter German, but last night we were Polkaing and Waltzing, first Charlotte and then me, for we thought it necessary to practise a little as we are going to be quite gay in the end of the week. I just wish we had George here to go about and enjoy himself with us.

When Paulizza came today he was in a great hurry as he had been sent for by the Archduke Ferdinand[3] who had just arrived, but he said he was thankful to say he is to depart tomorrow; our friend was consequently en grande toilette with his cocked hat and green feathers. He is such a curious person. He never goes anywhere in Venice but here and his affection for us is something quite extraordinary. He comes here continually and would do any thing for us in the world. I put his devotion to me however to some proof last night. My Gondolier's brother has

[1] Before modern methods of antisepsis, leeching was the only means of letting blood without causing septicaemia.

[2] Joan, or Joanna, remained with Rawdon Brown until 1864 when she retired. Ruskin augmented the small pension Brown gave her by a banker's order for £5 to be paid to her every Christmas.

[3] The Emperor's cousin who was in command at Treviso.

been marked in the conscription two or three days ago and
appointed to join Count Wimpffen's regiment at Trieste
directly. His case like that of hundreds is very hard; they
cannot be taken into the Gendarmerie for fear of plots and this
poor Giuseppe Parmo must leave his wife and family and go
and serve as a common soldier in Dalmatia. My Carlo came
to me in a great state of distress and begged me if I had any
influence over the Austrian to speak of his brother to him. I
did, and discomposed Paulizza not a little. He twirled his
moustaches and looked very uneasy; he said, "You know (and
I thought this in Perth would sound so funny) that every
thing you say is to me a command and that I will occupy myself
in whatever can promise you happiness, but in this thing I have
personally no power; I will write a petition to the Governor
and try that, but certainly it will be of no avail for if *one* is kept
back, hundreds ask for the same advantage and it is impossible in the present state of things to act otherwise." I saw he
was quite right and told him not to put himself in a disagreeable [word omitted] in any way, but he would do it and I hope
for poor Parmo's sake that he may be successful, and from the
peculiar way in which I first became acquainted with Paulizza
I shall not feel if he succeeds that I am under any other obligation than thanking him for his trouble.

Yesterday we went across to St. Servia [Servolo] and paid a
visit to my kind friends the Fate Bene Fratelli. We walked
through their Hospital, one of the finest salons I ever saw containing 300 sick, all so clean & well cared for that when one
speaks of the dirt of the Italians I will always remember this
well-aired Hall attended by these twelve good brothers. The
whole of the little Island is theirs, and contains, besides the
Hospital and the Monastery, the Lunatic Asylum. Some of the
maniacs greeted us through the windows as we passed and we
saw and heard nothing unpleasant. The garden was beautiful,
and in summer with the Trellises of vines & roses and the splendid view over the boundless Adriatic, St. Servia must be a
delightful retreat. Padre Prosdocimo, the Prior, and another
Monk, walked for half an hour with us and seemed greatly
delighted to see us. Mr Brown said that one of the subjects of
his & our visits was to ask the Padre about the propriety of my

going on Wednesday Evening to a Military Ball[1] after the
leeching today; if there was, to put off the leeching, but they
all said Oh! no, that it was four days till Wednesday and I could
go perfectly well. I was so amused at the Monks in their black
cloaks and cowls being so exceedingly anxious for me to go.
"Indeed," said the Prior who was very Jolly and well bred, "I
think young people should enjoy themselves. The Dama must
certainly go, but not drink any spiritous Liquors at supper."
At this we all roared as you may suppose, and Mr Brown
replied that although I was full of faults that was not one of
them. The Prior also warned me not to dance myself too hot,
and he bid us adieu at the door. He was a good-looking man,
between forty and fifty, and looked and laughed so merrily that
I thought but for his dress he might have liked a dance very
well himself. Mr Brown is very very fond of them and gets
them cases of instruments from England. He said he thought
them so sensible and so free from bigotry.[2]

We sailed across again and landed at the Palazzo Wetzlar. We
went up and the old Baroness received us and said she was

[1] The invitation to this ball was in French and she enclosed it in her letter.
It was to take place at the 'Palais sur la petite Place des Lions à St Marc'.
The only palace then, as now, in the Piazzetta dei Leoncini is that of the Patri-
arch. It seems a strange place for a ball, although it has a Great Hall of
Ceremonies. The neo-classical façade of the old palace was completed only
in 1850, so perhaps the ball was an inauguration.

[2] In November, 1852, Effie sent out some snuff from London for the
Prior, but more important she sent Prosdocimo some chloroform which she
managed to get from Dr Simpson. She wrote to Rawdon Brown that she got
it 'with some difficulty as it is so dangerous a medicine if improperly used
that it is only sold to the Faculty, but upon my explaining who the Friars
were and that it would be first sent to you—you may do with it as you think
proper. But if properly administered they will find it the greatest blessing
in relieving suffering and will wish for more. It is used universally now in
Scotland in cases of operation of every kind, and in England much more than
formerly. The best way of giving it is to pour a few drops on a sponge and
hold with a handkerchief over the Mouth and nose so that the patient may
inhale freely, the *pulse* being carefully felt at the time. This is the great care
required.' She packed the little bottle carefully in tow. In February, 1854, she
was writing to Brown that she was very sorry she could not get a chloroform
inhaler for 'the dear Monk' but at Savory & Moore's she had been told that
as no better way of giving chloroform had been found than dropping it on
a handkerchief they had ceased making them.

enchanted to make our acquaintance. An Aide de camp of the
Governor's was sitting with her and he said our names were
down for invitations to this ball (the said card I enclose) and
it was soon arranged that we were to go with her, and she ended
by asking us to an evening party on Saturday. She is a very curious old Lady, a sort of character in Venice where she has
resided for twenty years. Every body knows the Baroness
Wetzlar and as she is very rich and receives every week we shall
see no end of people at her house as long as we remain here.
She speaks English perfectly and so does her daughter who
looks an old woman while she looks about fifty. She is very
clever and a first rate musician which accounts in some way for
"Thalberg's" genius. I suppose in her youth she was not quite
correct but all the world knows he is her son; that is ages ago
and she is much liked in Venice. She was railing away at the
fine she has to pay, as being a resident in Venice throughout
the Blockade, of 40,000 zwanzigs [about £1,400], and she a
German too.[1] The Aide de Camp sat and laughed. I daresay he
thought she never would pay. Her room was well and richly
furnished, heated with a stove and perfumed with essence.
Two Italian Greyhounds were running about. She had on a
black worsted cap and gold pins, German fashion, in her front
hair. Really one sees odd looking as well as odd acting people
in this place. Her dress was a mantel of silk and curious sort
of dressing gown under it but her hands were covered with
splendid rings and still small and pretty. She talked very amus-
ingly indeed, a mixture of Italian to her grown up grandson,
German to the Officer, English & French to us, all well.

I think it will be great fun to go to this Ball for once to get
a glimpse of foreign manners. As it is given by the Austrian
Officers, & not public, we must dance with every body who
ask us without any introduction, which I was glad we were told

[1] She was in fact Hungarian. Born Baroness Julie Bidescuty d'Eyb, she had
in 1820 married, as his second wife, Baron Ludwig Wetzlar (1775-1858), a
Major in the Austrian Army and grandson of a poor Polish Jew who went
to Vienna at the beginning of the eighteenth century, made a fortune,
became a patron of the arts and was created Baron Wetzlar in 1777. Baron
Ludwig and the Baroness had three daughters and a son. The Palazzo
Wetzlar is now the Gritti Hotel. It was in part of this palace that Effie and
John lived when they next came to Venice.

before. We go by Paulizza who seems to be afraid we shall get
into some scrape. He says he is going to dance with me a little,
the first time for seven years, and with Charlotte a little; for
the rest he is going to look after us I believe. John goes with
us but will not stay all the time.

Charlotte is going to put on her black tarletan with scarlet
& white crape scarf and flowers to match in her hair. I am
going to wear my white glacé silk with white lace flounces
which Miss Rutherford put on before I came away. It was
trimmed with rose velvet ribbon but when John saw it on he
said it was like brick colour and says he will make me a
present of any trimming of flowers I like as he wants me to look
nice. Mr Brown is going to send us bouquets and hopes we will
enjoy ourselves very much, is he not kind? He does every
thing he can for us. Madame Mocenigo wrote to him the
other day to bring me to a raffle for a picture at her house. We
went and found a company of great Italian families assembled.
The old Lady was in great force and more in state than on the
former occasion. She was much grieved at gaining the picture
herself. The Count was very agreeable but a very bad looking
man, as you may suppose. I find my knowledge of French
stretched to the utmost in this kind of society, for here every
one forgets their particular tongue and conversation always goes
on in French so that you don't know whether you are speaking to an Italian or Spaniard or Russian or who....

Tuesday. The Padre was here yesterday and he thinks the
Leeching has diminished the inflammation a good deal. I feel
quite well and I hope in a short time to find that I am really
better.... It still continues extremely cold and the Canals are
full of floating ice; nevertheless in the sun it was quite warm.
The band was playing the first time for long and we walked up
& down with Mde. Nerly who, seeing Charlotte and me alone,
kindly left Taglioni, Prince Troubetzkoi and the children to
come to us. Taglioni's little son George was running up and
down with little Fritz Nerly[1] and I was greatly delighted with
his handsome, intelligent healthy countenance. The Prince is
a very nice looking young man indeed. I daresay we shall be

---

[1] He became a landscape and marine painter in Rome.

dancing together tomorrow evening as he knows who we are and told Mr Brown he should get us tickets for a ball they were going to give Radetzky early next month. Here a Ball is a political measure greatly and the Austrians are most anxious to get all the Ladies they possibly can. We hear the Baroness Wetzlar is going to have quite a Fete in honor of us on Saturday. I suppose we shall meet some curious and remarkable enough people in their way there. It is a great advantage to us seeing something of foreign manners.

DANCING WITH THE MILITARY

ↄ

My Dearest Mama
... By the time this reaches you it will be dear Papa's birth-day. I hope you will wish him every thing that is good and kind from me and tell him that he shall not be forgotten in a toast from me and a bumper pledged to his health from John on the tenth.[1] John's own birthday is on the 8th when he will be 31....

The Padre was here today. He thinks of putting on nine more leeches on Wednesday as he thinks they have done me so much good and hopes another application may still further advance my cure, and I am willing he should try although I must confess my throat to all appearance is not so far dimin-ished in redness as I had hoped it would have been. George will be comforted to see in my last letter how nicely I was attended by Joan and not by Paulizza. I assure you that John and I had more than one good laugh at his anger at the Austrian, and John declared he would not be George's wife when he got one for something if he was so jealous as to be terrified to trust her in other people's society.[2] Paulizza did not mean to be in the least impudent when he asked to put on the leeches, but spoke gravely to John upon the propriety of doing so, so that I really think John would have had no objections if I had not had very considerable ones. George would indeed be dreadfully shocked if he saw the way in which Charlotte & I are put under his care, for John has as high an opinion of his moral as his intellectual character.

The other night John left the Ball at eleven and Charlotte & I enjoyed ourselves till between one and two. I have written

[1] His birthday was in fact on the 17th when he became fifty-two. Mr Ruskin sent him a bottle of thirty-year-old rum as a birthday present.
[2] George never married. He died at Bowerswell in 1924 aged ninety-five.

some little account of it to Mr Ruskin which you will receive.[1] We enjoyed ourselves exceedingly and we were greatly delighted with the appearance of the Gentlemen. I danced so much, indeed I could not help myself; that my big toes have been sore ever since, and here they dance so fast, Prince Troubetzkoi danced the galope with me twice as fast as Lord Charles.[2] He is a fine young man and very gentlemanly in his manners. It was so odd to be dancing with him vis à vis to Taglioni. He was introduced to me by Paulizza and he afterwards made him present him to John whom he thanked for the Honour of dancing with me. He gave a very fine supper to the company at one, and I was engaged to him two Polkas after, but by half past one I made Paulizza bring us home as I felt tired. Next day, the Prince walked with me and gave me a rowing for not coming to supper, but gave me credit for a love of early hours. Besides dancing with him I danced part of the waltzes with Paulizza, and lots of other Hungarians & Germans with different uniforms and names enough to break one's tongue. A Baron Holbeach spoke very good English but the rest, Holzammer, Damrends and other unpronounceables, spoke German only or French, but I prefered German.

We did not go to the Baroness Wetzlar's on Saturday. One of her servants died and the party was put off until tomorrow night. The Comte Ürmenhy,[3] my handsome old friend who lives here in the Hotel, Prince Troubetzkoi and a number of the young

[1] Mr Ruskin wrote to John on his birthday that he had just received 'Effie's beautifully written and graphically given account of the Ball'. John intended to quote in *Praeterita* this letter from his father (a delightfully warm one saying how much happiness his son had given him in thirty-one years) and had therefore made a note on it: 'The "Effie" of this letter is the Phemy for whom *The King of the Golden River* was written when she was twelve years old.' At the end of his letter Mr Ruskin sends his kind regards to Miss Ker. Here John's curious note is: 'Not Mary Kerr, neither Alice of Huntley Burn.' Could he have forgotten Charlotte Ker?

[2] Lord Charles Ker, son of the 6th Marquess of Lothian by his second wife. He was in the Perth Militia, and had lived close to Bowerswell at Kinnoull Cottage which had been sold the year before when he moved from the neighbourhood.

[3] The Ürmenyi were Hungarian Barons not Counts. Effie's friend was Baron Francis (1780-1858) who had been Governor of Fiume. He was extremely rich and unmarried.

Officers are going. Holzammer wrote Paulizza a letter to tell us not to come in Ball dresses as it was only a Soirée, and although we were to dance not to come as if we expected a ball. The interest the people take in us here is very amusing. We are all sorts of characters in our way and receive great attention. We have received another invitation for another Ball the same as the last, which is on Wednesday evening. John is going to take us as he thinks the dancing does me a great deal of good and I do not stay late and it does not take up so much of his time as going out to an evening party. I shall postpone my leeching till next morning.

Yesterday we were taken by Paulizza to the Island of St. Giuliano from which place he threw all the Bombs into Venice. I never in reading realized what War could do till we saw this place which you will see is very important as commanding one side of Venice. Seven months has scarcely elapsed since a nice house stood there and a beautiful garden full of trees and flowers; now one sees four sentry boxes and pools of water frozen over earth embankments, shot, cannon and, I suppose, mens' bones lying about, a most perfect picture of desolation every where but still interesting. Paulizza, his Officers and men, were there for three months without ever leaving it or lying in a bed; often 24 hours without food and constantly some falling by the shot from the enemies' batteries. Some of them had no shoes, he amongst the rest, and at last they were so swollen that he could hardly stand. Fortunately it was summer or else many more would have died, but as it was, 700 did on that little piece of ground. Their powder magazine also caught fire and blew up & killed a great number.[1]

[1] San Giuliano is an island on the edge of the lagoon near Mestre, just south of Malghera. The Italians secretly evacuated Fort Malghera and Fort San Giuliano on the night of May 26, 1849. They mined San Giuliano and a number of Austrians were blown up when they took possession of the fort next morning; this is no doubt what Effie meant by the powder magazine blowing up. Paulizza must have stayed there until the final capitulation at the end of August. San Giuliano was the nearest point to Venice in Austrian hands, and it was from there that the final bombardment against the city was launched in the last days of July. The guns were dismounted from their carriages and placed on wooden platforms slanting at an angle of forty-five degrees. By firing high in the air a range of three miles was obtained and the

From St Giuliano we crossed to Terra firma and walked a long way across the Marshes to Malghera where we saw other Fortifications, enough balls, bombs & shot for another Blockade, saw a Soldiers' barrack, and taking our Gondola at Malghera we reached Venice before dinner-time. The day was lovely but cold, although in the sun it was quite delicious, but Paulizza declared it would be cold sailing so long, even though shut up, and would not go away without a *hot bottle* under his grey cloak for my use. He is always at John for allowing me to sit over the fire, but highly approves of the bottle which I thought you would highly approve of; but I suppose George would have considered the five hours spent in speaking German & sailing in a Gondola improper and dangerous in the last degree, but seriously don't let George be angry because we are in so talented a person's company. I wonder, considering the work he has to do, that he can be troubled to be so much with us, but as I have said in my other letters, John would require a wife who can take care of herself and I have all my wits about me as you say. All the other officers and Italians that I know make as much of me as Paulizza, only he has the entree here which they would have if we stayed a little longer now that we are acquainted with some of the rest of them, only one would always have much more respect for Paulizza because he is so distinguished a man. Amongst his other accomplishments he was telling me yesterday that he could knit & sew very well & make shoes. I don't know what he can't do, and when he was younger he played and sung better than anybody else. John says he never saw anybody like him. He goes to his house and sees all his studies. He did something against Venice very wonderful with Balloons but I could not exactly understand what,[1] but tell George that John is

---

shells all but reached the Piazza. Because they were fired from such a distance, however, they seldom penetrated more than two storeys of a building and the damage they did was less than was at first expected by both sides.

[1] Before the intense bombardment at the end of July, the Austrians had attempted aerial bombardment. On July 12, twenty air balloons were sent up from four ships anchored outside the Lido; most of them exploded in the air or dropped into the lagoon, but a few, driven by the wind, sailed over the lagoon and the city and burst amidst Paulizza's own men on San Giuliano. General Pepé, Commander of the Venetian forces, thus described their mechanism: 'Under these balloons was a large grenade full of combustible

perfectly satisfied with my conduct in every particular and is
kinder to me & fonder of me every day, and when I find a good
husband I hope I know his value properly and appreciate him
enough. John is particularly flattered with the attention they
pay me, and when I go out would give me any thing I liked
if he thought it would make me look better.

This morning I set out with John about eleven o'clock to
go and see the Pictures in the Barbarigo Palace (vid Murray).
The Manfrini Palace has been shut up since the Blockade
and the desolation of the former Palace is quite dreadful.
The Saloons are full of pictures of the greatest value but the
damp has destroyed them greatly and as the family is extinct
& the whole belongs to the Count Giustiniani he would willingly sell them all. One Titian, a Magdalene, is the finest in
the collection and in rather better preservation than the
rest....[1]

Charlotte is sitting darning black cotton stockings which
occupation she appears extremely partial to as I always see her
with something of the sort in her hand....[2]

We enjoyed our party [at Baroness Wetzlar's] very much
indeed last night. The company was very good and the rooms
well furnished, lighted, and warmed. The night was bitter
cold but dancing soon warmed us. We had Princes & Princesses,
Counts & Hussars, all dancing and enjoying themselves with
an energy and love for the exercise that would have done the
nonchalant English noblesse good to see. The party was not

---

matter, suspended by a sort of cord, also filled with combustible matter, which
cord, after a certain given period, was calculated to consume itself. As soon
as this happened, the grenade fell, and, in its fall, burst against the first object
it struck.' Paulizza may well have been responsible for their design.

[1] The Manfrini Palace, being on the Cannaregio near the station, was very
much exposed to the bombardment. After the Accademia it housed the best
collection of pictures in Venice. It had been entirely restored by 1852. The
Barbarigo della Terrazza Palace is on the Grand Canal at the corner of the
Rio San Polo. Many of the pictures Effie saw there were sold in 1850 to Tsar
Nicholas I for the Hermitage in St Petersburg.

[2] From the picture Effie draws of Charlotte it is perhaps not surprising
that she never married. In a later letter from London Effie told her mother
that Charlotte got very stout in Venice and 'her things were a good deal too
tight for her'.

large, about fifty, but the Ladies, mostly Italian, were much better looking than the Germans at the ball and well dressed like Frenchwomen. Two or three of them had magnificent pearl necklaces of four or five rows fastened with Diamonds. The Austrian Officers don't like dancing with them at all, for all Italian Ladies keep such bad time which I remarked at once and which is curious considering their knowledge of music.

I had a great deal of talk with Count Ürmenyi, the Hungarian who is so rich.... Near us, standing in black lace with a great quantity of blonde curls, a niece of Kossuth, an agreeable looking girl, the Count & Countess Zichy, the former, brother of the present Princess Metternich, a very disagreeable dissipated looking man who I have avoided knowing.[1] I danced further with Baron Holbeach and the young Officers Holzammer, Montzig & others, besides making an agreeable acquaintance with the Saxon Consul, Mr Becker, who having been in England speaks perfectly, a great comfort to Charlotte. He is very sorry I have not my habit here as he rides his three horses here every day on the Champ de Mars and we might have had a gallop.[2] We had no regular supper but refreshments the same way as you have at home, but never any wine, always Ices or Sorbet. We had most exquisite Paté de foie gras, the first time I ever tasted that delicacy so I did not take much of it. I enjoyed the party quite as much as the Ball. Paulizza was not there; he had no invitation & was ill and has been for some time with his head; he studies too hard....

Danieli's Hotel, 9th Feby. [Saturday]

... How very nice it was of Sophia to think of Venice in the fine day. These two last here have indeed been beautiful and everything has looked lovely and it is quite wonderful to me the difference of heat and cold. I look so much better when I am

[1] Melanie, Princess Metternich, third wife of the former Austrian Minister, had four brothers, all married.

[2] In 1806 the monastery of Santa Maria Maggiore was given to the military who turned it into a ten-acre parade ground, the Campo di Marte, where the Austrian officers exercised their horses. Civilians were also allowed to ride and walk there. It was at the extreme west of the Zattere and now comprises a gas works and maritime station.

heated & my blood in circulation. The Count Ürmenyi was
paying me a visit this morning and he was complimenting me
on my bon mien which fresh complexion is not common here
in the morning as the people keep such late hours and are
naturally pale besides. He informed me that the third Military
ball next week is not to take place as the Cavalchina is to be
given in the Fenice. This Cavalchina is the old masked Ball of
Venice which finishes the Carnival and they keep it up till the
morning and then Lent begins on Ash Wednesday [the 13th]
which is next week. The immense Theatre is boarded over and
the boxes hung with mirrors and the masks enter the boxes &
do anything they like. We may take a turn or two amongst
them but it is not considered comme il faut for Ladies to mask
or dance. As we have never seen anything of the kind it will
amuse us I believe. We first go to a Ball at the Baroness
Wetzlar's and then to the Opera to see the masks. Every body
that night considers themselves privileged and a little insane.

The last Ball [on the 6th] went off with much greater éclat than
the former and we enjoyed [it] much more. John stayed & was
much amused till twelve o'clock and he & Paulizza stood together
and made remarks. With the latter who brought us home about
three I did not dance at all.[1] He was not well with his head. He
has never been well since he was wounded with the Bomb at St.
Giuliano and has fears for his sight which would be dreadful; his
eyes are so exquisitely beautiful and so clear & bright that it does
not look well, and then men are so stupid; the Doctor tells him
he should do nothing, and he is so clever and so full of genius
that he is inventing and drawing and studying till all the hours
of the night and then he cannot sleep at all.

Since writing the above he was taking tea with us last evening
and says he is much better. As he was so ill he put blisters
behind his ears and they have done him a great deal of good. He
is so amiable and thoughtful that I am sure if George was here he

---

[1] Effie's conduct in allowing Paulizza to take them home did not go
uncensured as is shown in a letter to Rawdon Brown after she got home.
' ... which offence', she wrote on July 2, 'you pointed out to me in the gravest
colours and I would not therefore repeat, but I had never been but to two
Balls in my Life brought up in *that northern land* Scotland and did so by
my husband's desire, he being as unsuspecting of harm in the said deed as
myself'.

would be very fond of him. I have not been ill lately so that I have had no more notes from him to send for his perusal. He was very angry the other night with Prince Troubetzkoi who promised to let him twice have a turn with me in the waltz, and danced the whole time although Paulizza was waiting and never told me. I believe they had a few words about it and Troubetzkoi begged pardon but Paulizza is hot and the Russian good tempered and they have always been intimate.

The Prince introduced me to Count [Emile] Wimpffen, elder brother of Alphonse and the handsomest young man I have yet seen. He talked perfect English and I found him agreeable but I think I like Alphonse best. He and the Prince were with me at supper and the latter kept on such a chatter of French, Russian, which he declared I understood perfectly, Italian and German and broken English that I could hardly keep my own with him, and he was very furious at Wimpffen and me speaking English against him he declared at last. He began making love [to] me so cleverly that I retorted and returned to the Ballroom with Mr Nerly who the Prince had told to take me to supper. He could not do so himself as it is not etiquette here for an unmarried man of whatever rank and military to take a married Lady to supper. Taglioni was ill and was not at the Ball....

The day before yesterday we went with Paulizza to the Armenian Convent across the Lagune [on the island of San Lazzaro]. The Armenians are Turkish subjects and not confined by monastic vows to any one place but travel every where & are celebrated for their knowledge in Languages. We saw printing machines for twenty-four modern Tongues which most of the Priests speak. They also have a college for the Education of Armenian Boys and they are immensely wealthy. Their dress is all black with long white beard and moustache. The Priest, who Paulizza knew before and who talked English with us perfectly well, was evidently a very clever man but so old that his powers of mind were diminished and one could not help seeing the frailties of age. He told us he was a native of Angora and had travelled in every country and remained three years in England & Scotland. He taught Lord Byron the Armenian Tongue and showed us a translation he had made of Milton's Paradise Lost into that Language. The Brethren are not at all popular in Venice as during the Famine they shut themselves up on their island with plenty of good things and never assisted the poor who were dying of cholera and starving by Thousands in the City. My friends the Fate Bene Fratelli were very different and nearly killed themselves in their devotion to the sick during the time the Cholera raged.

This is Ash Wednesday, the first day in Lent, and all our gaiety is over for the present. We had a most charming dance at the Baroness Wetzlar's last night which we kept up with great spirit till two in the morning. The toilettes were more beautiful than any I have yet seen and the scene was exceedingly gay as it is the custom here on the last night of the Carnival to dress in grande toilette to go to a ball and then adjourn to the Cavalchina. The young Countess Zichy looked well. She was dressed in rose colored watered silk with Brussels Lace Berthe, diamonds & crown of roses. The Baroness Gras du Barry, a Scotch woman married to a Frenchman, just from Paris, a dashing woman attended by a handsome young French Count, the kind of person I particularly dislike to see any countrywomen of mine become, was very exquisitely dressed and altogether well got up. Her dress was rose silk with frills to the waist of shaded Lace from white to red, put in waves all round the skirt at intervals, and berthe to correspond with two frills of the same, hanging loose in a point behind and before, no ornaments but a pearl necklace and a white Feather on each side of her head, a mode which is very fashionable just now and extremely becoming. Two or three Ladies had them last night of colours to suit their dresses and all looked well; the ends of the feathers are placed in the plait behind and hang down gracefully at each side of the face.

Madame Taglioni was dressed in white damask silk with bouquets of roses down each side and a Diamond & Turquoise comb with roses in her hair. On one arm she wore two serpents, one entirely comprised of diamonds with emerald eyes encircling the arm twice which John said was worth going to see, and a Turquoise beside it of the same make. John & I both agreed that she was the best mannered and most agreeable person there for her age [forty-five]. Her daughter was there also and is very much thought of; she is so natural and simple in her manners and so entirely without affectation, that one cannot help thinking her very good indeed. Her mother has had her very carefully educated; she speaks four Languages with great ease.[1]

As usual I danced considerably with Troubetzkoi, who, with the Marquis Selvatico, are coming here this evening by John's invitation to tea and to see his [Turner] drawings. We then adjourned to the Fenice, and Paulizza and the Comte Ürmenyi soon joined us. Paulizza had come punctually at twelve to meet us and it was two when we came. We walked down into the parterre and soon were joined by all the Officers & Ladies from Madame Wetzlar's which we almost regretted having quitted, the scene was so melancholy. Nothing could be more beautiful than the Lighting of the Theatre, and if the place had only been as in former years the coup d'oeil would have been magnificent, but, only fancy, the Thousands and Thousands of wax lights and mirrors and the splendid band playing to about four boxes full of people, and in the Salle de danse two or three hundred men and about twenty women, 6 of whom were masked and interested me highly. Every one spoke to them and they spoke to every body, but the rules are that nobody touches a masked person or walks with them without permission.[2]

One Lady in a black Domino with the face masked with Black Lace and a little black velvet hat just on one side, moved with great grace. Her figure was something like this [a drawing]; there was something solemn in her figure and I know more about her than perhaps she would have liked to know. She is a

[1] This girl, Maria Hedda, who was then not yet fifteen, had been adopted by Taglioni's husband. Two years later Prince Troubetzkoi married her.

[2] Flagg wrote in 1853 that Manin's Republic had prohibited the mask in Venice and that 'the prohibition then imposed has been continued; so that, at the present time, even amid all the madness of the carnival, the mask is banished by Austrian, French, Tuscan and Neopolitan authority at Venice, Rome, Florence, Naples—from every city and every face in Italy!' John evidently did not go on to the Fenice. Mr Ruskin wrote to him on February 15: 'I rejoice to see your sense of your more important station & calling & destination as a writer saves you from entanglement & poor attraction & frivolities of Foreign Society—& that by God's goodness you are likely to move unscathed through Carnival & all manner of Dissipation.'

German Baroness whose name I don't know but she is a widow and has been for some years, but only this winter in Venice. She is madly in love with Paulizza and does every thing she can to become acquainted with him. She has asked several times to be introduced to him and he has refused as he says he cannot think of marrying her and he won't know her. I am very sorry for her & so was he till yesterday he heard she would not go to the Wetzlar's because he was not going, and sent him intimation that she was to be at the Cavalchina in such and such a dress, which Paulizza thought was rather too much of a good thing. She, seeing him with us, could not speak and I suppose he & me were the only two who knew who she was. I have known about her for a long time as I constantly saw her walking about in all places where we happened to be, and she has another Lady always with her. I can't help teasing Paulizza a little and saying he should marry her for she has a sweet looking face, very rich and not older than him, and then he could leave the army and stay beside his old mother to whom he is devotedly attached, but he gets angry and says, "My sword is my mistress and with this coat I have lived and with this coat I will die."

We then came home and John and I had our quiet breakfast together this morning. He is greatly amused to find how I thrive after dancing; he says I am a complete Salamander and thrive in destructive elements. But now goodbye.... Direct next letter Poste Restante *Verona*....

Danieli's Hotel, February 18th, 1850

Dearest George,

... At last the warm spring weather has come and any thing more perfectly delightful than living in Venice in this sort of weather I cannot imagine. It is not too hot and fresh breezes are wafted every moment from the Adriatic, and the Italians in the Riva below are all lying in groups sleeping and smoking on mats, and hundreds of chairs & little tables are placed under the awnings in front of the Coffee houses where men sit lounging Italian fashion all day making remarks on the crowds of people continually passing and repassing, and with the hot weather one forgets entirely that the Italian windows and doors we have been abusing all winter are so badly made.

I will not call on Taglioni as my mother seems to object, but Venice opinion of her is that she is well behaved and I know her well enough now without calling upon her, but she does not behave half as badly as many others, Italians, for I never hear a thing against the Austrian Ladies who appear more like other people, but as far as I have seen they are a very plain set and queerly dressed. The Italians are better dressed and better looking—Mother says tawdry but they are not that in good Society; they are very beautifully dressed & their hair is generally simply dressed, with bright flowers in it, but the Austrians say they are very bad dancers and have not the slightest idea of keeping time.

The Marquis Selvatico, a gentleman who has written a work on Italian Architecture,[1] and Prince Troubetzkoi spent the other evening with us. Troubetzkoi is extremely clever and the Italian & he got so energetic in Politics before tea was half over that John & I fairly at last gave up all share in the conversation and kept laughing to each other. It is most amusing to see these foreigners how hot they get even when they perfectly agree upon all points which these two did but they all talk far too much to act well. Talking of France, Troubetzkoi said he had been some years of his young life brought up with the President Louis Napoleon, whom he now every day expected to hear of being shot. His ambition, he says, is immense, but whenever the moment came for him to act he always wanted to procrastinate for a six weeks or so. Now he has not a sou and an English-woman, a Mrs Howard, is ruining him or has ruined him already.[2] Troubetzkoi has been often in London and generally

---

[1] Marchese Pietro Selvatico Estense (1803-80) was an architect and President of the Venetian Academy. He built several neo-Gothic churches and villas and published over fifty books including, in 1847, *Sulla Architetture e Sulla Scultura in Venezia*. Ruskin wrote in his preface to the first volume of *The Stones*: 'The work of the Marchese Selvatico is, however, to be distinguished with respect; it is clear in arrangement, and full of useful, though vague, information.'

[2] This was hardly true. Harriet Howard, who had been on the stage, met Louis Napoleon in June, 1846, at a party in London at Lady Blessington's soon after his escape from the Fortress of Ham. They fell deeply in love; she accompanied him to France in 1848 and gave most of the money she had amassed from former lovers to help his political campaign.

goes over for the season and enjoys the grouse shooting in
Scotland very much. He has been several times with Lord
Breadalbane and Lord Kinnaird.[1] He gave John some valuable
hints about Byzantine architecture, and they left about ten.

Talking of Lord Kinnaird, curious enough his first love is one
of the Ladies the worst in character, at least I would naturally
say so, in Venice. She was a niece or Grand-daughter of the
late Earl of Hertford. Papa I daresay will know the surname,
hers being Strachan. She was & is still wonderfully beautiful,
but the Earl had some quarrel in politics with Lord Kinnaird
and the match was broken off. The confidant in the affair was
a certain Count Berchtold, a Hungarian, who was also in love
with her and married her.[2] It must be years ago as her sons are
five in number and the eldest about twelve. Mr Brown told me
this as well as a great deal more about her, and one incident I
thought peculiarly characteristic of Continental morals which
had it not happened here some few years ago one could hardly
believe, but Mr B. knows the parties well. An Italian nobleman
and a young Hungarian Prince of very gallant character and
who had distinguished himself extremely (& Mr B. said he had
seldom seen a more noble young man) were in Venice and both
in love with Mdme Berchtold, she encouraging both. They felt
that one must go out of the way, and instead of sending each
other a challenge to fight, which at any rate was against the

[1] The 2nd Marquess of Breadalbane (1796-1862) was Lord-Lieutenant of
Argyllshire. Lord Kinnaird, the 9th Baron (1807-78), was Lord-Lieutenant
of Perthshire.
[2] She was Matilda, eldest of the three beautiful daughters of Admiral Sir
Richard Strachan, Bt, best known for his failure as commander of the
Walcheren expedition of 1809. His wife, née Louisa Dillon, had for some
time before his death in 1828 been the mistress of the enormously rich and
reprobate Marquess of Hertford who died in 1842. Charged by Sir Richard
on his deathbed, Lord Hertford undertook the guardianship of the three
girls who, with their mother, accompanied him to Naples where they all
lived for some years. Lady Strachan bought property there and the title of
Marchesa di Salsa, and even after her marriage to a Signor Piselli, Lord
Hertford continued to provide generously for his wards and gave each of
them a dowry. Count Antoine Berchtold (1796-1875) was an Imperial
Chamberlain. Lord Hertford described him as 'a handsome likeness of
Leopold [Queen Victoria's uncle] in his best days, supposing him to have
swallowed a poker'.

law, and make the affair notorious, they quietly met and agreed to draw lots which was to survive the other. The lot fell on the Prince who went into his room and shot himself through the head. Do not mention these events as such things are better not talked of; but can you conceive any woman having a moment's peace after such an event, she being certainly the most guilty of the three?

I could not help thinking the recklessness of the young men as extremely characteristic of the present Continental infidelity and the perfect want of consideration of any thing like an after state. I think it would be perfect egg and milk, as Mr Capes says to My mother, to hear Paulizza discourse on the state of the Romanist Church at the present day ... with true Roman Catholic doctrine of believing in work, he thinks he does his duty so perfectly in his life & morals & to his country, and in living always as if he might soon die, that he is sure to go to Heaven, and certainly as far as his light goes he follows out his own rules and is entirely separated from his brother officers and never frequents the Cafés or gambles, but studies continually. John however has great fears for his eyes and if he loses his sight I do not know what he will do. He says he thinks God very merciful and he puts himself entirely in his hands. As for his devotion to me, as Charlotte says it is enough to make any one cry, and what he is to do when we go away I don't know. John is very sorry for him, and so am I, and I am so amused with John who says he respects me much more since he finds a man so talented as Paulizza likes me. John says Paulizza is exactly like him in mind & character, educated in different circumstances and brought through a much harder ordeal.

We all went to Lido on Saturday. It was a most exquisite day and the Adriatic lay stretched out in one unbroken sheet of blue. John and the Austrian walked one way along the shore discussing the formation of sand banks and the theories of the tides, and Charlotte & I went in the opposite direction for above two hours and lastly lay down amongst the long grass and gathered shells until our Handkerchiefs were quite full. The gentlemen then joined us and we had great fun catching little crabs which were feeding on the mussels in scores. We each caught one and setting them in a row made them run races.

The way in which some of them shewed fight with their claws
and would not walk a bit was very fine. The two men were
exactly like children and John [her brother] & wee Melville
would have been greatly amused with the boat races they had
by drying the large empty shells and setting them to sail on
the water. It was dinner time before we got back and any
thing more lovely than the setting sun I never saw. We passed
a great Austrian man of war covered at the top with Sailors clus-
tered like bees about the rigging and singing to their hearts
content.

   In the evening Charlotte and I thought we would send and
take a box in the Fenice as I wished very much to hear Elizabeth of Valois, a new Opera by a Signor Brizzia, a Venetian,
whom I heard play some of his own music at M. Marzari's
concert.[1] John said he had too much to do but that we might
go if we liked. I said I would go but would put Domenico [the
Valet-de-Place] at the door not to let any one in. John laughed
and said I was very cruel but I might do as I liked if I did not
think it proper to receive visits when he was not there. I sent
a note to Paulizza to remain at home that evening which he
did. Charlotte and I went and enjoyed the music very much
shut up in our box. It was most amusing to hear the various
altercations and desires of admittance to Domenico outside
from the Prince [Troubetzkoi], Holzammer, the Saxon Consul
[M. Becker], Mr Blumenthal and others of our acquaintances,
which I suppose were rather angry than otherwise as such a
thing is against all rule here as the Ladies go regularly to
their box every night and the most visits they receive the
more fashionable they are considered, but I have no wish for
such celebrity; besides one goes to hear the music and not to
keep up a chatter for five hours of French, German & English.
Two boxes from us sat the Duc de Bordeaux, and in the next was
Taglioni and her family. They looked so nice and homely, and

   [1] It was Antonio Buzzola whose third opera, *Elisabetta di Valois*, was performed for the first time at the Fenice on February 16, 1850. The autographed
score is preserved in the Fenice archives. Born in Adria (where the Conser-
vatorio is still called after him), Buzzola came to Venice in 1830 at the age
of fifteen and became violinist and flautist at the Fenice. He took to
composing and had his first two operas performed at the Teatro Gallo in
Venice.

my pet, little George, ordinarily so frolicsome & wild jumping up to me on the Square and begging a kiss, was on his good
behaviour and eyed me with discretion & looked rather frightened than otherwise. I was much interested in observing
Taglioni during the Maywood's dancing in the Esmeralda
which is very beautiful. For a long time Taglioni looked with
great attention but showed no signs of pleasure till at last she
joined with the rest of the house in a long and loud applause,
clapping her hands in which the two children joined her with
unfeigned satisfaction....

John's work is coming fast to a close here and we leave
Venice on Saturday week for Padua where we remain two or
three days, and the same at Vicenza before arriving at Verona.
I hope you will be able to read all this crossing but I have written as distinctly as I could and only wish the contents were
more worthy your perusal. I was much obliged to you for your
epitome of Pendennis. I suppose it is now nearly as popular
as Vanity Fair. John intends, I think, to cultivate Thackeray's
acquaintance on his return as he says he has learnt a great deal
from his books which first I could hardly get him to look at....[1]

Danieli's Hotel, 24th February, 1850

My dearest Mama
   ... We heard from Mr Ruskin yesterday ... that the Count
& Ctsse Béthune and Mr Domecq[2] are to be their guests for
some months from 16th April so that we shall find them at
Denmark Hill when we return. Mr R makes no comment on
the cause of their visit and I am rather astonished at their
coming at that season. John is "very glad they are going, as he
is fond of them, which he says he is of very few people,"
(copied from John's letter to his father of today) which is quite
true and may amuse you for he read it to me and I begged to
copy it. It goes on, from last sentence about his liking the
Domecqs, "You say I am kept by a sense of my position and

[1] Effie met Thackeray at a dinner party in November and wrote to her
mother, 'I did not like him. I thought him loud & vulgar in manner & fond
of good living like a constant diner out.'
[2] Brother of Mr Ruskin's partner, Peter Domecq, who had died in
December, 1839.

calling out of Entanglement of foreign Society—but unhappily
it is to me no entanglement at all. I most heartily wish I could
feel as much interest & pleasure in seeing and talking to people
as would enable me to receive from them the information
which I might—or to do them the good in my power. But
Operas, drawing rooms and living creatures have become alike
nuisances to me. I go out to them as if I was to pass the time
in the Stocks and when I am in the rooms, I say and do just
what I must and no more: if people talk to me I answer them,
looking all the while whether there is any body else coming to
take them away. As soon as they are gone I forget their names
& their faces & what they said and when I meet them next day
I don't see them. When I walk with Effie she is always touching me and saying that is so and so—now don't cut him or her
as you did yesterday—Then I say *Where?*—like Mr Winkle with
the partridges [*Pickwick*, Chapter XIX]. Then she says *There*—
then I make a low bow to somebody whom I never saw before
in my life, then they stare—and Effie assures me that so & so
has gone away very much offended. But I never saw any thing
like Effie—she sees the tips of people's shawls and the rims of
their hats down a couple of streets and round a corner and is
perfectly alive as she walks in St Mark's Place to every thing that
is going on at St Giorgio Maggiore."

John excites the liveliest astonishment to all and sundry in
Venice and I do not think they have made up their minds yet
whether he is very mad or very wise. Nothing interrupts him
and whether the Square is crowded or empty he is either seen
with a black cloth over his head taking Daguerrotypes or
climbing about the capitals covered with dust, or else with cob-
webs exactly as if he had just arrived from taking a voyage with
the old woman on her broomstick. Then when he comes down
he stands very meekly to be brushed down by Domenico quite
regardless of the scores of idlers who cannot understand him
at all. Not withstanding the above against society in general he
sometimes does enjoy himself. The other day he took Paulizza,
Charlotte & I to Torcello. George, John and the two Gondoliers
rowed us so that we went very fast. The day was cloudy but we
were afraid to put off the day in case another opportunity
should not occur again; the sun broke forth warmly and the

afternoon was charming. Charlotte & I ran into the quiet churchyard to see if the violets were yet in flower but we were still a little too soon and only found a quantity of fresh leaves. At three o'clock we sat down in the same place as before,[1] leaning against the old Monastery of the Brothers of Torcello now filled with slag; a black lizard roused by the sun's heat fell from above on my shoulder but was gone before I hardly saw it. George laid out the cloth upon which he spread cold fowls, Parmesan cheese, Italian bread, beef, cakes, Muscat & Champagne Wines—and a copper vessel full of cold water from the draw well completed our bill of fare. John & Paulizza were in the greatest spirits and nothing could be merrier than the two. After dinner, to show us that the Champagne which they certainly did not take much of, had not gone into their heads, they ran races round the old buildings and so fast that one could hardly see them. Paulizza looked so funny with his sword jumping at every step and Blue spectacles on, which he has been wearing for some days and finds his eyes greatly better. He does not wear them in the streets but when he comes into the sun. He is in great distress just now because, from not being able to use his eyes for work, he has not finished some writings which have been sent to him to do before he goes to Verona, and he does not think he will be able to go there yet for a month, and he will only see us for a week longer which he seems to consider a very dreadful prospect.

This morning I was at the German Church which I always attend on Sunday forenoon as it is the only service at all like our own in Venice and I like it very much.[2] Charlotte likes it too although she does not understand one word, and it is short.

[1] There is no record of a previous visit to Torcello. However, she had written a long letter to George between the 3rd and 10th of December which has not survived, and which presumably contained her description of it. There does not seem to be any other letter missing.

[2] It was in the Scuola dell'Angelo Custode in the Campo Santi Apostoli. During their next visit John wrote to his father on October 11, 1851: 'Effie is gone to her German church—her knowledge of that very disagreeable dialect enabling her to get a Protestant service from which I am debarred.' By 1860 there was a service in English every Sunday in the Palazzo Crivan, but it was not until 1893 that an English church, St George's, in the Campo San Vio, was consecrated. It has a memorial window to Ruskin.

I sent the Gondola home as it was cold and walked back through the crowded thoroughfares to the Hotel....

Radetzky comes here for a week on the 4th. I am very sorry that we go just two days before but if they get up any entertainments for him the Officers will send us invitations and John I daresay will bring us back from Verona for a day if there is any thing particular. I was walking with Madame Nerly today who is in a great state because they have put 250 Croats into the Pisani Palace of which they occupy one suite of rooms. The consequence is that today coming through the interior of the Palace yard she says she saw a number of them at the well almost naked, washing themselves. I said it was very disagreeable but I was thankful to hear they washed themselves at all.

I think you should put your feathers in your bonnet again as they are extremely à la mode at present and yours are quite the thing.... At three I go to see the Baroness Wetzlar who has been ill but has appointed me by Lt. Holzammer to see her today. I enclose a card or two as you seem to like to see them. The Count Mocenigo's is a very proud card but fine and he has every right to the title as he is a descendant of so noble a house.... [1]

What you say about Paulizza was very just, he is singularly good in his way and a perfect jewel of a man as you say in his disposition. I am very much afraid however that he has a dark future before him. His eyes were very bad yesterday. I walked with him for two hours in the shade and it was perfectly melancholy to hear him speak of the beautiful work he used to do with his eyes and now he can do nothing the whole day. He cannot read, write or draw; the only thing he does is to lie with a wet cloth over his eyes, and then when he thinks, he becomes so dreadfully melancholy that he appears to me to lose the power of reasoning entirely and from bitter thought to become almost insane. I cannot think of him without the greatest

---

[1] His card is engraved with the single word Mocenigo. The old Countess's is engraved Lucia Memmo Mocenigo and the young Countess's Comtesse Mocenigo, née Comtesse Spaur. On the back of Holzammer's card is written: 'Madame la Baronne Wetzlar vous attende mardi le 26 Fevrier 1850 entre 2 ou 3 heures après midi.' These cards are now among the Bowerswell Papers. They are all of glossy white pasteboard.

distress, for when we go away he will be so entirely alone that I have a very great fear he will shoot himself. He is naturally extremely melancholy and one of his Brothers shot himself and these foreigners have not the same ideas of suicide as we have. When he is with us after a little while he seems to forget his sad state & to become quite cheerful and happy. He says he would like to be with us every moment in the day. He is very fond of me, and, as you say, were John unkind to me and not so perfectly amiable & good as he is, such excessive devotion might be somewhat dangerous from so handsome & gifted a man, but I am a strange person and Charlotte thinks I have a perfect heart of ice, for she sees him speaking to me until the tears come into his eyes and I looking and answering without the slightest discomposure, but I really feel none. I never could love anybody else in the world but John and the way these Italian women go on is so perfectly disgusting to me that it even removes from me any desire to coquetry which John declares I possess very highly, but he thinks it charming, so do not I. I tell him every word Paulizza says to me and tell the latter so too, so that they perfectly understand each other and after me I think Paulizza likes John better than any one else here. However, be sorry for Paulizza if you like, but do not fear for me. I am one of the odd of the earth and have no talent whatever for intrigue as every thing with me must be as open as the day.[1] I believe I can keep other people's secrets if necessary but I am thankful to say I have none of my own.... I never let Charlotte write any thing about Paulizza and me in her letters home as one does not know, amongst so many, what construction might be put upon what she says, and she agrees with me that it is best not to speak about us. She is quite well and enjoying herself as usual exceedingly.

---

[1] Yet when Effie left John on April 25, 1854, it was with the utmost secrecy. She made out that she was merely going on a visit to Bowerswell, and John saw her off at the station in the morning with her sister Sophia who had been staying with her. Twenty miles out of London her father and mother were waiting, and when the train stopped, Sophia jumped out and Mrs Gray got in beside Effie who gave her father a packet containing a long letter, her keys, house-book and wedding ring to be delivered to Mrs Ruskin that evening. At the same time her solicitor served a Citation on John.

Venice, 3rd March, 1850

... We ought to have left this yesterday, but Radetzky's promised visit has made a good excuse for staying two or three days longer, and John has found some work which he must have left undone about St. Mark's unless he had stayed. I cannot tell you how sorry I shall be to leave Venice. London will look such a black uninteresting whirling sort of place after this where one enjoys the greatest freedom of action of any place I ever saw....

We got the Padre Prosdocimo the other day to meet Paulizza here to look at his eyes and he pronounced them quite sound, but that the loss of sight proceeded from the wound in the head and overwork, and he told Paulizza that he must not think of work for a month to come which puts him into perfect despair, but he leeches himself and told us yesterday when he dined here that he felt lighter and better in his health although his eyes were the same.

About nine o'clock Charlotte and I went to the Fenice. We shut ourselves up as before and no one came near us. Paulizza was there also but not in our box. Madame Danieli before we went brought me a most beautiful present of pale pink Camelias which she had received that afternoon from Padua which Charlotte and I decorated our hair with and John was greatly pleased with their effect. The night before John took us to St. Benedetto[1] to see an Opera which George said was very charming, the sce[ne] being in Venice, but I did not enjoy it very much as we had not read the Libretto before going and a great deal of it was in Dialogue. We had a number of visitors in the box, amongst others P. Troubetzkoi who said he suppose he should see us soon again as he was to leave for London next month.

5th. Yesterday we went at eleven o'clock to St. Mark's to hear the Te Deum sung, being the first anniversary of Emperor's Coronation. We went up into the stone galleries above the

[1] This theatre, near San Luca, built in 1756 by the Grimani family, was the only one in Venice until the Fenice was built in 1791. It was also known as the Teatro Gallo from the name of its proprietor. In 1875 it was restored and renamed Rossini. Recently it was demolished and a cinema, still called Teatro Rossini, built in its place.

aisle which was entirely left clear for the Military, the order being kept by Croats with box-wood sprigs in their caps. The procession of clergy and Officers from the Governor downwards was very fine; an immense number came and the different Uniforms, from the Generals' white coats & scarlet trowsers with gold to the dark blue and gold of the Naval Officers, was a very pretty sight. We saw a number of our acquaintances there, but not Paulizza; he said it was another piece of mockery in the Church which he did not choose to attend. A soldier was stilettoed in the night by an Italian from jealousy as he saw the soldier walking with his sweetheart. He died instantly. We hear that Rome is in a very unsatisfactory state, a number of soldiers and Officers of the French having been attacked in the streets....

I had a nice walk with Mr Brown yesterday. He has invited us to Lunch with him tomorrow before we leave Venice, and then is going to take me in his Gondola to the Railway, which last I suppose poor Paulizza would willingly send a few of his darling Bombs into it if it would keep us longer here. John asked him to dine here today. At first he refused but then he said to me, "I will come, only I must suffer a great deal." He wrote me a long letter the other day which took me a considerable time, as you may suppose, to read, and I made a legible translation of it for John and Charlotte's benefit but was worth the trouble. I do not know that Charlotte did not cry over it. He intends to write to us after we go but seems to think that small comfort as he says when once we leave Venice he never expects to see us again. One might not wonder at a young man being a little mad and absurd, but a man of 35, so talented and so esteemed and so well known, makes it much more curious, but he says he lives so solitary that he never before met with people he had so much sympathy with, and now in addition to his other trials he loses us also. He says he must surely be very wicked to be so severely punished even in this world. I am longing for letters from you which I hope I shall find at Verona....

THE JOURNEY HOME

Effie and John spent one night in Padua and one in Vicenza on the way to Verona. Effie found Padua very interesting but could see no beauty in Vicenza as she 'could not admire anything Palladio ever did'.

Verona, 9th March, 1850

Dearest George

I send this letter first to Perth as Mama may like to continue receiving letters from me regularly, and if I wrote to both I would only repeat myself....

In the evening after we arrived here we had a visit from the young Count Gianbattista Ferrari [Podestà, or Mayor, of Verona before 1848] who Mr Brown had written to, to call on us whenever we arrived. He seems an agreeable person, talks English fluently and professed himself entirely at our service all the time we stay here to show us any thing in Verona. We shall stay here about ten days. Our other friends, the Minischalchis, at last got their passports from Radetzky and are now in Paris on their way to London,[1] but we have three other letters so that I suppose we shall soon have some agreeable Italian acquaintances. The Count Wimpffen is also here, I suppose, and he we know already.

Radetzky returned from Venice yesterday; he now lives in the Palazzo Emilii a few doors from the Inn which he has taken for nine years so that we shall see his movements every

---

[1] It might have been better for the Minischalchis if they had never got their passports. Effie wrote to her mother from Park Street on May 24: 'I was very sorry to hear from Mrs Murray a very sad thing about the Minischalchis. They left their little girl of seven at Paris, and were going out a great deal here and the Countess much admired and feted when they heard that their child was taken alarmingly ill with brain fever and is now dead. It will be a terrible blow to them and she was the only daughter.'

day.[1] Prince Troubetzkoi was to accompany him from Venice and said he would see us here before we started for London. A great number of Military are here just now; every where grey coats are seen lying about in the sun or smoking in the streets; a great number of cavalry also are seen here and there. The table D'Hote down stairs is composed of nearly fifty Officers and no one else. Every day they dine at four which I think very sensible. The Marshall [Radetzky] shows the example going to bed every night before nine and receiving the Orderly in the morning at five. His hours never vary except from necessity....

We were very very sorry to leave Venice, and such a parting as we had with all the garçons, chambermaids, gondoliers, Austrians & Italians, you would have been perfectly melted had you witnessed it. Monsieur & Mdme. Danieli,[2] who had treated George like their own son, gave him a grand supper party the night before and had an immense bowl of mulled wine brought in to drink his health. They are wealthy people and their society much better than what George has been accustomed to move in. I was in their apartment one day and never saw any thing more beautifully furnished in my life; Mdme. Danieli's toilet table with silver was almost as fine as the Countess Mocenigo's. Well, at this supper they gave to George, he had to undergo a kissing, Italian fashion, from every one present. He told us afterwards he did not mind being kissed by the Ladies but that really the moustaches were too much of a good thing.

Paulizza dined with us and I intended to bid him goodbye early as I had to pack up all my things to start early next forenoon, when after dinner in walked the two Mr Blumenthals and, although very nice young men in their way, I knew when they did come that there was no getting them away. They stood and, better, stayed, and as they hate the Austrians, all Paulizza's politeness in speaking to them in Italian was but coldly received. John went away to pack up his things and left us to

[1] Napoleon had lived in the Palazzo degli Emilii, now a museum. The Ruskins were again staying at the Due Torri almost in the next street.

[2] These were not the founders of the hotel but their adopted daughter, Alphonsine Clément, and her husband, Vespasien Muzzaretti, to whom it had passed at Joseph Danieli's death in 1840.

amuse each other. Charlotte and I got dreadfully tired. I
could not help giving them a few hints and telling them how
I had every thing to pack &c; Paulizza twice whispered to me
in German that he should not be averse to send a few balls into
them. At last after eleven o'clock they actually went away
and John returned from his room. Charlotte had gone to her
bed the moment he appeared and we now bid Paulizza goodbye which was very unpleasant indeed. He siezed John in his
arms and kissed him over both sides of his face and lamented
our departure bitterly in Italian. John went away and his
distress with me was so great that I was almost thankful when
he was gone. I could not help crying when I saw this strong
man so overwhelmed with grief; the tears rolled through his
fingers and he said to me, "In battle I have never been afraid
or trembled but here I shake and tears come of which I am not
ashamed." I said to him that John & I would hear from him
occasionally and I hoped we would soon hear his sight was
restored to him and he could go on with his work, which would
be the best thing for him. John came in and Paulizza again bid
us goodbye; he formed our, John and mine, hands together and
wished us every happiness and told John to watch over me with
care as he would a treasure, for that I had certainly been sent
into Italy to preserve his life, and that humanly speaking he
owed it to me, and that he prayed every day that I might be
kept from the evil which is in the world. He could not bear,
he said, to think how lonely he would be when we went away.
John said he hoped soon to hear that he had found one of his
countrywomen with whom he might live happily, & in whom
he would find all he could wish, but he shook his head and
said he was no longer a young man, that he had lived thirty-
five years in the world without loving any woman, and he had
never seen any one he had sympathy with by [sic] his mother,
a sister dead, & me, and that he didn't expect to see any more
now, and he was very happy when he could work.

I thought we were not to see him any more but he could not
think of our being in Venice all next forenoon without seeing us,
and when I was in the middle of my packing he walked into my
room with John with a most exquisite bouquet he had brought
for me with a beautiful white Camellia in the centre. He stood

in a corner of the room, chatting with me until I had finished packing, and seeing us into the Gondola, and the last thing I saw of him was his saluting us as we passed under the Bridge of Sighs on our way to lunch with Mr Brown, who we found had prepared a most exquisite Luncheon for us. I never saw any thing more perfect, the glass, china we ate off, the little cups of black coffee, served in the most exquisite style, and then the little Liqueur glasses of Rossolio, and a most splendid bouquet in the centre for me which I think had stripped every Camelia from the Botanical gardens. In fact I was quite feted and the room we were in was a perfect museum of invaluable manuscripts, Armour and all kinds of curiosities.

After Lunch we were told that Radetzky was up stairs calling on Taglioni. We went out to the Balcony and then in a few minutes we saw him assisted into his Gondola by Prince Troubetzkoi and attended by Count Montemolin [Don Carlos II] and another officer with a Helmet. As no one was there but ourselves we saw him most famously and immediately afterwards we parted for the Railway which is an Hour's sail across the Lagune. Mr Brown on the way, as I was in his Gondola, presented me with a Brooch which he had asked John's permission to give me, and which is now the most valuable ornament John says that I have. It is a Head of Bacchus crowned with vines of the most exquisite workmanship in red coral, and Mr Brown declares it must have always been intended for me for he bought it at Naples the year I was born. Was it not very kind of him? ...

[Verona, March 11th]

Dearest Mama

I received your long and interesting letter yesterday the 10th.... A few lines to wish you many, many happy returns of your birthday on the 17th which we shall not forget I assure you when it comes....[1]

[1] Mrs Gray, who was going to be forty-two, was ten years younger than her husband. She lived until 1894, surviving him by seventeen years. At this time she was pregnant again, apparently unknown as yet to Effie. A boy, Albert, was born on October 10. She was to have only one more child, Everett (called after Millais), born in March, 1855.

I was very much obliged to you for all you said about Mr Ruskin. Indeed I can never sufficiently thank you, dear Mother, for all your kindness in this matter, and your acting with such perfect good sense must make Mr R feel it is better just to be quiet. I daresay now his health is better he will also feel more amiable and as I too am stronger I hope we shall be better friends.[1] For all I care they may have John as much with them as they please for I could hardly see less of him than I do at present with his work, and I think it is much better, for we follow our different occupations and never interfere with one another and are always happy, but I shall take care to let them be as little alone as possible together for they had far too much time for grumbling about nothing before.

We shall stay here till Monday next [the 18th] and then go to Mantua, hoping to reach Genoa and rest a couple of days there in the end of the week. Counts Emile & Alphonse Wimpffen come here every day or every evening, and when the Band plays in the Amphitheatre they walk with us. The former, with whom I danced with at Venice, is in the Cavalry and very handsome indeed but I do not like him so well as Alphonse, my first acquaintance. John likes both as he talks architecture with them by the yard.

Ct. Emile and the Prince Troubetzkoi have just left me, the latter gone to Mantua but returns here, I suppose. I was sitting alone yesterday when in he walked to my great surprize most beautifully dressed in a green uniform with white facings, a cocked Hat and beautiful white plume of Feathers, and covered on one side with Russian & Austrian Orders of high Merit. I begged him to be seated but he said he was just going to the Marshall and came to pay his respects to me and tell me he was in the room next to mine and hoped we should be good neighbours. In the evening Count Ferrari, Alphonse Wimpffen & he all came in at different times, each looking astonished to see the other, and remained two or three hours with us.

[1] This last sentence has been misleadingly quoted out of its context in *The Order of Release* (p. 152) so that the 'he' appears to be John instead of Mr Ruskin. It seems that only now had Mrs Gray thought fit to tell Effie something about the exchange of letters with Mr Ruskin in October and November—probably to prepare her for her homecoming.

Troubetzkoi as usual was the most energetic of the party and his cleverness and wittiness on every subject touched, made us wonder more than ever at him. He knows ever so many languages, architecture and painting, John says as well almost as himself but the most curious was to hear him talking on religion. We found that all of us belonged to different sects, Troubetzkoi, being Russian, to the Greek Church. Alphonse was expressing some of the Protestant tenets which he much prefered to his own Church, and Troubetzkoi launched out into a complete sermon on duty and faith so excellent and so well reasoned, notwithstanding all John's arguments against his different starting points just to see what he would say, that after he was gone John said to me that he would much rather hear Troubetzkoi in the East Church than Mr Anderson, but as this is not a compliment that gentleman would quite like you may keep it to yourself....[1]

Prince Troubetzkoi came to call on Effie in Park Street in July, but by that time she had formed a very bad opinion of him. No doubt she had heard disparaging gossip about him in London. She wrote to her mother on July 5: 'I was rather startled and agitated two mornings ago to hear a knock at the drawing room door and thinking it Melina called out "Entrez." A manly voice answering, "Je suis charmée de vous voir," I turned and was saluted by Prince Troubetzkoi with the politeness for which he is so remarkable. I said that he was rather late for the season; he answered he had been kept in our rooms at Verona for six weeks with measles, which rather made me smile as he is a perfect Hercules and never had an illness in his life. He said everything at Venice was as usual but that he was sure I would be sorry to hear of the illness of Paulizza which I allowed him to recount to me and expressed great sorrow thereat; then he gave me lots of messages from the Counts Wimpffen and said quantities of gallant things and finally said I was such a puritan that he must go home and read the Evangile which I took the liberty of telling him I thought he had much need of. He is going tonight to a ball at Grosvenor House and wanted very much for me to get an invitation from Lady Westminster or to let him get one, but I refused all his

[1] The Rev. John Anderson of Craigie Park was minister of East Church, St John's Street, Perth.

entreaties, for although he is extremely repondu in London and goes everywhere, I should not like people to think him an admirer of mine or to be seen with him as if I felt honoured by his acquaintance, which I certainly do not although he amuses me beyond measure and says the wittiest and cleverest things I ever heard.' Describing the same visit in a letter to Rawdon Brown she used stronger terms: 'I shall not see him again if I can help it. I think him a bad man as ever I knew; perhaps there are many as bad but greater Hypocrites than he.' And on July 25 she wrote about him to her mother: 'He is to Paulizza what a coal is to a diamond.'[1]

Paulizza had fallen ill soon after they left Venice and was in bed with brain fever for six weeks. His condition was wretched, for not only had he lost all his savings the year before through the failure of a Venetian bank but he was quite blind for a time and could do no work. He wrote to Effie in May to tell her this and she reported to her mother: 'He says his whole desire in this world is to see his Mother and us again. He says he owes us eternal thanks for making him better and softer in his feelings to mankind. He says he should like to resemble John whose mind he admires so much and whose spirit he says must be pleasing to God for he is so pureminded.'

Effie, to her great disappointment, had to leave Verona without being presented to Radetzky. Just as the long-sought introduction was at last arranged the old Marshal went off suddenly to Milan for a week. From Mantua she and John posted to Genoa, Savona, Nice, Cannes, Brignolles and Marseilles. From Marseilles they took the railway to Avignon and then posted on to Montélimart, Lyons and Bourges where they stayed two nights because John was so delighted with the Cathedral. They reached Paris on Tuesday, April 9, having come by rail in seven hours from Vierzon. Effie wrote four long letters home during the journey but they were mostly taken up with descriptions of the scenery.

In Paris, where they stayed again at the Hotel Meurice, Effie was to meet all five daughters of the late Peter Domecq whose estates at

---

[1] In 1852, the year of his marriage to Taglioni's daughter, Troubetzkoi was ordered by the Tsar to return to Russia, and when he refused, was deprived of his title and military rank. Two years later he was reinstated, rejoined the Russian Army and rose again to the rank of Colonel. In 1868 he became Russian Consul-General in Marseilles. He died in 1889.

Xeres produced the wine for Mr Ruskin's sherry business. Mr Ruskin was most anxious that John and Effie should show them every attention for, as he wrote to John, 'It is only by means afforded by them that either my House or yours is kept.' Peter Domecq had been half Spanish, half French, and his wife English. His daughters had all been born abroad and were convent bred, but he had bought a house in the Champs-Élysées from which to launch them on the world, and there Ruskin as a boy visited them on his first trip to Paris in 1833. The first sight of them 'sealed itself into' him, he tells us in *Praeterita*, 'for they were the first well-bred and well-dressed girls' he had ever seen. Dowries of £30,000 had secured for each of them rich or aristocratic husbands. The eldest was Diana who, in 1836, when the other four sisters went to stay with the Ruskins at Herne Hill on their way to a convent near Chelmsford, had just married Comte Maison, a descendant of General Maison who had served under Napoleon and been rewarded by Louis XVIII with a Marquisate and a Marshal's baton for remaining loyal to the Bourbons during the Hundred Days.

Mr Domecq died while the other girls were still in England, and the duty of marrying them off fell to his brother, John Peter Domecq. Adèle Clotilde, whom John had loved, was now twenty-nine; in 1840 she had married Baron Duquesne. Next came Cécile, two years younger and the beauty of the family, married to the rich Comte de Chabrillan; then Elise, a year younger, wife of the Comte des Roys; and lastly Caroline Béthune, aged twenty-five, whom Effie had already met and liked in London. Her uncle had had some difficulty in finding a husband for her, and in June, 1843, had written to Mr Ruskin: 'This young lady cannot make out her mind to live in Xeres, therefore I have no hope of seeing my late brother's plan realised which was to marry her to H. Peter Domecq, his Nephew & godson. It occurs to my mind she might like to live in London, in that case would it be agreeable to yourself & Mrs Ruskin to have her for your interesting & distinguished son? I would gladly not only consent to it but do any thing in my power to incline her to it. Your candid answer will greatly oblige me.'[1]

Mr Ruskin would have had no difficulty in being candid, and we can gather what his reply was from the fact that a year later Caroline married Comte Maximilien Béthune who, Caroline claimed, was

[1] From an unpublished letter at Bembridge.

'related to all the world in Paris'. Was John ever told of M. Domecq's offer? Was it he himself who turned it down? We do not know, but if he *was* told of it this may account for the special fondness he seems to have had for Caroline. From a worldly point of view she did very well for herself. The Comte de Béthune was descended from Maximilien de Béthune, Henry IV's Minister of Finance, who was created Duc de Sully in 1606. His father was d'Amaury, Comte de Béthune, and in 1886 he became a Prince when his elder brother succeeded his cousin, Prince Maximilien Béthune. He died in 1881. His and Caroline's only son was killed in the Franco-Prussian War. Effie remained friends with Caroline after the annulment in spite of the friendship of the whole family for the Ruskins. The last letter Effie dictated on her deathbed to her daughter Mary was to Caroline.

Ruskin described in *Praeterita* the coming of these Domecq girls to Herne Hill in 1836 as 'a most curious galaxy, or southern cross, of unconceived stars, floating on a sudden into my obscure firmament of London suburb'. It was these girls and their husbands who first drew him to socialism. In *Praeterita* he wrote: ' ... the way in which these lords, virtually, of lands both in France and Spain, though men of sense and honour; and their wives, though women of gentle and amiable disposition, (Elise, indeed, one of the kindest I ever have known) spoke of their Spanish labourers and French tenantry, with no idea whatever respecting them but that, except as producers by their labour of money to be spent in Paris, they were cumberers of the ground, gave me the first clue to the real sources of wrong in the social laws of modern Europe; and led me necessarily into the political work which has been the most earnest of my life.'

Paris, 14th April, 1850

Dearest Mama

... I have not been very well since I arrived here which is unfortunate. I think it has been caused by the weather & thunder but it prevents me going about as I would like, besides making me feel very weak and unable to take any exercise. It is continued British Cholera[1] or dysentery or any thing else you like to call it, keeping away when I lie down but troubling me when I move about and especially when I drive. I took a dose of Magnesia yesterday and I think I will take another today but

[1] The first symptom of cholera is a mild diarrhoea.

it is very troublesome and I am obliged to be very careful what
I eat. I am writing in bed so forgive mistakes. I was out late last
night and will not rise till the afternoon. We shall not be home
till the end of the week as we have invitations more than we want
until we go away. Paris is extremely gay and the season has been
most brilliant and the quantity of strangers unusual, Balls,
fetes, and Concerts, without number, and in the midst of political confusion every body (except the President who is hated)
enjoying themselves to their hearts contents and as only French
people could in such a state of things. I never saw people enter
so completely into the spirit of amusement and enjoy themselves
more thoroughly. The night after we came John took us to the
French Opera where we saw Der Freischutz [by Weber]
performed. The Orchestra was much more perfect than the
acting. The Ballet in which Cerito & St Leon danced was very
pretty, but I think the Maywood at Venice more of a genius still.[1]

We dined with the Béthunes yesterday at the Hotel Choiseul
[Rue St Honoré] where they have had a suite of apartments for
the season, with their own servants and cook. In the forenoon
the Count & Countess Maison called on me and asked us to
dinner tomorrow. She is Diana, the eldest, Spanish looking but
not pretty. I liked both. At Madame de Béthune's was Elise &
her husband, Count & Ctse. des Roys, a thin Ladylike person
very agreeable indeed in pale green striped silk with black
velvet coiffure; the Marquise de Restant, a friend of Mdme.
Béthune's, a very lively little person indeed, dancing about the
room and doing a thousand little things very gracefully which
on an English woman would have looked very ill indeed. The
dinner was in very good style with showy servants in the Sully
Livery; the first course was as many oysters as made the table
look like Billingsgate and the soup in the middle cooling without a cover; then followed all sorts of little dishes, half a salmon,

[1] Fanny Cerito (1817-92), born in Naples, made her debut there when only
fifteen. In 1845 she married Arthur Saint-Leon (1821-70), choreographer, ballet
master and violinist, as well as dancer. *La Esmeralda* was in their repertoire
for the 1850 Paris season so this was probably the ballet they were dancing
that evening as Effie compares it to 'the Maywood'. This was the last year
they were to appear together in Paris. In 1851 they separated in Madrid. Cerito
fell in love with the Marqués de Bedmar who had been Queen Isabella's lover,
and had a daughter by him.

quantities of wines, the Count Béthune beside me drinking a
whole jug of Burgundy to himself, like beer. He is the best of the
men belonging to the sisters and I like him very much indeed.
The rest are various degrees of Frenchmen with moustaches
and beards. The moment dessert was over they brought in very
fine porcelain cups & bowls with luke warm water with essence
in it which they all applied to rinsing their mouths, which fashion I did not like at all; then the Count gave me his arm and we
all went into the drawingroom where was black coffee on a
salver in small cups without cream, and beside it three very
large stone bottles of Liqueurs, Curaçoa, Aniseed, which the
French are so fond of, and Cognac. We drank our coffee and then
the Countess Béthune, Mdme. Elise, John and I, all went to a
concert given by Offenbach the famous violoncello player[1]
and a protegé of the Countess Chabrillan, Cécile. It was select
and I had a good opportunity of seeing some of the persons
composing *la societé* as Caroline rules it, but dreadfully warm
and we had a vast deal of crushing to go through to reach the
Countess Cécile who had seats for us near the performers.
She is one of the belles of Paris and leaders of fashion and has
a very splendid House in the Place Vendôme [No. 19] where I
believe she gives very brilliant fêtes to the first people in Paris.
She is extremely small and a fine face to the mouth, but bad
teeth and an uninteresting piece of well-bred life, but very beautifully dressed. She had a rich white glacé silk with two flounces
and small open berthe to match trimmed with white silk fringe,
a small white glacé silk polka, or little cloak, trimmed with
frills of white tulle and white satin ribbon with long hang sleeves
looped with green leaves of enamel and gold, as also down each
side of the front of the open cloak, about 18, and as they were
each about an inch square, and beautiful work, they must have
cost something; her bracelets & brooch of splendid emeralds and
diamonds. Her head had been taken great pains with & was
striking, or, as John says, elaborate, her own hair smoothed
very tight on the forehead and two immense false plaits put on
each side, above which was a coiffure of scarlet silk ribbon in
bows and green leaves immensely large on each side, and at the

---

[1] Offenbach was not yet known as a composer. He was at this time giving
society concerts.

top a small fichu of very fine lace hanging over the back of the head. Through the leaves and ribbon were small loops of white pearls, the whole very beautiful.

Behind us two or three seats was the Baroness Duquesne, John's former Belle; she is now much the plainest of the whole of them and I believe fashionable and wordly but she did not strike me so and I liked her. She was much disfigured by a violent cold and inflammation in her eyes which are fine and large. She was dressed in white & blue silk with a white lace coiffure & blue ribbon in her hair, and a white satin Jacket entirely braided over with white silk braid, very handsome.[1]

For the rest I was much disappointed with the people there who were of Faubourg St. Germain notoriety. I did not think hardly any well dressed and all plain nearly excepting Ctses Caroline & Cécile. I did not think the children in the Tuilleries at all well dressed. The Ladies tell me that there is a rage just now for dressing all like the English children and certainly they have succeeded. As to fashions, particular plainess seems to be the thing and very rich cloaks with splendid lace, bonnets with no trimming at all, plain cased silk or crape, mostly white, very round & open & extremely large are all I can see or get. I have got little blue silk bonnets for Sophia & Alice & a pink one for Eliza [Jameson] as I thought they might be as useful as any thing for them, but I am afraid you will think them very plain and so do I but I can get no better. Silk Jackets with lace Worsted, very pretty, the same colour as the dress, much worn, and excepting for very full dress, tight high body and long

---

[1] Ruskin had thought Adèle less beautiful at eighteen than at fifteen, and Effie later reported that when he saw her in Paris he took no interest in her. After Effie left John, Mr Ruskin told David Roberts, the painter, that John had been trapped into marriage and might have married a French Countess. This was passed on to Rawdon Brown who was in London at the time, and he in his turn passed it on to Effie in Perth. She wrote back on May 3, 1854: ' ... the wicked old man I knew would be too angry not to say some ridiculous things which would only serve to show his own dreadful nature and bad heart. The idea of the *French Countess* made me smile. The lady was only plain *Miss Domecq* but her fortune procured her a French Baron for a Husband of very questionable character, but I understand that they have bought an estate, and as they are now older I daresay she has given up Balls as he has gambling—so that anyway the title of Countess was out of the question.' Mr Ruskin might have been referring to Caroline not Adèle.

hanging sleeves with net sleeves inside same shape, with two rows of broad lace, this is very pretty....[1]

The Baron Duquesne, who is particularly civil to us for some purpose unknown, and particularly to me, heard me say I should like to see Prince Louis Napoleon, the President. Today he & Mdme. Adèle came to call and he said if I still wished, that he had a plan in hand with the Countess Beauharnais, the cousin of the President, to take me with her to a Ball given by him on Thursday when I would have the best opportunity possible in his own house, and all the world besides, which I at once said I was most grateful for his attention. He said he would tell us tomorrow decidedly whether he received on Thursday or not, for in these days I suppose he is not very sure of anything, but it is a first rate chance for me which I may not have again in my life, and very interesting at such a time, and Mr Ruskin will like us to go as he was much disappointed at our not seeing Radetzky which I am so yet. All your letter yet unanswered and I at the end of my paper. Your account of poor Mrs Jones touched me much and I pity her most sincerely for she must be very unhappy at present and the future so uncertain....[2]

[1] Effie bought in Paris two day dresses, two ball dresses and two bonnets which are described in detail in a letter to her mother after she got home. For her birthday on May 7 John gave her ten guineas because he knew she had overspent in Paris.

[2] Mrs Jones, a niece of Lord Campbell, was to become the last love of the Duke of Wellington. She lived at Cupar, Fife, Mrs Gray's old home. She also had a house in London, and being very rich could, according to Effie, get anybody she liked to come to her parties. The Duke died, aged eighty-three, on September 14, 1852, and afterwards Effie wrote to her mother: ' ... as far as he is concerned it is much better he is dead for this love affair he had with Mrs Jones during this last Season was very unbecoming. He always was in love with someone but had never made himself ridiculous till this one which was a source of grief to his family and made him laughed at by every empty headed fool in London. They say that he never passed a day without seeing her and every where she went she took him with her and sometimes took him to very queer places. At every party Mrs Jones and the "Dook" were ushered in together as she has never been known to blush since she came to town. I daresay she will feel no remorse at all for making the last days of so great a Hero contemptible when perhaps she might have done him some lasting service, but everyone rejoices that he has not lived longer on this account.'

Paris, 17th April, 1850

... We have been busy driving out and seeing things ever since we came. Yesterday John and I, after being some places, took a turn in the Louvre where I wanted to see the Portraits of Giovanni & Gentile Bellini painted by the former and a great pet of mine. We met there Lord & Lady Ruthven and had some talk with her for some little time for I suppose poor Lord R. only looks sad and doesn't talk. I had never spoken with her before and her volubility astonished me not a little and I could hardly keep from laughing although it made me melancholy to see her, for she looked so curious, shabbily dressed and untidy, and didn't know where she was going, whether farther or not, but had come from Boulogne and was going out a great deal in Paris as there are quantities of English here. She asked me if I would permit her to take me on Monday Evening to Lady Elgin's where I would meet all the Philosophers but I thought one at a time was enough and said we were going to London on Friday. She said she hoped we would visit her at Ireland when she returned but I suppose she will never be able to live there again.[1]

We dined in the Afternoon with the Baroness Duquesne; the party were the Count & Ctsse. Duquesne, another brother, very rich and formerly Captain in the Prince de Joinville's ship. He said when he went to England with Louis Philippe the Officers at Portsmouth nearly killed him with kindness when he was there.[2] Count & Ctsse Maison were also there. The dinner

---

[1] Mary, daughter of Walter Campbell of Shawfield, N.B., had married, in 1813, 5th Baron Ruthven (1777-1853). He died without issue and the barony devolved on his sister, Mrs Walter Hore. They lived at Freeland House, Perthshire, and Mrs Gray served on several charity committees with Lady Ruthven who was well known for her kindness and hospitality. The family today are not aware that she ever lived in Ireland, let alone knowing of any reason why she could not go back there. It was perhaps on account of the potato famine.

Lady Elgin, née Elizabeth Oswald, was the widow of the 7th Earl who had bought the Elgin Marbles. He had died in Paris in 1841, and. she chose to stay on there for the rest of her life, keeping a *salon* at 29 Rue de Varenne.

[2] The Prince de Joinville was the third son of Louis Philippe. It was his ship which had carried Napoleon's body from St Helena in 1840.

was very beautiful and the glasses and china and real flowers on the table exquisite. The gentlemen rose with us and in the drawing-room we found Elise, Mdme. & the Count des Roys, who were going to a Soirée. She looked very well indeed in a pale blue & white rich damask dress with magnificent diamonds and bunches of white Marabouts on each side of her hair mixed with little silver things.[1] Madame Duquesne's little girl, only eight and speaking English perfectly, played with a doll Mrs Ruskin had sent her like Sophia's. She was dressed in Maroon velvet with white chemisette and sleeves, the same as Sophia has. Madame Duquesne has just sent me a very beautiful and old painted fan which she brought with her from Spain. I would send you her note but I am afraid it is too small for you to read & in French. She encloses a note to the Duchess de Coigny from Lady Normanby,[2] the former having presented our cards to the Ambassador & he & she having sent theirs to us today as a matter of etiquette, and you will see by it why, for want of time in applying, we cannot go to the President's Ball tomorrow night which is a pity but cannot be helped. Had it not been for that we should have gone.

We go to Boulogne on Friday and shall be at Denmark Hill on Saturday evening. Today the Count Maison & Baron Duquesne took me to see the Tomb of Napoleon now building in the Invalides, like every thing else now built a great waste of money and marble & no genius, not even a good copy of an old thing. Tomorrow they take me to see the Musée d'Artillerie and Hotel de Cluny. They will both interest me but how Frenchmen do talk. They are perfectly stunning. I would not give one Austrian for six Frenchmen. Goodnight. I hope soon to hear you are all well. I shall be very glad to get home as I am out of Italy, but I shall return soon I think, at least next year D.V....

[1] Effie got an identical head-dress for herself in Paris and another one of gold net with pearls and broad gold fringe. She told her mother that John was highly pleased with them.

[2] Maria Liddell (1798-1882), eldest daughter of 1st Baron Ravensworth, had married in 1818 1st Marquess of Normanby, Ambassador in Paris, 1846-52. In London, Effie had met two of her brothers who were John's great admirers. The Duchesse de Coigny was the daughter of Sir Hew Dalrymple-Hamilton, Bt.

Paris, 18th April, Thursday

I merely write a line to ask you when you write to me to enclose Lady Normanby's note as I think Mr Ruskin would like to see it. I think he will be much disappointed we cannot go to-night as we missed Radetzky's Balls which might easily have been managed after all. I think he will be much more sorry than us; indeed if we had gone I do not know how we should have managed as we must leave tomorrow at 7 in the morning in time to catch the Boulogne boat which crosses at two. We shall sleep at Folkestone and go up to London next morning and go to Denmark Hill to dinner and I suppose stay there till Monday.

Charlotte and I took a drive yesterday after we had done our shopping to the Bois de Boulogne; not many carriages there although a great number in the Champs D'Elysees. The prevalence of white bonnets is quite remarkable. Every person with dark hair seems to wear one with no colour about it.... We afterwards called on Madame Chabrillan who is married to the Rothschild of the family.[1] Their house in the Place Vendôme is splendid and most luxurious, all the furniture and walls covered with the richest satin, and statues, china & marbles of the finest kind everywhere. The rooms all opened into each other and at the end of the suite we found Cécile, the beauty, in a luxuriously furnished apartment lounging on the sofa. She always receives at four and there were several people there when we entered but they left. She is an exceedingly calm tranquil person, looks younger than Madame Béthune & has not her mind at all.[2] She was dressed à la Française in a sort of elegant dressing gown but tight to the waist of checked fawn & green glacé silk trimmed richly with black lace, open at the neck showing an exquisite lace chemisette, and in front of the skirt a petticoat of white thick muslin with flounces of coarse work all the way down, long hanging sleeves showing her arms and hands like snow, with a scent bottle hanging from one finger, and

[1] The Count's father had died in August, 1847, and left him over £60,000.
[2] Effie wrote to her mother on October 27, 1848, about Caroline Béthune when she first met her on their return from Normandy: 'I do not like her face but her hands and arms are quite perfect.... At Paris she goes to balls three times a week, the intervening nights to the *spectacle*.' And in a later letter: 'So much gaiety makes her look 30 and sallow.'

a large coiffure of white lace with quantities of cerise satin ribbon & velvet mixed. She took us into her rooms which she had furnished according to her own taste. Her bed room was one mass of crimson satin & Venice glass, the coverlet of the bed and curtains being rose silk covered with fine Lace, and on the wall a large crucifix in Ivory with a large Christ and other subjects from scripture of rare value. I never saw such a luxurious little creature. Of course her husband never enters these appartments excepting to dine with her and take her out in the evening, but has his own rooms and servants at another part of the house. They are the best friends in the world & think highly of each other. I suppose most of the other sisters live in the same way. John has just come in to go with us and the Baron Duquesne to the Hotel de Cluny....

LONDON AGAIN

❦

Effie and John got home on April 20 and went to Denmark Hill for a few days before returning to Park Street. Mr Ruskin was very pleased with Effie and wrote to Mr Gray that she had made her birthday on May 7 one of the pleasantest days of his and Mrs Ruskin's existence. George Gray, who came to London in June for a visit, declared that she was looking very well and that there were few like her and none so well dressed in London. Yet she was not in good spirits, and wrote to Rawdon Brown soon after getting home that although John agreed to take her out occasionally in the evenings, he intended to go to Denmark Hill every morning after breakfast until dinner at six for there was no light in Park Street and he had not got his Turners.

She made many new friends that season; rode the brougham horse every day in the Row between five and six when the band played and went to some of the smartest parties, including a breakfast on June 15 at Lady Westminster's where 'six saloons … were filled with the elite of London … and all the beauty and talent of the year'. On June 20 she was presented at a Drawing Room at Buckingham Palace by Lady Charlemont, a lady-in-waiting to the Queen, whom she had met through Lady Davy. (John could accompany her only as far as the door of the throne-room as he had not been to a levee, but on July 3, sponsored by his Oxford friend, Lord Eastnor, he made his bow.[1]) Lady Charlemont, who had lost her own four children, treated Effie like a daughter and took her everywhere with her, and Effie was able to ask her advice on all points of etiquette.

In May she met Edward Cheney and his elder brother, Robert-Henry, a distinguished artist, who became her great friends. Another interesting new friend was Richard Ford, who had published a

---

[1] Mr Ruskin paid £21 7s. for John's Court dress. A previous entry in his account-book reads: 'Effie Court £20'. This seems a huge sum for a dress considering it was made at home by Melina, but no doubt it included other items such as feathers, gloves and shoes.

Hand-book on Spain, having lived there for many years. Effie does not say where she met him but she first lunched at his house, 123 Park Street, on June 7 and wrote that she found everyone there distinguished except herself. The guests included the Prussian Ambassador, Chevalier de Bunsen and his wife, who thereafter asked her to all their parties at the Embassy. She also became very friendly with Mr Ford's two elder daughters (he was then a widower twice over but was soon to marry for the third time) and 'matronised' them to balls although they were older than she was. It was not until the following year, however, that she met his only son, Clare, then a spoilt, wild, dissipated young man of her own age, who fell in love with her. She lectured and admonished him on his way of life until he declared she would die of propriety; nevertheless, under her influence he gave up his commission in the army, and after a quiet period of study abroad, embarked on a diplomatic career which in due course led to the Ambassadorships of Madrid, Constantinople and Rome.

But of the friends she made at this time, the one who was to have most influence on her life was Elizabeth Eastlake. A daughter of Edward Rigby, an obstetric physician, she had married, in 1848, Charles Eastlake, the artist, who was knighted in November when he became President of the Royal Academy. It was Lady Eastlake who was later to discover the terms on which Effie was living with John and put into her head the idea of obtaining her freedom.

In spite of the excitements of the London season, Effie was already by July pining to get back to Venice, and writing to Rawdon Brown that she had been asking John ever since their return when they could go back there. In July he told her definitely that it could not be until the following year because of his book.

In the middle of August they went to stay for a few days with some friends of John's, the John Pritchards, at Brosely in Shropshire, and then (reluctantly on John's part) to the Cheneys at Badger seven miles away; and at the end of the month to Bowerswell. John stayed only a very short time but Effie remained for two months, and was there when Mrs Gray gave birth on October 10 to her son Albert. From Bowerswell Effie wrote in an undated letter to Rawdon Brown: 'I quite think with you that if I had children my health might be quite restored. Simpson and several of the best medical men have

said so to me and your gracious permission to me against your pre-
judices amuses me not a little, but you would require to win over
John too, for he hates children and does not wish any children to
interfere with his plans of studies. I often think I would be a much
happier, better, person if I was more like the rest of my sex in this
respect.'

On her return to Park Street she wrote to her mother on October
26, 'John was perfectly enchanted to see me again and said he never
saw such a difference in any creature in two months.' They found
their first happy daytime occupation together in rummaging in
secondhand bookshops in Charing Cross Road. They would walk
there in the mornings for exercise, and after half an hour or so Effie
would be sent home in a cab with their finds while John went on
to Denmark Hill. In November John wrote to Mrs Gray that Effie
was more cheerful and strong than he had known her since their marriage and she had been able to go out to several dinners (*without*
him—much to his content and profit). He encouraged her to see her
friends to keep her from fretting over her incapability of doing any
serious work—in his opinion the worst symptom of her illness. All
the same he hoped she would not spend another season in London
and felt she would only be well in a country home with the exercise
she loved.

For New Year, 1851, she went on her own to stay with Lady de
Salis at Dewley Court, Uxbridge. This lady and her charming
family, who each thought the other perfection, had been introduced to Effie by Lady Charlemont. She was the third wife, and
widow, of Count Jerome de Salis, a Count of the Holy Roman
Empire though a British subject. Effie went to two local balls
while she was there and thoroughly enjoyed herself in this happy,
informal, family atmosphere.

John gave her instructions to refuse all invitations for him until the
season started when he would be obliged to go out with her a little,
so she went out alone or with Lady Charlemont; she was always sure
now of meeting people she knew wherever she went. She would not
accept any invitations, however, unless she had been properly introduced to her hostess and John had also been invited, even though he
did not go. The convenience of having Effie alone must have added
to her success. A pretty, lively, intelligent, respectable young woman
who was willing to go out without her husband would have been a

godsend to any hostess. Moreover, she could always be relied upon to pull her weight, whereas John, unless his interest was particularly engaged, could be a great boor at a party.

In February she decided to give a series of At Homes at Park Street every Friday from 9 to 11 p.m., beginning on the 28th and continuing through the whole of March. She had 'such a quantity of clever and nice acquaintances' she told her mother that she was sorry she had 'not more room to make them meet together'. These parties were a great success and about thirty people came on each occasion, and stayed till midnight. (Dickens and Thackeray were among those asked to the first party but they were unable to come.) Effie, herself, made the tea and had coffee handed round by Melina and George. She wrote that John enjoyed himself very much but that she found the parties fatiguing.

On March 3 the first volume of *The Stones of Venice* appeared, simultaneously with John's anti-Puseyite pamphlet *Notes on the Construction of Sheepfolds*. Effie's only comment on *The Stones* was that it made a handsome book. Later that month she complained that much of her time was taken up sitting to G. F. Watts and Thomas Richmond (George Richmond's little known younger brother) for her portrait. Mr Ruskin had commissioned both these pictures which were exhibited in that year's Academy.[1] It was after this exhibition that Ruskin undertook his defence of the Pre-Raphaelites which brought him into touch with Millais.

On April 3 Effie and John attended a Drawing Room at Buckingham Palace together. Soon afterwards they went to stay at Cambridge

---

[1] Effie described the Watts picture, for which Mr Ruskin paid forty guineas, as 'a masterly drawing' and 'a grand sketch in chalks the size of life'. It is now at Wightwick Manor, Wolverhampton, occupied by Lady Mander. For the other portrait Mr Ruskin gave Thomas Richmond £20 in wine. According to Clare Stuart Wortley, Thomas Richmond's picture was given to Charlotte Ker, who took it with her when she went to live near Bath where she died. She had promised to leave it to Mary Millais, but never did. It seems more likely that it was the earlier picture by Thomas Richmond, painted in December, 1848, (see p. 28), which was given to Charlotte, for it is hardly conceivable that Effie could have taken the commissioned picture with her when she left John, nor that Mr Ruskin would have sent it to her after she left. We do not know what became of it, however, except that it was hanging at Denmark Hill while John and Effie were in Venice for the second time. The publishers would be grateful for any information about either of these Richmond pictures.

with Dr Whewell, the Master of Trinity, and then on to the Francis Fawkes's at Farnley Hall near Leeds. Mr Fawkes's father had been one of Turner's earliest patrons, and John, during the few days he was at Farnley, helped to re-hang two hundred Turner pictures. From there they went for twenty-four hours to Badger where they found all three Cheney brothers.

On Thursday, May 1, soon after their return to London, came the opening of the Great Exhibition. Mr Ruskin had procured a season ticket for Effie which enabled her to attend the opening. Even without John, who refused to go, she reported that she had three gentlemen to look after her whereas most gentlemen had four ladies apiece, and a wonderful view from the judge's stand where she could hear every word of the Queen's speech.

On this same day, John, at Denmark Hill, was writing in his diary: 'All London is active and some part of all the world & I am sitting in my quiet room, hearing the birds sing, and about to enter on the true beginning of the second part of my Venetian work. May God help me to finish it—to His glory, and man's good.'

At the end of May, Mr and Mrs Gray and George came to London to see the Exhibition and stayed until July, so we have no record of Effie's activities during that time except for one letter to Rawdon Brown. Her parents stayed with her at Park Street. She had warned them that they would not be very comfortable although she could offer them the luxury of a cold bath, presumably from the spring in her kitchen. To Brown she wrote on June 2 that she was going out very little as John was too busy to take her. 'I am very sorry not to take so great an opportunity as I have now of seeing a little of London life but Mr Ruskin dislikes it so very much that I suppose I never shall at present. I am sorry, as I am yet young and enjoy myself very much, but I suppose it is better for me not to have every thing my own way & it is very kind taking me to Venice which I love a thousand times more than I ever could this place.' Yet John complained vehemently to his father when they got to Venice that it would take him six months to recover from the social life and late nights of London.

As early as April Effie was asking Mr Brown if he could recommend suitable furnished rooms for them in Venice from the first week in September until March. John did not intend to stay again at the

Danieli as it was too uncomfortable and expensive, but was leaving all the arrangements to her as he did not want to be troubled. Mr Brown suggested rooms in the Casa Wetzlar which the Baroness was willing to let for six months. In a later letter he gave particulars of four other sets of rooms but on the whole advised 'the Wetzlar' as the Baroness could keep them *au courant* with what was going on and it was nearer the Piazza than the others. It was these rooms they decided to take.

Then, in the middle of July, Rawdon Brown himself turned up in London to see the Exhibition, and stayed with the Cheneys at 4 Audley Square. It was the first time for fourteen years that he had been in London and he was enchanted with everything, except the weather, and found everyone so improved. Effie took him to the Exhibition and sat with him in Kensington Gardens. John was at Malvern with his parents and Rawdon Brown was the only man she allowed into Park Street while he was away—an uncertain compliment. Brown went back to Venice before they left London to get everything comfortable for them.

Effie and John had now been home fifteen months and there had been no further deterioration in Effie's relationship with the old people. If anything they were getting on better, and if Mr Ruskin did send any letters to Perth abusing her they have not survived. He often gave her little presents,[1] took her to concerts and to The Trafalgar at Greenwich where they dined off 'a whitebait'—a variety of fish dishes, of which whitebait was only one, served together, most appetisingly arranged. Mr Ruskin was very proud of Effie's success, though later he was to criticise the flamboyance of her taste in dress. On one occasion when she dined with Admiral (later Sir Houston) Stewart to meet three Cabinet Ministers, John called for her at half past ten, before the gentlemen left the dining-room, so that she had no chance of being presented to these eminent men, none of whom had sat next to her at dinner. Mr Ruskin was very angry at her missing this opportunity and said that John was never to call for her again. Her comment on this to her mother was, 'Just fancy the touch of pride.'

It was evidently her mother who offered gently admonitory advice

---

[1] In his account-book is noted for May, 1851: 'Effie's birthday £10'. She does not tell her mother that he gave her this sum. The year before he had given her only a guinea.

about her behaviour, for Effie wrote to her shortly before setting out for Venice: 'What you say is perfectly true and I am so peculiarly situated as a married woman that being much alone and most men thinking that I live quite alone I am more exposed to their attentions, but I assure you I never allow such people to enter the house and stop everything of the kind which might be hurtful to my reputation and I would not for the sake of improving any person destroy or impare the only fortune I possess, viz—a good name—which if you inquired here amongst the people calculated to know you would find that I had never been spoken about with anyone—if I was, the most respectable women in London would certainly not give me their daughters to Chaperone, and although you think me unsuspicious I am quite quick enough to see, observe or hear if any one thought lightly of my conduct. I know quite well that George [her brother] has been gossiping to you about Clare [Ford] as Mr Furnivall did to him. I soon got to the bottom of that & the result nothing at all excepting that John was very angry with Mr Furnivall for putting such ideas into George's head, merely thinking him jealous of Clare, whom he does not know & cannot indure.'

Effie's indignation against George in this letter did not prevent his believing for the rest of his life that John had deliberately tried to compromise Effie with Clare Ford. On May 3, 1910, when he was eighty-one, he was writing to his niece, Mrs Stuart Wortley, when sending her the Bowerswell letters, 'yr father's [Millais's] letters, some of which I have just looked at, show JR up as a proper scoundrel. I supposed as much before your Father came on the scene for both in Italy in Venice & in Park St with Clare Ford as a frequent visitor his (JR'S) schemes were very apparent & your Mother was quite aware of them.'[1] Effie's own words seem to refute this accusation completely.

On Monday, August 4, they set out for Paris. It was the end of their life in Park Street. This time they took no carriage of their own, and no friend to keep Effie company, but they had with them Effie's new maid, Mary, as well as George Hobbs. Effie also took her riding habit and 'a nice saddle and bridle' in the hope of getting some riding in Switzerland and Venice. The old Ruskins were very distressed at John going off for six montbs. He wrote to his father from Boulogne

[1] From unpublished letter in the Bowerswell Papers.

on the first evening, 'I was very sorry to leave my mother & you: and would not have done so for any pleasure of mine: nor of Effie's, which is the same thing. But I think I ought to finish my book & I cannot finish it properly but at Venice.'

All John's letters to his father on this journey (and he wrote practically every day) have survived and are now at Yale. Whenever a letter of his written from Venice is quoted, it is from J. L. Bradley's edition published by Yale University Press. Mr Ruskin wrote almost as often, but only comparatively few of his letters have been preserved. They are now at the Ruskin Galleries, Bembridge, and the extracts quoted from them have never before been published.

Effie from the portrait in chalks by G. F. Watts, exhibited in the Royal Academy, 1851

Effie in 1860 , bust by J. E. Boehm

Drawing of Effie by G. F. Watts in 1851

*First photograph of Effie,
taken in London by
daguerrotype in 1851*

John Ruskin in 1853, from a drawing by J. E. Millais

John James Ruskin in 1848, from a picture by George Richmond given by Mr. Ruskin to his son as a wedding present

The only known picture of Mrs. J. J. Ruskin, from a portrait by James Northcote painted in 1825

The Verona-Venice train, carrying a private carriage, crossing the post road at Mestre

The first train arrives in Venice at the new station, in 1846

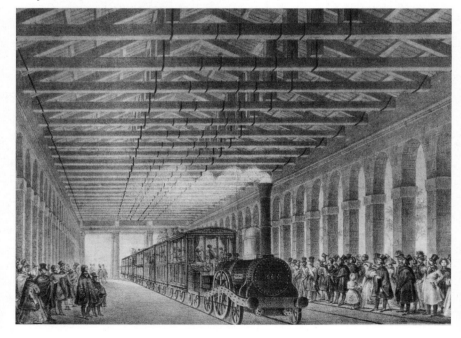

Adam and Eve on the corner of the Doge's Palace: daguerrotype from Ruskin's collection, probably taken by his manservant Crawley under Ruskin's supervision

The Danieli in Effie's time. The Ruskins' sitting-room windows are at the far end of the prin-cipal floor. From a drawing by G. Pividor. Right: the hall of the Danieli as it looked towards the end of the nineteenth century.

The Casa Wetzlar in 1851, now the Gritti Palace Hotel. Effie's 'dear little room, four feet square, built in one of the balconies' is on the right of the main floor. The Ruskins occupied the whole floor except for the room on the left.

1848: in St Mark's Square

Above, the bombardment of Venice in 1849, with Paulizza's balloons visible in the sky and seen from Mestre (below)

*The Grand Duke Constantine in 1850.
'He was in Russian uniform which is
hideous . . . those who wear it look as
if they have no neck at all.*

*The Grand Duchess Constantine in
1850. 'Youth and refinement and considerable beauty.' (Ruskin)*

The Fenice Theatre during a performance in 1851. 'Having a box at the Opera is the cheapest way for all to see people and society.'

The scene of the Emperor's arrival in Venice as described by Effie in February 1852

*The Emperor Franz Josef in 1849.
'The Emperor is very like his
portrait, a tall fair young man.'*

*Field Marshal Radetzky in 1849.
'Much better looking than I
expected and a perfect wonder
for his age.'*

PART
TWO

THE SECOND JOURNEY

 ✌

In Paris, where John and Effie stayed at a little hotel at No. 3 Rue Mont Thabord, the Meurice being full up, they were joined by Charles Newton of the British Museum, an old Christ Church friend, and the Rev. Daniel Moore, of the Campden Chapel, Camberwell, who were to go with them to Switzerland. After two nights in Paris they took the recently opened railroad to Sens and then to Dijon from where they posted to Champagnole. There they ran into Mr and Mrs Pritchard with whom they had stayed for a few days in August, 1850. John Pritchard was M.P. for Bridgnorth and a rich landowner in Shropshire; his wife was a sister of Osborne Gordon, Ruskin's private tutor at Oxford. The whole party went on to Chamonix together, stopping at Les Rousses and Geneva on the way.

Montanvert,[1] 15th August [Friday], 1851

My dear Mama

You will be rather astonished to see the date of my letter. I asked for one from you at Geneva but was disappointed in not getting any. I hope however to hear of you at Vevey where however we shall not be till Wednesday next [20th] as we have to return to Geneva to pick up our clothes which we left to wash there. Geneva was looking most beautiful, and while there I got a very nice English mare to ride on which, after many assurances of its safety, John allowed me to have. I rode to Bonneville [about eighteen miles] and enjoyed it exceedingly as the animal

---

[1] The starting-point of many climbing expeditions above Chamonix. The inn where the Ruskins were staying was built in 1840 to supersede the eighteenth-century *Temple de la Nature*, one of the oldest refuges in the Alps, which has been preserved as a national monument. The shell of Effie's inn can still be seen. It is a stone bungalow consisting of four bedrooms, dining-room and kitchen.

was exceedingly quiet and only annoyed by the flies & a very
bad cold which made it sneeze continually. Next morning we
started at seven for St. Martin's and, it being rather early for
me to ride, George mounted on my saddle to go on for half an
hour. We came up to him on the road and found him without
his cap, the horse having run away with him and when he got
it stopped, after many frantic efforts of pulling the Bridles round
the saddle, he got off in a most dreadful fright. I did not
believe in the least that it was any thing in the horse, which
perhaps had been stung & set off, & then George being afraid
of falling off had irritated its mouth exceedingly, for Mr
Newton rode it to Clues and said it never moved out of the way
with him. I would then have ridden it but I found with
George's adventure that the saddle had skinned all its back, and
being in delicate health I thought it more prudent to send it
back as it might have got worse and then we might have had
more trouble. I was very sorry as it was so nice riding behind
the carriage and seeing the country which is more lovely just
now with the vines at their brightest green, the flowers in
every garden, Hops & every kind of fruit getting ripe.

We left St. Martin's and arrived at Chamouni in time for the
Table D'Hote [at the Hotel de l'Union] at two. We found Couttet had started on a Course of a fortnight round Mont Blanc &
Monte Rosa with Sir R. Peel, who enjoys a very bad reputation
in these parts as a few years ago he lost in Gambling at Chamouni
to the Master of the Casino 25,000 francs, and the man, having
several times asked payment, Sir R. Peel said that if his Father
knew that he had this debt in addition to others he would dis-
inherit him and prayed of him to let it stand until he had some
money in his own hands. The man said he would destroy the
paper and trust to his honor. Wh[en] his Father died the man
wrote and received [no] answer, and last week when he came here
and the man met him, Sir R. declared he did not know him &
had never seen him & did not owe him a farthing, when they
had a complete row and the man spoke so to him that he had
not a word to say excepting that he would revenge himself on
him.[1]

[1] The 3rd Baronet (1822-95) had been Secretary of Legation in Switzerland
and was now M.P. for his famous father's constituency of Tamworth.

When Couttet heard John was coming he tried to get off his engagement but could not, and after our dinner John set off by way of the Glacier des Bossons with Mr Moore and Mr Newton, & I came up on a Mule[1] with Judith Couttet. I found John had nearly killed with fatigue his friends who were drinking Brandy & water and Mr Newton calling him an enragé. We slept here all night and were only disturbed by a storm of thunder & lightning very fine indeed. Today the gentlemen went an Excursion to the Aiguilles above and left me to go to Chamouni at four with Judith if the weather continued fine. If not, I was with them to sleep here again, but it is a splendid day & I have been sitting outside the house working on the bank surrounded by Goats and watching the people coming up in such quantities as makes it quite an Exhibition of the Nations. Mr & Mrs Pritchard are also just come up and are now on the Mer de Glace. Albert Smith and two other artists ascended Mont Blanc the day before yesterday & had a most splendid excursion, not a cloud in the sky and they slept in their Plaids on the snow and found it so warm that they had to open them to get air. They sketched at every point and are now returning to Lecture on the Cocknies ascent of the Mountain....

Albert Smith, then aged thirty-four, the son of a Chertsey doctor, had abandoned medicine for writing, drawing and lecturing. He made his high-spirited ascent of Mont Blanc on the 12th-13th August in the company of three other Englishmen he had fallen in with, sixteen guides, eighteen porters, a number of volunteers who had joined them and a vast quantity of wines, spirits and provisions. The party descended by various routes, some sliding, some skating and some rolling down, to be greeted by all Chamonix with triumphal music and flowers—the cost of which was added to their bill of 2,338 francs. On his return to London, Smith proved a clever publicist for both himself and Chamonix with lectures at the Egyptian Hall in Piccadilly, an illustrated book on the exploit and even a

---

His father had been thrown from his horse on Constitution Hill on June 29, 1850, and on July 2 died from his injuries.

[1] It then took two and a half hours to reach Montanvert on a mule. Now the journey is done in twenty minutes by mountain railway.

highly successful 'New Game of the Ascent of Mont Blanc', rather like Ludo. In 1857 he accompanied the Prince of Wales to Chamonix; three years later he died after a short illness.

The Ruskins returned on the 19th to Geneva where Mr Moore and the Pritchards left them, and next day went to Vevey by boat. Effie wrote home from Vevey but the letter has not survived. On July 9 she had written to her mother from Park Street describing a day spent at Dawley with the de Salis's and some young friends: 'A number of them were talking of the various routes they intended taking for the summer and the most said they intended to be at Vevey the 1st week in August to see the Fête des Vignerons which only happens once in twenty years. We intended to be there just at that time and when I came home I told John I would like to set out a couple of days sooner as he was anxious to see it also, but when I inadvertently mentioned that some people I knew were to be there he vows that nothing will persuade him to go, and got quite into a bad humour because the English even went to the places he is fond of which he says they have not the slightest business to do as they do not enjoy the Country. I said, "But you ought first to turn out the Swiss for they do not care about the beauty of the Alps at all but English travellers do and you need not see more of the English than you like." He said "Oh! you collect such a quantity of people about you wherever you go that I am determined I won't be bothered in my pet places", so I suppose we shall miss it altogether.'
Evidently they did miss it as they were not there until the third week. This festival is still held every twenty-five years. The next will be in 2005.

Aosta [Piedmont], 24th August, 1851
My dearest George
I hope you have not thought me unkind in not writing to you before but I could not as I have been so much occupied. We have had several interesting days from Vevey to the St. Bernard— which we descended from yesterday. I had rather a hard day from Martigny to the Hospice, first five hours of Char a Banc[1] and

---

[1] The char-à-banc road went as far as Liddes; thereafter the road was impracticable for any sort of vehicle. The carriage road was not completed until 1893 on the Swiss side and 1905 on the Italian side.

then five hours to the Hospice on Mules, John walking and Mr Newton and myself riding, but we were well repaid for the trouble, the scenery is so beautiful.... The monk received us very kindly and soon after we had souper, which, being a maigre day [Friday, 22nd] we had soup with milk, macaroni, salt fish, fritters and very bad wine. We all agreed the establishment was going to the dogs. The place was filthily dirty, so were the dogs, and the smell was like a kennel. We got fleas and I was starved with cold. The monks were delighted to get me to play the most unclerical tunes on the piano and said they would be glad if we would dance, for in fact it was Liberty Hall and we could do what we liked.[1] The Gentians were growing beautifully blue but the place was so deserted that I could not live there a month I think at the very most.

We descended to this place yesterday. Very hot it was getting into the Valley.... John says this town is improved but the number of Cretins and Goitred persons is perfectly dreadful, every fifth person I should say was one or other of these or both, and not with bad expressions but very horrible notwithstanding. We saw a couple of children's funerals. I never saw anything so dreadful; the little Coffins where the children lay were covered over with Weddingcake finery and little boys as bearers. A fat Priest led the way with the Cross and was followed by a quantity of Cretins and horried looking men and women, all looking as happy and goodnatured as could be and laughing like anything....

They stayed two nights at Aosta, the 24th being a Sunday, a day on which they never travelled if they could help it. The night of the 25th was spent at Ivrea.

[1] John wrote on the 23rd: 'Effie & the monks got on capitally—& she made one of them play and *sing*—I was afraid we should have more banishments to the Simplon.' This, of course, refers to Father Barras who was banished to the Simplon for dancing with a lady at Geneva. According to Murray the room at the Hospice appropriated to visitors was large and convenient and 'hung with many drawings and prints, presents sent by travellers in acknowledgement of the kind attention which they have received from the brethren. A piano was among the presents thus sent, from a lady.' This piano, on which Effie played, came from Amédée Thibout & Cie of Paris. It has now been relegated to the sewing-room in favour of one presented by Edward VII.

Vercelli, 26th August

Dearest Mama

I hope you got my last letter from Vevey telling you how much
I admired it. Since then we have got on very well, crossing the
St. Bernard, sleeping at the Hospice which we found unusu-
ally full and very cold, and a question arose as to where Mr
Newton was to be stowed away and whether in the same room
with George Hobbs, when one of the Monks proposed by way
of solving the difficulty that the Le Domestique of Monsieur
should occupy the same room with *La* Domestique of Madame
so as to give Mr N a room to himself. We informed the worthy
Monk that such things were not done in our country which he
seemed rather surprized at.[1]

Mr Newton left us at Ivrea this morning being obliged to go
as far as Turin [capital of Sardinia] to get a passport to go to
Milan tomorrow with us. What a bother these passports are.
John is turning Republican he is so disgusted with the useless-
ness of them.[2] We came all through the Val D'Aosta yesterday.
The beauty of the Valley is not overrated.... I never saw such
Luxuriance in Nature, but the people are monstrous & horrible. How they keep their Land so perfect is a marvel. Here it
is different. The people in this fine old town are pure Italian,
walking about with large green fans because of the heat. I
never feel the heat. I am much stronger—fancy me getting up
yesterday at 3 1/2 and not stopping till 7, and today again from
10 to 5, with very hot sun. I wear a white dress and a large round
straw hat which I got at Geneva. Young Italy here were much

---

[1] John wrote on November 8 about Mary, the maid: 'Just fancy her fixing
the great St Bernard as the place, of all she has seen—where she would most
like to live! And yet there was nothing even of the usual look about the
place— it was dirty—doggish—commonplace—Even *I* was not sorry to find
myself on the way down.' Murray tells us that the Hospice was 'capable of
accomodating 70 or 80 travellers with beds'.

[2] John wrote on November 16: 'Effie says, with some justice—that I am
a great conservative in France—because there everybody is radical—and a
great radical in Austria, because there everybody is conservative. I suppose
that one reason why I am so fond of fish—(as creatures I mean, not as eating)
is that they always swim with their heads against the stream. I find it for
me the healthiest position.'

astonished at me this evening so that at Milan I must, I think, modify my Costume. In five days more we shall D.V. be at Venice....

The letter from Effie announcing their arrival in Venice is missing, but we know from John's letters that after staying two nights in Milan, one in Brescia and two in Verona, they arrived in Venice on the evening of Monday, September 1. There they were greeted with the news of Paulizza's death. He had died in July but it is not until Effie's letter of October 27 that we hear any details of his death. It must have come as a complete surprise to her. On March 25 she had written from Park Street to her mother, 'I had two most charming letters from Paulizza yesterday, one in Italian and the other in German. He says his eyes are much better and he has a great deal to do as he is made Inspection Officer of San Francesco della Vigna.' And in April she received another long letter from him, the last.

The Ruskins stayed with Rawdon Brown at the Casa Businello until September 9 when they moved into the Casa Wetzlar (now the Gritti Hotel). They had not intended to stay with Mr Brown but were having a fight with the Baroness over an extra room for John to work in, and looked at other lodgings until she agreed to give it to them. Their rooms in the Casa Wetzlar were on the first floor on the side nearest the mouth of the Grand Canal. The Baroness's own rooms were on the same floor, on the other side. Their rooms comprised a study, a hall dining-room, a drawing-room thirty feet long, double bedroom and dressing room, and, on the ground floor, three servants' rooms and a kitchen, all for £17 a month. (These details we know from John's letter of September 24 which also gives a plan of their accommodation.) The drawing-room and study looked on to the Grand Canal, and the bedroom on to the Rio dell' Albero, the canal which divides the Palazzo from what is now the Grand Hotel. There was a water entrance on this canal which can still be seen but is no longer in use. The land entrance gave then, as it does now, on to the Campo Santa Maria Zobenigo.

Casa Businello, 7th September

My dearest Mama

I was very much relieved by the receipt of your letter yesterday because we were getting very anxious about every body, not having any from Mr Ruskin until today when there is an agreeable letter from him also and now our minds are at rest on that point, but John went fancying all manner of improbabilities, not one under that his father or his mother must be exceedingly ill &c and would listen neither to Mr Brown nor myself when we said the contrary....[1]

We are not sure yet whether the Young Emperor intends coming or not but great preparations are being made for a sort of military Fete at Verona on the 15th for which the music [the band] has gone from here and most of the Soldiers too for Venice is very quiet and yet generally improved. The place is cleaner and the Literature sold on the Porch of St. Mark's Church is of a purely religious character. We have got our rooms at Mdme. Wetzlar's and will be into them in a few days. Some of our things have come from England and a most important piece of furniture for the winter will I fear turn out a failure. John said in London that he would buy the Grate which Mr Brown recommended we should have for our room. Out it has come and such a thing! It proves that talents have been wisely distributed and that a man who can write the 7 Lamps is not fit to choose a fire grate. It is so small that one could nearly put it in one's pocket and John now confesses he bought it for old iron and it only cost 5/- without any fender, poker or tongs! Fortunately before leaving I said to Mr Ruskin that I thought he had better send a second one for our bedroom so that I hope it will be more useful than this one is likely to prove.

The cook here [Nani] also is to be our cook and comes to us so many times a day providing every thing himself for so much per day. I have got a servant named Beppo who is my valet or any thing, row the prow oar and is to do any thing from roasting coffee to sweeping the rooms out, in fact to work at every thing that is required. Carlo is John's man and is the Stern Oar. We have to dress them, which we do in dark blue cloth with red waistcoats and Fez caps. Their wages are not very high, 16d a day each, but making our arrangements with the aid of Mr

---

[1] It appears from John's own letters that he was quite ill with fretting at not hearing from his father. The reason for the delay was that they had changed their route and gone faster to Venice than they had intended. When Mr Ruskin heard of John's anxiety he suffered it all over again himself.

Brown's experience, the saving of cheating and story telling is immense, for every one here respects you in proportion to the way you keep yourself from being taken in, but they are so polite and nice that it is easy to forget that & so spoil them which John invariably does [2]....

Before getting into the apartment John had written: 'The quantities of questions about bills and kitchens and beds and things of which I know nothing are inconceivable,' to which Mr Ruskin replied most unjustly, 'These questions surely should be Effie's & the maids & George's affairs not yours—unless Effie takes to a little Housewifery & Housekeeping you will find living abroad a sad bore & taking House worse than Hotels. Foreigners are too sharp not to see who are managers & will pluck you dreadfully.' One hopes John had the tact not to show this to Effie.

[2] John wrote on September 24: 'Effie cannot succeed in getting her gondoliers to dress well—This is much my fault—unavoidable, as I keep one of them lounging about all day with the boat wherever [I] may happen to want it—and this spoils both his clothes and his habits.'

AT HOME IN VENICE

∾

Dearest Mama

I received a second letter from you today.... We are now fairly established in our house, and the occupation and managing and seeing about every thing has been such hard work that I think I have been all the better for it and my arrangements are now getting completed. Mary I find very useful and ready to do anything. She & I together have made a whole set of curtains for my bedroom of muslin which I cut out, and the edges lined with Pink calico, festooned and hung in festoons, looks very pretty indeed. The Drawing room is a beautiful large room with windows and Balconies on the Grand Canal and it is nice and warm in the morning, and tomorrow we have received orders to hang out Curtains and Tablecloths all along the Canal and make it look as gay as possible [for the Emperor's visit].

10th. This morning we were awoke by the Cannon firing and shaking every house in Venice which must do a great deal of harm to the Ducal Palace. I was up at six, and about eight I went into the Square and getting up to the first Storey of the Campanile I got outside, where I commanded a splendid view of the whole Square lined with troops, and St. Mark's, before which were lying purple cushions. Immediately after the young Emperor stepped out of the Church and attended by all the clergy in their purple robes and his magnificent suite they then received the benediction of the Patriarch, every one being on their knees as well as himself. It was a beautiful & impressive sight. The troops then defiled before him and he stood out touching his hat to every officer that saluted him as he passed. Radetzky stood beside him all the time, and his magnificent Jaegers wearing scarlet dresses & Polish hats with white cloaks

lined with fur and embroidered in gold thrown over their
shoulders. The Emperor is very like his portrait, a tall fair
young man of 20,[1] a very handsome figure, tall & straight,
walks remarkably well & has very neat feet. His face is pleasing and from the way he moved about and spoke to people he
appeared to have very easy affable manners. We then got into
our Gondola and accompanied him in company with thousands of Gondolas to the Railway when he went to Verona to
meet, it is said, nearly all the Princes in Italy for a very important congress the result of which will appear shortly. The
Reviews for him at Verona are to be on a very grand scale
including 40,000 Troops & Artillery. Many of the Gondoliers
were very gay in their dress this morning with bright blue Jackets and sashes with gold ends hanging down and white
Trowsers....

We had the Dean of St. Paul's,[2] Mrs Milman and their son to
tea last night, and Mr Cheney and his nephew Mr Capel Cure.
Mr Brown did not come because he thought I had asked Lady
Sorell a woman he dislikes, which certainly I had never dreamt
of doing. Charlotte will recollect her, and as Lord Glenelg
wrote to her about me she called on me.[3] I have not made any
acquaintances and my next door neighbour whose Palace window look into my room curiously enough happens to be the

[1] He was in fact twenty-one, having been born August 18, 1830.

[2] Henry Hart Milman was Dean of St Paul's from 1849 until his death in
1868. In 1824 he had married Mary Ann Cockell. Effie had first met them
in May, 1848, when Milman was rector of St Margaret's, Westminster, and
had written home that it was a capital introduction. They were extremely
kind to her after she got back to London in 1852 and gave her two of the
coveted places in St Paul's for the Duke of Wellington's funeral. They remained staunch to her through the annulment, never having cared for
John, who abused St Paul's to the Dean.

[3] Lady Sorell, born of an old French family, was the widow of Lt.-Col. Sir
Thomas Sorell who, from 1834 to 1846 (when he died, aged sixty-nine), had
been British Consul-General to the Lombardo-Venetian Kingdom. She
lived in Venice and had two daughters. Charles Grant, Lord Glenelg (1778-
1866), had held various minor appointments until his retirement on a
pension in 1839. He was created a baron in 1831. Effie had met him dining
with Sir Robert Inglis (M.P. for Oxford University) in December, 1848. He
hesitated to take sides when she left John, but eventually wrote her a
sympathetic letter.

Countess Wimpffen but she is in London seeing the Exhibition. I have got a beautiful Piano and a Master to teach me to
Model. John has just been reading to me his account of the
Emperor this morning. I have desired him to send it to Perth
for it is so like him. He was so sulky at the whole thing and
always is at every thing of the kind that it is rather amusing to
hear his remarks, for I don't mind his growling at all; it doesn't
do any body any harm....[1]

Casa Wetzlar, 19th Septr.

Dearest George
    Many thanks for your nice long letter.... We are so com-
fortable that really I am quite astonished in how little time we
have got everything in order, and go on quietly with our different employments. I take the entire charge of the accounts and
John has nothing to do but go on with his work. I find that one
can live here as comfortably and even luxuriously upon very
much less than in London, and much better in every way.[2] I pay
in addition [to] a Donna and two Gondoliers, a modelling
Master for myself three times a week who teaches me to make
at present ears & toes, and the Cook I pay 16 Zwanzigers a day
to, or 11/-; for this he feeds Mary & George, a dish at breakfast
for us, two at Luncheon, & then our dinner at 5, which is
every day varied in the most wonderful manner. Yesterday we
had 1st, Macaroni soup; 2nd, fish of Tunny; 3rd, small leg of
Mutton; 4th, cold veal in jelly beautifully made; 5th, sweetbreads
fried; 6th, roasted Larks & Blackbirds; 7th, sort of Spanish
Fritters—and every day this sort of thing, and he leaves us to Cook

---

[1] John described Radetzky and the Emperor going about together 'looking just like a great white baboon and a small brown monkey; a barrel organ
would have made the thing complete'. Mr Ruskin was 'gladdened by' his
'delightful account of the Emperor's arrival'.

[2] John was writing on September 26 that Effie thought their household
expenses would come to 800 francs (£32) a month, which, although rather
more than he expected, was still much less than at Danieli's. In the following January he wrote, '... I thought "living in lodgings" in Venice would be
so delightfully cheap that I need not mind paying a good rent for the
rooms—It turns out much the same as Park St. I am especially puzzled
because it seems to cost nearly as much as when we had Miss Ker with us
and two carriages and lived at an hotel.'

Mr Brown's dinner so that he only takes half an hour to get
Mr Brown's ready and ours about an hour.

We rise at 7 and I do Italian with John till 9 when we breakfast which Mary prepares, Beppo bringing in fruit, milk and
ice for the butter. These things cost little, a dish of figs 2d, of
grapes and Peaches which serve for Desert. After breakfast John
reads Pope or something else; at 10 we have Prayers; at 11 I
model and practice or work. I go out after Lunch & John is
out all day till 5. After dinner we go into the Square at 7 and
sit or walk hearing the Music and meeting Mr Brown & Mr
Cheney....

You would hear of Paulizza's death from my former letter to
Mama [the first missing letter]. I suppose the wound in his
head was the cause. I do not know when it happened or where
but I hope he died at home and was cared for by his Mother
to whom he was devotedly attached. I have no doubt his
melancholy temperament had a good [deal] to do with hasten-
ing his end as he was so convinced that he was not to live. I
am very glad you like my picture....

This picture, now belonging to Mr Raoul Millais, was 'a small and
very finely finished drawing', as Effie described it, which Watts
had made of her at the same time as the portrait exhibited in the 1851
Academy. She had sent her mother a daguerreotype of this drawing
for her birthday on March 17 and, shortly before she left London,
the drawing itself for safe-keeping. Ruskin wrote on September 21:
'Watt's Effie is lent to her father until we come back—and we hear
it is much admired by everybody and thought quite perfect—I
should have fancied it would have been too fine for them.' And on
November 10, 1852, he was writing to Mr Gray: 'I am glad you like
Watt's sketch of Effie. It is very sweet & very like, but does not satisfy
me in the least. He had from the beginning a false ideal of her face—
which depends on colour even more than on form, and will never
be properly done till the *eyebrows* are as much cared for as the eyes.'
Nevertheless Mr Ruskin wrote that he would give the large one for
the small one. The large one he described as 'like a befloured miller,
or a baker, who has seen a ghost'.[1]

[1] See plates 1 and 3.

Casa Wetzlar
Sta. Maria Zobenigo
[*Postmarked 22 Sept., 1851*].

Dearest Mama

... John has gone as usual to Murano and draws there till dinner-time....[1] Mr Brown & Mr Cheney were here yesterday. They have been going four nights to see Rachel in Les Horace & Phèdre and think her very grand. They wanted me very much to go and John offered to give me a Box and ask Lady Sorell to Chaperone me, but I did not encourage him unless he had offered to go himself and then I might have cared, but Rachel they say is such a very bad person and although only 32 she looks much older and is killing herself by drinking gin to excess. I thought her very pretty in London this year but she looked what Lady Ruthven called her "a beautiful shadow" or more correctly to my idea a pale shadow.[2]

I am much obliged to Lord Glenelg for letting me know Lady Sorell. She talks a little too much and for that reason, as Mr Brown says, you would not make her yr. bosom friend but she has, as Mr Brown says, always conducted herself with the greatest propriety and she knows everybody in Venice and is a very proper person to take me anywhere, to tell me the shops, where to get things and what to do, which is invaluable as an Englishwoman sees things with such different eyes to a foreigner, and being resident here always knows the people and their ways so that she is of use to me in many little ways & is charmed to help me in anything.[3] She introduced me the other day to

---

[1] A whole chapter of Volume II of *The Stones* is devoted to Murano.

[2] Rachel was appearing at the Teatro San Benedetto. She was then only thirty and was already ill with consumption. She had had a two-month engagement in London that summer ending on July 29, but Effie must have seen her during the period when her parents were staying in London and there were no letters from her.

[3] Lady Sorell had more birth than rank, according to John, and although the kindest person in the world, found her chief pleasure in life in knowing everybody who *ought* to be known. She had a jointure of £570 a year out of which she managed to save £50, but had incurred a debt of £200 when she was turned out of her house in Venice during the revolution and forced to get another in Trieste. All this we know from John's letter of May 16, 1852. She went out of her mind in 1854 as a result of financial worry and grief over the death of a daughter, but subsequently recovered.

Marshall Marmont who I talked some time with, a wonderfully young man considering his years and the time that has elapsed since the Duke beat him at Salamanca.[1]

Venice is very quiet, all the people in the Country till November. They say the Emperor returns and they have put large gas lamps in the Square, but nothing is known for certain.... I am so glad we did not go back to Danieli's. This house is so comfortable and quiet & warm, and when it gets colder they will put down carpets for us and with our coal fire we shall not feel the cold of the winter as we did in the Inn....

Casa Wetzlar, 28th Septr.

I received your letter yesterday with much pleasure and relief to my mind, but do not let three weeks elapse without writing because I can't help wondering what can be the reason of such long silence and your letters are such a pleasure to me that you cannot fancy how disappointed I felt at the end of each day's journey to the Post Office to find no letter from you—although in this instance I knew from Mr Ruskin that you were all well. He mentions having sent you John's letter also with the Emperor's visit, and you will probably have a second shortly as yesterday a notice was out saying that the Emperor is to return in a few days to stay a day or two on his way home, and that an illumination is to take place in St. Mark's Square and all the Canal Grande the same, so that we shall be put to the expence of some wax lights to do honor to the Caesar. The Fenice is also to be opened and illuminated. He has been very well received every where and his appearance, whatever John may say, is extremely in his favor with the Italians who admire exceedingly his active habits, insensibility to fatigue and his horsemanship, which are a striking contrast to the last German Emperor who was crowned amongst them, almost a Cretin and could hardly walk, but this change to the Bavarian race is thought well of and was become indispensible.

We have had the Sirocco blowing violently for two days accompanied with the heaviest showers of rain I ever saw so that this morning the sea is above water mark and it has to rise a

[1] Marmont was then seventy-eight. He had been badly wounded at the Battle of Salamanca in August, 1812.

foot and a half higher by twelve o'clock. I intend to go into
St. Mark's Place as it will probably be flooded. I go out every
afternoon to take my walk with Beppo but I find that I am
rather inconveniently placed now as to a walk for I am so much
farther off from the public gardens than I was at Danieli's and
by the time I have got to the end of the Riva I am tired
enough & want to return home. After dinner we sometimes
go out in the Gondola and row out towards the Lido....

I find that my letter to Lady Sorell will introduce me, if I
wish, into all the best society of Venice this winter and of which
I saw & knew nothing when I was here before as nearly all were
away and are just returning by degrees. The two or three that
are here have kindly requested to know me and I went yesterday and paid one or two visits, on the Countess Esterhazy who
receives all the best Austrian society. Her son [Valentin] was
attached to the embassy in London & is now Minister at
Munich. She was ill & I did not see her.[1] I then went to the
Princess Hohenlohe whose husband is cousin or something to
the Queen. She, I thought, a most charming person, with the
remains of great beauty and although no longer young has only
been married a short time and has a beautiful little child
about 18 months old. I was very much struck with the sweetness and Grace of her manners and she is so good that I
believe the people here have been indebted to her good offices
in Venetian affairs more than once as her father was Count
Thurn, 25 years Governor of Venice and died just before the
Revolution. The fate of Venice might have been very different had he lived during '48 and '49—but every one has their
trials and the Princess waits constantly on her mother who is
confined to her bed quite childish, and also a cousin who she
takes care of who is rather out of her mind, which society must
have a depressing effect on her mind. Her husband is a very
amiable like man and they said when they returned from
Trieste that they would come & see me.[2]

[1] Countess Esterhazy, born Anna Ungnad Countess Weissenwolf in 1795,
had married in 1812 Count Valentin Philip Esterhazy de Galantha of the well-
known Hungarian family. He had died in 1838.
[2] It was another branch of the family, the Hohenlohe-Langenbourgs, who
were connected with Queen Victoria through her step-sister. The Princess

Today I am going to see the Infanta of Spain by her desire as she remembered me in London and desired her Lady-in-waiting, Mlle. Garciamartia, to tell me that she would receive me at two o'clock today, so as that is a command I must go although I do not know what I am to say to her as she can only remember me as having known her husband, Don Juan, but as she thinks of nothing in the world but him I suppose she likes to see me. He is in London. She lives very quietly with her two little children, goes out to her Mass in the morning and sits entirely alone all day, but likes English Ladies to call on her....

I went and saw the Infanta at two; she is much thinner than when I saw her at Ld. Lovelace's but still graceful and very tall. She received me very kindly and said how well she remembered me and that I was dressed so and so, being in white with white roses in my hair. She begged me to take a seat beside her and as she is deaf, although quite a young person [twenty-seven], the conversation was not so interesting to me as half a dozen other stupid people were in the room and she spoke to me as much as good breeding demanded. I liked her very much and played with her pretty little boys who are between two and four years old and call[ed] Monseigneurs Alphonse and Charles. They were very prettily dressed in white frocks trimmed with coarse open-work all round the bottom and short sleeves with bare necks, large rose coloured knots at the sleeves and broad sashes, just like English children. We sat till the servant announced another visitor and then we all curtsied and she said something kind to

---

Hohenloe whom Effie met was the wife of Prince Egon Hohenloe-Waldenbourg-Schillingsfurst whom she had married in 1849. She was Thérèse, daughter of Count Thurn-Hofer-Valsassina, and had been brought up in Venice at the great Palazzo Corner. Now she lived in the lovely little Contarini-Fasan Palace on the Grand Canal, and there her husband died in 1865. Their real home was the Castle Duino, in the Bay of Panzano, north of Trieste. The Princess was thirty-four at this time and had one son, Fritz, born in August, 1850. She was so popular in Venice and so beautiful that during the revolution she went out without wearing the Italian cockade and was never insulted, although an Austrian. Her spinster cousin, Thérèse, who lived with her, had had an unhappy love affair which had partly deranged her mind.

each and we all left together, observing to walk out backwards which is easy enough without a train.[1]

When the Duchesses of Angoulême and Berry return and the Duke de Bordeaux, I shall be presented to them and it will be interesting for me to make the acquaintance of the Daughter and Daughter-in-Law of Louis XVI and Marie Antoinette, and if I had only the pen of a ready writer I would have towards the end of the winter plenty of materials to write you something very curious about all the people here who are Royal in reality although not recognised as such....[2]

I was sure you would be sorry to hear of Paulizza's death. I have not heard from his mother and do not know how to get at any information about his death. We shall never see any body like him again for wonderful intellect, great humility and the sweetest disposition. John said yesterday that he never felt surer of any one's being in Heaven, and I have the same hope. Such entire want of selfishness I have never seen in man, and the earnest desire he had for the good & happiness of others at the price of his own was only the result of this absence of self. Many things that he said & did for us I have forgotten but his love and gratitude for our friendship only make me wish we had done more for him than we did when we left Venice....

There is a letter missing between September 28 and October 10 but we know from a letter of John's to his father that Countess

---

[1] The Infanta was born Beatrix d'Este, sister of Francis V, Duke of Modena. She had married Don Juan in February, 1847. It was in May, 1850, that Effie had met her at a party at the Lovelaces, 'a handsome person in Pink silk, black lace and diamonds'. Don Juan asked to be introduced to Effie at this party. He spoke only bad French, but with the help of his attaché they had some 'very amusing conversation'. Effie addressed him as 'your highness' and he said that if ever his brother regained the throne of Spain they must come to Madrid and he would give them a suite of rooms. On the death of his brother without issue in 1861, the Carlist claims passed to him.

[2] The Duchesse d'Angoulême, then aged seventy-three, was the daughter of Louis XVI and had been imprisoned in the Temple with her parents. In 1799 she had married her cousin, the eldest son of Charles X, brother of Louis XVI. He had died in 1844, the last Dauphin of France. The Duchesse de Berry was not Louis XVI's daughter-in-law but his niece-in-law, having married Charles X's second son.

Esterhazy and Princess Hohenlohe called on Effie on the 19th and that the Infanta left her card on her on October 1. John wrote on that day: 'It is rather curious that while living in lodgings is considerably cheaper than living in a hotel, it is also so much more respectable—Effie is now looked upon as a Venetian Lady—before she was merely a traveller: and no one took any notice of her.' It seems, however, to have been the introduction to Lady Sorell, who took a great fancy to Effie, rather than the fact of living in lodgings that gave her the entrée into Venetian society.

Her account of the Emperor's second visit must be in the missing letter, but John wrote on October 3 that he came on the evening of the 29th and that they, with hundreds of others, went to the station in accordance with his express wish that everyone who had a gondola should go and meet him. The crowd of boats was such that for a quarter of an hour their gondola was pressed up against that of the Emperor.

Casa Wetzlar, 10th Oct.

Dearest Mama

... For the whole of this last week I have been suffering very much from a kind of intermitting fever common here and caused by the changeable weather from Sirocco to rain, very trying to strangers during the Autumn. I have felt quite well during the day but about one in the morning my sufferings, for really they were so, began and continued till about eight when tired out I fell into a drowsy sleep and not being able to get up & dress till 11—the symptoms were excessive sickness and diorrhea, constant internal pains & Rheumatism and shivering, no joke at all. All the middle of each night no sleep, and one night John was quite frightened for I called him out of his bed to find me fainting and moaning on the floor. At last by Lady Sorrell's advice I have taken her Doctor for she says that the fever goes on until it is checked and he is giving me Tamarinds—teas—and other slight remedies, recommending me to keep in bed and as warm as possible. I am better tonight. Mary has had the same kind of thing but I gave her some Magnesia & I have heard no more of it....

I have made the acquaintance of the English Consul and his Wife, Mrs Clinton Dawkins, who is a very pretty woman

married about a year and has a large fortune. He has also
£1200 a year for being Consul so they ought to be comfortable.[1] I also called upon the Lutheran clergyman [Mr Wittelieu]
and his wife today because I sit in his German Church &
wanted to know him, & Lady Sor[ell] took me who knows
every body here. Although Hungarian, they, as well as every
body here, think the Demonstrations for Kossuth when he
arrives in England excessively wrong.[2] He has very grave faults
of character and both he & his Wife were far more personally
ambitious than Patriotic—and he is supposed to have carried
of the Crown of St Stephen which disappeared under his
temporary government. Ld. Palmerston is making the position
of the English here in Italy every day more uncomfortable and
if they can be rude to the English they are so—& thoroughly
our ministers deserve it. I have no patience with our Ministry
either in religion or Politics—and our Country is surely in a
very bad state not to be able to furnish a more upright man
than Ld. Palmerston to manage foreign affairs and keep up the
English Character.

Two or three days ago a Mr Gibbs brought me a letter from
Mr [Richard] Ford's niece; he is the person appointed to
succeed Mr Birch in the charge of the young Princes and has
been chosen by Prince Albert because he is a Lawyer. He is a
good looking very nice man about 30, exceedingly knowing &
well informed upon everything, very anti-puseyite and happy

[1] Clinton Dawkins was Consul-General from 1846 to 1852. All the Consuls
elected to remain in Venice throughout the siege and bombardment although
they were given the option of leaving before May 20, 1849. Unlike the
French Consul, Dawkins was decidedly pro-Austrian. Flagg recounts that
one night during the bombardment 'while lying in bed, flat on his back, a
ball not only pierced his roof and perforated two terrace-floors above him,
but incredible to relate, penetrated the coverlids and passed down between
his legs into the apartment below; and, still more incredible to relate, yet
doubtless not the less true, without inflicting on his person the slightest
injury, save a contusion, which for some time caused him to walk lame'.
[2] Lajos Kossuth (1802-94), the Hungarian revolutionary leader, had fled
to Turkey on the collapse of his insurrection in August, 1849, and was imprisoned there. He was released in September, 1851, and arrived at
Southampton on October 23. He toured England for three weeks making
speeches and, as the majority of the British public was violently anti-
Austrian, he received a hero's welcome wherever he went.

tempered.[1] I go about with him every day and he comes here
to tea as well as young Brinsley Marlay who I may have
mentioned to you in London. His sister, Lady John Manners,
is ill at Milan & he left her & her husband there while he came
here for a week.[2] He knew Mr Gibbs at Cambridge [Trinity]....

Casa Wetzlar, 14th Octr.
... We have not been doing much lately as I have been ill, but
Mr Gibbs & Mr Marlay have been almost living here for the last
week. John asked them to Lunch and take tea here every night
after the Labours of their sightseeing days were over and they
were most glad to do so.[3] Mr Gibbs is gone but Mr Marlay fell
ill with a little attack of the Fever yesterday and having got the
Doctor to dose him he says he is much better and will now possibly be able to join his mother & her party at Turin. He was
telling me rather a good thing yesterday: Mrs Loudon & her
Daughter have been here for the last week at Danieli's. You know
she is the florist who writes Botanical papers, and her Daughter I have heard of in London as rather a clever accomplished
girl who writes pretty children's stories, but is rather senti-
mental withal. Somebody had passed through here dangerous
in his opinions named *Loudon* and the Police, thinking it the
same name, stopped the Ladies' Papers and books, amongst the
rest the younger Lady's Journal, and coming in the first Page

[1] Frederick Waymouth Gibbs took up his appointment in the following
January, and strictly supervised the Prince of Wales's education for the next
seven years.

[2] Brinsley Marlay, born 1831, was the son of Lt.-Col. George Marlay. In
1847 he had inherited the entailed portion of the estates of the last Earl of
Belvedere, including Belvedere House, Mullingar. His only sister, Catherine, had married the Duke of Rutland's second son in June. They had a son
in April, 1852, and she died two years later after a long illness. It was
Thomas Richmond's portrait of Lady John Manners that decided Ruskin to
have Effie painted by him.

[3] John had his reasons for this unusual display of hospitality. '... my time
has been a little trenched upon in the evenings lately, for a gentleman was
introduced to us who is going to be Tutor to the Prince of Wales: and I
thought I might as well get some hold in that quarter—might do a great deal
of good—So I let him be asked to tea, and found him sensible—and have
given him several lectures on the Renaissance, which I think he will not
forget' (Letter of October 14).

on the name of a Hungarian noble, a refugee, thought the manuscript dangerous, and what the embarassed young Lady had never even read to *her Mother* was carefully translated into German for the Austrians who I daresay had a good laugh over its contents.[1]

The Galignani[2] of each day retails in Venice to the readers the farther progress of feeling in favor of Kossuth in London and no one conceals their disapprobation of Ld. Palmerston's conduct in permitting him to be so received. The Austrians if such things go on much longer will certainly doubt every English person & possibly a continued residence in Italy to many may become precarious....

                                  Casa Wetzlar, 20th Oct.

... Quinine & dry weather have helped to make me better but I cannot go out in the open Gondola or take any liberty with myself as these fevers come back on the slightest indiscretion, and still they do not make one look in the least ill, for though sometimes I felt as ill as ever I did in my life, I quite surprized Mr Gibbs & Mr Marlay who said they could not understand it for every day I looked quite well. We have lost them and now we have Count Strzelecki, a very clever man who first made known to Sir Roderick Murchison the probability of an Australian California. He is with Lord Overstone and going to winter at Rome with him and his family. You know I suppose that Lord O.'s only Daughter, Miss Jones Loyd, is to have three million if she marries with her Father's consent,

[1] Jane Loudon (1807-58) was the widow of John Claudius Loudon, the landscape gardener and writer on horticulture, who had died in 1843. As well as writing many books on gardens and gardening, she had edited in 1841 a weekly magazine, *The Ladies' Companion to the Flower Garden*. Her only child, Agnes, was nearly nineteen. She had published *Tales for Young People* and *Tales of School Life* in 1846 and 1849. She began keeping a journal—a tooled leather album—in 1849. After some disappointing love affairs she married Markham Spofforth. Mrs Loudon was travelling as a measure of economy, having let her London house, 3 Porchester Terrace, for two months.

[2] *Galignani's Messenger*, a daily paper in English, published in Paris, had been founded in Paris in 1814 by an Italian, Giovanni Galignani, and continued until 1904. John subscribed to it until March. Mr Ruskin wrote on May 1, 1852: 'Mama & I have treated ourselves to a Quarter of Galignani, 28/6, that we may read what you read.'

and if Strzelecki were not quite old enough to be her Father,
I would think it a capital parti for him as he is quite clever
enough to make himself very agreeable to a young Lady of
sixteen.[1]

Earl Gifford, Lord Dufferin & Sir Francis Scott are also
here.[2] I don't know the first but the two others are very
agreeable and dine with us today. Young Englishmen always
show their eccentric habits and their energetic ones in contra-
distinction to Italian laziness and these young men are not
being idle at all, and wanting exercise after studying the fine arts
all the forenoon go out on the canals and Lagoons in the afternoon in two of these inflated india rubber life boats just large
enough to sit in and propel themselves sitting straight in the
middle by throwing a single *double* oar from side to side, a very
graceful and efficient exercise. They told me they had been
out in rather a rough sea on the Adriatic and even with a sail
they were perfectly safe and they believe that nothing could
destroy them but perhaps rough breakers stunning the rower....

You ask what I am wearing, but nothing very particular as

[1] Harriet Sarah Jones Loyd was in fact not even fifteen. Her father,
Samuel Jones Loyd (1796-1883), had succeeded to his father's business, the
London and Westminster Bank, in 1844 and been created Baron Overstone
in 1850. His only son had died in 1833 and his daughter was his sole heir.
She married in 1858 Robert Lindsay, grandson of the 5th Earl of Crawford
and Balcarres, who was created Baron Wantage in 1885. They had no children. She lived until 1920, a much loved, attractive old lady. Paul Edmund
Strzelecki (1796-1873), a Polish count, had been naturalised British in 1850
through the good offices of Lord Overstone. In 1839 he had found gold in
New South Wales but at the request of the Colonial authorities had kept it
secret for some years. At the time he was in Venice, Sir Roderick Murchison, the geologist, made a statement about this discovery.
[2] The Earl of Gifford (1822-62), eldest son of the Marquess of Tweeddale,
died before his father. Lord Dufferin (1826-1902) had succeeded as 5th
Baron on July 21, 1841, when his father, a Captain in the Navy, had died
suddenly from an overdose of morphine on board the steamer *Reindeer*. He
was to have a most distinguished career, becoming Viceroy of India and
Ambassador at St Petersburg, Constantinople, Rome and Paris. In 1888 he
was created Marquess of Dufferin and Ava. Sir Francis Scott, 2nd Bt (1824-
1863), had been at Christ Church. John wrote to his father about him on
this same day: 'I found him a very eager fellow in my own way, who had spent
the time when he ought to have been reading for his class at Oxford in studying architecture and may be very influential in England.'

no society goes on here until the French people return. I am
not buying any thing but wearing what I brought from London
which however are very much admired here. I have a white Lace
bonnet covered with small white flowers all over the outside,
a bright blue corded silk & mantilla with broad blue fringe,
and my grey moiré which I think you saw. I have also a pink
gauze ribbon & tulle bonnet. My things are all pretty, and for
the winter I bought in Milan what is very cheap, a bright snuff
brown velvet which they make there. I enclose a piece and if
you do not think the quality suberb for 10/- a yard I shall be
surprized. I intend bringing some for you or the children
(but if I do I shall have to cut it to save the duty but which
won't matter) any colour you like....

I am not overpleased with Mr Ruskin for writing to you
that I am more domestic here than in London. It is not his
saying this but his underhand manner I dislike. He always
says something or other when I am far away which he never said
or hinted at when I was at home. What going out I had in
London might be counted and was during May, June and July.
What does he make of 13 months before during which time John
was always with them and I at home alone many & many a day
from morning till night, and even during last season? They are
strange people and I am free to confess I do not get fonder of
them as I get older although we get on better. I suppose you
know they are coming to Switzerland in the Spring and John
is to travel with them wherever they like? I never heard a word
of it until it was all settled, and the letters between John and
his father are sometimes de trop what between sentimentalism
& duplicity on Mr Ruskin's side, abusing everybody who stays
with them & yet keeping them, and on John's side an obedience "sans bornes" and making an excuse for everything he does
and everybody he sees here as if he was doing harm—for fear
the old people should think he leans too much to what I say.
Certainly things went on very differently at Bowerswell *between
all of us*, and these [*sic*] family put me a good deal in mind of
the Duncans [Melville Jameson's in-laws] with their speeches
and manoeuvrings. I detest anything like a want of openness....[1]

[1] Mr Ruskin for his part was always complaining of a lack of openness in
the Grays. It was on September 26 that John had written: 'Effie is getting

Casa Wetzlar, Sunday, 27th Octr.

Dearest Papa & Mama & George

Your letters all require answering and as I do not think I can answer all three separately I shall let one do just now and write you the oftener.... I wish you could all step over here for a couple of weeks and see how we get on in our Palazzo. Papa's inquiries about the Duchesse d'Angoulême come sadly enough just now when I have just heard of her death. I had hoped very much to have known her this winter but the other day a letter came to the Infanta saying that on the 15th she had taken to her bed having a presentiment that she was going to die. Brain fever came on & this morning I heard of her death.[1] Marmont and a number of French are gone to Gorizia to meet her body and where she is to be buried beside her husband and Charles X. They lie in a Convent situated beautifully on a hill overlooking the town. A Martyr all her life she, the last of her family, has now found those dear to her gone before. Her loss will be deeply felt both here & at Gorizia where her Charitable disposition made her much loved. All who knew her here loved her very much. The Count de Chambord always treated her as sa Majesté but she in turn always addressed him as king and rose up when he spoke to her. He comes here immediately after the Funeral but I should think this death would sadden both the Duchesse de Berry & himself too much to be gay this winter.

It is very interesting my knowing Marmont and he comes and talks to me whenever I go to Mdme. Esterhazy's[2] when he is very agreeable except when he gets on Ld. Palmerston who is

so domestic that we really have no news for you.' He had arranged before leaving that his parents should meet them in Switzerland in the spring, but it is quite possible that he had only just told Effie about it. The plan never materialised. On December 18 Mr Ruskin wrote to say they would not come as he was afraid it might be 'another Salisbury', where they had all been so unhappy in July, 1848.

[1] She died at Frohsdorf, near Vienna, where the Duc de Chambord had his court. The Infanta Beatrix was the younger sister of the Comtesse de Chambord.

[2] Marmont lived above Countess Esterhazy in the Barbarigo Palace on the Grand Canal at San Vio, now the Venezia Murano Company with its façade covered with mosaics of 1887.

too generally detested here to make Marmont's abuse particular. He must have been very good looking when young and has very polite manners but all the people here have so much more so than in France. Here politeness and kindness of heart go together and a perfect want of formality which is very comfortable, and as to the morality which exists, I should say it was quite as good as in the same circles in London. Nobody in fact do I hear of bad character but Prince Troubetzkoi who is well known & not likely to pass the winter here. Of course the Italians are not to boast of but they are not in society in Venice because they don't choose & the Germans are well conducted without exception and the Governor Gorzkowski a most excellent man.

I am going tomorrow to be presented to Countess Pallavicini, a very nice person I believe and half Irish being the Daughter of Marshall Nugent now visiting the Queen in London. He and his son return this way so that we shall hear their ideas of England. He has been a brave officer to Austria for more than 30 years....[1]

Lord Dufferin went off to Rome two days ago. I sent his pretty Mother, who you know is Mrs Norton's sister, some tea for which she was abundantly grateful.[2] I went about with him as well as Beppo and Nani the Cook who is an Antiquary and took us to all sorts of odd places where I chose for Ld. Dufferin all manner of old carved frames—Venice glass—& Pictures,

[1] Laval, Count Nugent, born in Ireland 1777, had entered the Austrian Army at the age of sixteen. He had first distinguished himself at the Battle of Marengo. In the revolution of 1848-9 he had commanded an army corps in Italy and Hungary. He had married in 1815 Jane, only child and heir of Duke Riario Sforza, a very gay and fascinating woman. They had three sons and three daughters. Jane Lilla, their second daughter, was married to Count (later Prince) Antonio Pallavicini-Fibbia who died in 1860. His palace was in Bologna but they lived in Venice so that she might be among her compatriots. She became Effie's best friend in Venice.

[2] Helen Dufferin and her sister, Caroline Norton, were daughters of Tom Sheridan, son of Richard Brinsley Sheridan. Helen had married Lord Dufferin in 1825. Effie had met her at a party at Lady Westminster's on June 15, 1850. In 1862, twenty-one years after her husband's death, she married the Earl of Gifford who had been in Venice with them and was only four years older than her son. She married him on his deathbed and died herself five years later.

and although he is a very clever talented young man I had no opinion of his taste in the fine arts, therefore pointed out all that he should take which he did most obediently, I getting them much cheaper than he would have done, and I think his house in Ireland will be none the worse of some of the things. He was very sorry to go away and said nothing could equal Venice....

Excuse my writing but I am in bed not very well today but intend getting up to tea as we have some more English here, Mr & Mrs Gambier Parry and Mr & Mrs Watts Russell. I have not seen them yet. The gentlemen are Christ Church friends of John's.[1] A great many English seem to be coming to Italy this winter and the Converts to Romanism in England form quite a little society of most bigotted Romanists in Rome, such as Lord & Lady Campden, Ld. & Lady Feilding[2] and others, very bad for the other English there as they are most strict and devoted to Rome—and the Society in Rome I am told is extremely respectable, quite different from Naples and Florence which is the worst....

I had a long letter yesterday from Gratz from Paulizza's Mother which being in German character took me some time to decipher but was wonderful for a woman of 72. It was very sad to read it. She says she cannot get the better of his death. He died away from her in Venice for what I should think must have been three strokes of a sort of Paralysis. He lived seven days after and then a friend of his wrote to her when it was all over. She says in the winter he stayed with her four months and got much better. In the winter evenings he used to sit with our picture [they had sent him a daguerreotype from Verona] before him and tell her all about John and me, and when he left he took the picture with him and she does not [know] where it is. She says what an invaluable son he was to her and also helped to maintain herself and unmarried Daughter—& now she is old, a widow, and has lived to see the most of 16 children die before

[1] Thomas Gambier Parry (1816-88) was the inventor of a special process for painting frescoes. He had been at Trinity, Cambridge, not Christ Church. For Watts Russell, see p. 209.

[2] Viscount Feilding was the eldest son of the Earl of Denbigh. Later he tried his best to convert John and Effie. Viscount Campden was the eldest son of the Earl of Gainsborough.

her. Poor old Lady, I know you will feel for her—she writes most affectionately to me and says how much she feels my sympathy and that it is a comfort to her to open her Mother's heart to me & that those that knew & loved her son must ever be dear to her. It is quite dark & my dinner is lying cold besides me....

From John's letter of December 7 we know the actual day of Paulizza's death: 'I had certainly no presentiment of Paulizza's death—He died the night that you and my mother and I slept at Leamington on our way to Malvern'—that is, Friday, July 11. And from John's letter of December 28 we learn one more detail: 'I shall come back to it [the cemetery at Murano] some day, at evening—and speak of Turner then—and perhaps also name Paulizza—who is buried there: and has no tomb.' He never did name Paulizza again in writing. The old cemetery at Murano, at the northernmost tip of the island, is still a wild and beautiful place, but years ago Paulizza's body would have been dug up and his skeleton added to the great mountain of uncovered bones on the island of Sant' Arianna. Every ten years the graves of Venice are emptied to make room for new arrivals.

ARRIVAL OF THE RUSSIANS

ℰ⅋

Casa Wetzlar, All Saints Day, 1st Novr.

My dearest Mama

... We have had such rain for three days that I have been sitting seeing nobody and looking out from my projecting window on the Grand Canal & seeing nothing but the sea-gulls crying and the Gondoliers rowing through the rain with their hoods over their heads and the water so high as almost to be in at the doors to divert myself and to take exercise I alternately cleaned my window and the furniture and having made myself warm by that I returned to my sewing which is furnishing my project-ing window very prettily for the winter. It is such a dear little place and is in fact a little room four feet square built into one of the Balconies with nice seats all round and a Ledge with cush-ions and where I have some nice plants. All the sun comes in and it is always cheerful and a lovely view.[1] In the roof I have put a hook and hung a crimson Lamp with little chains which lights it very nicely; then I have a white rug on the floor and I have the drawingroom curtains hanging over the entrance and in the middle an orchidaceous plant hanging down very grace-fully. I am now covering the cushions and seats of the Belvidere, as they call the little place here, for many houses have them, with a sort of dark brown and rose Damask, with white muslin curtains to keep out the sun and rose silk ones instead [*sic*]. It does not take much and it will look warmer in the winter than the Baroness's white Dimity. I have also two fine Camelias full in bud with about thirty buds on them and the enclosed Trum-pet flower in great beauty, one or two Geraniums, a poor little pot of Mignonette not like yours I am sure but then it will flower

---

[1] This little wooden room built out of the window can be seen in the print of Casa Wetzlar, plate 13. The belvederes have been removed from the present Gritti Hotel.

all the winter which yrs. won't, and two Aloes complete my
little garden which is a great pleasure to me and fills one of
the Balconies which looks very pretty in the room when the
window is open. I have got all the Carpets down with plenty
of Hay under them so that we are now almost independant of
fire—and every body compliments me on the order of the
rooms and say they never saw the Baroness's rooms look half
so well before and that she has given me things she never gave
any body else, but the fact is that the covers & curtains I
brought from England with my pretty cushions and a handsome Viennese Piano make all the difference—although we
have made some changes all of which the Baroness does at her
own cost and her Porter is a very nice man and whenever I want
anything done I send for him when he expresses himself my
devoted servant (servito devoto) and does what I want, which,
as I sometimes give him a Zwanzig [rather less than 9d.] for
his trouble, is always well done....

I am very glad to hear you are no Kossuthities. I think the
Austrians are very sore as far as I hear about our treatment of him
and do not understand that the best classes look on him in his
true light. They only look at what is permitted and the difference between Haynau's reception and his is sufficiently striking.[1]

The other day I was calling on the Countess Pallavicini,
Marshall Nugent's daughter, a very plain but Lady-like amiable
person and young, married against her will to an Italian nobleman very rich and very stupid. She was for long very unhappy
but she has a child [a girl] now and she is much happier but
brought up amongst the Austrians she lives here as much as

---

[1] Field-Marshal Baron Julius von Haynau (1786-1853) had been nicknamed the 'Hyena of Brescia' from his atrocities in that city after its
capitulation in March, 1848. He had been in command of the siege of
Malghera and if he had not been called away to succeed Baron Weldon as
Commander-in-Chief in Hungary, Venice might well have suffered the
barbarities inflicted on the Brescians and Hungarians. In Hungary he had
ordered the flogging of women which gained him such an odious reputation that when, during a visit to London in September, he went to inspect
the new brewery of Barclay & Perkins at Southwark, the draymen, recog-
nising him from his long white moustaches which he refused to cut in
spite of warnings, attacked him with whips. He was rescued from serious
injury only just in time by the river police.

possible to be amongst them and has one room covered with their pictures—I should think every distinguished man she has known, two or three hundred, beginning of course with the Emperor, then Radetzky, Wimpffen, her father, so on. Sitting with her were two oldish brave looking men, Marshall Falkenhayn and Baron Reischach,[1] decorated with orders and who listened with grave attention while we discussed Kossuth. She said her father had enjoyed his visit in England very much but had gone over to Ireland as he would not be in England when Kossuth, against whom he had fought several battles, should be so received. Marshall Marmont and several of the French have gone off to the poor Duchesse's Funeral and not come back yet.

I told you that the Watts Russells were here. John left his friend rather a rosy, red-haired well bred young man at Christ Church; now he finds him with a sickly wife and half a dozen children, a pervert to Rome and moreover a Renegade Priest for he was in the Church of England and looks old & broken down.[2] They have taken a house very dreary at the top of the Grand Canal for three years. I think they must be very weak people to take a house for such a time without knowing the severity of the Venetian climate, for John says she looks in a consumption, and for their children they could not have chosen a worse place for education for the Priests are notoriously scandalous and San Clemente, an Island here, is full of all the Priests who have committed crimes, a sort of Botany Bay and a more horrible looking set of villains you never saw.

[1] General Baron Siegmund Reischach (1809-78) was a Knight and Grand Cross of the Order of Malta. The fact that his hair was quite white made him seem older than he was. Count Eugène Falkenhayn (1792-1853) was a General of Cavalry, not a Marshal. He was second in command at Venice. Both these men are frequently mentioned in Effie's letters.

[2] Michael Watts Russell had been Rector of Benefield, Northants, and had married Augusta Barker. On November 19 John wrote to his father: 'You ask if Russell is an Oxford made Roman—No—only "prepared" at Oxford—the finishing touches given after he had taken duty at some English rectory.' In his letter of November 1, after his first duty visit to them which he had intended to be the last and during which he discovered they were Catholics, he wrote: 'They are to stay here for the winter and I am very glad of it for through them I shall get a good deal of information which would otherwise have been inaccessible to me, and they are too far off—and too sickly to require any rudeness in keeping them out of my way.'

The Bishop of Verona is just elected as Patriarch[1] here which the Venetians don't like as every town in Italy dislikes the other, and because the Veronese are more pious and attentive to Fête day, they dislike them and say they are Bigots. How is such a country fit to govern itself? But the Bishop will keep things in better order and St. Mark's is much cleaner this year—but I do not know any Italian here who believes in his religion. They all say what is yr. religion and when I tell them they say, Ah! that is much the most rational. They appear to especially abhor confession & I have not met with one yet who has confessed since they were children. The Perversion of the English is most wonderful, and how when they are here they still remain blinded is a miracle....

Sunday [*the 2nd*]. This morning when we got up we found we could have no breakfast for some time to come as the water was a foot high in the yard & no entrance to the Kitchen so we called a Gondola and Beppo carried me from the house into it. We rowed to the Piazza and getting on to the Procuratie we walked all round the Square which was under water and St. Mark's reflected like a Lake and numbers of boys running about splashing each other and Gondoliers carrying across people twice their size for which they were paid a centesimo....

Casa Wetzlar, 6th Novr.

When I wrote to you last Sunday I gave you a description of the water & rain which has not abated—at least the rain which is doing immense harm on the Terra ferma, and in Padua the water is up to the first storey in the houses, and the Count Gritti, one of the richest nobles there, has had all his this year's corn swept away. The poor are worse off & Mon. Saint Maure, who was with the Duchesse D'Angoulême in her last moments, told me he & Count Zen were in the water all night on the banks of the Brenta helping the poor people to save their furniture and now they have left their houses altogether and are living in Tents on the hills, enough to kill them all in this rain. The Bridge over the Tagliamento has had both its ends carried away while 67 persons were on it who were kept there two

[1] Petrus-Aurelius Mutti was Patriarch of Venice until his death in 1857. Like his predecessor he is buried in the crypt of St Mark's.

nights and two days till they were taken off, and tonight we hear the Brenta has burst its banks which will do a great deal more harm. M. St. Maure has been collecting for them, & John & I have contributed & will do so further if he asks again.[1]

It is a great pity I had not had the privilege of seeing the Duchesse before she died. She seems to have been much loved…. They were saying Masses for her today and I intended going to such with Mdme Pallavicini but the weather was too bad. Last night I was at Countess Esterhazy's and all the Ladies were in different shades of mourning, grey barege, white silk, black and purple; it was a very nice party and a very pretty one. The house is beautiful and the Hostess is very kind.[2] The people here are so polite and so easy in their manners. I like what I see of them very much. I do not think our most cour-teous English are equal to them at all in grace of reception, and certainly in conversation we are far behind.

The conversation here has more solidity than the French and I have never seen society more rational or that I more approve of. They never invite you but tell one or two people whom they chance to see; they tell the others and you go or not as you like at eight o'clock, when tea is handed round, and about ten— cakes, fruit, preserves &c on beautiful Dresden China & gold plate. Last night there were about forty people to meet two Florentine Ladies, Countesses Orsini & Meyendorff, the former Rossini's pet pupil and the finest private singer in Italy and of whom he said had she not been Grand Dame she would have been the finest singer in the world. She is a large fat bold looking woman of thirty, dressed in plain white Glacé & flounces with magnificent black hair plaited round her head. She sang very easily & with every variety of power long pieces from the Operas and yet not disagreeably loud for I was sitting close to the Piano and was delighted. She had brought with her a

---

[1] The Byzantine picture of the Virgin, La Nicopeia, in St Mark's, said to have been painted by St Luke himself and to work miracles, was carried in procession round the Piazza during this dreadful season of rain.

[2] Ruskin, who called on her for the first time on February 21, described her house as 'the prettiest thing I ever saw on a small scale—only wanting some Turner pictures to complete its perfection'.

protégé, a pretty little boy whom I heard play wonderfully in the Theatre at Milan & who played several pieces. Mr & Mrs Dawkins & her sister were there & Lady Sorell & her daughter, some Russians & French, Count & Ctsse Pallavicini, Countess Babbi, and the room looked gayer from some few Austrians of distinguished rank & moustaches immense & perfectly distinguishable at any distance. I never saw such wonderful things and so beautifully kept. Baron [Count] Falkenhayn's I should think almost six inches on each side.

I was presented to a very handsome Colonel of Hussars commanding at Vicenza, a very young man to have so many orders and so high a position but I daresay he may owe something to his rank as the Ctsse Pallavicini told me he belonged to one of the oldest families in Hungary.[1] Having been in England & Scotland he immediately launched out upon Kossuth whom he said even before the Revolution of '48 was known as a democrat & a robber to the Hungarians, and then abused Lord Palmerston and asked if I did not, being Scotch, blush for the English. I said certainly I was ashamed but that the upper classes took no part.[2] He said, "Ah! but they do not like us in England that's clear." I said it was true there was a great prejudice against Austria in London. We had a great deal of conversation & I was amused at his manner. He did not seem to care much for such difficult matters, of course, speaking to other people at the same time. I was quite amused and then continued my talk with him as if no interruption had occurred.

I talked some time with Marmont who is a great admirer of mine, I presume because I always speak very loud to him and attend to all he says. He said he was coming to call on me whenever he could get out and pronounced my Toilette ravissante. I had on my black velvet because it was mourning & besides warm, with high body and open in front to the waist and [end of page torn and some lines missing] from a picture of Giorgione which I admire very much. I had a gold net on my head and a

[1] He was General Count Tassilo Festitics, born 1813, son of Count Ladislas Festitics and his wife, *née* Princess Josephine Hohenzollern-Hechingen. Effie often mentions him hereafter.

[2] John wrote on November 12 that it was very difficult to give the Austrians any idea of the independence of the lower classes in England.

thick roll of hair all twisted with large pearls round the top of my head beginning from each ear, and the same round my arms and a row round my neck so I looked like a Magpie all black and white and awed the Florentine ladies who stared at me through their glasses....

Casa Wetzlar, 17th November[1]

... Write to me what you like. I destroy all yr. letters immediately and what you say about the R's [Ruskins] is very true & sensible. To be open with them and never to mind their peculiarities, at least as little as possible, is the only way to keep oneself tolerably happy with them, but they are most peculiar. John sometimes tells me he does not know what to write to his Father about, for one thing would make him uneasy, another thing suspicious, and yet John thinks it all perfectly right to know this. Mr Ruskin writes to him in this comforting manner at which I could not help taking a good laugh the other day: "Mama is glad to hear you have a good appetite for all your meals, she says it is a proof you have no disease in your constitution." (Comforting that, isn't it?) Then follows rules à la Mrs. Ruskin for all the things he is to eat from breakfast till tea, and when his stomach is out of order another diet and so on.[2]

John writes to them as if he perfectly attended to everything they said but in reality I think they would be altogether shocked if they saw him, for he is beginning to think highly of the water cure, for rowing several days in the rain till he was soaked through and yet warm like Papa in bad weather at Golf, he changes his clothes and feels delightfully comfortable. He is always much better when away from their over care and attention which, as he is naturally extremely nervous, makes him ill

---

[1] There is a letter missing between the 6th and 17th.

[2] Mrs Ruskin's diet sheet was intended for Effie not John according to Mr Ruskin's letter of October 31 in which it was enclosed. John had complained to his father of a bad taste in his mouth, nervousness, quickness of pulse and other ailments, all of which he attributed to having had to sit up so often until past midnight for the last six months in London. He believed it would take him as long to recover, for he looked upon it as a fixed law that the time taken in recovering from mischief should be *at least* equal to the time taken in doing it.

by such constant enquiry, but by habit he is so infatuated that
when with them they can make him do any thing they take into
their heads, and that Old Ann is nearly the same—he delights
in her and does not mind her hypocritical ways or any thing
although he knows very well what she is—but then she was his
nurse and that makes a great difference.[1]

But now I must get on with my letter as I have a good deal
that is interesting to tell you, and by the bye I enclose £5 for
you to buy yourself a Christmas present of any thing you
may be in want of for the winter. It will be many months before
I am home and if you want a cloak of black velvet you had
much better get it with this and be sure and always get what
you want. You are far too shy of asking me for things and you
know it is the greatest pleasure I have in this world to think
I can do anything for you or my Father or the children. Do
you think it would ever be possible for me if I gave you everything I have to repay in the least your love for & care of me
during my Life? You must often have little wants that I could
relieve if you would only let me know. I am sure I often trouble you and you like to be troubled, so do I....

The other day [we] dined at Mr Cheney's where John went
as he did not wish to offend Mr Cheney by refusing so often.
There was Mr Brown, a Baroness Meyendorff,[2] the same that
I met at Ctsse. Esterhazy, and Count Calani, Chamberlain of
the G. Duke of Tuscany. We had a pleasant & elegant little
dinner as Mr Cheney has everything perfect in point of Menage.
The Lady [the Baroness], a clever woman, copying pictures in
the Churches here, after dinner recited to us in the manner of
Rachel, & quite as good, extracts from Les Horaces, Phèdre,
Attalie and other pieces. She entered so into the spirit of de-
clamation and tragedy that at one time I really thought she was
crying and I must say that as far as her acting went she quite
equalled Rachel. The same Master taught both and she said

[1] Ann, or Anne, Strachan had first entered the service of John's paternal
grandfather when she was fifteen. Effie grew to dislike her more and more,
and thought she was a great mischief-maker.
[2] Born in 1800 Countess Wilhelmine de Buol-Schauenstein. In 1830 she
had married Baron Pierre Meyendorff, an Imperial Russian State Councillor
and diplomat. She died in 1868.

that she practised every day in Paris for some hours with little indian rubber balls in her mouth which makes the voice very clear. She praised my toilette and complimented me, but to me she was quite [rep]ulsive, immensely fat and dressed in a very decoltée manner. Her English friends, Lady Holland, Ladys Ailesbury & Castlereagh,[1] don't speak much for her and when she said she would come and pay me a visit I determined to be out if possible.

The Grand Duke Constantine and his wife and suite of 50 Russians [page torn] two days ago for a visit of 5 months in the Imperial Palace in St. Mark's Square. They are said to be both sick and have come for their health but they looked extremely well. Mdme. Pallavicini sent to know if I would like to see them arrive as Count Falkenhayn, the 2nd in command here, had got her a room in the Palace. We went and were politely received by Baron Baumgarten (Gorzkowski's adjutant) in his rooms from whence we looked down into the gardens of the Governor.[2] Ct. Falkenhayn brought us great rolls of scarlet [word missing] and white cloth, the Imperial colours, which we hung out of the windows to make a demonstration. In a little the Steamer came in surrounded by Gondolas, and the Duke and his wife were received by Gorzkowski. The servants were all in beautiful Livery, the Gondolas covered with pale blue silk and the Blue, red & white Russian colours flying. The pair looked well. He was in Marine uniform and looks about 23—she about the same and pretty. She wore a white satin bonnet with pink roses inside, a black velvet cloak nearly to her feet surrounded with a narrow band of sable all round and a bright blue dress. I hope

[1] There is no record of Effie having met these two last ladies, but on July 25 she and John had been to a grand party at Holland House. She was enthusiastic over the beauty of the house and garden, and described Lady Holland as 'a pretty, gay little thing, not at all affected'.

[2] The gardens are now public and the Governor's palace houses the Correr Museum. General Charles Gorzkowski, the Polish Civil and Military Governor of Venice, had been the last of the five generals to take over command of the army besieging Venice, and on August 28, 1849, had entered the city as conqueror. He had previously been Governor of Mantua and. returned there for about a year before becoming Governor of Venice. He was a huge man and as popular with the Italians as any Austrian could be.

they will do something for Venice by making more Russians take Houses here for the winter.[1]

The Russian Consul & his wife, M. & Mdme. de Gnostoff, called on me. They will have some parties for the Ladies who accompany the Duchess here to which I can go if I like. They gave themselves great airs because the Grand D. has come and I saw her promenading with her children just now in the Square. The children were the queerest looking antics in this cold winter day you ever saw, green satin bonnets like large Mutches,[2] tight pink merino spencers, and white merino frocks, quite short with trowsers to match. Can you conceive any thing more hideous? Now goodbye....

Venezia, 25th November, 1851.

I tore up your last letter and fear that this may contain some unanswered questions, but as long as I remember I must thank you and Sophie Alice & John for the delightful Blueberry Jam you sent me and which arrived in the Madonna della Grazia two days ago....

The Grate is also in the Drawing room and when a fender is made & coals brought in I shall be much better with a fire than the stove which makes the room so close that it gives headache and on going into my cold bed-room invariably Rheumatism in the shoulders, but there is a difficulty about getting coal as they are not inclined to sell us less than a Ship load as they say that it would not be worth selling a few Tons which seems very odd.

['The grate is up,' John wrote, 'and we had a coal fire yesterday, all owing to Mr Brown's kindness, for the coal-merchant told us that unless we wanted a *shipload*—it was not worth their while. Under such circumstances—as it was Mr Brown's suggestion that we sent the grate, we applied to him to tell us how to fill it—and on his personal application to the coal-merchant's feelings, we were allowed

---

[1] Constantine, born September 21, 1827, was the second of the four sons of Tsar Nicholas I. On September 11, 1848, he had married Alexandra, born July 20, 1830, daughter of Duke Joseph of Saxe-Altenburg. Constantine commanded the Russian fleet in the Baltic during the Crimean War and was Governor of Poland 1862-3. He died in 1892.

[2] Mutch is a Scottish word for a baby's bonnet or close-fitting cap for an old lady.

to have a couple of tons—There were still Tongs, poker—and shovel wanting to our establishment which Mr Brown raked up out of his stores—and sent us, and we had a nice scene at the first lighting of the fire—for our gondolier servant Beppo had never seen one, and did not believe that coals would burn; and Bastian, Mr Brown's servant—who came with the fire irons, thought it necessary to instruct George that the poker "was to break the coals with"—on which George immediately asked him in a humble manner—the use of the tongs; which Bastian having explained with great gravity—George proceeded to enquire that of the shovel; but then Bastian found him out—and appeared for a moment disposed to let him feel the weight of all the three. It was quite a little bit of Molière.']

By the Bye you were asking about the Watts Russells who had taken a house here I told you for three years. I heard she was ill and went several times but never saw her. John did and said she looked very consumptive and breathed with difficulty; she told him that she had been imprudent in going to Mass one very cold day & I then heard she had taken gastric fever. One day lately about three o'clock I asked for her when they said she was better and her sister, wife of an Austrian General Martine, had come from Milan to see her. At seven I heard she was dead. I sent John directly to him and he said he had been expecting her death for a year and that the Doctors had given her up at Turin & Rome, but what he is to do I know not with a number of quite little children, the eldest about 9—and nobody with them. I have not seen him yet and John says he has not yet determined what he is to do. Poor Man. John says he always sees priests about the door.[1]

I never saw such a place for Priests as my Kitchen. I never go in or out but I meet one or two going or coming from the Kitchen. They are very polite to me, so I suppose *Nani* feeds them, and having nothing to do with the eatables down stairs all that they get must be at his expense. The fact is that his son is a young priest and I suppose he brings his friends, but you would

[1] John wrote that if instead of the thirty-nine Articles, Watts Russell 'had been taught a little Christianity, he would not now have been consoling himself for his wife's death by the help of a copper image of the Virgin' (Letter of November 25).

think one kitchen held the whole parish sometimes. When I want to speak to Mary, who sits in an Inner room, I have to pass Nani, Annetta, Beppo, Carlo, the Priests, the Ironing woman, the Porter, his family, Nani's daughters, some of Annetta's children, George and his violin which he scrapes on all his leisure time, and stray Gondoliers & women whom I never saw before. When it is a *Maigre* day, which they don't like at all, Nani makes them a great dish of Fish seasoned strongly with Garlic and the smell is something too dreadful if one happens to pass by the door, but such contented, lounging, goodnatured people you never saw, so fond of gossiping & never working but when they are obliged. The Lower Venetians are very devout and yet if you question them they don't seem to believe any thing particularly but are superstitious by habit. My Beppo is very religious and always takes off his hat when passing a Church, and when I go in to see any of the pictures he takes the opportunity of saying his prayers. Today a crowd passed us of priests carrying the Host and followed by a train of women & children. Beppo and all the men took off their hats. I said, "Why do you take off your hat Beppo?" He said, "Always eccza (short for Yr. Excellency) when the *Lord* (il Signor) passes." I said, "But he is everywhere Beppo, don't you think so too?" He said, "Oh, yes, you have reason, Signora, but it's just a habit with us"....

I never saw any place so profoundly still as Venice at night. After it gets dark people seem all to stay at home, and in so thickly populated a town, with so many thousands of Soldiers, one never meets one. Sometimes I go to tea at Mdme. Pallavicini's at eight o'clock and I put on my cloak & hood and with Beppo I go through the streets on foot, which in the day swarm with people, and I never meet anybody hardly. The Venetians are very proud of the security and quiet of Venice. They say it has always been known for its quiet at night and at two in the morning it would be the same thing. Last night I walked home from Mdme. P's with the Princess *Yablouknoffsky*[1] and three

---

[1] This was Princess Jablonowska (as it will be spelt hereafter) who in 1841 had married, as his second wife, Prince Louis Jablonowski, thirty years older than herself, of a very aristocratic Polish family. She had been born, in 1813, Louisa Nobil Donna Marini, one of the great Venetian families.

Austrian Counts at midnight all talking German in the dark & lonely street with hardly any sky visible and no sound excepting their Lingua Brutto as the Italians say and the clinking of Sabres on the stone.

I go every two or three nights to Mdme. Pallavicini to tea, take my work and we pass a couple of hours very agreeably chatting as they have incorporated me into their little circle. I always meet the same half dozen and these are always the Princess Jablonowska & sometimes her niece with another unpronounceable name—myself and Mdme. P., Count Falkenhayn, Count Festetics (the Col. of Hussars at Vicenza), Ct. Thun,[1] who being the youngest is called the *Thé Comtesse* because he makes our tea, & a very nice Bohemian, Count Wrbna[2] (pronounced Vurbna) who has the charge of the Grand Duke Constantine and his Wife—that is to say that the Emperor puts him here to see that they have every thing they want, arrange their dinner and be in fact in place of himself as they are his Guests while here. Poor Count Wrbna is immensely bored as you may imagine as his duties are begun at ten by going to Mass with them and waiting on them until 9 at night, but he is very good and well bred and I have no doubt they don't see how gened he is.

The other night we were all sitting as usual at our tea and talk and he did not appear at 9 as usual; when, in a little, he appeared at the door dressed with unusual care and covered with orders and his sword drawn. He announced the Arch Duke Albert, the Governor of Hungary. I was rather amazed but got mechanically on my feet and put on my gloves. The Officers presented arms and he did something in return which I did not see but he begged them to lay down their sabres in a corner and being all introduced our chat went on just as before. The Thé Comtesse made him a cup of tea and we laughed & talked as

[1] Franz, Count Thun, born 1826, was son of Count Johann Thun and his wife, *née* Countess Nicolasine de Baillet Latour (sister of the Minister of War who was hanged by the revolutionaries in 1848). He was a Captain in an infantry regiment and A.D.C. to Radetzky. Before the Ruskins left Italy he was to challenge John to a duel.

[2] Eugène, Count Wrbna and Freudenthal (1822-80), was the son of the Imperial Master of the Horse, also Count Eugène, and his wife, *née* Countess Barbara Erdödy. He was a General and A.D.C. to the Emperor.

before he came. You may be sure I was much interested in conversing with the son of the great Arch Duke Charles. He appeared about 34 and very Austrian in the face, the heavy mouth like the Emperor and fair hair, plain looking but evidently a very agreeable man and they all seemed so fond of him and so familiar & easy with him.[1] He teased me well about Kossuth & when at last I said, "Well I am Scotch,"—he said, "Oh, if he went to Scotland, at Glasgow they would receive him just as they did at Birmingham [where he had had a particularly warm welcome] in company with Mazzini & Gavazzi to bless them."[2]

He was very sorry to go away but said that Steamers & Railways waited for nobody and he was going at midnight to Trieste on his way to Hungary. Mdme. Pallavicini told me that she has known him 18 years and they used to play together at Battledoor and Shuttlecock at Vienna when they were children. He always comes to see her and he was just passing through from being at Verona with Radetzky so he came. I could not be better placed for seeing Austrian Society and I really admire them, so easily amused, so kind and goodtempered & so eminently wellbred. I never am with them that I don't feel myself brusque and awkward and they are so different from the French who are so heartless with their politeness. But they like my out spokeness & I make them laugh immensely, I don't know why, but my ways are altogether different from theirs and Mdme. P. comes and begs John to let me come when I sometimes refuse, for she says I make her happy. It is a Capital thing for me, for

---

[1] Archduke Albert (1817-95) had served with Radetzky in the Italian campaign of 1848-9. He was the Civil and Military Governor of Hungary from 1851 to 1860 when he took over command in Venetia. In 1866 he had married Hildegarde, daughter of Louis, King of Bavaria, niece of the Emperor's mother. He was the eldest son of Archduke Charles (1771-1847), brother of Francis I and Napoleon's most formidable enemy.

[2] In April, 1851, Effie had written to her father: 'I went the other day to hear Gavazzi, the Italian Priest who is giving lectures on Popery, himself still a priest but a Liberal against the Pope, the Jesuits and the Austrians. He is a wonderful orator and I listened for two hours to his Tuscan, understanding nearly all without tiring. I am going again tomorrow.' Gavazzi had in fact in 1850 joined the Evangelical church, and until 1860, when he served under Garibaldi, was organising the Italian Protestants in England. Mazzini was also in exile in England.

I learn so much more of French, German & Italian than if I
always was by myself....

John wrote on November 20 that Lady Sorell had told him that Effie
got on very nicely with foreigners—not being stiff or shy like most
English. We know from this same letter that she met Archduke Albert
on the 19th. John wrote about him: 'He is a great admirer of Palladio at Vicenza—so it was just as well it was Effie there, and not me.'

Casa Wetzlar, 30 Novr.
... I send you Today's bill of fare. Don't think any of this is
wasted; it is all sold or feeds the servants. The wonder is how
Nani can give us so fine a dinner for so little money & every
day different. I wish you were all here to partake.

1. Vermicelli Soup
2. Red Mullet
3. Filet of Veal
4. Stewed Hare
5. Sweet Bread in Sauce
6. Roast Chicken
   Potatoes
   Beans
7. Spanish Fritters

... The Grand Duke [Constantine] and his wife live here very
quietly and walk about in the Merceria by themselves looking
in at the shop-windows like children. He is very like a clerk,
insignificent looking & pale and short, the least goodlooking
of all the Emperor's sons. She is only 20 [in fact 21] and tall and
handsome and striking looking. She is always magnificantly
dressed in ermine & velvet from head to foot, but she does not
look clever. She has left two children in Russia, the youngest
three months old only.[1] They are so much in public in Russia
that they have come here for perfect quiet for some months so

[1] Olga, born September 3 and Nicholas, born February 14, 1850. Olga
married King George I of Greece when she was sixteen and was the great-
grandmother of the Duke of Edinburgh. Their next child, Vera, was born
in February, 1854. After that came two more boys, Constantine and Dimitri.

that they do not receive any visits or give any parties which the Austrians seemed to hope they would. They have a little Steamer here and Russian crew very beautifully fitted up, they tell me, which they travel about in from one place to another as it suits their convenience. They talked of going to Palermo but seem happy to stay here for several months yet. Count Wrbna is always in attendance on them. He is obliged to intimate wherever he goes & what he does if he wishes to get away for an hour or two. He told the Grand Duchess the other night that he could not pass the Soirée with her as he was coming to me with Mdme. Pallavicini, Count Falkenhayn and General Reischach. They and Mr Hope Johnston & Mr Cooke[1] came to tea, also Princess Jablonowska. John was out at the Nerlys but came in before they went[2] and Mr Cooke brought all the paintings he has done since he has been here to show them as he is going to London in a few days to prepare them for the Exhibition next year—they are oil paintings of different views here and very beautiful. The Austrians & the Ladies were delighted with them and I have since asked Count Falkenhayn to get me an order from the Governor for Mr Cooke to take his paintings out of Venice without being searched which will save him much trouble and a good deal of money too.[3]

My Soirée was very agreeable and I enjoyed it very much. The Ladies had their work, the gentlemen talked and I made tea, and had besides for them fruit and preserves, for some of them take tea, others a pear, or like Mdme. Jablonowska who

[1] Edward William Cooke (1811-80), the marine painter, had just been elected A.R.A. He went drawing with John to Murano.

[2] John wrote: 'Effie had some of her friends to tea last night [26th]—but I only condescended to go in at the end of the evening—merely to show that I wasn't a *myth.*' It must have been on this occasion that Countess Pallavicini saw Effie's bath. John asked his father on December 7 to get one for her just like it at Matthew's, Charing Cross, the Indian Rubber place, and described it as being circular, inflatable, about four feet over and folding up into a small space for carriage. On January 3 Mr Ruskin reported having sent it off by sea and debiting John's account £3 10s.

[3] John had written on November 15 about Cooke: 'You will have the exhibition full of Ducal palaces next year—such as they may be. But Cooke has taken great pains—and though raw and cold and meanlooking—his drawings will be more accurate in detail than any that have yet been taken.' He exhibited only two pictures of Venice in the 1852 Academy.

only eats grapes, and they were very happy. They looked at all the English things in the room & were charmed with the comfortable coal-fire. The handsome Hussar, Ct. Festitics, was at home at Vicenza and did not come. He was here yesterday. He comes every week to Venice and favours me with a call. He looks very grand and noble, & his beautiful dress covered with gold and silver passementerie and buttons and gold cords round his neck upon pale blue cloth, sets off his fine person to advantage, as you may suppose, which, added to his rank as being one of the first of the Hungarian Magnates, has given him an enviable position in the eyes of the world, not I should say to the improvement of his character as a man, for he seems to me to have been very much spoiled all his Life by having had every thing he could desire, and being immensely proud he has no humility. He said to me yesterday, talking of people often going wrong, and looking at the same time perfectly dignified and grave, "As for me I have never repented of any thing I ever did in my Life," but you know the Hungarians are very proud & they say even the Hungarian Horses hold their heads in a different manner to other horses. This man naturally is a fine animal, but he is spoiled, and I should think not likely to be happy or a good man now, for he is too old to mend in his situation & position at seven & thirty. Count Wrbna I like much better and he more respected than Ct. Festitics.

I think I should write a book about the Austrians I meet for under that name are all nations, I think. General Reischach is another curious example. He is old [in fact 41] and a Chevalier of Malta. He wears the White Maltese Cross on his uniform & I asked him what his vows were—he said one of his family had always belonged to the Commanderie and he being the Cadette of the family as usual had followed the Custom of his house. He had taken the vows many years ago which consisted in his laying down on the floor of a Cathedral Church; the Priests chanted the prayers for the death & Miserere over his body, he being covered with black clothes; he then rose up, swore the vows of Poverty, Chastity and Obedience and to die to the world. He looks excessively jolly notwithstanding and is very rich for the poverty only means that after he is dead, excepting his sword and Horse, his property goes to the order. He can read the Mass and receive confession but not marry or even speak much to women, which I am sure he breaks through for he talks immensely and came walking on the Square with me next day until I went away. He is a great story teller and friend of Radetzky's—who, the Arch Duke Albert said, hardly liked to be separated from Reischach for he told such capital stories and amused him so much.

I have to go to Madme. Pallavicini's tomorrow night to meet her brother, Ct. Albert Nugent, who has come here for the winter, also the Prince Pallavicini, her husband's brother. I have not seen them yet. Mdme. Esterhazy has given no more Soirées as she has been ill, and this evening I am going to sit with Mrs Dawkins who has also been three weeks in the house. The cold is intense and the wind bitter cold. I walked home from the German Church so very fast this morning that I almost ran and believe I have hurt myself a little for I feel as if my legs were broken to pieces and I have been sitting shivering over the fire for an hour. I always feel the worse of walking very fast beyond my strength, but since my seasoning to Venice by the fever I have been quite well and able to row a long way in the Lagunes....

I see Mr Cheney and Mr Brown very seldom. I think they have got some idea about us that I can't make out. They always were satirical to John and laughed at him because they were in reality angry to find he knew much better about art here than themselves and now they have a very queer manner to me. Mr Brown never asks me to come and see him although I call regularly on both as politeness requires but there is something about them both that I can't make out at all. However it is not of much importance as we are quite independent of each other, but Mr B. has been so kind that I am sorry to have any disagreeable feeling between us....

Effie had her ups and downs in her relationship with Rawdon Brown, but in the next few weeks their friendship was strained as it was never to be again. He was very reserved about himself for it was not until Effie met a friend of his in London on her return from her first journey to Venice that she discovered he had a mother and two sisters living.

On April 21, 1852, John wrote about him: 'He is as *kind* as ever, but we see little of him, for he is as jealous as he is irritable—he has quarrelled with everybody who lives in Venice and does not come to see us lest he should meet them in our drawing room ... but if anything is to be *done* he is always ready and so are we.'

Effie had been on excellent terms with the Cheney brothers in England, but an extract from a letter from Edward Cheney to his friend Lord Holland gives his opinion of John: 'Mrs Ruskin is a very pretty woman and is a good deal neglected by her husband, not for other women but for what he calls literature. I am willing to suppose he has more talent than I give him credit for—indeed he could not well have less—but I cannot see that he has either talent or knowledge and I am surprised that he should have succeeded in forming the sort of reputation that he has acquired. He has so little taste that I am surprised he admired Holland House.'[1]

[1] Unpublished letter from Venice of August, 1851, in possession of Mr Nigel Capel Cure.

KINDNESS OF THE AUSTRIANS

❧

Casa Wetzlar, 7th Decr.

Dearest Mama

Not having heard from you since I wrote last I have nothing to answer and shall tell you what we have been doing here in the cold. We have no snow but bitter cold thick frost, the worst of all. Last night Mr Foster, an English-man in Austrian Service,[1] came in shivering and we both declared we had never been in such a climate. We were at Mdme. Pallavicini's where were several Austrians all talking about the French affairs which they all *seem* to approve of as every thing seems on the side of order, therefore quite in their own way of thinking but they say that it is impossible to account for any thing now in France and are sur-prized at the troops preferring Louis [Napoleon] to their Generals.[2]

Mdme. Palla[vicini] has only begun to receive again as she has met with a very great loss in the death of her mother's Aunt, the Princess Montléart, by whom she was educated and who was more than a Mother to her. She & the present Queen of Sardinia were the Princess's pupils and remained under her care until they were grown up. She must have been a woman of very religious mind & noble character, and had great trials in this world. She was Charles Albert's mother by her first Husband, the Prince de Carignan, and when a still beautiful widow at Paris she was saved from the fire which Prince Schwarzenberg's Ball occasioned by M. Montléart whom she married out of

[1] This was the first meeting with Mr Foster of whom much more will be heard.

[2] Louis Napoleon had brought off his *coup d'état* on December 2. It was followed by fighting all over France. Exactly a year later he proclaimed himself Emperor.

gratitude.[1] Charles Albert might have done better had he seen more of his Mother but Mdme. P says he had little heart and never saw her for 16 years before he died. She lived in the Tyrol quietly superintending these two girls' education in which she has succeeded, for they say that the present Queen of Sardinia is a most excellent woman, her husband inferior to her—and Mdme. P. is the best behaved & cleverest of all the Nugents. She is in the deepest mourning and told me that nobody could know what she had lost. She said every thing she did she wrote to the Princess and took her advice on every occasion and her great desire in this world was to make a journey to Paris to see her for which she was carefully collecting money, for the Count is such a miser that he doesn't give her any thing, and I find it is not to her who d'Aspre left his fortune but to her handsome sister, the Marchesa Strozzi, who is suspected to be his Daughter.[2]

Her brother Gilbert Nugent is here for the winter. He lives with Count Falkenhayn on the Grand Canal very near me. He is here for his health and I fear consumptive. He has a splendid voice and a very handsome person and kind to his sister now he has come.[3]

I never see Pallavicini; he never comes into the Drawingroom when we are all there. I asked her yesterday when we were

---

[1] Marie Christine, Princess of Saxony and Courlande, born 1779, had married Charles-Emmanuel-Ferdinand, Duke of Savoy-Carignan, who died 1800 when their son, Charles Albert, was not two years old. Queen Adelaide of Sardinia, Princess Montléart's grand-daughter, had married in 1842 her first cousin, Victor Emmanuel. On July 1, 1810, Prince Charles Schwarzenberg, the Austrian Ambassador in Paris, had given a huge ball on the occasion of Napoleon's marriage to Marie Louise. As there was no room large enough at the Embassy, a ballroom built of wood and decorated with flimsy materials was erected in the garden. This caught fire during the ball and many guests lost their lives.

[2] Countess Beatrice (Bébé) Nugent was born 1822. Her first husband, Maximilian, Marchese Strozzi Sagrati, had divorced her and she was now living a very gay life in Vienna. Constantin, Baron d'Aspre, born 1789, was one of the bravest and most brilliant Generals in Radetzky's army. He had been Governor of Padua, and had died there, unmarried, in May, 1851.

[3] Count Gilbert, born 1821, the second of Field-Marshal Nugent's three sons, had been a Lieutenant in the Imperial Army.

alone where he was. She said, "Oh! he remains up stairs—he never does anything." I said, "Does he never read?"—"Never," she said. "Could you not make him do something?" I said— She said, "I tried for seven years different occupations but he was only worried and he is happy left alone to do nothing." One would really think he was silly but all the time he knows what he is about and adores money. Ct. Falkenhayn says he has no head or heart for any thing else and most Italians are the same. The contempt the Austrians have for them is wonderful and really deserved. Fancy Count Wrbna telling me that when he was sent to Vicenza during the Revolution to treat with the Italians, although he had a Safe conduct &c the Italians all came out to the streets and spit on him & whistled & cocked their pistols and guns at him, he being perfectly alone & unarmed. Last night he had on, tied round his neck with scarlet ribbon, the magnificent order of St. Anne given him by the Emperor of Russia of red enamel and large diamonds with a little figure of St. Anne in the centre. He wears it always when dining with the Grand Duke out of compliment to his father.

I see the death of Marshall Soult in the papers. Marmont was speaking rather against him as a general last night. He said that he lost armies without making them fight....[1]

I am very glad to hear you are so satisfied with Delphine [the new French nursery governess]. John is sorry to hear she is not pretty as he is very partial to pretty French girls but I can conceive no more dangerous thing in a household than one. They are always so intriguing, as witness Melina who, if I would have let her have her way, would in a short time have ruled everything. John thinks it capital for the children, and now to talk French in society of any place or kind is necessary....

Casa Wetzlar, 14th December, 1851

[1] Marmont and Soult had quarrelled in Spain. Although Soult had made peace with the Bourbons and was Minister of War under Louis XVIII, he, unlike Marmont, had rallied to Napoleon during the Hundred Days and lived in exile after Waterloo until he was recalled in 1819 and again appointed a Marshal. He was Minister of War 1830-4 and 1840-4. He had a splendid old age and managed to retain most of his Spanish loot. He was eighty-three when he died on November 26. There was a big sale of his pictures in Paris the following May.

Not being very well, and unable because of the damp to get out to my German Church this morning, I shall begin my letter to you hoping that the afternoon will bring some news from you, and I am also anxious to hear how Delphine goes on and what Papa thinks about La Grande Nation now. We hear by Telegraph that they are still fighting in Paris; is it not a disgrace to them all to allow themselves to be scrambled for in this manner? I was at Ctse. Esterhazy's the other night where were two or three gentlemen, amongst others Ct. Festitics and Marmont. The latter was talking so cleverly about Fra[nce] and saying he had never imagined that there was half [the] cleverness in the President that he has shown there is—but said had the two parties, the Bourbons and Orleanists, followed Guizot's advice and been at unity amongst themselves it would all have been different....

Marmont is now Senior Marshall of France since Soult is dead. I understand that he is much disliked in France because of his conduct with Charles X—what it is I don't know, but every body likes him here and I think him wonderful for his age and he is very happy here.[1] He has nice rooms and gives beautiful little dinners to one or two people every day. He has not asked me as I could not go without John, who has never called on him. The gentlemen here are very goodnatured, I think, for when they come to see me they leave their cards for John and say all manner of Civil things too of him and he cuts them all on the street unless when I am with him and make him, and he never calls on anybody. I believe they think him very good & eccentric and never mind. Yesterday was the Old Countess Mocenigo's Fete day—Sta. Lucia, Lucia being her name—and everybody went to see her. Not being learned in the Romish Calendar I did not know until four o'clock but sent my cards and compliments by Beppo.

[1] Marmont had been created a Marshal in 1809 and Soult in 1804. Marmont was now the sole survivor of Napoleon's twenty-six Marshals and the only one to be born an aristocrat. He was detested in France by both Bonapartists and Legitimists, having gone over to the Bourbons in 1814 yet failing to hold Paris at the time of the 1830 revolution when he had been Governor of that city. He was driven out of France never to return; his name was expunged from the list of Marshals and his portrait in the Salle des Maréchaux at the Tuileries covered with a black veil.

I am good friends again with Mr Brown because I go to take tea with him sometimes without being invited. I never knew anybody so peculiar or so touchy or yet so agreeable when in good humour, but it is very troublesome to be so changeable— he says that I prefer bad company to his and how I can endure to know both he can't imagine. I say there is only one step be- tween the sublime and the ridiculous and he probably considers himself belonging to the first. He says he does [page torn]. I answer that, being a person of wonderfully staid [t]aste, I also like the other and that I suppose he has nothing to say against their birth or manners. Oh, no, he says but they are all such idiots and fools &c, and so he rails against everybody whom he don't in the least know....

The Little Watts Russels are coming with their [page torn] to Lunch with me tomorrow. They are nice little children and it is so sad to think of them being without a Mother all so young, but they seem very happy and don't look very sad. They had been expecting her death so long that I suppose they had prepared themselves for it. The little girls row the Gondola very nicely. They don't know a soul here but ourselves although they had letters to Mdmes. [page torn] and Esterhazy, & are surrounded with priests. Count Wrbna said to me on my saying so, although he is a very good Catholic, "Ah! when our Priests get hold of an English Convert don't they grip him fast—they never let him go out of their clutches." I am aston- ished at the Austrians; they seem so well aware of the bad effects of their religion upon all classes, especially exemplified in the Italians, and yet they never seem to see the necessity of having any other and better system and go on without think- ing much about it, and if you press them they only shrug their shoulders like Frenchmen....

The other day Beppo went with me to St. Mark's and when- ever I sit down he goes to an Altar and says his prayers regularly & devoutly. At Dinner I asked him what he said. "Oh, several Paters & Aves." John said, as he began to declaim Latin, "But what do they mean?" Beppo replied, "Oh! Pater noster means *Padre nostra*." "Yes," said John, "go on, what does 'Qui in coeli est' mean?" He could not tell, nor any other part, nor the prayers to the Madonna—he had never been told a word of what they meant. The same day was the Fete of the Madonna of the Intercession and Beppo assured me gravely that if any man or woman fell into the water on that day they would not be drowned. I said, "Do you really think so, Beppo?" "Oh, certainly, Signora." I said, "Then please jump in and I will pay for your wet clothes." He said it was rather too cold. I went in the evening to Mdme. Pallavicini's where were two or three Austrians and I told them these things. They laughed and said it was all the Priests' fault who taught the people to be superstitious. I said, "And yet you Austrians protect this system," and they shrugged their shoulders. The Ladies were doing no work because it was a fete day, and on Sundays they all sew and do crochet work....

Casa Wetzlar, 20th December
... I have been what you would call rather gay this week. On Wednesday [the 17th] Mdme Pal—her name is so long I shall always in future call her Jane—wrote to me saying they were going to see the Russian steamer and would I go. I was in bed and said I couldn't, but at one, whilst I was eating my lunch, Ct. Falkenhayn & Gilbert Nugent came in & insisted that I should come. I went below and found the Russian ship's boat and Mdme. Gnostoff, the Russian Consuless, waiting. It was very famous to be rowed out on the Lagune by 21 Russian sailors and a Pilot who directed them. They were dressed in blue and checked shirts with open collars and a handkerchief round their necks, the ends pulled through a sort of brass ring with a stone in the middle, rather pretty. They row tremendously fast but very ungracefully, throwing their bodies and heads forward at the same moment and using their whole strength. You would think half an hour a day at such work enough. When we arrived at the Wladimir we were received by the Captain, Count Rasinski, and his Officers and all the Crew, 280 Russians on deck. As it was the first time in my Life I had seen any Russians you may be sure I was much interested, and an uglier looking set of men I never saw. I think them the ugliest people I have seen, something between Chinese and negroes, but that is the Mongol type and they have all kinds of beauty and

ugliness. Their Language however is lovely. It is as soft as Italian and as fluent as French. I was charmed with it. The Captn. could only speak English and Russian & showed me every thing—every thing being English—Cannon, Ship, Plate, Coals, newspapers even, and everything made in London. The fittings were plain & substantial and he showed us the Grand Duke's bedroom and the Ladies' room and Ct. Wrbna's &c.

They all went away last night, the whole Court, to Trieste for three days for the Duchess to shop as it appears the shops there are much better and she is fond of toillette and pretty things. She is very handsome and looks nice & is, I fancy, a great talker. I saw her yesterday on the Square by herself, very richly dressed, rather too much so. She had on a dark maroon tartan velvet dress with a black velvet Polka [a tight fitting jacket] trimmed with sable and a white satin bonnet covered with Brussels lace. Wrbna told me the other day how they spend their time. They walk after lunch till four and dine at five. At six the gentlemen go to their rooms for an hour to smoke their cigars, and at 7 the Duchess walks on the Square for an hour till tea time with Wrbna. I said, "In the Dark?" & he says, "Yes, every night, the Doctors have ordered." At 8 tea and at nine she ought to retire, but it appears she must be fond of chatting with the Count for when they first came he used to come to us at the Ctsse.'s at nine, and the other night he did not appear till half past ten which annoys him not a little for he daren't stir until she does, and although he says she is of "une amabilité excessive" he naturally likes to choose his society, and yet I don't wonder at her liking him he is so nice and so perfectly comme il faut, but he is a little accustomed to it now because he says he is always obliged to give up his own pleasure when he is with the Emperor who naturally often wants and has to go one place when his aide de camp has plans of his own.

On Friday, being the Emperor of Russia's Fête day,[1] they had a beautiful parade on the Square in compliment to the Grand Duke. I went into the Palace of the Governor with Jane

[1] St Nicholas's day was the 6th, but the Russians still kept the Julian Calendar which was twelve days behind the rest of Europe: Effie must, therefore, have meant Thursday.

and Princess Jablonowska and Falkenhayn and Gilbert Nugent. We ascended the stairs with Radetzky and Prince Liechtenstein.[1] The former talked to Jane all the way up, and if the Marshall had been at his ease in a Russian uniform he had on out of compliment, she would have introduced me, but he had on Marshall's boots and the poor old man could hardly get up stairs and Count Thun was obliged to help him on one side. We had a beautiful large room given us and when the wonderful Band began to play below [the palace windows look on to the Piazza as well as the lagoon], Count Nugent and I had such a Polka round and round on the green cloth in the middle. Wrbna came in to see if we were well placed before he went to join the staff. He had on the most beautiful dress of his Regiment, the Polish Lancers. It was all green and red & fur and plume of feathers, but we only saw him a minute and I was so amused at seeing so many orders that I was counting them and looking about for more amongst the Ornaments of his dress. He had two Hessian orders besides the Iron Crown, St. Anne, St. George and I can't tell you the names of all the enamelled birds & men and women in medals. When he was gone Count Nugent sighed and said, "Just to think of Eugène being three years younger than me, 27 that is [he was in fact 29], & me 30, and look at him with his position and all these orders." It appears that Marshall Nugent won't give his son the means to enter the Diplomatic Line and he is here doing nothing but attending to his health. I like him much better as the affectation wears off and his real talents appear. He sings and speaks every Language and dialect known and plays beautifully—and paints equally well. He says he is going to paint me one of these days.[2]

After the Parade, in the evening they had a Serenade in the Square by Torchlight but I did not go as I was at a Soirée at

[1] Probably Prince Francis, a brother of the reigning Prince and a Lt.-Field-Marshall in the Austrian Army. Liechtenstein was then part of the German Confederation It became independent in 1866.

[2] Gilbert Nugent had served for three years in Croatia in command of a troop of Cavalry, until one day his servant shot him in the arm by mistake. He was obliged to leave the army after being eight months in bed. He eventually became a Knight of Malta.

Jane's. I thought there would be nobody there except Gilbert and Mdme. Jablonowska. I put on my white Cashmere dress, which I had washed and embroidered it anew myself and is quite beautiful, because he said he was to put on his dress of Hungarian Magnate which I was very anxious to see. I was amazed when I went in to find a dozen Austrians. They all surrounded me & examined my uniform, as they called it, and the gold net and diamonds in my hair and the gold cords & tassels round my waist. Nugent's dress is black velvet all ornamented with Turquoise buttons, and black trowsers with buttons of the same at the ancle; small boots with gold fringe hanging down and spurs of gold, the shape of a cockatoo's head; a gold belt all inlaid with Turquoise and an upper cloak of purple velvet with a deep border of crimson; large white hanging sleeves and Hungarian velvet cap with a jewel on the side and a black eagle's feather. You may fancy the effect on the handsome Count with his immense height, black eyes & hair and pale face. He looks to my mind like the Master of Ravenswood exactly....[1]

Any thing equal to the kindness of the people here I never met; they never do any thing without asking me to take a part, and were I the Grand Duchess they could not be more obliging or more ready to serve me, and always offer me the best places and the prettiest things and are really so good to me you have no idea, which I appreciate very much as it is refreshing to find people who don't flatter like the French nor say things they don't mean & yet such good breeding. One only requires to take care what one says as they tell each other everything, and were it any thing illnatured I don't think they would, but if any thing to give pleasure they repeat directly. Observing at Jane's that a gentleman whose name I had forgot at the moment was not there, I said, "Mais ou est donc Le Monsieur avec les jolies mains?" which of course was repeated and now he never gets another name but "Le M. avec les jolies mains".

Your letter has come à propos about Marmont with whom I was with last night at Ctsse. Esterhazy's in full possess[ion] of his two arms. That he was wounded there is no doubt, and

[1] The hero of Scott's *Bride of Lammermoor* which Ruskin was reading at this time.

I believe two of his fingers still show a little bruise, but the arms are perfect and he himself as gallant and [page torn] as possible....[1]

We have bright, cold Christmas weather and are to dine on Christmas Day with the Dawkins. I get on well with Mr Brown now as I take tea with him. His friends the Minischalchis have been here for a week bidding goodbye to her Brother, the Count Guerrieri, who is sent to the fortress of Olmütz for six years[2]— only fancy what a trial to his mother. Count Festitics was here today from Vicenza, he comes every week—Le beau Huzzar as Falkenhayn ca[lls] him. He has offer[ed] me a place in the Marine College at Trieste for a boy whom I wanted to place there, the son of the Lutheran Clergyman, who, poor people, want to put their son in the Austrian Marine and Festitics' family have two nominations. If I did it myself, as I made Wrbna enquire for me, it would cost £50 a year for four years which I never could dream of—but still less would I accept Festitics' kind offer because although it would cost him nothing farther than a letter to his homme-d'affairs at Vienna to arrange, I could not put myself under so great an obligation to a stranger, especially to so young a man, so that the affair is finished, much to Festitics' displeasure because he said, "If the boy

---

[1] Mr Ruskin as well as the Grays doubted that the Marshal Marmont Effie knew was *the* Marmont. Indeed Mr Ruskin believed he had proof of his death through William Harrison, John's old editor of *Friendship's Offerings* who had now joined the Crown Life Insurance Co. 'Harrison knows he is dead,' Mr Ruskin wrote on November 21, 'for his office had an insurance to pay on his life.' And even when they were at last convinced he was alive they went on maintaining that he had lost an arm at Salamanca. Even *The Times* stated this in its obituary notice of him on March 13, 1852. When Effie met the 2nd Duke of Wellington at a dinner at Mr Ford's on January 21, 1853, he told her that Marmont's arm had been condemned at Salamanca, 'but they were forced to make so hasty a retreat that the arm was uncared for and grew well'. Greville recounts in his *Memoirs* that when Marmont came to England in August after the surrender of Paris in 1830, he went down to Woolwich on the 29th 'and found the man who had pointed the gun which wounded him at Salamanca, and who had since lost his own arm at Waterloo. Marmont shook hands with him and said, "Ah, mon ami, chacun a son tour."'

[2] Count Anselmo Guerrieri Gonzaga (1819-79) had been sentenced for his part in the 1848-9 risings. The Fortress of Olmüz (now Olomone, Czechoslovakia) was the most important prison in the Austrian Empire.

has not an excellent education it is your fault, Madame"—and
John also urged me as it cost nothing but I said I could not
feel myself justified in accepting so much from the Count, and
as the people knew nothing about it, it did not signify and we
have not spoken since about it. But I would have been so glad
had it been Falkenhayn; then I think I might without impro-
priety have accepted—but you know John does not think
about these things and I always find it best not to consult
people at all unless I have the highest respect for them which
naturally I have not for anybody here, as I don't know them
enough, but I try always to do what I believe to be right and
if I do wrong or think wrongly, I am perhaps the greatest
sufferer. But now adieu....

                                        Venice, 28th December
    As I received your letter just after I had begun mine to you
I have nothing to answer, but will tell you how I have passed
Christmas week which I felt more like Christmas time than
when I was here with Charlotte as the German customs are
more like our own, and I saw several trees and gave several
presents myself to the Children on Christmas eve. Lady Sorell
had one for her little granddaughter & Jane one for her child,
but her presents were numerous & costly, and all her family sent
presents, and all of them in the house to each other for which
they had been preparing for months before and some of the
things were lovely—and the drawing room was like a Bazaar.
Falkenhayn gave the child a beautiful case of silver spoons, knife
& fork, and to Jane a steel glacé silk dress, and to Gilbert
curtains for his windows. The Ct. Pal. gave to Falkenhayn a
complete new set of English steel & Leather Bridles, and the
Queen of Sardinia sent a beautiful inlaid wooden workbox with
silver mountings to Jane with, inside, a dress of white muslin
tamboured with scarlet for the little Marie, and there were lots
of bracelets, toys &c from other people whose names I forget.
    They wanted me to come in the evening when the tree was
lighted to see the presents all divided, and I intended, but
having gone with Mary to St. Mark's to hear the Virgilio Mass
there was such a crowd that seeing the pew-opener I asked for a
place, and as every body calls me Excellency and treats me as if

I were a Personage, what did he do but take me inside the Choir and put me the opposite pew to the Grand Duke which was doubtless a great Honor but very inconvenient as I could not get out until he moved first and that was not till seven, but we heard the music beautifully and Mary was so astonished that for her she got quite excited, and as she never moves out of the house by any chance, the moment she returned she fell fast asleep in the cold Kitchen and awoke with such toothache that she had to go yesterday to the Fate Bene Fratelli and one of them pulled it out, the tooth, very well indeed for her. She said they were so kind and she behaved so ill, she was so nervous at the thoughts of it, that she tried to get out of the room & they wouldn't let her so she had to return & get it out. She was also astonished that they would take no fee. The room was full of people who had come to be cured by them.[1]

On Christmas day all the Romanists went to their three Masses and there was also Service in the German Church but I stayed at home as John read the English service and in the afternoon we dined at the Dawkins who have got a most beautiful appartment in the Barbaro Palace which they are just now putting in order. They have got in their Ballroom the most lovely frescoed and stuccoed walls and ceiling I ever saw, and they are preparing it for us to have a dance there on the last night of the Year.[2] The dinner included Mr Cheney, ourselves, a nice family of O'Connors who live here and are just returned for the winter and themselves. A number of foreigners came in the evening and it was rather stupid as we did nothing, and it

[1] Effie does not mention a visit she herself made to the Brothers. John wrote on the 21st: 'She was paying a visit yesterday to her old doctor— padre Prosdocimo—at the convent of the "Do Good" brethren— on these occasions she collects most of the monks, and the Prior and has a chat with the whole of them—Yesterday they complimented her on her better health and looks—"but"—said the Prior—"you will do yourself a great deal of harm at the Carnival"—"How so?" said Effie—"Why," said the Prior—"there are so many balls at the Carnival—and *we all know* what a dancer you are." Fancy Effie's fame as a dancer having extended to the brethren in the Island Convent!'

[2] According to John's letter of the 26th, two old brothers, the last of the Barbaros, still lived in a garret of this palace. There are two Barbaro palaces. The one next to the Cavalli (now Franchetti) had a ceiling by Tiepolo, so presumably this was the one in which the Dawkinses lived.

would have been much better had they made some of us play or
asked Nugent to sing which he always does with great good-nature
whenever he is asked. Some of the gentlemen had a rubber but
I left at half past nine as John looked bored as he sat in a corner
reading by himself, but he never talks to any body and he says
his great object is to talk as little and go through a dinner with
the smallest possible trouble to himself—and I suppose it is best
just to let him do so although I think it a great pity that he does
not exert himself to speak more as he speaks so well.

Last night was the St. Stefano day when the Carnival com-
mences and the Fenice opens. I had not intended going as John
likes attending to the music and does not like the box filled with
people talking so I did not intend to ask him—but Ct. Wrbna,
thinking it a pity I should not go, asked if I would like to go.
I said, "Oh! yes, but I could not go alone." He said, "Oh? I'll
manage all that in five minutes," and in a very short time
Princess Jablonowska sent me a note saying that Falkenhayn had
sent her one of the Emperor's boxes which are at the disposal
of the Suite of the G. Duke and would I accompany her. I went
with her. Nugent & General Duodo, whom we met, took care
of us and I was very glad that Wrbna's kindness has enabled me
to go for I never saw any thing so brilliant in Italy, every place
was filled and the crowd in the Parterre innumerable. I was next
box to the Governor [General Gorzkowski], and in the middle
of the House the Emperor's box was brilliantly lighted with the
Grand Duke in Austrian uniform [he was Colonel of an
Austrian infantry regiment] and the Duchess, who looked very
handsome in Pink glacé with low body & short sleeves and most
splendid pearls almost covering her neck, her hair with two large
plaits on each side. Behind her sat Wrbna and on the other side
of the box the other ladies and gentlemen of the suite. The
Opera was Semiramide [by Rossini] and the Music very fine....

We came away before the end as it was so long. I wish they
did not talk so much in the Theatre for it is impossible to pay
any attention to the Opera, for first came Nugent talking
English as fast as he could, at the same time the Princess talking
her Venetian and General Duodo replying—then came
Falkenhayn with his German & Wrbna with his French making
your box a sort of Babel, and as it would be considered quite

contrary to etiquette that Ladies should ever be left alone in
their box, whenever one gentleman has paid his visit of a quarter of an hour or so another arrives to take his place and you
never have a chance of being alone a minute. I complained of
it last night to Mdme. Pal. and they were all against me; they
said that the Theatre was public property and every body had
a right to call upon any body that they knew, and as most people
went every night for an hour it was economical as it saved them
lighting their rooms at home, and that having a box at the
Opera was the cheapest way for all to see people & society.[1] I
thought the system quite wrong as people who cannot see
their friends at home ought not to have a box &c but it is useless
arguing with people who have been brought up to a different
set of rules & who are happy in their mode of Life, such as it
is, and I never saw better behaved people—but for my part I
think their visiting in the Theatre quite superfluous; for
instance if, as in London, you did not see your acquaintances
often it might be allowed, but here I see Jane or Nugent or
Wrbna or Falkenhayn or Mde. Jablonowska every day, and
some of them always walk at three on the Square where I can
join them if I choose, but I prefer walking alone with Beppo
and when the Band plays I go up to the Gallery [of] the Ducal
Palace and walk up and down in the sun where I hear the
music delightfully without being near the crowd.

   Ct. Festitics has just been here and says he would not be the
reader of this crossed letter for anything.... A Happy New Year
to you all. I have on the 1st, forty Gondolier families to dinner
at eight o'clock & snap dragon.

Casa Wetzlar, 4th Jany. [1852]

   It was curious enough in your last letter your recommending
our making a new agreement with Nani. I proposed it to John
some time ago and he said, "Oh! Just let Nani alone"—but

---

   [1] The Fenice was then owned and operated by its box holders, originally
Venetian patrician families who had financed the building. A number of these
afterwards sold their boxes to foreigners but it was not until after the first
World War that ownership of a box became a liability. The holders then
handed over their rights and responsibilities to the City authorities who still
own the theatre.

when he began to be ordering more casts to be taken from the Ducal Palace and want all the money he could have,[1] I made an arrangement with Nani by which we have not so good a dinner but quite sufficient. I gave up my meat in the morning and thus save a £1 a week, a very considerable sum. It is a great mistake in most English coming to Venice, they live the same as in England. Here not much meat is required and no wine. Whenever I taste sherry I get heated but a little Port is considered good as it keeps away fever in damp weather which we have in perfection today.

John has just come in and says I am beautifully dressed and he hopes somebody will call on me to see me, which interruption however I would gladly dispense with as then I will get my letter written to you. The dress which excites John's admiration is the brown velvet I bought at Milan made with a body open in front with little tails round, à la Basquine, under which a blue satin waistcoat fastened up to the Throat in front with Pearl buttons, with frills of Valenciennes round the top at the sleeves, a coiffure of white Lace & blue ribbon. Nani's daughter, although only a common working girl, is as clever at dressmaking as any one I ever saw. I just require to show her any pattern I like in the Journal des Modes, or out of my head, and she does things very perfectly which saves me some trouble as Mary is very good but cannot learn anything of the sort although I have been teaching her ever since Melina left me.[2] Tell Sophie that I do not know where Melina is or any thing about her—I hope I shall never see her again. I think she was dreadfully intriguing. I am thankful not to have any body like her near me.

We had a very nice ball at Mrs Dawkins on the last night of the year. The rooms were most beautiful and it was only a pity the company was not more numerous because the place was large enough [for] more, at least 200 people more than were

---

[1] John had so far spent £25 on casts. On January 16 he packed up to send home '21 pieces of Ducal palace capitals &c.' By the end of February he had already spent £800 on that journey, including the rent paid up to March 9. He was deeply apologetic about being such a continual drain on his father while giving him nothing in return.

[2] After her marriage to Millais, Effie often made the costumes for his historical pictures.

there. There was an especial want of Lady dancers, and as I made a point of dancing every turn at the beginning with all the different gentlemen, who were numerous, so as not to let the party get dull, not having danced for some time I got such a pain in my side that I was glad to sit down. Mrs Dawkins looked very well. She is very handsome. She had on a pale blue glacé with a number of flounces, a Brussels lace Berthe and most superb shawl of the same.

The next evening we had even a merrier party here for I gave the Gondoliers a Fete in the Kitchen which they enjoyed immensely. They had dinner at eight o'clock, about 40 of them, and after our tea Princess Jablonowska & Jane, Nugent, Wrbna, Thun, Mr Foster, John & myself went down to see them dance. Their national dance, the Manfrina, was going on with my Mary in the middle dancing most vigorously with a nice little Gondolier of Mdme. Esterhazy's whom she had never seen before with her hands clenched on both his shoulders. All the lot were dancing a sort of rustic Polka, very badly I must confess, but in such spirits. When we entered there was such a rush to kiss our hands. The washerwoman, the belle of the evening, fastened on Mdme. Jablonowska and wrung her hands saying, "Oh, Cara Principessa—che Allegria &c." The Austrians did not seem to put them out in the least. They shouted out my name and hurraed, and Nani's son, the handsome young Priest, made an apology for not dancing the Polka because he was Religious, but said he had written a Poem in my honor which he repeated to the great delight of the party and the equal delight of the Austrians who have been teasing me ever since with lines out of the production. After we were gone, however, the Priest, not being a St. Anthony, gave way to the temptations of the dance and Polkaed till past twelve o'clock.

Count Thun went next morning to Verona. Before going he said he hoped that I would come to the Marshall's Balls of which he gives three. I said perhaps I might as Mr Ruskin wished me to know him before I left Italy and if he wanted me I would come. Today General Reischach came from Verona to invite me in the Marshall's name. He said he never sent written invitations to anyone but that I might consider this perfectly formal. I gave my thanks and will go on the 26th....

You ask about John—he is very pleased at having been made one of Turner's executors and to find that the fortune and gallery are all left to the nation so that they will not be dispersed, and he hopes that the other executors will give him all the trouble of forming the Gallery and seeing that a proper one is built. Some are anxious for him to write Turner's Life but he thinks not, and I dissuade him from it as what is known of Turner would not be profitable to any lady, and he has left no rules for painting or any memorial that would be any good but his great gift to the country. The sooner they make a Myth of him the better.[1]

John is busy at his drawings and books, writing beautiful descriptions and very poetical—he goes out after Breakfast and I never see him till dinner time. I am occupied all day till 4 o'clock and then I am at home to any body who calls. Some one or another always comes and it is agreeable to have a chat of an hour before dinner time. I can go out every night if I choose with my work any where I like but it is cold weather and I just go when I feel inclined. I have not been again at the Fenice, and these are all my doings. My music is my greatest amusement. I consider I have gained a great victory in converting my Italian master to Mendelssohn but we play all sorts of music. He is such a good little man and very clever. Although he is only 24 he arranges all the Fenice rehearsals &c. He seldom speaks but never tires playing. He says very simply that he is sure I will play music in Heaven some day because I am Buonissima Signora, but he is in horror when I come to play with my black dress lined with orange—the Austrian colors. He once hinted that it ought to be burned and when I told him that I was very fond of it, he said he could not play with me in it for I took up so much room and the sleeves were large enough to hold a Breviary inside each—now he makes a little face when he sees it and says nothing. Now goodbye....

---

[1] Turner had died on December 19. Effie, with John, had first called on him in Queen Anne Street on May 3, 1848. Thereafter she visited him frequently and was proud to be one of the few 'ladies' allowed to enter his house. In his will he expressed the wish that a special gallery for his pictures might be built on to the National Gallery, or his own house be turned into a gallery.

While Effie and John were staying with Mr Fawkes at Farnley Hall in April, 1851, she had written on the 16th: 'I play on the piano which delights Mr Fawkes immensely. He is very fond of my music and would have me playing all the evening if I could. John thinks much more of my music now, especially since I came here because one day when I was playing out of my head, he put a Turner drawing before me and told me to play a piece descriptive of the scenery & the water &c. which I did and he was so astonished and thought it so much more wonderful than it really was that he said he would give me any instruction in music I liked, & which I shall take advantage in the winter when I am in Italy. D.V.' In February, 1853, she sent a dressing case to Venice for her music master, Signor Busoni.

Casa Wetzlar, 10th Jany.
Although it is rather late to begin a letter to you on a Saturday night at half past ten, still I may not be able to find a better time as John is still in his study, I don't know what about, since half past eight—for Count Wrbna came to pay me a visit and after John had almost annihilated him in abusing his belief in the Priests and the absurdity of his remaining under the teaching of a Church in which he could not trust, he walked out of the room with a great Book of History under his arm and I have not heard of him since. The Count came here to see some old Venice glass which I had got to sell, which I daresay astonishes you but I know a Jew in the Ghetto (or Jews' Quarter) who collects these things. I have bought some beautiful wine glasses and the other day he brought another set of the same and as I had no desire to buy more Ct. Eugène took them for his Menage in Transylvania. What a Col. of Lancers has to do with rococo things like Venetian glass I don't know, but I suppose he will establish himself some day like other people & have a house,[1] so at least seems to think the Grand Duchess whose Christmas day was two days ago [in fact on the 6th] when she had a most splendid Tree all hung with every kind of fruit and Bonbons for the two or three children belonging to the suite, and on tables were laid all the presents for her Ladies and the

[1] Count Wrbna never married. He became a General and died in 1880, aged sixty-two.

gentlemen and nobody gave presents excepting herself and the
Grand Duke. They gave to Ct. Wrbna a Tea Service in Silver,
and Coffee Pot as well with his Arms & Motto engraven in
Russian letters—two Superb China vases and some drawings
in Water Colors by the Grand Duke. All the other presents were
magnificent and costly. The same day the G. Duke caused to
be distributed through the Russian Consul sums varying in size
according to the case to all the poor women in Venice. George
said the number who received was immense—but they could
hardly do less than give away a large sum of money in one way
or another for the Emperor furnishes them with everything
they have, and if they gave parties it would still be at the
Emperor's expense.[1]

By the bye can I never make you believe that Marmont is here
& in possession of two arms, both made of flesh and blood
with all the fingers on all, made of the same material to
match? He came to wish me Happy new Year the other day but
I was not at home and he left his card which I send to you....
John wanted me to send it to his Father who is not more believing than yourselves on this point, excepting Papa who seems
to have taken my word for it at first, but send the card to Mr
Ruskin as it will perhaps convince him.[2] I shall be amused to
hear what you say now for although you don't seem to doubt
any longer that he is alive his poor arm you will insist to
have been left in Spain. Ct. Festitics the other day was greatly
amused when I told yr ideas. He says Marmont used to visit
his Father in Hungary when he was five years old, now 30 years
ago, always with the same arms on as far as he can remember....

My next gaiety will be the Marshall's Ball at Verona on the
26th. General Reischach came the other day from Verona to
invite a few people here in the Marshall's name—I hope the
Dawkins will go and regret that Mdme. Pallavicini's mourning
will prevent her this going out this year. Prince Jablonowski is

[1] Edward Cheney wrote to Lord Holland on January 7 that 500,000
Austrian lire (£17,000) had been distributed by the Russian Consul in
presents and charity.
[2] Marmont's card has been preserved:
                    Le Maréchal
                    Duc de Raguse

still in Vienna which will prevent *Her* going which I also regret
as she is such a good nice little woman. Ct. Nugent & Ct.
Wrbna say they go and I know several people at Verona, so that
after I leave my card on Ctsse. Radetzky every thing will be
done. John says he goes the day before as he has a good deal
of work to do there and he would have had to have gone at any
rate. I have persuaded him to leave the servants here as I
think it nonsense having the expence of them....[1]

George seems to think Uncle And [Andrew Jameson] severe
against my friends the Austrians on account of their Religion,
or rather their defending & supporting the Roman Catholic
doctrines. I think him quite right as far as I know them and I
have daily opportunities of seeing some of them. Their only Religion is Honor and a strong feeling of love to the traditions of
their families mixed with Moyen-age sentiments of Chivalry
and knowledge of the Art of War, and our country people who
settle here show them no better example but do every thing they
do and are perhaps worse after a time. They think me dreadfully
rigid because I don't let any one in on Sunday, or walk to hear
the Music on the Place or go to the Opera or pay visits—and read
a sermon to the servants in the evening. They call me "Kitzerin"
[*sic*], or the German for Heretic, and say if the Priests only
knew how I argued with them that they would be glad to burn
me. Although so clever about every thing else, in Religion they
are deplorably ignorant. I think most children of Sophia's age
knows more than they do. It would perfectly surprise you. For
instance one of them came in yesterday and I was reading the
Bible—"Qu'est-ce que c'est ce livre la?" said he. "C'est Le Bible,
Monsieur Le Comte." "Le Bible? Je n'ai jamais entendu parler
du Bible"—he had never heard of it he said, and appeared never
to have learned any thing but the Priests' Catechism....

The weather is very cold & fine, but rain is wanted as the
wells are empty and we are obliged to buy water as it is six
weeks since we have had a shower of rain....

---

[1] It was difficult for Effie to do right in Mr Ruskin's eyes. He wrote on
February 11: 'If you went to Verona without George & Mary in order to
save—Mama and I would rather live on Bread & water than that you
should do same.'

The wells in every campo, including the two famous ones in the courtyard of the Doge's palace, were public cisterns filled with rainwater filtered through sand. Horatio Brown wrote in *Life in the Lagoons* in 1884: 'When little rain has fallen and the wells run dry, the contractors who are bound to keep four and a half feet of water in every well, find themselves obliged to carry the fresh supply from the Brenta, past Fusina, into the city.' Ruskin in Volume II of *The Stones* mentions the 'large barges laden with fresh water from Fusina in round white tubs seven feet across'. Flagg in 1853 described how all day long the water carriers—chiefly female peasants from the Friuli, with naked feet and short bright-coloured skirts, wandered about the narrow lanes, uttering their mournful cry of *acqua fresca* at one centime a cup, their pails suspended from a yoke on their shoulders. They can be seen in many of the old prints of Venice. Since 1884 drinking water has been piped from the mainland.

Casa Wetzlar, 16th Janry.
I am going out to tea to Mdme. Pallavicini's but have time to begin my weekly budget before I go. We are neither of us very well but I am the worst. I am perfectly exhausted this evening from want of sleep and John the same. Fancy us both laying awake all night and getting up at four this morning, he to put on his clothes and write, and I to dance about in my nightgown till I was fairly done up which procured me an hour and a half's troubled slumber....
We have been much shocked by the dreadful loss of the Amazon with our friend Eliot Warburton on board. I am so sorry for his poor young wife and infant children.[1] I had a long letter from Lady Eastlake today which mentions that there is no

---

[1] Eliot Warburton, born 1810, was the author of *The Crescent and the Cross*, an account of a Near Eastern tour, published in 1844, which had caused as much stir as *Eothen* which came out the same year. Effie had met the Warburtons when lunching with Mr Ford on January 2, 1851, and 'did not think much of them'. Nevertheless they came to two of her Friday parties. The *Amazon*, a 2,250-ton steamship, the latest built of the Royal Mail Steam Packet Co., had left London on the afternoon of January 2 bound for the West Indies. Two days later, just entering the Bay of Biscay, she had caught fire and only 59 were saved of her 161 passengers and crew. Warburton went down with the ship after rescuing a number of women passengers. In 1848 he had married Matilda Grove. They had two sons. She married again in 1857.

hope of his having been saved—and which I think worth enclosing to you, she writes so exceedingly well and tells me about
just all the people I want to know. John thinks it a delightful
letter, too, but is angry at her for writing so of Turner as he
thinks one Turner equal to many Amazons and says that many
ships are lost and mines explode and because the people are
not fashionable, or known, no work is made about them. But
Lady E seems quite right about the confusion of the will and
I don't think things will be cleared for many a long day....[1]

Who do you think we are going to have for a visitor to
occupy our pretty little spare room and French Bed?—Mr
Newton who is coming out immediately on his way to Mytilene in Lesbos to which place he has been appointed Consul
by Ld. Granville immediately on his coming into office, as
Newton wants to leave England and thinks he can gain many
treasures for the British Museum in Greece and Asia Minor
which I have no doubt he will do—but I am very sorry he is
leaving London. He is one of our best friends there and we got
so fond of him in the summer when he was with us [in Switzer-
land]. *Romance* is at the bottom of it—which I think he might
have cured without exiling himself in this way but other causes
combined. His health is very bad and the constant six hours
daily drudgery at the Museum annoyed & worried his mind full
of more intellectual subjects. I shall be very glad to see him
again and John has never ceased longing for him to show him
one thing after another since we came here but this about
Newton entre-nous as I do not think it is known yet.[2]

[1] Turner's will was contested by his relations and litigation went on for four
years.

[2] John thought Newton's appointment not good enough—he could not
do much with £250 a year and there was always a risk of fever. He wrote on
January 15: 'How would mama and you do—if you were *his* father and
mother instead of mine, having seen him for about a fortnight once a year,
since he was at college—and now having to let him go to the Troad.' Mr
Ruskin thoroughly disliked Newton and had written to John about him on
August 14: 'The Elgin Marbles petrify him & as he so hates children he will
never marry other than Niobe after she is thoroughly done with her young
ones—thoroughly done into alibaster in a state fit for him & the Museum.'
In 1861 he married Mary Severn, an artist, daughter of Joseph Severn, the
friend of Keats, and sister of Arthur Severn who married Joan Agnew,
Ruskin's ward and cousin.

John and I had a little walk on the Square yesterday as he wanted to see the Grand Duchess whom he had admired at a distance. He was much disappointed when he got nearer, and said as an Austrian said to me the other day remarking her, "Il faut etre bien indulgente aux Grand Duchesses", but we had not far to go before we found her as she walks up and down amongst the people with her husband who is dressed in common Austrian uniform by her desire, she being very young and far too striking for this season. Fancy a beautiful pale pink glacé silk dress, full skirt, with a black velvet Polka surrounded with sable, and black lace and pink satin bonnet, for walking in the street in the middle of January! She constantly comes out in a change and they tell me she has 9 cloaks of velvet all trimmed with splendid furs and 40 dresses which I believe may be quite true—but she has certainly a very handsome figure and only 20. John wants me to be presented to her—but I dislike all Russians and I don't like the trouble of arranging to do it. I would much rather go to the Duchesse de Berry and the Ct. de Chambord when they come. The latter however is still at Prague as they say he does not like coming because the Grand Duke is here because of the etiquette of visiting together, but his mother is coming almost directly.

I was out last night at Madame Esterhazy's where I conferred with Marmont whose two arms looked perfectly sound and well. Madame E. has fixed now to receive every Friday which is very nice as it collects all the people together. Last night was the first, and the result was a very brilliant Soirée of all nations I should say—and I thought the people excessively well dressed & well behaved. The rooms hung with crimson damask & gold & white painting made the people look so fresh and gay, and the numerous Austrian uniforms contribute very much to the gay appearance of the room.

Adieu
Effie

RADETZKY AT LAST

❧

Effie's next letter was to her father. It bears no address or date but is postmarked 'Venezia 19 Gennaio'. In December there had been two more inflammatory letters from Mr Ruskin to Mr Gray accusing the young people of extravagance, and Mr Gray had evidently relayed much of this to Effie. Mr Ruskin also criticised her taste for 'gay colours' in dress which Mr Gray had tact enough not to pass on.

Dearest Papa

Many many thanks for your delightful long letter just received ... but I am very uneasy at your constant confinement to the Office.... I wish May were here and George in Perth to relieve you, or, to return to the old story, that I had been the Boy and never left you—which I believe in the end might have been better for all parties, for then the Ruskins would not have had me to grumble at and I would always have been with my mother and you and amongst the places I shall always love best. But then poor John would not have been so happy as he is with me and it is always something that he thinks me perfect—as long as he is not with the old people—but there is the rub— and as his Father trys every point to blame me on and pretends to be very fond of me all the time, every time John is with them without me his mind is poisoned.

Thank you very much for your remarks about our expences which is only another form of Mr R's continued and never-ceasing disappointment of John's marriage with me instead of Miss Lockhart or some person of higher position and more fortune. How he can accuse me of extravagance is to me too strange. He never accuses frankly and openly but I have seen it in some of his letters to John for a week past. They have given John most expensive habits which added to his generous mind entails on him the loss of quantities of money. He has a perfect mania for buying old books to aid him in his Book on Venice which I know Mr Ruskin will lose a great deal on, as it is not selling at all and the beautiful plates which cost £30 & £50 each engraving, and are invaluable as records of Architecture, are not sold as the public are not inclined to give £12 for a work in which they are not interested in and which if they get the loan of they still like to see.[1] These losses annoy and disappoint Mr. R, not so much I believe really for the money as that he is exceedingly proud & cannot bear to think that the fame of his son is declining—which is only in the natural consequences of things as no Author enjoys continued popularity—but John's mind is more vigorous & strong than ever it was before, and that will pass.

But to return to the point—John has a man constantly taking casts for him from Ducal Palace &c to send home which must cost him a great deal more than he thinks. I have remonstrated with him but in vain. He only replys, "Just think what treasures these would be to the British Museum were the Austrians to blow down St Mark's some day." I say, "Yes, if we had money." He says, "Oh, we have plenty for that and I must always have everything proper for my work, even should we live in a Garret." "Well," I said, "I shall not assist you. I shall give up my modelling Master," which he willingly assented to. I also wished to give up my music lessons but he decidedly refused. This is the only expence I have. I have wished him to send away the gondola and Carlo—to whom I pay 14 Zwanzigers a week for being with John about two hours a day—but no, he says he must have him. Then my quarterly allowance is due for some time and I do not intend to ask him for it.[2]

Our acquaintance here cost us literally nothing—I never give parties and there is no expence attending my visiting as I brought a good supply of clothes from London. I have bought

[1] The first volume of *The Stones* was selling very badly. The large plates, *Examples of Architecture of Venice,* had been issued at the same time in a separate folio volume. It was intended to issue twelve parts at a guinea each but in fact only three were published with five plates in each part. Later the success of the three volumes of *The Stones* was such that in three years Ruskin made £3,069 profit from the 1886 edition alone.

[2] She did not get her full quarter's allowance of £25 until April 10, her wedding day.

nothing to speak of here and I am always better dressed than any body else because I can, thanks to Mama, do without dressmakers and can arrange my toilettes to look like new. But the Ruskins do such strange things & show no ideas of economy. Mr. R. bought the other day another new Turner, cost £170 guineas. John was angry and said it was worth to him about £80.[1] Then Mr. R. *writes* that when they come abroad in May to travel to Switzerland, and perhaps Italy, that it would be *so sad* to cross the water, and land at Calais without John, that we must come home and meet them and return directly with them to Switzerland—at any rate John—but I may either stay with you for a couple of months (which I believe they would prefer) but I said to John, "Just fancy the expense of our crossing the Alps twice and for what good?" "Never mind," says John, "it must be done—it does not signify whether it is folly or not if they want it. What will you do?" he said. I said I would do what was most economical and that I had quite made up my mind a year ago never to return to Perth (much as I should like to be with you) unless he accompanied me. Nor would I ever again permit him to be travelling months with his parents without me. He seemed satisfied and pleased & will probably leave Mary and me some where in May whilst he goes home for them. Are they not strange people? Write to me all you think. John never sees your letters and I never speak on these subjects unless I am obliged....

John had written on the 15th: 'I don't think Effie will stay in Scotland this time—she did not find it so pleasant before—and besides people made so many impertinent remarks to her, and talked so much scandal that I don't much wonder at her not choosing to do it a second time. And the *travelling* with Effie is just what I wanted to save you by your meeting us, for she is slow and must stop to lunches and cannot rise early—and in fact—would not fit with our ways of doing the thing.' Effie's belief that John thought her perfect was ill-founded. Mr Ruskin had written a month before this to say

[1] This was Carisbrooke Castle, a drawing Turner had executed for his *England and Wales* series. John had told his father on December 27 that it would be a good buy at £50 and an ill one at £80. Before this letter arrived his father had bought it for *105 guineas*. Mr Ruskin had already, apart from this, spent £650 on pictures that year.

that he was *not* coming to Switzerland, a fact which John does not
seem to have told Effie.

    Casa Wetzlar, January '52 [Postmarked Venezia 26 Genn]
My dearest Mama
    ... I go tomorrow morning to Verona for the Marshall's
Ball in the evening which is expected to be very brilliant and
will include amongst the guests the Arch Duke Charles Ferdinand,[1] brother of the A. Duke Albert whom I met in
November. I am the only Lady going from here. The Dawkins,
foolish people, ought to have gone too but they seemed to
think it a slight not having a special invitation from Radetzky and now when the thing is explained it is too late for them
to make their preparations. Mr Foster—hearing their objections which he thought very absurd after General Reischach
had been here on purpose to invite us—wrote to our nice little
friend Count Thun, the Marshall's Aide de Camp. He wrote
back yesterday saying, "I have just shown yr. letter to his
Excellency the Marshall who begs it to be distinctly understood
to the Ladies in Venice that it is impossible for him to send
a few written invitations, much as he should like to do so, as
he would then, being Governor of Lombardy, be obliged to
write all the Ladies of Milan, Vicenza, Padua &c and there
would be no end, besides he has the misfortune not to have
a large enough house to contain them and he could not ask
them to come to the uncomfortable Inns unless they chose it—
but he adds that all who will come to Verona shall have a
proper invitation the moment they are in the Town and shall
be received and entertained with every possible attention."
    I am in great hopes to find that the Minischalchis will go,
as two days ago the Emperor has granted to the Count Guerrieri, her brother, a full pardon. As you know he was
condemned to six years in Ölmütz fortress—and Ct. Minischalchi is now in Vienna to thank the Emperor. She, it is said,
will in consequence go to the Ball, and if she does the other
Veronese Ladies will also. I think she could hardly do less
notwithstanding her hatred to the Austrians....

    [1] Second son, aged thirty-three, of Archduke Charles; a Lt.-Field-Marshal
and as yet unmarried (see note 1, p. 284).

The Grand Duchess has had visitors this week in the persons of the Duke of Parma and the Ct. & Ctsse Trapani—he, you will recollect, was the intended at one time of the Queen of Spain & is youngest brother to the King of Naples. She is a daughter of the Grand Duke of Tuscany and about 18 & plain.[1] They were all in the Theatre on Friday [the 23rd], when I was there, sitting in the State Box. It was interesting seeing them all together, so young, none of them thirty. They behaved well and seemed to enjoy themselves. When they got tired they went into a little room which they have at the back where Punch, ices and Coffee was served to them. The Grand Duchess looked very handsome. She never wears any thing on her head but two large plaits of hair on each side and a blue & white striped silk dress with a white waistcoat & jacket very open at the neck.

I asked Wrbna last night how all the princes amused themselves. He said he was thankful to say they were gone; as for the Duke of Parma he was like a Laquais, & the Trapanis could not, he was certain, amuse themselves any where for they were like Idiots and such manners—he was quite astonished. They did not know how to conduct themselves in a Salon at all (you must know the Austrians are full of etiquette and beautiful manners) but it appears the Grand Duchess asked them to dinner—they dined at five and it lasted till six. Then the etiquette is that they should stand for a minute and then take leave, but they stood and stood until seven o'clock, dying to get away and yet not knowing what to do, till at last the Grand Duchess, being quite fatigued standing, gave them their Congé herself. The Duke of Parma, who is a great rattle, talked for the whole party—but should you not have thought, considering the rank of the pair, that they would at least have known the ordinary courtesies of the Drawing-room? The fashion here with every one is to withdraw immediately after dinner and to

[1] Isabella, Countess Trapani, would not be eighteen until May. She was a daughter of Leopold II, Grand Duke of Tuscany, and his second wife, a sister of King Ferdinand II of Naples. In April, 1850, she had married her mother's youngest brother, Count Trapani, born 1827, who had been one of the two candidates favoured by the British Government for the hand of another niece, Queen Isabella II of Spain. (The Pope may give dispensation for such consanguineous marriages among royalty.) For the Duke of Parma see note 2, p. 280.

return at nine o'clock if there is a Soirée afterwards, to which they are separately invited. It is much better than in England making a Dinner party an affair of four or five hours. I think an hour is much nicer and then you have all your evening free....

I heard of Mrs Macdonald's having a son and am very glad.[1] I think it will do them both much good. I am trying to impress on John that he ought to write a note to Mr M on the event— which he seems to think will be a great bore as he can't understand what people have sons for, turning their homes topsy-turvy and making a disturbance. He says in a very doleful tone, "Must I begin, 'my dear Macdonald, I hear you have got a Baby—I hope you have got a good wetnurse for it?'" I cannot help laughing at him but he considers children of tender age like so many Kittens or Puppies—but he is delighted when you tell me about all the children at home and all their little stories.[2]

I am glad the Major [Guthrie, a very old friend of the Grays] has paid his bet about Marmont with whom I was the night before last. He certainly has no Gutta Percha arm. He says he is going to the Military Ball here on Wednesday to see me dance and begged that I would look my best for the Occasion. I said certainly if I was not too tired after Verona and back in time. You have no idea how Lazy I am. Although I am going in the morning at ten I have not put out one of my things nor decided what to put on except a coiffure I have made for myself which John says is decidedly Moyen-age and the prettiest thing he ever saw. It is a piece of scarlet velvet with a fringe of large & small pearls all round; a point à la Marie Stuart comes in front,

[1] In June, 1849, William Macdonald had married Clara Brownlow, daughter of 1st Lord Lurgan by his second wife. Effie had attended the wedding at St Martin's near Perth while John was abroad and had written an account of it to Mr Ruskin at Chamonix. This letter is now at Bembridge.

[2] Effie was not fond of babies either. When John's cousin, Mary Bolding (*née* Richardson), had a son in May, 1848, Effie wrote to her mother: 'I tried to enforce on John that we ought to call on her but he won't as he says he cannot bear lumps of *Putty* as he terms babies and I think as little of them excepting the little ones at Bowerswell as he does.' She went on that Mrs Ruskin was very indignant with him for she loved babies with all her heart. When he did at last go and see the Bolding baby in November, Effie reported, 'He likes it a little because he says it is not like a baby at all and has eyes like rat's fur and a black face like a mouldy walnut, which is a great deal for him.'

and it covers all the head, with the hair plaited in bows low on the neck behind and my braids in front—but further than this I have done nothing, but when once I begin I don't take very long. I shall be quite delighted to see a little country Landscape again.... I shall probably have Cts. Nugent & Wrbna with me in the Railway [the bridge had now been repaired] as I saw them at a distance today which showed me they were not gone. I wish they were, for it is so tiresome talking to people in the Railroad. Ct. Eugène, being Court bred, does every thing so properly & quietly, but Nugent having English at his command argues upon every subject grave & gay. He bores John as he will talk Architecture.

I am very glad to hear you get on with yr. French. I have great practice here & make much progress as I read an hour to John every night and nothing else is generally spoken here.[1] I am very sorry not to have the opportunity of acquiring more German but none of the educated Austrians ever talk their own Language in society and I do not like to insist upon their speaking with me as I make so many faults and conversation does not go on so easily. I must now conclude as John calls me to stop....

Casa Wetzlar, 1st February

I have been stopped from beginning my letter to you at least an hour ago by a visit from Lady Sorell who always talks so much & so agreeably that when she does not go on too long she generally makes me laugh at her stories.... You will be glad to hear that we enjoyed our visit to Verona exceedingly. We went on Monday [the 26th] morning at ten and you may imagine I was tired and hungry enough when we arrived at Verona at three for Cts. Nugent, Festitics & Wrbna came into the carriage beside me, and John, knowing that they would talk the whole way, went into another part to study. I took refuge in my work and spoke no more than I could help, but they were so anxious to show me all the places where they had bivouaced during the war, what Bridges they had blown up and where they had slept months in the open air that I could not be dumb altogether. Arriving at the station we found Ct. Thun waiting to receive us

[1] She was reading to John *Histoire des Croisades* in six volumes by J. F. Michaud.

with a formal invitation from the Marshall for us which I daresay Mr Ruskin will send you—so that you see he lost no time in doing every thing that was polite, and Thun added that we had better come as soon after eight as possible as the Marshall was so punctual and liked every one to be there at the hour invited.

Our old rooms in the Due Torri were occupied by the Governor and they gave us very good ones at the back, but John was very displeased as he likes to look at the beautiful Monuments in front.[1] They said the other room in front had been kept for Count Wrbna. I went and told him that with his permission I would order his bed to be carried out as I knew he didn't care in the least for any Monuments in Verona & would prefer the comfortable sofa in the other room where he could smoke after dinner at his ease. He replied in his usual manner that he was my "très humble serviteur" and to dispose of him in every way I should think best. I must say that their words are not words only; they all came one after another and begged to know if they could be of any use, all saying, "Madame, je suis tout à fait à votre disposition &c". Mr Foster brought me a beautiful bouquet of flowers, red & white Camelias, Myrtle, Carnations &c. I was very sorry some of the other Ladies had not come, for they seemed to think it so polite in us coming, & said the Marshall would be so pleased. He inhabits the same Palace which Napoleon had and it is very richly & beautifully furnished without any pretentions to effect or show—the Pictures, China and furniture all good & the latter of dark crimson velvet in some rooms, and green & gold damask in the other, very handsome. The Ball room, white & gold, with a gallery above for the Musicians and lighted by Candelabra from the roof and innumerable wax lights, filled with hundreds of men in every Austrian uniform of Cavalry or Infantry, looked exceedingly brilliant.[2]

On entering the house the stairs all lined with Crimson

---

[1] The tomb of Castelbarco above the cemetery gate of the church of St Anastasia which Ruskin described in Volume I of *The Stones* as 'the most perfect Gothic sepulchral monument in the world'.

[2] The Palazzo degli Emilii is now a picture gallery. The furniture and decorations appear to be unchanged since Effie's day but a false ceiling must have been put in the ballroom for there is no place now for a minstrels' gallery.

cloth and Orange trees and plants at each side. We passed through some rooms filled with people amongst whom at a glance I recognised Ctsse. Minischalchi who looked handsomer than any one else & very happy—and Cts. Wrbna & Festitics talking with Princess Esterhazy and her daughter. The former was Ambassadress in London for long & her son is married to Lady Jersey's daughter.[1] Her dress was magnificent, of blue & white Moiré with Brussels Lace flounce, a beautiful Coiffure of Gold Lace, and on each side of her hair in front a pearl pin surmounted by a little coronet of diamonds. Each pearl of pear shape was as long as that line [about 3 inches]; I never saw any thing to equal them; nevertheless she said to General Reischach when he was admiring them that she would willingly exchange all she had for my Youth & looks.

We gained the Ballroom where Count Thun presented me to Radetzky who looked very glad to see me, & taking my hand instantly turned round and presented me to the Arch Duke Charles Ferdinand which I believe was a very distinguished honor. He then took me the length of the Ballroom to the Countess Radetzky who also received me very kindly and I talked with her till Ct. Festitics came with some half dozen of his children as he calls his Officers and I was soon dancing away with people of all nations and tongues. Baron Diller, the Marshall's other Aide de Camp, had the arrangement of all the dances—& Thun that of the tea-making, which he did till 12 o'clock. He sat at the head of a long table and made tea for every one who came in. Every one sat down and every thing was so comfortable & well arranged. On my way with General Sternberg to see how he was getting on we passed the splendid present given to the Marshall by the Emperor & the Army, a sort of trophy made in Metal and gold, beautifully wrought with Cannon & little groups lying round of all the different

[1] Sarah Villiers, born 1822, eldest daughter of 5th Earl of Jersey, married in 1842, Prince Nicholas Esterhazy. She died in November, 1853. Her mother-in-law, Marie Thérèse, born 1794, daughter of Prince Charles Alexander of Thurn and Taxis, had married in 1812 Prince Paul Esterhazy, the most popular of all the Austrian Ambassadors to London. They had two daughters, both married, but the one at the ball was more likely to have been Countess Cavriani whose husband was in command of a brigade at Como.

uniforms in the Army. Lying on the top were two Marshall's
Batons, one given by the Emperor, the other by the Emperor
of Russia. Both were about a foot & quarter long surrounded
by wreathes of Laurel in green enamel & diamonds. The
whole was in a large glass case. At the side of the room was a
glass cabinet full of cases which I hope to see on a future occasion, containing all the orders and presents Radetzky has
received from every power in Europe.

On our way to the tea room, Wrbna came up to us as I had
not yet spoken to him and I could not help saying, "Mais
comme il est beau." "Pas de doute," said Sternberg. "Eh bien,"
said Ct. Eugène, "je puis retourner votre complément avec
vous; il a decidé avec L'Arche Duc que vous êtes La Reine du
Bal." Of course I said I was glad the Marshall was pleased and
then proceeded to examine his dress to amuse myself. Perhaps
I admired it more because it was the only one of the kind, being
Aide de Camp of the Emperor, & the decorations were so
numerous and so valuable & quaint that I have not time to
describe it all, but I counted ten Orders, some in Diamonds,
and I finished by telling him that now I neither wondered at
his taking an hour to dress nor bringing his valet with him from
Venice for the purpose—for they were all so surprised at my
being able to dress myself without a maid.

The supper was at twelve and was very interesting. All the
Ladies sat down; all the gentlemen, except the Arch Duke who
was the only gentleman to sit down at the top of the table, a few
Generals and one or two more who remained, were all the rest
supped in another room. The table was covered with Candelabra, Baskets of flowers or bon-bons and Bottles of wine, very
pretty but nothing to eat—but for it we were handed cups of
delicious Hot Soup, cold meats and Creams &c, all very good.
The Kitchen was next to the supper room & here was the
Marshall in his element. He kept going about helping & seeing
every body helped, going twice into the Kitchen to bring out
things for people and acting exactly like the head waiter, no
body interfering with him. Count Thun, who was standing
behind my chair, said, "Now the Marshall is in his element; he
is indefatigable and arranges every thing here himself." He
came up at that moment & gave Thun three plates, telling him

to go about & see that the Ladies had all enough to eat. Thun went away saying, "Le Maréchal a toujours peur que tout le monde va mourir de faim ici."[1] He told me next day that he [Radetzky] had remained till 3 on his feet and at 8 o'clock was transacting his usual business. This at 86 is wonderful. He is never ill and does not like to be asked about his health at any time. It was worth going any distances to see the dear old Man and hearing every one tell some traits in his character and goodness or kindness to all around him. For instance his two Aides de Camp, Diller & Thun, who naturally see most of him, are so happy with him & fond of him, and he indulges them just like children. They wanted very much both to return with us to Venice to go to the Military Ball on Wednesday & did not like to ask both to get away, so they resolved to speak of the Ball before the Marshall at dinner on Tuesday. Diller said, "Quel dommage que nous ne pouvons pas allé tous les deux à Venise demain." "Pourquoi pas?" said the Marshall instantly attentive. "Parceque il faut que une reste pour la service," replied Thun. "Allons donc! mes Enfants," said Radetzky, "vous etes fou. Allez-tous les deux a Venise"—which they both did and enjoyed themselves very much, only they were in such spirits that they talked all the way back to Venice, not only they but Mr Foster, General Franco and Ct Festitics who came in at Vicenza, and when I arrived at home I was quite done with fatigue.

No sooner had I arrived when Falkenhayn & Wrbna came to see if I was safely returned. I said to John, "This is really too much, you had much better divide me into 20 pieces at once & give a bit to each of my Austrian acquaintances," so I told

---

[1] John in his letter of January 27 had only a few touches to add to Effie's description of the ball. He was struck by the fact that there was entertainment for *everybody*—even 'a library for the readers, with all manner of valuable books laid open, so that instead of having to stand with my back to the wall in a hot room the whole time, I got a quiet seat—and a book of natural history'. He was also struck by the tea-making—'not tea handed over a counter by confectioners' girls, as in London, making the people's houses look like railway stations, but tea made at a large comfortable table where people sat down and talked—and in large cups'. Mr Ruskin wrote back on February 5: 'I never heard of anything so beautifully managed or so rational—so true it is that in all true greatness—there is simplicity'.

George not to let any body in till the end of Carnival which is a month, as I go out often at night and then I meet them all and also often in the street, so that I may be absurd in making this rule but I shall have my days uninterrupted. John says I am very cruel, but if I let one I must all, and sometimes I find it inconvenient now the fine weather has come to be home every day at 4 o'clock. John never speaks to any body or troubles himself to speak at all unless it happens to amuse him at the moment and fortunately for him he is not expected by any etiquette here from going out at all which agrees perfectly with his taste although not with mine. John made some nice sketches from his room-window at Verona and if we return again will finish some more....[1]

[1] We know from John's letter of February 24 that he did make another drawing when they went back to Verona for the Marshal's third ball. He described it as more satisfactory to himself than usual.

SHINING IN SOCIETY

❧

Since December John had been writing to his father about the question of where they should live when they returned to England. It was his intention to settle there for about eighteen months while finishing *The Stones* and *Modern Painters*. On December 27 he had declared that he had had too much society in the past three years and could do nothing right but when he was quiet and alone. He wanted to live somewhere near his parents—not in the same house, for 'that would cause dispeace' between Effie and his mother, and not next door 'for then whenever we dined by ourselves—you and I should both be thinking—why in the world dine with a partition between us?' Mr Ruskin had therefore been looking for houses in the neighbourhood of Denmark Hill. In this same letter of December 27 John wrote: 'I do not speak of Effie in this arrangement—as it is a necessary one—and therefore I can give her no choice. She will be unhappy—that is her fault—not mine—the only real regret I have, however is on her account—as I have pride in seeing her shining as she does in society—and pain in seeing her deprived, in her youth and beauty, of that which 10 years hence she cannot have—the Alps will not wrinkle—so *my* pleasure is always in store—but her cheeks will: and the loss of life from 24 to 27 in a cottage at Norwood is not a pleasant thing for a woman of her temper—But this cannot be helped.'

And the next day: 'I believe the *proper* thing would be for me and Effie to live at Denmark Hill as long as you stay there—while I am working on my two books—only I am afraid Effie would succeed in making my mother and you both so uncomfortable—if she chose—that you could not bear it.... *I* could do perfectly well—and if you and my mother could treat Effie with perfect coolness—if she was late for dinner, let her have it cold—without comment or care—and if she chose to be out late at night—let her own maid sit up for her—content—so long as she did not set the house on fire—that she was either out or in, I believe all might go perfectly well. Effie would not be more uncomfortable than in the cottage at Norwood—and I should save money.... There is indeed no question but that Effie is wrong—but—for want of the Fixed and understood code of right and wrong—it is impossible in the present state of her conscience—to convince her of it. Her duty is not determinable by an established law—and probably the world is nearly equally divided in its opinion respecting us—one half of it blaming *me* for neglecting *her*—the other half blaming *her* for neglecting *you*. Then in the second place, we are always too little disposed to allow for different nature and education. It may literally be as impossible for Effie to *live solitary* without injury, as for me to *go into company* without injury: *I* feel—because I am older, that there is Wrong in *my* case—She does not yet feel that there is wrong in hers: I, at 21 was just as self-willed as she is—fretted myself nearly to death—tormented both you and my mother into grey hairs—yet never would allow that I was wrong—Allow for difference of education and Effie's 23 may well be rated as correspondent to my 21; And I recollect perfectly well that no good was ever done me by any scolding, however well deserved: Scolding only does good to good people—or people in a good state. Bad people—or people in a bad state—can only be benefited by Kindness—or letting alone—(unless they come to that pitch of badness that they must be punished for the sake of society—I don't mean that Red Republicans are to be won by kindness—or mended by letting alone). Therefore I am always either kind or indifferent to Effie—I never scold—simply take *my own way* and let her have hers—love her, as it is easy to do—and never vex myself—If she did anything definitely wrong—gambled—or spent money—or lost her character—it would be another affair—but as she is very good and prudent in her general conduct—the only way is to let her do as she likes—so long as she does not interfere with *me* : and that, she has long ago learned—won't do—So that—really, I believe the question of whether we could live with you at Denmark Hill or not—is much more for your consideration than mine.'

Mr Ruskin replied by return: 'Mama pronounces *definitively*—she and Effie could not be in one House. Consider this at once impossible for though from Mama's very unselfish character she may be thus decided partly in sympathy with my feelings, yet *decided* she feels it a duty to be for all our happiness.... I could not be satisfied as you propose to sit down to meals & not wait—I should be devoured with chagrin at being put in the position of doing a rude & unkind thing.... Most painful the conclusion is but more, much more, painful would the scenes be that might lead to separation of families with aggravated feelings of enmity—whilst by judicious avoidance of disturbance on one hand or Interference on the other we may all live in love & harmony.'

Eflie's next letter reveals what *she* felt about these arrangements being made for her future.

Casa Wetzlar, February [8th], 52

Dearest Mama

... I only wish you could bring all yrselves and Bowerswell here during the Carnival that I might return a few of the parties I am invited to, & you to see & know the people I am amongst. I am very glad Papa was pleased with my letter; indeed it is only too true that these Ruskins are what the French would denominate "des gens impossible". I assure you the letters that pass between them and John are the most extraordinary productions you ever saw. The father, who writes sermons sometimes almost to John and is pathetic and almost like a Martyr when he considers the iniquity of the world, says yesterday, speaking of Mr Munro and angry because he won't sell the pictures of Turner to Mr R cheap, "that he is a miser & that much as he, Mr R, dislikes executions generally he would with pleasure go and see said gentleman hanged"[1]—then both he & Mrs R send the most affectionate messages to me and all the time write *at* or *against* me and speak of the hollowness of worldly society and the extravagance of living in large houses and seeing great people, all of which is perfectly true if

[1] Hugh Andrew Johnstone Munro had been a great friend of Turner's and the chief collector of his pictures. What aroused Mr Ruskin's indignation was that he had asked £200 for a picture which had cost him only £80. 'I cannot even hate him,' he wrote on January 31, 'for he is a Christian—I doubt *that*—but were he to be hanged at the Old Bailey on Monday week—albeit I dislike Executions generally I should attend his with the greatest pleasure imaginable.' John's reply was mild: 'I have no right to abuse him because he—with his fortune—perhaps no whit larger than mine in proportion to his habits—does exactly as I would do with mine—Only I should be more extortionate.'

it applied in the least to us, which it does not, for as I said before—I have spent nothing on dress, and the Gondola is kept for John *not* me. If I had not one I could still go every where here on foot.

They always put themselves in the position of the injured party who give up everything to please us, or rather *me*, and then they have got so much power over John by touching his feelings. They arrange and manage everything, and Mr R has been looking at all the houses near to fix us down beside themselves as they say that they think society ruinous for his mind and health, and when I ventured to say that I ought at least to have been consulted, John said he *never intended as long as they lived to consult me* on any subject of importance as he owed it to them to follow their commands implicitly. Neither they or he think that he has any duty to me in these things at all. At present they annoy me little but were I settled down only amongst them and no others, I'm afraid my equanimity is not great enough to endure such an existence altogether with happiness, but then I have always you and my father and the children which are great blessings to be thankful for, and John, as long as I never interfere, is kindness itself to me were that all that one wanted.

He is, like all men of genius, very peculiar but he is very good and considerate in little things and I think for my own peace of mind the best thing is to let them all take their own way and I try to be as happy as I can. If I don't always succeed and have some times forebodings rather gloomy I perhaps forget often the many blessings I have, and certainly at the present moment if anyone was to come in Venice and be asked who they would pick out as the happiest person here I am convinced they would say me. For everybody is fond of me and pets me; I am the Belle at all the Balls and the people respect me for being virtuous and occupied. The women are not jealous of me because I pay them every politeness in my power and the men adore me, one & all, because, I suppose, I like none better than the other and it flatters their vanity that being admired by Radetzky & the Arch Dukes, and complimented publicly by Gorzkowski, the Governor, on my looks and taste in wearing the Austrian colours, and dancing and talking with all & sundry without distinction, I have sufficient means and Liberty to do whatever I choose—therefore sometimes when I am a little dull I feel very much ashamed of myself for if ever I ought to be thankful it should be now when I have so much influence and the power sometimes of making people not so fortunate as myself a little happier or more contented with their lot. If the Ruskins think I have no heart, and in fact if you asked them tomorrow what they thought of me I am sure they could not tell you. They are so peculiar that, as Newton said to me when we were travelling together, he could not understand how I got on so well—he thought two days at Denmark Hill with Mrs Ruskin without prospects of release would really kill him and yet he thought her a very good woman but very queer—but he advised me never to let John away again for so long with them without me. He said it did us both a great deal of harm and he knew the effects it had on all our acquaintances, & he is going to Mytilene by Malta and wants John to meet him at Corfu. John is enraged and won't write to him; he says "The idea of my leaving my work to go to Corfu," and then Mr Ruskin writes, "For Heaven's sake, my dearest John, never whilst I live dream of going into a vessel with steam in it. Ever since the Amazon burning I have never had it out of my head. Pray write us directly a long account of your Health—Your Pulse—Meals and sleep—perspiration etc. I am sure you cannot be well in Venice—it is the Holland of Italy."[1]

I am sure this will make you laugh and when I tell you this kind of thing nearly every day, interspersed with *lines from* Mrs R [added to Mr Ruskin's letters] in a style almost of amatory tenderness, calling John her beloved and Heart's Treasure and

[1] Mr Ruskin also wrote (on February 3): 'Mama wants you with her because she thinks she can comfort & soothe & strengthen you ... I am as sure as I am of my existence that your Existence is owing to tenderness & watchful care & that under a coarse roughing mother you would long since have gone to Heaven... It is well for you that you were born this side of the Tweed.' Mrs Ruskin evidently had no faith in Effie's care of John for she had written to her husband on January 31: 'I should be very uncomfortable about his health if George were not with him for I desired George to be sure and write if he saw anything amiss.' John himself gave a 2,000-word report of his health in his letter of February 8, going over his symptoms for the last eight years.

a variety of other terms which only, I believe, a lover would
do in addressing a Sonnet to his Mistress—but enough, poor
people, if they are happy in such a life they may call John any
thing they like & I am sure I hope he will always be a comfort
and source of happiness to them but they really torture themselves and I don't know but that I have quite come to the
conclusion that people blessed *with one child* is a very great misfortune to the child afterwards. John has given up all idea of
writing to Mr McDonald to congratulate him on his son's
birth. He says he has no friends and that he never will have
any and that the world and every body in it are all going
wrong but that he is right, and then he sits and writes such
accounts to Mr R—of the state of society both here in Venice
and in London and thinks himself an excellent judge, although
he knows no one and never stirs out.

Mr Brown has taken one of his fits of sulleness again. I have
not seen him since Christmas day and have called upon him
without him having ever returned my visits. He was so rude and
insulting to me one day in the Ducal Palace that both John and
I think I have done all I can and unless he comes I will not go
near him again. You know the Band plays on Tuesdays and
Thursdays between two & three. When I went on the Square
I was instantly surrounded with Austrians and Ladies & could
not hear a tone of the most beautiful music in the world; I
therefore found out that the open Gallery of the Ducal Palace
was a delicious promenade in the sun. The Porter gives me
a chair and a mat and there I sit or walk as I please; nobody
knows to this day where I go and I have been for months
doing this. One day Mr Brown in his peregrinations tumbled
upon me; he asked what I came for; I told him—but he
declared that he did not believe me, that he was convinced I
came for some reason—that I walked with some one, or watched
some one on the Place and that he would soon find out. I kept
my temper and said that as he did not believe my word, nor
walked, nor watched any one, that so neither could I walk with
him and begged to bid him good morning. I believe he questioned my friend, the old Porter—who is quite enlivened by
my visits—but Mr Brown I have heard nothing of since. Was
it not too impertinent to impute such motives to me? John

was very angry but I do think Mr Brown is mad and not accountable.

I was at a beautiful Ball on Thursday night at Mrs Dawkins— our Consuless. The whole of the society here was there. Mdme. Pallavicini was quite gay and danced till 2; the Princess Hohenlohe appeared for the first time since her confinement. She is still very pretty and had on her neck a splendid necklace of diamonds with a Saphire pendant sent her the other day by the Countess de Chambord who stood Godmother to the baby.[1] The rest of her dress was very pretty, two skirts of white silk embroidered with groups of flowers of different sizes. They were all well dressed but they were all in admiration at my dress which was my green satin Court dress you will remember with white satin in front and velvet leaves.[2] My hair was all plaited through with large pearls and Lace Lappets and the little pearls you gave me with an emerald heart on my neck. I am going to a Military Ball on Wednesday when I shall wear it again as it was so much approved of.

The next evening we had a large and brilliant Soirée at Ctsse. Esterhazy's which the Ladies of Honor of the Grand Duchess honored with their presence—the first time they have been seen in Society here. They were attended by Count Wrbna who is dreadfully offended with me because I do not let him in. I said, "Why pray should I let you in and shut every body else out?"—which you know I have done for ten days— "Oh, because," said he, "I like you as much as all the rest put together." I answered, "Je vous demande bien pardon M. Le Comte, but it appears to me that you like me much less, because did I permit you, you would spend part of every afternoon in my drawing-room which to say the least of it would be very idle, and the others at least don't interfere with my occupations which you would if you could." "But then am I never

[1] This baby must soon have died, for there is no record of it. The Comtesse de Chambord, known as Gegina, was Princess Hohenlohe's greatest friend. They wrote to each other every day, signing their letters 'la Sua Fida Inseparabile'.

[2] Effie wore this Louis XV-style dress at the second Drawing Room she went to on April 3, 1851. Like her first Court dress it was made by Melina. Everyone she knew at Buckingham Palace admired it and wanted to know where she had got it. She had in fact copied it from a picture.

to see you?" "In society yes," I said, "but until the end of Carnival not in my house." So he is furious because he considers himself a person of much importance and went away saying he would revenge himself. I said, "What, will you send for your 1,500 men to keep me in order?" "No," he said, "but I certainly will revenge myself for your injustice—and if any thing happens to you remember it is yr. own fault." I told him not to talk such bavardages because his amour propre was hurt.

The Ladies were charming. One of them is the Princess Troubetzkoi, sister-in-law to the Prince that I knew before & who cannot on account of his connection with Taglioni return here at all while the Grand Duke & suite remains. The young Lady, Mdlle. Wayancoff, was pretty and very lively and desired to be presented to me and we had a long chat & some fun. They say she is immensely rich and if so I think from her repartee she is quite able to take care of herself. She said she had for some time desired to make my acquaintance as Mdme. Pallavicini had spoken so much of me &c....

Casa Wetzlar, Feby. [Postmarked 16th from Venice]
My dearest Mama

I think we are beginning, like you, to have spring at last.... You have no idea what delightful singing birds there are in these Palaces for it is so rare in Italy to hear birds sing as I think they shoot all the pretty little creatures to eat up, but the number who have fled to Venice for security from the Sportsman exactly as did the Venetians of olden time from the scourge of Attila, and they now live here and build their nests in peace and waken me every morning with their singing, so that sometimes I cannot believe that I waken in the midst of a large & populous City....

We go on Monday again to Verona. The Marshall had his second Ball last Monday which was also very brilliant. He was so polite as to regret our non-attendance to several of his Generals, and he called Mr Foster twice to him and said, "Mais, cher Foster, ou est donc Madame Ruskin, votre jolie compatriote?" and begged General Reischach to tell me that he hoped very much we would do him the favor to come on the

3rd [ball]. A number of the gentlemen came from Verona on Wednesday last to attend the Military Ball here which was given in the Hall of the Knights of Malta, a very beautiful room and from the walls being white and covered with the shields of the Order, painted in Fresco, and plenty of wax lights, every one looked very well.[1] I saw the husband of the Duchesse de Berry there, the Count Lucchesi, a large dark Italian looking man all in black with the order of the St. Esprit in Diamonds. They have three daughters and a son almost grown up.[2] I am going on Tuesday to call on her Dame de Cour, and will be presented to her in a few days afterwards when she fixes, but I must go in black which is doleful enough.

Today Madme. Pallavicini sent to say that Mdlle. Wayancoff, the young Lady of the Grand Duchess, wished to pay me a visit and they would come at 4 o'clock. They came and told me that there were masks in the Square and if I liked they would take a couple of turns with me to look at them. I was delighted and went, but the Square was so full of people that we went up in the Palace and came out on the Balconies of the Anti-chamber where we saw beautifully. The masks were walking in single file to music, two companies of 30 each with dresses of red and black, and black masks with long noses, with tight stockings. They spoke & threw bonbons—but the mob pressed on them so much that they could hardly walk. I thought it a very melancholy spectacle and no fun as the people are sulky about it & it is all done by the Governor to promote good feeling and gaiety during the Carnival without success. The crowds

[1] The hall and church of the Knights of Malta are in the Corte di San Giovanni di Malta, next to the Scuola di San Giorgio degli Schiavoni. They were re-opened and redecorated in 1839 after being suppressed by Napoleon. They can be visited on request.

[2] The Duchesse de Berry had secretly married on October 14, 1831, Count Lucchesi-Palli of an old Sicilian family. He died in 1864. Their three daughters, Clementine, Isabelle and Francesca, and their son, Adinolfe, all eventually married Italians. The Order of St Esprit had been the senior Royal Order of France, its sash being known as the *Cordon Bleu*. It was suspended in 1791, resurrected in 1814, and finally abolished in 1830 by Louis Philippe. The exiled Bourbons, however, went on giving orders to their own adherents.

were immense but all of the lower classes & quantities of
little Boys whistling and making a din through wooden penny
whistles.[1]

I heard some one speaking behind me to Mdme. Pal. &
turned round. It was the Grand Duke in the Austrian uniform
which he nearly always wears out of compliment to the Emperor
& to please his wife. I made him a reverance which he returned,
and then she came into the room when they both left it to go
and dress for a dinner at the Duchesse de Berry's. We then went
to the young Lady's sitting room where we found every thing
very comfortable and nicely arranged. She gave us bonbons and
oranges and on her writing table had portraits of most of the
Imperial family. Two or three Russian attendants were loiter-
ing about the room and some of them came out of her bedroom
which I thought odd, but as usual with me remarked all the
differences of customs to our own and held my tongue until
she said that although Venice was so charming she should be
very glad when they left, at which I was amazed for she
complained of the excessive dullness. I said as much and asked
how she could be dull when there were about 14 of the Suite
and constantly people coming to see them and at the Opera
every other night. Oh! she said she was so lonely from 2 till 4
every day alone in her room with not even a cat in the room.
I thought to myself that it would be well for her if no greater
misfortune happened to her than having the good fortune to
have two hours solitude per day. But certainly they ought all
to be as happy as possible if prosperity, riches, good fortune &
youth could make them so, for there was the appearance of
every thing that money could procure, crowds of servants,
and Croat soldiers on guard at every passage, and all so quiet
and well managed under the direction of my connaissance the
Ct. Wrbna who was lounging out of the window of his appartments as we passed—but having quarrelled with me, because
I would not consider him or treat him as I suppose he considered the Emperor's Aide de Camp ought to be treated, &
did not show us out of the Palace which it would have been

[1] Edward Cheney wrote to Lord Holland on February 14: 'The Carnival
has begun—but Mazzini gives the orders that it shall not be gay & he is better
obeyed & more feared than the Emperor.'

polite to have done, but Nugent took care of us through the crowd.

After dinner John & I went out to see if it would get gayer as it got dark but the canaille, not the masks seemed to have increased and I was glad to return home. In one of the narrow streets I met four female masks very nicely dressed with sort of moorish dress and blue satin little cloaks with black masks. Some Venetian passing spoke to them and asked for bon-bons. I asked for some too when the Mask very politely held the Handkerchief which was full of sweeties to me saying in Venetian, "Resta Servita Signora"—Be served Lady!—I took some and thanked her. I sent George & Mary out but they found the Square almost impassable with the crowd and very few masks. It is a pity it is not popular as the people are so naturally polite that there would be great fun. I must conclude. John calls me *Mrs Scratch* he is so tired hearing my pen scrape across the paper and back....

Casa Wetzlar, 20 Febry
... I am rather tired today as I was up late last night, John & I having taking [*sic*] it into our heads that we would mask and have some fun as these last days of the Carnival a good many have appeared in the evenings. We hired a couple of Dominoes, black with black masks and white gloves, and reached the Square about ten. I laughed so that I could scarcely go on, and John, who was as grave as possible, did the thing capitally. We found quantities of masks in Dominoes and fancy costumes of all kinds parading about and entering the Cafés to throw Bonbons. Plenty of men spoke to me—what they said I don't know, but I replied by uttering the usual cries of the other masks and shaking hands with one or two. These people seemed all of the Lower orders but so well behaved and rather too quiet as if they had not quite got into sufficient good spirits to mask generally. We wandered about till half past eleven when John wanted to take me to the masked Ball [at the Fenice] which used to be attended by everyone in Venice, but this year as I heard of no one going I went home and sent John first to see if I could go. He soon came back and said it would not do for the music was bad and the dancing worse, and half the

people were in plain clothes so I was very glad to go to my bed.[1]

On Wednesday [the 18th] the Military gave their last Carnival Ball which was very well attended and very elegantly arranged. In the morning I made Mr Foster send a Telegraphic message to Verona to ask General Reischach and Ct. Thun to dine with me as they were coming at any rate for the Ball. They came with great pleasure as well as Foster & Nugent—and we had a very nice dinner much enlivened by the wit of Reischach who is a great character and would delight Papa. John says he never saw anything to equal him, his head is constantly framing the most drole and original ideas and he talks on every subject with equal facility and is never at a loss for an answer as you may suppose. Truth is perfectly disregarded if it suits his purpose and he does not in the least mind what he says to the young men who are alternately furious at him or amused as he teases all and sundry alike and yet they all like him....

But to return to my dinner, we all enjoyed it very much and the conversation was very interesting. It turned upon Gipsies, and Thun & Reischach both being Bohemians told us many interesting things about them, one thing I do not recollect to have heard before—that they prefer eating animals which have died a natural death to those killed, and nothing pleases them so much as a Malady amongst the sheep or Cattle as they say what is killed by the Almighty must be better food than what is killed by man.

We all went to the Ball at nine. Thun brought me from Verona such a beautiful bouquet of six camelias of different colors all surrounded by Orange flowers and violets. I had on my maize colored Tarletane with red roses and the same in the hair. As I had only ten minutes to dress after dinner I said, "What shall I put on?" Reischach said, "Ma chère Dame, if you were to roll yr. hair into a knot and go in robe de chambre you would still be prettier than them all so it doesn't signify"— but as I was of an entirely different opinion I dressed myself very well.

---

[1] Not only did John refrain from mentioning to his father that he had put on a mask and domino, but he wrote on February 20 that he had *taken Effie* to the Fenice the night before.

The Grand Duchess looked most lovely; she was so exquisitely dressed I never saw any thing half so pretty; she looked the most beautiful and most modest of Sir Peter Lely's beauties stepped out of their frames, a style which admirably became her style of face & figure. Her head was covered with innumerable little ringlets before and behind of all lengths with a rose, put coquettishly on one side, and the other a bouquet of Diamonds and Emeralds and behind a Comb of the same; on her neck and fastening her sleeves and the front of her dress Emeralds & Diamonds forming fruit and Diamond leaves, each emerald as long and as broad as that [a line an inch and a half long]. John could hardly believe them real but they are so, and she had a set of sapphires equally enormous, but fancy the dark green upon a very rich pink satin dress, the under dress covered with one piece of Lace and the upper a sort of full Hoop petticoat held up at one side with an immense Bow of ribbon and the effect was exactly like the pictures à la Watteau.[1]

The Princess Hohenlohe was also beautifully dressed in *almost* red corded silk trimmed à la Louis XV with Mechlin Lace and her magnificent diamonds on black velvet on her head and neck. These fine ladies as you may suppose get every thing direct from Paris and seem to spare no expense on their toilettes and never appear twice the same. Don Ferdinand of Spain begged to be presented to me and the reigning Prince de Reuss. They were both astonished to hear I was married. The former is the second son of Don Carlos.[2]

On Monday we go to Verona for the Marshall's Ball and on

[1] John took Effie to the ball at nine o'clock and left her there at ten. He was as impressed as Effie with the Grand Duchess and wrote on the 19th that there was 'a row of six or seven emeralds clasping the dress from the neck to the waist—each about the length of a small walnut... In our society a duchess is usually a fat old woman, worse dressed than anybody else and highly painted—and with a whole jewellers shop of diamonds shaken over her till she looks like a chandelier, but here there was youth and refinement, and considerable beauty: and though there were at least £20,000 of stones on the front of the dress they were not put on so as to catch the eye.' Mr Ruskin replied, 'I was as much amused with your account of Duchesses & Jewels as with a number of C. Dickens.'

[2] In fact the third son, born 1824, younger brother of Don Juan whom Effie had met in London. Prince Heinrich XX of Reuss, born 1794, had succeeded his brother as head of the main branch of the family in 1836.

Tuesday return. I would like to have stayed a day or two at Verona but on Tuesday the Ctsse Esterhazy gives a Soirée Poudré which is sometimes done on the Night of "Mardi gras". After which people go to the Cavalchina or Masked Ball in the Fenice—that is to say you go into your box and see what goes on below, and so ends the Carnival and Ash Wednesday brings Lent—but this Soirée is a great bore and gives one immensity of trouble for nothing. I hate dirtying all my hair with powder and tried a peruke but it is not nice and I must just submit like the rest. Many of the Ladies have rococo dresses. My green and white [her Court dress] with high body open in front, sleeves to the elbow & ruffles is the very thing, but my hair is a great trouble and will put it quite in a mess. We have very fine cold weather but the want of rain makes the wells dry up and some people are busy emptying a Boat full of fresh water, a precious article in Venice in dry weather....

Mr Ruskin writes constantly to John & such letters about his health and spirits, which are both perfect, that I think both Mrs R. and he, from having John so long *really ill* when he was younger, can never be persuaded that he has grown out of it. I expect them bye and bye to send him parcels of Medicated food as their riches [?] must surely soon come to an end they send him so many.[1] But now goodbye.... I admire yr. prudence about my letters. Of course I always trust to yr. discretion in everything I write....

> Casa Wetzlar, Febry 24th, Ash Wednesday[2]
>
> ... On Monday [23rd] we went to Verona and arrived there at three. We found Ct. Thun waiting for us and soon afterwards General Reischach came to ask for us. The Dawkins being in the same Hotel I went to ask for them and Mrs D. kindly sent me her French maid which I was grateful for as I was ready for the Ball a few minutes before eight.[3] The House was as beautiful

---

[1] Mr Ruskin had written on February 14 that Dr Grant, his old friend, recommended for John 'a *little* meat at Breakfast—*no* lunch to carry you on to 5 o'clock—an alka soda—or a glass of Selzer Water 3 hours after Dinner'.

[2] Ash Wednesday was the 25th in 1852.

[3] This shows that Effie did not take Mary on this visit either in spite of Mr Ruskin's protest. They may, however, have taken George.

as formerly, and having paid my respects to the Countess and the Marshall, who was so delighted to see me and asked if I was enjoying myself and paid me so many kind little speeches that I was quite charmed with him, I had a long talk with Ct. Minischalchi who was exceedingly kind.... The Ladies were very handsomely dressed but I have not room to specify. I had on my Tulle dress covered with all the innumerable colors that Melina made and which I have not worn before—it was very much admired.[1]

Thun came to dance with me. He had given me a beautiful Bouquet and I said, "You look rather put out, what's the matter?" "Why," he said, "Baron Diller is still unwell" (I had heard about a fortnight ago that he had tumbled down stairs and hurt his arm) "and I have to arrange everything." I said, "Is he confined to Bed still?"—"Oh! no," said Thun, "he is going into the musicians' gallery to look down at us just to have a peep."—I said, "If he is able to do that why don't he come and arrange the dancing even if he can't dance?" Thun turned off the conversation and it did not strike me as odd. This morning by mere chance I have an explanation: after we returned from Verona the first time George told his master that he had heard that a duel had been fought at Verona about me, and an officer killed. I laughed at the thing as perfectly absurd. It is a point of honor amongst Austrians never to speak about affairs of that kind and probably every one knew but me. But it appears that Diller had some words in the ball room with another officer about dancing with me—who the other man was I don't know—but they lost their tempers, went out next evening, and Diller got a very severe sabre wound all down the arm and cannot appear in the Marshall's presence until his arm is quite well. Did you ever know anything so foolish? I think these young men think as little of Duelling as they do of smoking a

---

[1] John wrote about Effie's dress: 'It was very simple—but quaint, white, with little rosettes or bows or knots of divers coloured riband fastened over it, on the gothic principle of no one colour being like the next to it. It was Carnival time, and she looked as if she had just sustained a shower of sugar plums. She received many compliments—and the old marshal expressed to her in very touching terms his regret at being too old to dance with her' (Letter of February 23). It was this 'want of quietness of Dress', as he called it, that Mr Ruskin disapproved of so thoroughly in Effie.

cigar and feel no responsibility in such behaviour. I am very
glad I had nothing to do with it and that I neither said nor
did anything to provoke such conduct. Baron Diller is the
Marshall's other Aide de Camp with Thun and is as sweet,
gentle, well behaved a young man as can be. Radetzky asked
him of the Emperor two years ago and he is a great favorite,
but the Austrian army, I think, rather encourages duelling, and
such things are of frequent occurrence. I only hope he will soon
be quite well for he is the sort of lad whose Mama would be
in a dreadful way about him and I daresay as he gets older he
will avoid getting sabre wounds.[1] As was to be expected he did
not call on me which otherwise would have been his duty and
when I see him again I shall say How do you do &c and
Goodbye as to the others and the thing will be forgotten, but
poor Thun has had double duty for three weeks and could not
return with us to Venice which he regretted exceedingly as John
& I had a plan in our heads to mask at the Cavalchina. I had
a blue dress & Domino and John black, and I had a Cerise
costume for Thun who makes a capital Lady as to size, and I
intended that Foster should go with him and we should have
great fun and tell nobody, but the Marshal is so kind that he
gives the young men permission whenever they ask any favor
which makes them very particular what they do ask, and
Thun did not think he ought to ask, upon which we
commended his prudence.

As I thought I would be tired next day I left the Ball before
any body else by at twelve o'clock having danced since eight,
four hours being I think perfectly enough dancing, for they
never let you miss a dance by any chance and as they are all
so kind I make a point of being introduced to every person who
wishes it and dancing with all who desire it. But when the
Austrians have a Ball they make it last as long as possible and
all the rest went on till four in the morning.

We started for Venice at eleven next day and were a pretty
large party all together, Mr & Mrs Dawkins & her sister Miss
Dent, Ct. Falkenhayn, Festitics and young Baron Meyendorff,

[1] Baron Ludwig von Diller, born 1830, was the son of Baron Joseph
Herman Diller and his wife, *née* Antonie von Hess, sister of Field-Marshal
Baron Hess.

son of the Russian Ambassador at Vienna, and several others. These gentlemen came and placed themselves beside me. Notwithstanding the Governor of Vicenza's detestation of me he condescended to bring his handsome person wrapped up in an enormous cloak of fox skins opposite to me all the way to Venice and we chattered away very agreeably.[1] A Tube broke in front and we were kept from reaching Venice till five o'clock. At Vicenza Festitics' horses and Aide de Camp were waiting for him, his equipage the prettiest thing I have ever seen, his Coachman a regular Hungarian dressed in that Costume, and the little horses, two of which were in Harness. He is far too great a gentleman to be vain of his position or wealth and when I said how beautiful they were, he merely curled his moustache and said, "Oui, ils sont très gentile," and rolled his cloak over himself and me to keep us warm. He then said, "You know I can do anything I like here in my territory and it would give me great pleasure to order you to be hanged." I said, "In order I suppose to show the Vicentins what a fountain of justice and honor they have in their Governor?" He said, "Yes, but you know I have motives of Hatred to you." I said, "It is an honor sometimes to be disliked by certain people. I consider you and yr. friend Ct. Wrbna pay me a very high compliment." Falkenhayn sat by and was much amused at us, for he is so good and so ugly that I would ask him to serve me a turn when I would have none of the rest and because he is so old, and he [is] always very pleased when he hears me uttering, as he says, my good principles.[2]

Then we all went asleep till we arrived in Venice. You may imagine I had not much time to prepare my toilette as I had to dine and put it all in order before nine, and I had never seen powdered hair excepting on footmen & did not know how to do my own. My dress also had to be considerably arranged. I got Mary to stand still. I put on [her] my white satin Petticoat

---

[1] As well as being a great friend of Wrbna, whom Effie had offended, the reason for Festitics' half playful anger against her must have been that she had refused to accept his offer of a nomination in the Marine College at Trieste.

[2] Falkenhayn, who was sixty, had only another eighteen months to live. He was a widower with four sons.

and over that my green dress and looped it up in five places
with velvet ribbon and pearls so that it was like a Hoop;—two
large bunches of red roses at the bottom of the green and one
on one side of my hair, and on the other pearls, and a large
rosette on my throat and hands of cerise colored satin ribbon.
You have no idea how beautiful it was and my powdered hair
turned back in the way I had in London with two little patches
on my face and my toilette was perfect. I also had my Chate-
laine and fan. I went to show Mdme. Wetzlar myself before I
went and she was so much pleased that she jumped about the
room & finally got Mrs Swift and the servants to see me.[1]

I went out in such a gale to Mdme. Esterhazy's that I thought
that powder, Gondola and all would have been at the bottom,
but I landed and the servants received me, they all in Livery
and powder. I entered alone and Marmont poudré welcomed
me saying that I was "si bonne et si belle" that it was quite a
delight to him to see me. The Salons looked quite wonderful.
The Ladies were not too numerous to destroy the effect of the
other, and I felt as if I were at Louis XIVth's Court it was so brilliant and picturesque. Every Lady was in the richest costume of
the time, and the many uniforms took away from the sombre
line of the rest of the gentlemen in black coats. The Countess
Esterhazy looked exceedingly well (all the fat Ladies nearby did)
—she had on a white damask petticoat with peach color Hoop
and her hair powdered over two cushions with a veil fastened
at the top descending behind and these caught in front with a
Brooch, most magnificent Diamond flowers all ornamenting her
head and the Bows which looped up her dress. The Princess
Hohenlohe had a Costume of corded Cerise silk and six Sapphire
brooches with diamonds in front, ear-rings and Diadem and
three rows of diamonds round her neck. The jewels of the
Ladies last night far exceed any thing I have ever seen in
England. Our Ladies at the Drawing rooms are without

[1] Mrs Swift lived on the floor above. The Casa Wetzlar was subsequently
called the Palazzo Swift. John wrote on February 25: 'Effie looked excessively
nice—very simply dressed—hair very white indeed—and a scarlet ribbon
round the neck and wrists—her court dress with the ivy leaves tucked in some
incomprehensible manner into an ancient form. She went out—at 10—to
Mme Esterhazy's—and I to bed.'

compare with them. I was presented to the Marquesa Anna Pallavicini who has just come here for a month or two. Her upper
skirt was covered with one single piece of ancient Brussels
point. Every one was looking at it. She said she inherited it from
her Aunt, the late Electress of Bavaria, who had had it presented
to her by the town of Brussels. It was quite a work of art.[1]

We left gazing at each other after about half an hour and sat
down in groups like Watteau's pictures to chat. I had some
agreeable talk with the Prince de Reuss and we were sitting
together when Festitics & Wrbna, who are never separate, came
beside us, also Sternberg & Meyendorff, what Reischach calls
"ma cour". The Prince de Reuss stayed beside me as he evidently
enjoyed excessively the battle that went on between Festitics,
Wrbna & myself—which I would willingly have avoided but
could not escape, being so hemmed in. Wrbna said that their
Vengeance wasn't quite ready but they were preparing it and it
would fall on me all at once. I said I had plenty of friends. He
said, "Oh, none of them will be able to help you." He said, "You
know the Barber of Seville?" I said no—He said, "It shows
what calumny can do, and already Gorzkowski has a bad opinion of you. Both Festitics and I hate you but we have not
confided to each other yet why." Festitics joined in and said, "Oh
yes! Je vous dis tout bonnement que je vous deteste and I only
speak to you because you are pretty and à la mode." I said, "I
know perfectly well that you only consulted yr. own interest
and fortunately for myself every body in Venice knows you and
the Ct. Wrbna and I have not been here five months without also
being known. Excuse me, but all you have said only shows pique
and a want of esprit in you both to bring your quarrels with me
into Mdme. Esterhazy's drawing room before your equals. It is
more than a month since I had cause of complaint against the Ct.
Wrbna particularly and no one ever heard of it until he by his
own conduct has shown it to every body." As to the Ct. Festitics,
his anger and hatred are merely imaginary and both perfectly

[1] The seventy-year-old Elector of Bavaria, Charles Theodore, had, in the
vain hope of producing an heir, married in 1795 as his second wife the
nineteen-year-old Archduchess Marie Leopoldine of Austria-Modena. He
died in 1799, and five years later she married her chamberlain, Count Louis
Arco, uncle of Marchesa Anna Pallavicini. The Electress died in 1848.

indifferent to me even if real. I asked Falkenhayn afterwards what
he thought, if they could harm me or not. He laughed at the
idea. He said, "As Austrians they dare not—& in the second
place they are only piqued because you do not permit them to
vous faire la cour. In reality they feel all the respect for you which
you merit and if they were so bête as to say any thing against
you nobody would believe them for an instant. You should
just laugh at them and return their persiflage as you did tonight."

I went with Pallavicini and he to the Cavalchina. They put
me in Mr Dawkins's box beside Princess Hohenlohe and Miss
Dent [Mrs Dawkins's sister]. The Theatre was illuminated
from top to bottom, everybody in grande tenue, and five or
six boxes full of our party with powdered heads who I think
created a much greater sensation than the crowds of masks
below. It was very brilliant but it was easy to see the upper
classes were not masking.[1] Pallavicini left us and I only stayed
a few minutes because I did not like keeping Falkenhayn who
had to be at Padua to exercise Cavalry at six in the morning
and he hardly ever goes out late at night. I was much obliged
to him and was in my own bed about one—most of the people
spend the night there.

I am much better of having been at Verona and John pro-
poses going soon again for he finds he can write so much better
when he returns with a fresh eye; he writes much more vigorously.... Of course all our gaieties are now over and we shall
be very quiet during Lent. The Emperor comes on Saturday,
and in a few days two more Grand Dukes of Russia, younger
brothers of G.D. Constantine. The Infanta [Beatrix] of Spain
is here. I am going to her in a day or two, and the Duke &
Duchess of Parma & children are coming also, a great family
gathering....[2]

[1] Edward Cheney wrote to Lord Holland on February 26: 'The Duchesse
de Berry appeared at the cavalchina in deep mourning & without a mask!—
anything for an outing!'

[2] Charles III, born 1823, had succeeded to the Dukedom of Parma on the
abdication of his father in 1849, and was a cousin of Queen Isabella of Spain.
He had married the Comte de Chambord's sister, Louise, in 1845 and they
had four children. He died in 1854. It is his grandson, Prince Xavier, who
inherited the Carlist claims in 1936 and who is the father-in-law of Princess
Irene of the Netherlands.

Saturday [*February 28th*]

Today the Emperor arrived from Trieste. Nothing could be more beautiful than his arrival, the Palace and Church covered with people and the Square filled with troops, all the Gondolas with flags and sailors to the top. I was ready to go out to meet him at 8 this morning but he did not arrive till two, but Venice is a charming place for such things and is never kept long waiting. The Cannon always let the whole town know by firing at Malamocco, and one has always an hour after that before the Emperor comes to scramble off to any place to see him.

I returned after 8 quietly to my usual avocations till 11 when I had a visit from Ct. Thun who had arrived from Verona with Radetzky the last night. I hear Diller has also come which showed he is quite well, but Thun had been sent to me by Radetzky to express his great regret that he could not pay me a visit [in] person in return for my visits to him, but that his time was altogether at the disposal of the Emperor while here, and he hoped I would believe that were it otherwise he would have done himself the pleasure to come and see me.[1] Is he not polite? However his worthy Aide de Camp made himself as happy as possible and I gave him his lunch which he said would make him receive the Emperor much more satisfactorily. He said I must come to a room in the Palace when I heard the guns fire from which we could see the review, & I went and ascended the Emperor's staircase covered with green cloth & lined with Croats and Gens d'Armes. They were very polite and said they had orders to conduct me to the Saloon where I found Ct. & Ctsse Pallavicini, Nugent, Thun & Falkenhayn, who had put mantles for us on the Balcony, but as there was still some time Falkenhayn took us into the Emperor's private appartments which were close by his. Valets and Chamberlains were standing about ready waiting. I walked into his bedroom which was clean and neat, much more couldn't be said—no Luxury excepting a very comfortable red Morocco arm chair, a clean little Bed with[out] any canopy or hanging, and a Chest of Drawers. We heard a Cannon and rushed to our window before I had time to look into his sittingroom.

[1] John reported this to his father and was evidently much impressed by the Marshal's courtesy.

He walked along the Place with all his Generals and the Grand Duke Constantine. He looked well and handsome and I always admire his walk which is so perfectly graceful and dignified at the same time.

In the middle of all this display and sunshine I heard that Marmont was very unwell. I went directly to ask for him and was told he had been bled in the night having had a stroke of apoplexie. This is the second he has had but I hope he gets over it, he is so strong. I sent again this evening and they said he was better. Now goodbye....

                              Casa Wetzlar, 7th March
... Since writing to you poor Marmont has died [on the 3rd] and is very much regretted. His doctor thought at one time that he would have recovered but severe vomiting came on and afterwards congestion of the brain which ended fatally. He was quite sensible almost to the last and was attended by Ctsse. Esterhazy and Mdme. Sturmer who never left him. He lived above the former and as they had been constant friends for 36 years and she just like a daughter to him it is a great loss for her, but not so great as if she had died & he had been left. He could never have survived it. He has left no fortune but some 6,000 francs to his Maitre-d'Hotel who was an old and faithful servant. He had left instructions with him in the event of his dying suddenly what was to be done with his remains. He desired to be embalmed after the method of Gannal and after six months to be transported to France and buried in a little monument he had built for himself near Châtillon where his family property had been but which, with the Chateau, had passed into the hands of strangers.[1] They say that he spent all his large income, which was in pensions, in Venice. He had a dinner every day and

---

[1] Marmont had been born at Châtillon-sur-Seine. He was the first of the twenty-six Marshals to know Napoleon. As young artillery officers they had been stationed in adjacent garrison towns; Marmont had befriended him and taken him home to meet his parents. Jean-Nicolas Gannal (1791-1852) was a surgeon and chemist who first studied methods of preserving corpses during Napoleon's retreat from Moscow. His arterial system became famous in 1840 when he successfully embalmed the body of the Duc d'Orleans after a carriage accident in Paris. The methods followed today in Great Britain and France are derived from his system.

never went out without having his pockets full of little sous pieces which he gave to the poor, and he gave immense sums in Charity. He has left some trifling debts here. They say his plate &c is to be sold to Liquidate them. If so I should like to buy some little Memorial of the kind old Marshal who was always so very amiable & kind to me whenever I saw him. So great was the interest excited by his illness, and people sent so often to ask during the day, that there was a bulletin issued twice a day. Afterwards most of the Ladies saw Mdme. Ester-hazy but as I am comparatively a stranger I did not go although I sent to ask for her every day as I did not like calling while the Body was still in the house, but tomorrow I am to be presented to the Duchesse de Berry when I must appear in deep mourning. I will take the opportunity of calling afterwards [a few words obliterated here and on following pages] and show my respect for the deceased by going to her in black. People think a great deal of these little attentions here and certainly I am most glad to sympathize with them when they are in distress for they have been most kind to me.

The Emperor went back to Vienna in a dreadful storm the other day [the 4th] quite by his own desire, for seeing how the sea was rising and having a great wish to be out in a tempest, he wanted to set off the moment he arrived from Verona the night before, but we heard yesterday from one of the Steam-ers which had been driven back here with her Funnel broken that the Emperor only reached Trieste yesterday having been driven down to Pola on the Dalmation Coast, and instead of five hours to Trieste he had been two days and two nights, so I hope he is satisfied. Count Wimpffen and others who suffer dreadfully from sea sickness would, I think, be very ill pleased with the Royal Progress.[1]

[1] Count Wimpffen had now been made an Admiral although it was said of him that he had never been to sea. The military and maritime adminis-tration at Trieste had recently been unified under his command. On the night of March 4 there was one of the worst storms ever known in the Adriatic. The Emperor was on a war steamer, the *Volta*. Her sister ship, the *Marianna*, with eighty of the Emperor's suite on board, went to the bottom with total loss of life. Ruskin wrote characteristically: 'no one will hear of the vulgar calamity of the poor fisher population of Chioggia. Four hundred were drowned in that gale' (Letter of March 21, 1852).

The Emperor, it is said, is much in Love and anxious to marry his pretty cousin the Arch Duchess Elisabeth who although only 21 is a widow with a little girl, having been married to the Duke of Modena's brother, but I think this wants confirmation as he would not have left Venice just two hours before she arrived from Modena the other day. She has come to pay a visit to her Sister in Law the Infanta, so that I hope I shall see her some day soon....[1]

John is at last writing to Mr Macdonald. He begins by saying something about not writing for so long and then adds, "But let me beg of you to present my compliments to the young Laird of Rossie upon his arrival in a world which I sometimes think the greater part of his species had better have kept out of." Do you think Mr M. will think this complimentary, or otherwise? John is very much taken up with Politics just now. He is entirely disgusted with his country and thinks they are all going mad together. As he is a Free Trader he naturally thinks Ld. Derby's ministry will cause some confusion in the Country. He is at present writing a long letter to the Times on Taxation and Elections but whether he sends it or not I don't know so let it be entre nous.[2]

George and I have had a small skirmish for some few days for you must know George, who hates the Austrians, has however imitated them in one particular, viz—in a large black moustache which I consider entirely spoils his appearance, and I have told him that I believe he had also a design on his Master's chin for you never saw such a figure as John is sometimes in the morning, only half shaved for which I blame

[1] The Archduchess Elizabeth, born January, 1831, was a daughter of Archduke Joseph (a great-uncle of the Emperor) by his third wife. In 1847 she had married Duke Ferdinand of Modena, brother of the Infanta Beatrix and the Duchesse de Chambord. He had died in December, 1849, five months after the birth of their daughter Maria Teresa. In 1854 she married Archduke Charles Ferdinand whom Effie had met at Radetzky's first ball. Eight days afterwards the Emperor married another Elizabeth, his first cousin.

[2] John wrote three letters to *The Times* on the Corn Laws, elections and education, and took great pains with them. His father, however, to whom he first submitted them, did not approve and they were never published. As usual he took his father's criticism with very good grace. Lord John Russell's government had been defeated on February 20, 1852.

George as I consider he has his Master's person in [his] charge,[1]
but you will be glad to hear that John's long [hair?] is no longer
visible because he found so amiable a Barber who cuts his
hair so nicely & softly, telling him at the same time all the
gossip of the town and railing against the Priests that John
engaged him to come every Tuesday fortnight so that his Hair
is always in good order and he looks forward to the operation
with pleasure.

I saw the Grand Duchess today. She would enchant & astonish the Condies [rather vulgar Perth neighbours] and I think
from the Multitude of Her changes of dress that were she to
die her wardrobe might be found to contain, like Queen Elizabeth, three thousand Habits. Today she was walking about
with a maize colored silk with a trimming of black Lace in
front, a Mantle of purple velvet covered with superb black Lace,
a white Lace bonnet and white parasol. *He* was in his Russian
uniform which is Hideous, & from the epaulettes being so high
those who wear it look as if they had no neck at all. His
brothers, G.D.'s Nicholas [aged 21] & Michael [20], are expected every day. She likes going out and goes every night
almost to the Opera but is under orders from the Emperor &
her Doctor to keep early hours and not fatigue herself. She was
threatened with a disease in the throat but it had not declared
itself. Her color is too clear however for her to be very strong.

My friend Mdlle. Wayancoff is ill and Mons. Le Comte
Wrbna is far too much afraid of my raillery to trust himself
in my drawing room with me by myself without the aid of Ct.
Festitics so he does not come near me, besides his thinking me
a person of excessive bad taste because I won't let him call me
chère Ange & pay me compliments and make love to me—in
which meritorious occupation some of these gentlemen pass
their lives—"Pour faire le Cour aux Dames"—and they make
quite a business of it. I found that when I got angry with

---

[1] On February 11 John had written that the whisker on his right cheek grew
much more strongly than on the left which he hardly ever had to cut, so
perhaps George was not altogether to blame. Mr Ruskin expressed himself
on the matter with his usual vigour: 'I do hope you will always be able to
keep a smooth face—for I never see a man (not a Jew or a Soldier) with Hair
on his face that I do not set down as an idiot.'

Wrbna it quite delighted him, so for some time, as I know more about him now, I take the upper hand, make fun of him and rather laugh at him, treat him with perfect indifference which is the best way with such men, for it is, I believe, paying them a compliment to mind their badinage. Now I am left entirely to myself and every one is civil and Courteous to me....

END OF CARNIVAL

❧

Effie's letters between March 7th and April 3rd are missing, so we do not have her account of her visit to the Duchesse de Berry nor her presentation to the Chambords. We know from John, however, that she did call on the Duchesse de Berry on March 8 (no details are given) and on the 27th he wrote that she had been 'yesterday to pay her devoirs to Monseigneur: (Henri cinq) who has within the last few days arrived with the Duchess [of Bordeaux—Chambord's other title]. She was very much pleased with her reception—first of all, pleased by being *kept waiting*, for instead of there being a servant at the head of the stairs to receive her, as usual in great houses, when she got to the top of the first flight, there was no one to be seen—till—on advancing a step she found behind a screen the two laquais in waiting [so?] deep in a game of chess they had heard no call. They jumped up in great consternation, and ushered her forward—but one doesn't find English footmen occupying their time so well. She was much surprised by the excessively *quiet* look of the duchess and her ladies—she says they had not the least appearance of French women, no *paint* about them—no *putting on* of dress or coiffure so as to produce an effect, nor any of the piquancy in manner either—but exceeding quietness and simplicity—both of dress and *add*ress; like English ladies in middle rank of life—but *vraiment grande dame* nevertheless.... Effie declares the duke himself to be very handsome. I am rather doubtful on this head myself—having only seen him at a distance—when his effect was not striking. But everybody says he is very good. They made Effie sit beside them, and were much pleased by her recollecting having seen them, somewhere or other—on their visit to Scotland.' Mr Ruskin wrote back characteristically: 'I am deeply grateful for your interesting account of Effie's visit to the Mons Henri 5—party—I am also flattered by the Quiet look of the family, for you may remember—the Quietness of Colour & of Demeanour is a monomania of mine.' The Chambords lived in the Palazzo Cavalli (now Franchetti) opposite the Accademia. At that time it had a much larger garden which the Count had made by demolishing a palace.

On the 16th of March John heard that his father had taken for him and Effie a seven-year lease, at £95 a year, of No. 30 Herne Hill, next door to, and an exact replica of, No. 28, Mr Ruskin's own old house (which he still owned and let on lease), and had given Mr Snell, an upholsterer and house agent of 27 Albemarle Street, £1,000 and carte blanche to furnish and decorate it. John expressed himself 'a little vexed at the enormous sum spent in furniture' when he and Effie's tastes were so simple.[1] All the same, he wrote on the 17th: 'I have no doubt I shall be very happy there.... As for poor Effie—I am rather afraid; her London society will be out of her reach—and though we have worthy people in our neighbourhood—there is a wide difference between the society of the gentry of Camberwell— and the kind of companions she has had—more especially lately— who—however frivolous they might be—yet could hardly say anything even in its frivolity—was not interesting—owing to its large bearings. Last Sunday we had for instance—two generals and a commandant of a city—side by side on our sofa—and however the time might pass in badinage—things *come out* of the badinage of such men which are not to be had out of a decent teaparty in Camber-well; and after being made a pet of by Marmont—and able to run in whenever she likes in the evening to the drawingrooms of women of the highest rank in Austria, I don't wonder at her beginning to look a little melancholy at the idea of the seclusion of Dulwich.... We must be as kind to her as we can.' Effie was allowed one say in the furnishing of her new home. She 'bids me beg of you', John wrote on the 25th, 'to tell Mr Snell not to put a four poster—but a large French bed in the bedroom at Herne hill'.

John's fears for her happiness in the seclusion of Dulwich were gloomily reflected in a letter from Mr Ruskin to Mr Gray.[2] Mr Gray's reply, having done nothing to dissipate his forebodings, two more letters followed in which all the old complaints against Effie were reiterated. He pleaded guilty to being pleased with the young

[1] We know from Mr Ruskin's account-book that eventually he paid Mr Snell £2,327 10s. for altering and furnishing the house, and gave John £20 more for a piano.

[2] Bowerswell Papers, March 30, 1852.

people going into good society but maintained that it could have happened in a more prudent and economical manner. 'In fact,' he continued, 'had they kept a little back—had Phemy dressed much more quietly, they would have been at parties higher than they ever reached.' (He must have been thinking of London Society for Effie certainly got into the very highest society in Venice.) Quite rightly he feared for their happiness in the dull life at Herne Hill and was at his wits' end to know what to do for the best. To make them contented in the kind of quiet life he himself enjoyed with Mrs Ruskin seemed quite chimerical. 'They never appeared to me to have more than a decent affection for each other,' he wrote, 'John being divided between his wife & his pictures, & Phemy between her husband & her Dress.' As usual Mr Gray made more inadvertent mischief by passing on at least some of his criticism to Effie.

Casa Wetzlar, April 3, Saturday

Dearest Mama

I am glad my last letters have amused you and I think you will have been interested in my last about my visits to the Chambords. They are remaining here only a month and go on giving their Soirées, and expressed their regrets to Lady Sorell and Princess Hohenlohe at my non-appearance.[1] I suppose, poor people, their hopes in France become every day more faint as the President consolidates his power, and people seem to think he intends playing the Napoleon game all through—as soon as possible to declare himself Emperor and probably have a *Tug* for Italy with the Austrians as the Army will want some work and the French soldiers have not forgotten the pleasant Life in Italy. Poor Italy, what a pity it is that whenever any war is to be gone through, her plains and Cities should be made into battlefields to finish the quarrels of other nations.

I shall give your message to Reischach when I see him which may be today as he called yesterday, and if he has not gone again to Verona he will be sure to come again as I did not see him and he always makes a point of seeing me when he is in Venice as both John and I are prime favorites of his. He declares he has a *profonda Passion* pour moi but as he says this to every

[1] This was because the soirées were given on Sunday when Effie would not go out.

Lady whom he admires or likes I only laugh at him and we
always have some fun with him when he comes.... About ten
years ago he was staying at Gordon Castle [belonging then to
the Duke of Richmond] and Papa would be diverted to hear
him imitating perfectly the Highland reels he heard on the Bag-
pipes there. He likes to outshine the young men in which he
is perfectly able as with his wit he can at any moment turn the
laugh against any of them. I never see his nephew Wrbna[1] now
excepting when he is in attendance on the Russians. You
wonder what he will do? I suppose nothing because he finds
that I don't permit him to add to his reputation by being with
me and he had not the esprit or real gentlemanly feeling at the
bottom of his gallantry like Festitics to pay me a visit merely
for politeness sake. If he comes again to say goodbye when he
leaves with the Russians I shall certainly admit him as I consider him too contemptible to shut out, as if I did he would
say that I was piqued at his not having been for months.
However, he knows very well what I am about as the other
night he went up to Miss Dent (sister of the English Consuless, a very nice girl who has been here since I came and who
I often walk with) at the Ct. de Chambord's and said to her,
"Vous savez, Madelle., que vous allez a l'Enfer." "Why?" said
Miss Dent—"Ci ce que Mdme. Ruskin pretende," said Wrbna,
"that any body who amuses themselves on Sunday will certainly
go there."—"In the first place," said Miss Dent, "*at the present
time* I am not amusing myself at all and in the second place
I am quite sure Mrs Ruskin never said any thing of the kind."
Festitics is still in Hungary....

These last few days the weather has been quite mild and
balmy just such as you seem to have had. One day I went with
John over to the Lido and found such lovely violets amongst
the ancient Jews' burying ground. John said they smelt of *old
clothes* but I found them as sweet as growing in Christian
Lanes....

Not a single plank of the Marianna has been found and
Vienna has been full of the news and Lamentations. I suppose
the Grand Dukes have left [Vienna] by this time but they have

[1] Wrbna's great-grandmother and Reischach's maternal grandfather were brother
and sister.

had plenty of Fetes and amusement at Court for them. The Marquise Strozzi, Mdme. Pallavicini's sister, had been playing in a French Comedy with much success and she sent the lists of people who acted & the Programme acted by the nobles. It was very interesting reading over all the noble Austrian, Bohemian, Hungarian & other names in the Lists. The Dukes [Grand Duke Constantine's brothers] will be here after Easter & Marshall & the Ctsse. Nugent are coming with their youngest son [Arthur] all of whom I shall be interested in seeing as I have heard so much of them as they are all characters in their way.

I am glad to hear you are beginning to wear vests [waistcoats]. They are so comfortable and do with any dress. Princess Hohenlohe the other night at Lady Sorell's had on a Lilac watered skirt, white silk vest with emerald buttons set in gold, and a crimson velvet jacket with Ermine round it and a blonde Coiffure with crimson roses. I am glad to hear Papa was so gallant as to give you a present on yr. birthday [on March 17]. I hope you will get it nicely made up. Venice is a very bad place for getting any thing in, especially ribbons and gloves; the latter are so illmade & the former just like paper. All the Ladies get their Caps &c from Vienna where they are not dear and as nicely made as in Paris. They get beautiful little morning lace coiffures with colored ribbon in satin or gauze for about 7/-....

Casa Wetzlar, 6th April

My dearest George

... Venice is so tempting just now at night that it is hardly possible not to be imprudent—the full moon and clear air not cold is lovely on the Grand Canal, and last night, hearing at ten some singing and the splashing of oars, I went out on the Balcony at ten and saw passing under, the Russian Court in their Gondolas enjoying a Serenade along the Canals from two boats who accompanied them full of singers....

A good many Travellers seem passing through, just to judge from the English faces and dresses one sees. I find after living here some time that the moment an Englishman or woman sets their foot on the Square it is impossible to mistake their nation or origin. There is some[thing] in the bad dressing of the Ladies, particularly the way they put on their bonnets, and the gentlemanly air of the men with their well cut Paletots and generally well cared for air which is equally unmistakable....

All our gaiety is over for the present as it is the Sainte Semaine but next week Mdme. Wetzlar gives a Ball to which I shall go and enjoy as I have not danced since a good many weeks. General Sternberg & Mr Foster were calling on me yesterday, the former to wish me goodbye as the Emperor has told him to be near him at Vienna. He is like most Austrian Generals, a handsome, accomplished, middle aged man without much principle and very pleasing manners.[1] All these men liked Florence so much and regretted leaving it.[2] The reason why is because the Society is as dissipated as possible and they could do whatever they chose, but some of the young men who have more shame have told me that if they had sisters or wives they would not permit them to visit Florence, but the Austrians, generally speaking, are fond of amusement and do not in the least care of right or wrong. Mr Foster, however, would please you. He is an honest well bred English-man of the right thinking kind. The only fault John has to him is being too fond of horses. He spent a year in the desert in Algeria and tells us curious stories of his Life there....

Telegraphic Dispatch has just brought the Intelligence of Prince Schwarzenberg's death. The future Minister will prob-ably be Comte de Ficquelmont—Thun's Uncle who has lately written "Ld. Palmerston, Angleterre et Le Continent". It will make a great change in Austrian Politics.[3]

Casa Wetzlar, 12 April

Dearest Mama

... This is Easter Monday and a great Festa and every body is about doing nothing. John wanted his sculptor to take a cast for him in the Ducal Palace because the day was so mild but

[1] Leopold Count Sternberg was forty-one. In 1863 he married Princess Louise of Hohenlohe-Bartenstein-Jagstberg.

[2] The Austrians had some regiments stationed in Florence to help main-tain order.

[3] Prince Felix Schwarzenberg, who had been Prime Minister of Austria since 1848, was only fifty-two. He had introduced a constitution in 1849 which the Emperor abolished at the end of 1851.

Giordani said he could not possibly as it would shock the people so much were he to be seen working.[1] John said, "I suppose, however, they would have no objections to your getting drunk?" He said, "Oh! no, and one might break windows, do as much mischief as they liked but only they mustn't work." The day is beautiful and I shall go and walk in the Square to hear the music with Miss Dent at two o'clock. The people make to this a great day for eating and formerly they used to go to the Brenta to eat the large cakes with which Venice is now full. They look almost like large cushions and are in taste like Cookies without the Currants—and a great many Bonbons are sold & sugar Lambs and Doves. I bought a number and took to the little Watts Russells as I have not seen them for some time.

I shall be busy all today and probably not have time this week as I have the Nerlys to dinner, John having bought an old sketch of Tintoretto's from Mr Nerly and having invited him on the strength of it.

[John had first seen this sketch of a woman with two dogs—life size—on February 12, and had attributed it to Veronese. At the same time he had seen another sketch which he judged at once to be by Tintoretto—the sketch for the picture in the Doge's Palace of the Doge Alvise Mocenigo kneeling before Christ. Both these pictures belonged to Nerly to whom they had been given by Baron Rumhor, and John wrote to his father that he believed he could get them for 80 Napoleons (£64) but did not want to beat Nerly down as he had lost all his money in a bank failure two years before. His father was very distressed that he should now want to buy old masters and the matter was dropped until May 6 when he confessed that 'the other day' he had given £30 'for the—*not* Paul Veronese—but Tintoret as I afterwards discovered it to be by accident: It was put into a frame too small for it: in talking over it one day, moving it into the light, it slipped and came out, and behold, behind the frame, a piece of foliage and landscape which only one man's hand in the world could have painted'. We now know from Effie's letter that 'the other day' was at least three weeks before. John had evidently hesitated to tell his father of this new extravagance. His

[1] Giuseppe Giordani had made a plaster cast of Verrochio's Colleoni statue for the Great Exhibition.

father was not annoyed, however, and John subsequently bought the
other sketch which arrived by sea in June, 1853. This was bought for
£10,000 in 1910 from Mrs Severn, Ruskin's heir, by the Metropolitan Museum of New York. The first sketch, known as *Diana and
her Dogs*, is now in the Fogg Art Museum, Cambridge, Massachusetts. It was bought in 1915 from the Severns by Mr Samuel Sachs
who gave it to the Museum.]

There is also a Soirée at Lady Sorell's, but I shall not, I think,
go which she will be very sorry for but it has been so warm today
that it is too much to go picture hunting in the Churches with
one Lady, dine with another and take tea with a third. Lady
Sorell hopes that she will yet have the pleasure of being my
Chaperon one evening at the Comte de Chambord's as for two
Sundays they have given no Soirée and perhaps tomorrow,
when the Arch Duchess Sophie comes, they may arrange another
which I should like best of all as I should like to see the
Emperor's Mother in a room. She is coming to nurse her second
son, Maximilian, who is ill, & to take the sea baths herself.[1]
Schwarzenberg's death was awfully sudden. He died in an
instant, they suppose of disease of the heart, before the Emperor,
who was close at hand and called to him, could arrive. Nobody
seems to regret him and yet hard work for his country seems
to have killed him. He never went to bed till two or three in
the morning and was up early again at business but these
Austrians have constitutions of iron. Festitics has several times
told me that he has never been ill in his Life. His life has
been none of the quietest or soberest and he never goes to bed
till four and when in town at Florence was known to do this
for weeks together and be on horseback at five. I never saw him
dance, and at supper always moderate. I have seen many of these
men after several nights of hardly sleeping at all look as fresh
as if they had been in a state of forgetfulness for long, and Ct.
Wrbna told me that once in Bohemia he had slept only seven

[1] Archduchess Sophie (1805-72), daughter of King Maximilian Joseph of
Bavaria, had married Archduke Francis Charles in 1824. It was largely
through her influence that in 1848 he renounced his rights to the throne in
favour of his son. Their second son became Emperor of Mexico and was
executed in 1867.

hours in *ten* nights. I struck one reason that they do not look worn as English would is that they have arrived at the great philosophy of amusing themselves as much as possible, never being put out, and above all having no conscience. This is a very convenient code if one could believe it. Radetzky led this sort of Life when he was young and has arrived at a very old age without ever being ill.

They say that the Emperor passed here yesterday quite incognito under the name of a Colonel to Verona to consult about who he should choose for his New Minister. There are different reports about the way in which he took the loss of the Marianna. Some say he cried and others say he is hard & did not care. It is impossible to know the truth about these things. Radetzky comes tomorrow which will suit his Aides de Camp admirably as Madame Wetzlar gives a Ball on Wednesday and Ct. Thun & Baron Diller will be very glad of an opportunity to dance again in Venice.

I saw Mr Brown yesterday. He is in excellent humour again and has been so for some weeks; he said he was just in fun in the Ducal Palace. He is very dissatisfied with our cook Nani, whom his faithful Johanna [or Joan] declares that he puts stuff into the meat to make Mr B. ill and does not use proper food. I am of the same opinion as once or twice I have been sensibly ill after eating of his prepared dishes and I am going to send him away as I have felt very unwell for several days with pains in my limbs and stomach, and Mr Brown does not know what to do for he was ill for two days and yet not being able to catch Nani in the fact hates the trouble of changing. Johanna declares that once she was nearly dead with some strong medicine put in her food and that a man told her that Nani had made him get stuff from the druggist's and since then she has never eaten anything prepared by him; sure enough she was dreadfully sick & ill. This was last year and if so what his meaning is I can't understand but he bears a very bad character and if he has a Mania for Poisoning it is just as well we should dismiss him. He has always been getting more neglectful ever since we curtailed our expenses and perhaps wants to revenge himself, and yesterday morning I told him that for a week past he had given us very careless and badly cooked dinners, and knowing what he could

do, if he did not do better this week, and especially as we were
to have two people to dine, that I should dismiss him. Well, what
sort of a dinner do you think he gave us—a plain boiled fish—
a small piece of roast mutton—ditto of veal—ditto of Lamb and
a plain rice pudding—did you ever read such an arrangement of
dinner for company when he is known as an exceedingly clever
cook for the last twenty years and was in the Kitchen of the
Viceroy Eugène Beauharnais? ...[1]

Here I was quite shocked on Good Friday to see every shop
open and the whole town like a Fair preparing for Easter instead
of a day of solemn fasting and prayer as one has always supposed
this day in Catholic countries to be—the most solemn day in the
whole year. Now I must stop as George is going to the Post....[2]

Casa Wetzlar, 17th April

... I was very grateful for your long kind letter, the enclosure
to Papa's half sheet about the Ruskins about whom really I intend to take up very little space in my letter as it does no good
and it is as impossible to explain what they would be at sometimes as it is in endeavouring to please them when you think you
perceive what they want. I am very much obliged to Papa for
writing to Mr Ruskin and giving him a little bit of his mind. I
always told John that since they had taken the house it would
be much better to let them furnish it as they liked since they had
decided to lay out £3000, but they need not say they are doing
it for us since they know that we both are against so great an
outlay of money in such a situation of London where they
do not think of remaining themselves; then talking of our
expences is quite ridiculous since they sanction and encourage
all that John lays out here, and even now he has given a fresh
order to his sculptor to cast a number of the capitals of the Ducal
Palace, I believe at a further expence of £40. John gets quite angry
at me when I say that I think he is taking too many. I daresay they

[1] Eugène de Beauharnais, Napoleon's stepson, had been Viceroy of Italy
in 1805. Mr Brown kept Nani on, at any rate until February, 1855, for Effie
then wrote asking him if Nani fed him well. In the same letter she says how
sorry she is that Joan is ill, so perhaps she was still being poisoned.

[2] We know from a letter of John's that George always went to the post at
10.30, directly after morning prayers read by John and lasting half an hour.

would be valuable to posterity if the Austrians were throwing
Venice down but I do not know that any idea of future good
to others sanctions living beyond your means, but it is
nonsence representing this to the Ruskins as Mr R., only a fortnight ago, made an offer of £300 for some prints of Turner's
that John wanted to get.[1]

John last week bought a Tintoretto for £30. Now when they
think of incurring all these expences in which I have no voice
how can you deal with such people? Any little thing I buy I save
out of my clothes money which this year I have not had as regularly as usual owing to these expenses, therefore how Mr Ruskin
can talk I conceive not. I have no doubt they would like me to
be happy but I don't believe they ever can for after four years
experience I have found it equally impossible to be fond of Mrs
R or to trust Mr R. I always get on with them very well but it
is at a great loss of temper and comfort, for the subjection I am
obliged to keep myself in while with them renders me perfectly
spiritless for any thing else. One of the things that distress me
perhaps most is hearing them all railing against people behind
their backs and then letting themselves be toadied and flattered
by the Artistic canaille by whom they are surrounded. I am quite
of Mr Cheney's opinion that of all canaille they are the lowest
with very few exceptions. Considering all that John did both
personally and in his works for Turner and Prout, never to
leave him a stroke of their pencil is to me wonderful. The
letters that man Prout used to write John were quite disgusting
with flattery.[2] But there is no end to them and as any thing
I write to you about them must only distress you and only

[1] A book of the *Liber Studiorum*—drawings etched on copper—from
Thomas Lupton, the engraver.

[2] Samuel Prout, the water-colour painter, born 1783, had been a neighbour
of the Ruskins at Denmark Hill, and on February 7 had died of apoplexy
within quarter of an hour of dining there. John, who had greatly loved and
praised his work, was 'a little vexed' that he had not left him anything. Of
Turner he had expected nothing because only once in all the years had he
heard him say, 'Thank you Mr Ruskin', whereas Prout had 'made all manner
of speeches'. But Mr Ruskin's indignation was against Turner: 'He has left
£1000 to build a monument to himself & to you who have built a monument to him stronger than Brass—not a Sketch' (Letter of January 31,
1852).

serves by thinking over all their conduct to make me more dissatisfied I shall turn to themes more agreeable to myself and
more amusing to you.

But now I must go out as I have been sitting in all day which
makes me feel quite unwell without any thing else. I have seen
no one today but General Falkenhayn to whom I am very much
obliged, as by his kindness in doing me a somewhat valuable piece
of service I have been able to return one of Mr Brown's many
kindnesses to us. The other day there was a conscription in
Venice which always causes a great deal of grief to the men who
are obliged to leave their families, and they had drafted a certain
number of men into Ct. Wimpffen's regiment, amongst others
a son of Bastian's, Mr Brown's Gondolier. He came to me and
begged me to use my influence with the Austrians to get the man
if possible put into the Arsenal, as he is a good Joiner, as they
were in despair at his leaving Venice. I asked Falkenhayn who
said he did not think there was any chance as they did not let
Italians work in the Arsenal as they are dangerous. However in
two days he got it done and they are grateful you have no idea.

I wrote to Falkenhayn in French and thanked him very much
for his kindness to me all the time I have been here & he came
today to see me, notwithstanding that he has a great deal to do,
the two Arch Dukes & the Arch Duchess Sophie being here.
I was asking Prince Felix Jablonowski,[1] son of the Prince who
always lives here and who has attended them hither, last night
at Mdme. Pallavicini's if they were as good looking as the
Emperor. He said no and was complaining very much of their
growing so fast; he is obliged to order them new uniforms every
three months; (like John [her brother] darling man) he ought
to have their clothes made for growing. He himself is magnificent. If you did not know that he was not Emperor I believe
you would take him for one, such a fine tall figure and gentle
dignified manners with beautiful hands covered with Jewels, and
moustaches I do not exaggerate when I say eight or nine

---

[1] The stepson of Princess Jablonowska whom Effie met so often. He was
five years older than his stepmother, having been born in 1809, and head
of the household of Archdukes Maximilian and Charles Louis, the Emperor's
brothers, aged nineteen and eighteen. It was the son of this latter Archduke
who was assassinated at Sarajevo in 1914.

inches long from end to end sticking straight out far beyond each side of his face with no beard or whiskers. In the Austrian service nothing but Moustache is permitted unless you are a General Officer which he is, but still he had none. He showed me in a beautiful velvet box a present he had had from the Emperor of Russia of the Star & Order of St. Anne entirely in diamonds. I never saw anything more magnificent—the Star was as large as the top of a breakfast cup and getting larger the Diamonds as they approached the centre. The Order had also very fine stones with red enamel. The Prince defended Vienna against the Mob in '49 and it was an Ancester of his who saved Vienna from the Turks the last time they besieged it. He looked sad however and said during conversation, with a sigh, that Life was so long and one had so few happy moments in it. I refuted his Theory wanting to draw him out—but the fact is that he is "éperdument amoureux" of Mdme. Strozzi, Mdme. Pal's gay & charming sister in Vienna, but he cannot marry her as she has a small impediment in the way in the shape of a husband who lives in the Papal states from whom she has been separated some years. She was married at 16 and he treated her so badly that after suffering eight years she ran away to her father at Vienna. She is very clever and handsome and I suspect not equal to Jablonowski in character as they say she is coquettish. They are queer people those Viennoise—they have such very queer ideas of right & wrong.[1]

The Russians in the meantime are all away. They went to Verona to a Grand supper given them by Radetzky on their way to Modena on Thursday where they stay with the Duke of Modena till the 24th when the two other Grand Dukes reach them there and they all return here for five days when they depart finally for home, visiting Rome & Naples on the way. Baron Diller spent the other evening with me. He had come from Verona the night before for Madme. Wetzlar's ball which was pretty and made a great noise in the house. George & Mary had the benefit of all the music as it was in a Saloon next John's study. Col. Cameron brought some Indian Officers going home

[1] In 1864, after her husband's death, Countess Strozzi married the Austrian General, Prince Leopold Croy. She died in 1881. Prince Felix Jablonowski never married. He died in 1868.

on leave with him. I had such a Polka with one youth, a Capt. Keith, one of the Kintore family,[1] who perfectly astonished all the Ladies, because you must know that the Austrians, not particular in many things that we are particular in, are still very strict about their manners in society, and in dancing your partner holds you very nicely so that you can dance perfectly well and yet are quite far from him, but Capt. Keith danced in the usual London fashion holding you quite near and the hand immensely far out. The Ladies vowed we danced beautiful [sic] as they never dance Polka steps here & we executed every imaginable pas, but they said it was a wonder for they had never seen any manner of holding a Lady so as to entirely, to all appearance, to impede her movements. Two or three of them tried to dance with him and could not get on at all. I left at twelve being tired and they were all at supper diving into Patés and other eatable matters. Diller spent the next evening with me & told me that the Marshal is coming next week with his état major to take leave of the Arch Duchess Sophie for whom they have illuminated the Theatre tonight....

Casa Wetzlar, 26th April [Monday]
... Yesterday the Russians all returned accompanied by the two other Grand Dukes, Alexander[2] and Michael, who had joined the rest at the Duke of Modena's. Gorzkowski & his suite went at six to the Station to meet them and as they came down the Canal and under my windows all in open Gondolas attended by all the boats belonging to the Russian steamer which are all white, with the sailors all in white, with one Officer and Russian flag in each, the effect was most beautiful. First came the Imperial Gondola with the Grand Duchess and the three Grand Dukes all in Austrian uniforms of the Huzzar and Cavalry. They looked exceedingly well; one of them [Nicholas] looked exceedingly tall and a very fine face; they say he is the image of his father. After them came my friend, the little Wayancoff, who

[1] Charles Keith-Falconer, aged twenty, only brother of the Earl of Kintore, was in the 10th Hussars. Effie had known Colonel Cameron in Perth. He married Lady Sorell's younger daughter who died in 1854.
[2] Effie means Nicholas. Alexander was the Tsarevitch who became Alexander II in 1855.

kissed her hands to me and looked very happy attended by a
number of very fine looking Russians with helmets and
wrapped up in immense cloaks doubled with furs. They only
stay a week and then go home by the Black Sea.

Mr Cheney is soon going away. He is going to give up his
beautiful rooms here and return to England, selling most of
his furniture and taking all his pictures and articles of vertu
with him. His departure will be a great loss to Mr Brown &
Mr Dawkins, who are great enemies but curiously enough are
both great friends of Mr Cheney's. Mr Brown is in the greatest state of gratitude to me for getting the man into the
Arsenal. They tried him at his work and were satisfied and his
getting into the conscription, instead of being a loss to him,
may in the end prove the making of him as if he conducts
himself well he is in the way of being employed in the Austrian
shipbuilding there which goes on constantly....

Today I have a note from the Duchesse de Levis[1] begging me
in the name of Mdme. de Chambord to attend a grand Soirée
to be given tomorrow evening to their Imperial Highnesses of
Russia. As it is again on Sunday I intend to refuse but to ask an
audience of Mdme. de Chambord to thank her *for her extreme
kindness*, and after writing this in the morning I went on the Place
and met Mdme. de Levis, who accepted my excuse with all the
good breeding for which I find these French so remarkable.
She said that she feared I wouldn't come and that it was so
unfortunate that they had chosen Sunday again but that she
would let me know when Madame would receive and I could say
my adieux as they all leave on Thursday. She was walking with
the Marquis de Fontenil who is a very nice person. He knows
the Béthunes very well at Paris and says Mdme. dances herself
green every season. She does nothing all the time she is in Paris
but dance and dress. He thought it deplorable but said what he
wondered at much more was the influence she had over the
Count who never dances and goes to every ball with her and waits
till seven in the morning for her.[2] I hear a rumour that the

---

[1] Wife of Gaston François, Duc de Levis, who spent his life in the service
of the Duc de Chambord.

[2] When Effie first met Count Béthune at Denmark Hill in October, 1848,
he told her that in Paris married men never danced, married ladies always.

Duchesse de Berry is to have a Soirée on Tuesday which I hope
she will invite me to as I shall see the Russians and all together....

On Monday [May 3] morning I am going to see the last of
poor old Marmont. All this time his Body has been in a coffin
covered with black velvet and a crucifix lying on the top of it
in his Parish Church opposite here where I saw it the other day.[1]
On Monday they are going to place it in a raised Catafalque
covered with black velvet and silver and all the Church hung
with black for the funeral service when the Soldiers are to play
a military mass—it is all done by the Duchesse de Berry.
Next day the Body goes into France to be buried at Paris. A
Priest here whom I know goes with it. After it passes the
frontier the expence will be to the French government. He has
been well prayed for poor man. I know that every morning
Mdme. Esterhazy and Mdme. Pallavicini and others went and
prayed beside his coffin. Every body was very fond of him. I
always liked him from the first moment I spoke to him; he was
so thoroughly a French gentleman of the old Régime. There
are a good many Legitimists here just now. By the bye the other
evening I had a talk with the Earl of Denbigh—he is Ld.
Feilding's Father and I believe has not yet got over his son's
perversion to Rome. He seemed a quiet sensible respectable sort
of man and had been passing the winter at Gratz with his
family and came over for two or three days with his daughters
to show them the beauties of Venice....[2]

You want to know our plans. I hardly know them myself excepting that on the 17th of May we leave this house and go into
appartments on the Square for a week or two which will be
delightful as the warm weather comes and we can sit at our window and hear the Band in the evening. About the second week
in June we shall be in Verona for a little time; after that I do
not know when we get to London or how, but I should think
about the beginning of July. Of our House we hear almost nothing. I know, of course, what it is like and the size of garden

[1] In the church of the Rosario, usually called Gesuati, on the Zattere. It
was two months since his death.
[2] The 7th Earl of Denbigh (1796-1865) was a widower with five sons and
five daughters. The Ruskins were soon to meet Lord Feilding and travel with
him to Paris where he did his best to convert them.

exactly, as it is the one joining their old house in Herne Hill which you will recollect too,[1] but my idea is that they have taken this on purpose to come beside us and turn their tenant out after we are once settled. I think they will begin to expatiate upon the inconvenience of Denmark Hill and then quietly move up again to their old quarters.[2] I always burn yr. letters; you may always write exactly what you like to me as I read them over, mark what I have to answer and then burn your letter.... I hope I shall be able somehow or other to see you all this Autumn & retain some of my good looks not to disappoint Alice. I believe I look well just now and Falkenhayn says I am much fatter than when I came, but I don't feel quite well; my stomach always troubles me with pains— dreaming at night and feverish. I believe it is a good deal my own fault; I am not sufficiently careful of what I eat and take anything that comes until I am satisfied. My headache is better this morning but I passed a very bad night and although I bathed my feet feel unrefreshed, but I have constantly these little ailments and they just come & go....

Casa Wetzlar, 1st May

Dearest Papa

... John was much interested about your description of the Raphael and obliged by your defending him. Talking of pictures puts me in mind that I don't think I told you that about a month ago I told John that I thought he might try to buy some of the Tintorettos going to ruin here for England & that he ought to write to Sir C. Eastlake, and at the same time I proposed writing to Ld. Lansdowne[3] for a request from the National Gallery or the nation of £20,000. John did not like to

[1] Effie had stayed at 28 Herne Hill in 1840. It was there that she had first met John.

[2] Mr Ruskin had written on December 19 to say that Denmark Hill with its six women servants, two men servants and three gardeners was now too big for them. It was never his intention, though, to settle near the young people but rather to take over the new Herne Hill house when John and Effie moved out of it. He did not expect them to stay anywhere for more than a year or so.

[3] Henry, 3rd Marquess of Lansdowne (1780-1863), was a Trustee of the National Gallery. Effie had first met him at Lady Davy's in May, 1848, and

write to Ld. L. but I insisted as I know Ld. L. is fonder in reality of the Arts than politics and aspires more to be a Maecanus
than a Charles Fox. I wrote him a letter myself accompanying
John's more business like one and we got yesterday answers. It
appears that it interested him. Directly he called a meeting of
the Trustees but some being out of town they were to have
another meeting this week and Ld. L. says that he hopes very
much that Sir Charles will receive power to act and to give John
funds to purchase. But don't mention this, as if the Trustees are
shabby it may come to nothing, but it gratifies me to find that
I am not mistaken in what I have always believed—Ld. L's real
kindness and friendship for us which even the severe gout in his
hands does not prevent him from writing us himself instead of
making his secretary do so. You may like to hear his note to me
which is as follows—"Dear Mrs Ruskin, I assure you that I feel
much indebted to the Tintorets for having procured me a letter
from you, and tho I have written to Mr. Ruskin on the subject,
I must say that your eloquent pleading in their favour, adds
greatly to the desire that I feel to see them, if it can be accomplished, the property of the British Publick, whose taste requires
a frequent refreshing from such quarters to keep it sound &
straight, amidst all the vagaries into which it is apt to run—as
you will find if as I hope you will return to London in time to
see all our annual Exhibitions now about to open. Our friend
Lady Davy after a long hybernation at Bournemouth has just
come into full blow in town & is exerting herself as usual to
promote society. You must really not allow the lapidary charms
of Venice to retain you there much longer. Whenever you arrive
you will find friends impatient to see you and none more than
myself and believe me Yrs. Truly Lansdowne."[1]

---

thereafter he was unfailingly kind and hospitable to her. He even offered to
give evidence on her behalf at the time of the annulment. Sir Charles Eastlake, President of the Royal Academy, was also a Trustee of the National
Gallery.

[1] John wrote on April 30 that Effie was too proud of this letter to part
with it but she copied it to send to the old Ruskins. He does not give her
any credit for writing to Lord Lansdowne, nor indeed for the idea of buying
Tintorettos, but it may not have been her idea originally, for on March 10
John had written to Sir Charles Eastlake offering to buy some Titians and
Tintorettos for the nation.

If any thing is to be done about these pictures it may keep us a little longer here but at present we intend leaving for Verona the 1st of June or so. You may be sure that whenever I can manage it I shall take a run to Perth and during the autumn I believe I could manage as Mr & Mrs R. will never at any time, you may be sure, object to my visiting you as then they get John to Denmark Hill all to themselves. They are not coming abroad at all this year....

The Marshal is here from Verona attended by his two merry aides de camp, Diller & Thun, who paid me a visit last Evening but I did not receive them as I had a headache. They have come to pay their adieux to the Russians who sail tonight in their steamer after their residence here of four months. They have not made the most agreeable impression here. The Ladies of Honor have been pointedly rude to all the Ladies of rank here. I know one who wrote three times to the Princess Troubetzkoi desiring to see the Grand Duchess and never received any answer. They have equally offended Princess Hohenlohe, Mdme. Pallavicini, Comtesse d'Arco &c. For me they were always amiable and returned my visits regularly and politely. I never went until they had formally returned each call I made them and they knew that I had refused to ask them to be presented to the Grand Duchess because in truth I made up my mind at once, when I saw what sort of people they were, to act accordingly, which ends in me being the only Lady in Venice who has nothing to complain of, and the Grand Duchess staring after me whenever she sees me. It is not her fault as she is an immense talker and likes seeing people to show her jewels & toilettes and give them half a dozen kisses. As for kissing I never saw anything like these Russians. Comtesse Arco and I were quite amazed and amused at the scene the other day at the Station when the Grand Duke & Duchess, their Ladies and suite went to see their Brothers Alexander [Nicholas] & Michael and their suite off to Florence—such a kissing took place—I was glad not to be too near or might have shared in all the Imperial embraces which took place. I was quite astonished to see my little friend Madlle Wayancoff first in the arms of the Grand Duke Alexander who is very handsome, then Michael and then the Russian nobles who were with them. The Grand Duchess partook likewise. They did it quite as a matter of course and Mdme. Arco lifted up her hands in the evening to me and said, "À present tout passe dans le monde, personne ne se géne pour personne." The Marquise de Fontenil, dame d'honneur to the Ctsse de Chambord, said in France such things were never permitted excepting amongst the nearest relations, as with us.

Now Goodbye. May has begun with a little more East wind and rain which prevents a Picnic and Ball the Officers were to give us at the Lido which will be put off a few days. On Monday last I saw the last of poor Marmont. They had a grand funeral service for him—the Church all hung with black and his Ducal Arms painted every where. In the middle of the Church was a Catafalque with his coffin covered with gold & black Velvet—his Marshal's hat and his sword and orders all lying on the top. All the Bourbons and the Military Authorities were present and a fine Mass Chanted.[1] We all went in deep mourning. In the afternoon his Body attended by a Priest set out for France. It received no military honors in leaving because he had borne arms against Austria which I took the liberty of telling some of my Austrian friends was the most paltry thing I had seen them do yet—they ought to have honored his military rank whether as a foe or friend....

Casa Wetzlar [May 5]

Dearest Mama

... We have had such trying weather that really we have quite given up the idea of seeing any summer. The want of rain for so long, the cold wind and hot sun have retarded all vegetation so much that now in the country they are obliged to cut the young grain to feed the cattle, and the Polenta, which is the food of the poor, has risen 4 centessimi the pound which always makes a considerable difference, and the number of people who live here by charity is immense—30,000, out of a population of 70,000.[2] You must not suppose that many of these however do

---

[1] The *Gazetta di Venezia* of the time gives a long description of the funeral. As it took place on the 3rd and Effie's letter is dated the 1st, she had evidently been several days writing it as usual.

[2] Flagg in 1853 gives 'the ordinary population of Venice as 126,000'.

not live and bring up their families in comparative comfort. They are too proud or too lazy to work and they belong to different societies in Venice which, founded in the middle ages, are still enormously rich. Another of the blessings of the religion is that it encourages & maintains this vast body of idleness by making the present Italians pay for their sins by being charitable, and all this 30,000 in Venice are yearly clothed & fed by these means instead of being obliged to work and live in a cleanly, healthy manner. The evils of their Church and its inefficient teaching appear at every corner in some form or other, and although the nation groan under it, and since I have been here I have never heard a good word for the Priests from either Austrian or Italian, such is the curse and lethargy under which they lie that nothing is done by themselves or others to help them. How the English with their eyes open can be so blinded & enticed is quite wonderful. We often see Mr Watts Russell who is as anxious to convert John as John is to reconvert him. He often takes tea with us and they have long arguments and it is very interesting to hear them for they are both so gentle and so earnest and never lose their temper in the least.[1] Mr Russell is very kind and spends his whole time in the study of divinity and teaching his children but his mind is completely confused.... One of his grave assertions the other night was that the Roman Church had never persecuted or burned or killed a single heretic, that it was always the civil power, and that Priests were constantly interfering to save life—that history was very false and that the Inquisition in Spain was entirely the work of the Government. John quietly said that nothing would give him greater pleasure than to find out that the Church was innocent.

John got two copies of three numbers each of his large Plates from England yesterday. He gave one to Mr Brown as he had promised long ago, and he was so delighted with them that he has presented them to St. Mark's Library where they will be better kept and seen by all the scientific people who come to

[1] John wrote on May 23: 'I have seen a good deal of Russell and we have long arguments together. But when once people have taken that leap—it is like trying to pull them out of a well with a cobweb, to argue with them. They break line, and tumble back, the moment you pull.'

Venice.¹ The other copy John is to present to Radetzky when we return to Verona on the 1st of June. I intend taking my riding things with me there as I am promised some nice riding and the Country is so lovely that I should like to take advantage of a little horse exercise to see a little further beyond the town, and I shall probably sell my saddle which is beautiful and only been used once. Baron Diller told me to be sure and bring it for there were always people ready to have an English Saddle and if no Lady wanted it there he would buy it himself. He and Reischach were both at the Picnic at the Lido on Monday last but now the latter has gone to Vienna for a month. He left the key to his Opera box with Thun for me that I might go when I liked, and is to bring me his picture from Vienna, so that you see he is always very good friends with me although we dispute about religion sometimes. Falkenhayn is also going to get a Daguerrotype of himself done for me as I have a great respect for him. He is the best of them all and has always done any little thing he could for me. I made him ask the Governor Gorzkowski if any objection would be made on [*sic*] the Government to our bringing pictures from the town in case the National Gallery permitted John to acquire a few. They said there would be none so that I really hope when the Trustees have such an excellent opportunity that they will not grudge the money.

On Saturday next [the 15th] direct my letter to the Post Office as we leave this house [their lease was up] on that day for the Square, and up to the 20th you may write to me to Venice; then direct to Post Restante Verona. We have not decided on our route home yet. I want to see something of Germany but John is so wedded to old roads from no reasons whatever but custom that I don't know which we will take.² I am

¹ On December 10 John had asked his father to send these plates, *Examples of the Architecture of Venice*, and it is from their arrival that we can date Effie's letter, for on May 5 John reported having received them 'yesterday'. The copy presented to Mr Brown (the three parts in paper covers now bound in a hard cover) is still in the Marciana Library and bears the inscription: 'Rawdon Brown Esq. With the Author's sincere regards. Venice. 5th May. 1852'.

² John had written on April 27: 'I am thinking of returning over the Splugen by Schaffhausen and Strasburg—have you any objection to our

going this afternoon with Lady Sorell to the Cemetery to see where her husband lies[1] in order to tell Ld. Glenelg about it as they were great friends. She was yesterday with the Duchesse de Berry who said she would be glad to see me any day between twelve and one as I was going to leave Venice—so I shall go one of these days. I saw her three daughters, the Ctsses. Luchesi, the other day. They are very plain indeed with heavy pudding like faces and much more like Germans than Italians.

I went and took a walk to the Bersaglio[2] today [the 9th] where I found no less than six ripe strawberries. A Croat came and caught me in the act of stealing his fruit on Sunday and after regarding me with a slight air of suspicion began, when he found I understood his very extraordinary German, to help me to gather them. When I got home I took a funny little bit of Venetian Glass, rolled them in it with the leaves and sent them off to Mr Brown for a very nice dessert—in return for a present he sent me very appropriately on my birthday which I spent very happily, and after dinner John drank your health and said he was very much obliged [page torn] for giving me to him. Mr Brown's present was a beautiful box of Bonbons which came in this way—a young friend of his, the Prince Giovanelli, has just married a young Roman Lady of a great family, a daughter of Don Sigismondo Chigi, Prince of Carignano.[3] A great number of sonnets were made on the occasion on the different towns,

---

doing so? I am rather tired of the Geneva line.' He added that he wanted to see Constance which, since Turner painted it, he had longed to see. But by the end of the month he had changed his mind and decided to go by the St Gotthard and Basle to Strasbourg.

[1] In the Protestant Cemetery at San Michele. He has a very grand marble tombstone with his coat of arms carved on it.

[2] A shooting gallery by San Alvise at the northernmost tip of Venice. It is now a children's hospital with beautiful grounds, the greenest part of Venice except for the public gardens.

[3] Maria, aged sixteen, daughter of Prince Chigi-Albani, had married on April 21 the Venetian Prince Joseph Giovanelli, born 1824. Effie seems to have forgotten that she had met this young man, nicknamed Betta, with his father at a musical party at Signor Marzari's in January, 1850. They had no children. He died in 1886, and his widow, a year before her death in 1895, adopted a young man, Alberto, who in 1897 received the King of Italy's authorisation to call himself Prince Giovanelli. He was believed to be an illegitimate son of Prince Joseph.

Verona, Padua, Venice &c. and instead of sending Bride's cake
as the people in England do, they send Bonbons, copies of the
sonnets and a declaration of the marriage between the parties,
surmounted by all their arms and setting forth all their titles.
Nothing could be more pompous or more moyenage. I liked
it rather so Mr B. gave me the Sweeties and kept the Sonnets....

  I can now make bonnets and when I come to see you, will
probably be able to save you something in that line. I made
myself a most beautiful bonnet for 2/6 the other day. You will
be quite amused when I tell you—the Governor sent to invite
me to join his party in his little steamer to go to the Lido
Picnic. As we were to be rather gay and dance in a Marquee
all made of Austrian flags with the sides open to the air, we
were to dance in our bonnets, and I put on a Pink silk dress
with Lace Pelerine [cape] and had the day before no bonnet
prepared. I was determined to fabricate one and after thinking in vain I bethought me of my point lace Berthe. I made
a transparent frame and covered it with this which just fitted
admirably for frill and everything with out altering in the least.
I put white Tulle puffings instead [sic] and one very beautiful rose outside and others instead [sic] which I got in Paris.
Every one wondered where it was made and admired the
beauty of the Lace. I told them I made it but did not choose
to tell them it was my berthe which amused John very much.
The Picnic was very gay and everybody was there but it was
rather cold and our party at least had nothing to eat as we left
too soon, but I had some fun listening to Reischach's wonderful stories and dancing with Diller....

  Now I must say goodbye. I am tired and must go to bed. I
am beginning to be sorry every day as one little thing after
another shows me that we must leave Venice. The quiet of this
place quite spoils one for leaving [sic] in any other town and
if I allowed myself to think much about it I would soon fall
ill for I am as near you here I think as I am in London and my
Life will not be there what it has been here....

  Effie was evidently trying to shut out of her mind the thought of
returning. John had written on April 27: 'You say Effie and I seem
happier within the last few weeks. I am happier, just as in my first

letters, you will find I said I should be, as the effect of London society worked off, which I was sure it would take six months to do.... For Effie, I believe she is in better health than she was, but I cannot say she is quite as happy as I am. She looks forward regretfully to leaving Venice—and with considerable dislike to Herne Hill, and for the present avoids the subject as much as possible—to which I make no objection—for if she cannot or will not make herself happy there, it is no reason why she should not be happy here.'

THE ROBBERY

❧

Effie and John were both happy to move on May 15 to their new lodgings in the Piazza. 'We ... feel as if we had a new lease of Venice, and as if it were Venice itself again,' John wrote on the 16th; and again on the 19th: 'I am only sorry I did not live here all the winter. I like the small rooms much better than the large—and there is all the difference in the world between looking out on the Madonna della Salute, or on St Mark's.' He gives no indication of the situation of their rooms in the Piazza, but two of Effie's letters are headed Café Français (the others bear no address at all). The Café Français was at No. 110 San Marco, on the same side as Quadri's but further from St Mark's. Adjacent to it, at 109, in the little Corte di Maruzzi, was the Hotel San Marco. The conjecture is that although the hotel entrance was in the court, some of its rooms were next to, or above, the Café Français overlooking the square and that the Ruskins stayed in the hotel and had meals in the café which was said to have the best food in Venice. The numbers have not changed: 110 is now Salviati, the glass-maker, and 109 the despatch section of the Assicurazioni Generali, a great insurance company which occupies the upper floors of all the houses on the north side of the Piazza.

The beginning of Effie's next letter is missing but the following portion of it is postmarked 17 Maggio, 1852.

... we have moved into the Hotel on the Place and are very comfortably settled. Your advices for me to take care of myself were impossible. Yesterday you have not an idea what a day I had so that I feel a little tired today. We moved and the packing up I had all the forenoon was terrible. Mary is not of the slightest use on such occasions; she completely loses her head; I cannot trust her in a single thing. When I let her pack any box she wisely puts my Ball dresses at the bottom, and shawls and

Umbrellas above, so that now I am obliged to trust to myself entirely and only let her turn out the wardrobes and drawers which usually she only does half. I spent from 9 till half past twelve in this kind of work and when the rooms looked all dismantled and miserable and I very hungry, Mr Foster and Ct. Thun came in from Verona and were so sorry to see the desolation that reigned I told them they had better stay and lunch with me and amuse me for I wanted my mind turned to some Fresh subjects. I sent down to Bartholemeo the Cook[1] and he sent us in a few minutes a nice lunch of roast chicken, chops and peas and a delightful gooseberry Tart.

While it was preparing, Foster made his dogs go through all their tricks and Thun danced about, made Jokes and went into the fits of laughter for which he is famous. He brought me the kindest messages from the people at Verona saying how glad they were we were coming soon &c. I then left the Casa Wetzlar and came here. Mdme. Pallavicini sent to tell me that Count Nugent, her father, was at home and if I wanted to see him to come. I said I wanted very much but really could not as I was going to Mr Cheney's to dinner and to Mdme. Wetzlar's Soirée afterwards where we went merely out of politeness to say goodbye to her on leaving her house. She had a large dancing party but I only took two or three turns. Mr Cheney's house looks very dismantled but all concerning the dinner was perfect. Only Mr Brown was there; he was very quiet; he is really very fond of us I think and the idea of us all going and leaving him alone, for he has literally no one else, made him I thought very dull for he generally talks so much. I am going to take him some Jelly & Jam we have over to console him a little....[2]

I must now stop. It is beginning to be a little warmer; I have my windows full of Flowers looking out on the lovely Place & St. Mark's and sleeping all night with the windows open, but there is always too much breeze still to please me; I could bear many

[1] This is the only mention of the new cook. The missing part of this letter may have told of his coming and Nani's going.

[2] They also gave him as a parting present a picture bought at the sale of the contents of Mr Cheney's house. This we know from an undated letter (now in the possession of Mr Victor Cavendish-Bentinck) from Ruskin to Brown sent with the picture, but unfortunately he gives no description of it.

degrees more heat. I forgot to mention that I was at the Duchess de Berry's the other day to pay my adieux. They were very polite and said they were sorry I was going home....

Café Français, 23rd May
... Yesterday Ld. & Lady Kintore dined beside us in the Café—they are on their way home for her confinement. As she created quite a furore at Rome by her beauty I took a good look at her and was disappointed. Her extreme fairness of skin & hair is always considered a great beauty in South Italy but I thought they looked a miserable sort of couple. He is not bad looking but is, I understand, quite cracked & she unhappy. Her father & mother, Capt. & Mrs Hawkins, travel with them, have a suite of seven servants, a number of their own children and spend, of course, Ld. Kintore's money and are altogether so bad and so disliked that at Florence numbers of the people would not visit them and it was very much against the young couple. All the people from Florence during the winter have told me the same story and it is melancholy to see two such young people so badly matched, but as this is Italian gossip it might just be as well not to let it get North to Aberdeen.[1]

I want you if you hear of any nice Man servant to remember me—George will leave us when we return home. I believe he wants to marry & get into the London Docks, perhaps through Mr R's interest, but he is not being explicit and I don't ask him. I am not sorry he is going as both John and I find great trouble with his sulky temper although I shall be sorry to lose him for many little things and from the habit of him always being with us, but I think he has just been long enough and if he had stayed with us at Herne Hill I would have had no end of trouble with him so near Denmark Hill; he would have been discontented

[1] Francis Alexander Keith-Falconer (1828-80) had succeeded his father as 9th Earl of Kintore in 1844. He had married in June, 1851, Louisa Hawkins, his first cousin. His mother (his father's second wife, who obtained a divorce from him in 1840) was also called Louisa Hawkins, and it was her brother, Captain Hawkins, who was Lord Kintore's uncle and father-in-law. Lord Kintore's home was Keith Hall, Aberdeenshire. His heir, Lord Inverury, was born on August 12 of this year, 1852. He was to have another son and three daughters. Lady Kintore died in 1916.

with everything chez nous and have gossiped about everything with Anne, who is my bête noir there, and the rest of the servants. I never could get him to serve me the four years I have had him as he always considered himself John's servant not mine. Now I would like rather an oldish man who would be entirely for the house, and we shall have no Coachman, and I dislike young men in the house as they have amourettes with the maids. I suppose John will have a secretary or something of the sort to write for him at times when he is preparing for the press. We must either have that or two men in the House, for John has been so waited on all his Life that he quite spoils servants and requires almost one man to himself to run his errands, keep his clothes clean and all his things in order.[1] I shall also want a cook but as I do not know the size of the house cannot yet tell what women I may want. Every thing in England is so much more trouble of that kind than here where all sleep and feed out of the house and one has only to pay moderate wages once a week.

We are quite delighted with our change of quarters. The Square is a constant amusement, never otherwise than gay, always beautiful and at night with the music and crowds walking about quite delicious. John is quite charmed and is quite sorry he did not come sooner. The rooms are very nice and I sleep in a recess in the Salon. George was so disgusted at being put into a small backroom instead of a large one young [sic] with pictures as he had, that he sulked for four days although here he has nothing earthly to do and we never see him as Beppo sits outside my door and attends me like a Highland Gilly....

---

[1] George also copied out John's manuscript. This was sent in instalments to Mr Ruskin who called George a 'St George conquering the Dragon of an author's MS piles of scraps', in 'most *close, legible* & valuable writing'. Effie never could handle him and had had a great row with him in July, 1851, while John was at Malvern. He left a few weeks after the Ruskins returned to London and eventually emigrated to Australia where he became a Police Magistrate in New South Wales. He married and had seven children. He died in 1892. At the end of October, the Ruskins got a new *young* manservant, Frederick Crawley. He became devoted to Effie but fell out with old Ann at Denmark Hill because he would not gossip about his mistress. Nevertheless, he elected to stay with John after Effie left, much to her chagrin. He remained with John for years doing all that George had done.

John has had another letter from Sir Charles Eastlake saying that before they apply to the Treasury for a grant of money they would like Mr Cheney's opinion of the state of the pictures because although they are quite satisfied with John's account the Treasury never grant money on the application of one person. Mr Cheney wrote a capital letter but both he & Mr Brown have been discouraging John as much as possible because they say they believe it will be quite impossible to get Church property. I daresay there will be considerable difficulties in the way. The old Countess Mocenigo has a sketch by Tintoret of the largest picture in the world, his Last Judgement in the Ducal Palace. They would sell it [for £1,000] but John finds on examining it that it has been retouched and could not recommend it. I had a great battle the other day with John who in a pet wanted to throw up the whole thing. He wrote such an unbusinesslike letter to the Trustees that I thought if it went it might seriously hurt his character after promising to do all he could for the acquisition of these works to the nation. After some discussion I got him to write another letter which I hope will finish the money part & give him funds at least to try what he can do—but unfortunately he is very easily depressed, and he is so angry when he loses any time for his own work that nobody could be more unfortunate for such kind of business which requires all your time and attention and energy, and in fact all the qualities which Papa has & John has not. Every thing he does he requires to be pushed to, and he feels incapability in these things so much that he is disgusted with men and keeps away from them as much as he can.[1]

He is very nicely dressed just now. I bought him trowsers and vest of Turkish "gane", white crossed with black; it looks so glossy, clean & nice with a blue tie that I shall buy him another set as they are very cheap & nice in comparison with Stulz's.[2] Now goodbye....

[1] Apart from the sketch Effie mentions, John had an opportunity of buying for the National Gallery two Tintorettos—the *Crucifixion* in San Cassiano and the *Marriage at Cana* in the Salute which he valued at £7,000 and £5,000 respectively.

[2] John's tailor of 10 Clifford Street, *the* tailor of the day.

Café Français, 29th May

... We are still here and likely to be for a fortnight to come as John must wait Sir C. Eastlake's reply to his letter and then see about the pictures. We are quite delighted with our Lodgings on the Place and never tire sitting in our room which is most amusing and especially in the evening when the people all come out to enjoy the cool air and take their walk. I find the heat so strengthening and I have not been so well for long as these few last very hot days. I believe bathing at the Lido has a good deal to do with it. Nobody has begun, yet I thought it was quite warm enough and that it would be a pity to leave Venice without having a few dips in the Adriatic. Mr Brown kindly lent me two old sails with which my Gondoliers construct in a few minutes a very servicable sort of tent where, with Mary's aid, I undress & dress. The sea is delightfully warm and the bottom such beautiful smooth sand that I enjoy my bathe excessively. There is no one all along the shore and going about two I get back to dinner at five. It cuts up the day very much but just now there is nothing doing and many of the people who have been here all the winter are now returning to their different countries. All visiting is long since at an end and the only gaiety in the town is the walk in the evening....

John is very well. He is very busy drawing, rowing and buying little bits of antiquity which don't cost much and which he finds in holes and corners that no other Christian would put their foot into.[1] He eats quantities of strawberries and milk and cherries and says he has acquired a taste for two things since he came this time into Italy—viz. Oysters and Artichockes which he never could take before....

I had a very agreeable visit from Festitics just returned from his Hungarian estates.... His Castle I believe is very fine and always open to all travellers, who are served and lodged as long as they like and without distinction. In a country not much

---

[1] John reported on May 4 that he had got for a Napoleon (16/-) 'the Shadow of a head by Bonifazio', and on the 6th an ivory tabernacle of fourteenth-century Venetian Gothic work such as he had never seen outside cathedral treasurehouses, some Greek sculpture, and as much sixteenth-century Venetian glass as would furnish their dessert table on grand occasions—all for £20.

cultivated and where there are few Inns it is the fashion and a very good one I think. He wanted me much to come to Vicenza and ride with him, and if I was passing a day there I would do with pleasure but shall not now have time.[1]

Mr Cheney is still here [staying with Mr Brown as his house was dismantled] and says he is much out of humour at having to go away to England. I don't wonder; Venice is quite enchanting in the fine weather and not disenchanting even in the bad.... You must tell George to write to me how he likes Perth and if he was very sorry to leave Edinburgh....[2]

The beginning of the next letter is missing, but we know from John's that the remaining part was written on June 5 from Verona. John had to go there to finish some work and then return to Venice to await a reply from the Trustees of the National Gallery. They went to Verona on Tuesday, the 1st, and on the 3rd John was writing: 'We are excessively petted here—Marshal Radetzky sent Effie his picture yesterday with his own signature[3]—I wish I could write as well—as dashing and firm as if it had been written at thirty instead of 86, and his chief of staff who is not now in Verona—left his carriage for us—with all manner of insists on our using it when we wanted—and the Marshal's two aides de camp—and another young officer—came to escort us in our drive in the evening. It was pleasant—after being so long in Venice—to see the young men's riding—the nice—loose—cavalry balanced swinging seat, and the

---

[1] Count Tassilo Festitics died in 1866 after losing a foot at the Battle of Sadowa where he was commanding an Imperial Corps d'Armée against the Prussians. He never married. His nephew, also called Tassilo, inherited from him the estate of Berzeneze, on Lake Balaton, where he often entertained King Edward VII.

[2] George Gray had finished his apprenticeship. He never married and lived at Bowerswell until his death on December 27, 1924, aged ninety-five. When, in 1910, he sent Effie's letters to her daughter, Mrs Stuart Wortley, in London, he wrote that he had the sight of only one eye and would soon 'be as blind as yr poor Mother was in her last years'. The letters were despatched on May 3 in a small tin trunk, painted in stripes of green and russet, with a rounded lid. And in this same trunk they lie today at the Pierpont Morgan Library in New York.

[3] Effie sent this picture from London to her father and hoped it might be hung in the dining-room at Bowerswell.

horses as happy as their masters—but keeping their place beside the carriage to a hair's breadth.' And on the 5th: 'I am pleased with the young men; they are so highbred—so light-hearted—and so fond of each other, as well as desirous in every way to oblige us. Effie is a great catch for them, as they have no ladies' society here except one or two wives of the generals, who are very kind—but are forced to be always en grande dame.'

[*June 5*]

... Then Thun insisted we should breakfast with him in his rooms, where he gave us a breakfast as good as a Scotch one with Coffee and tea, anchovies, eggs, cherries, strawberries & cream and lots of things, and such a bouquet of Orange flower and carnations, made up in the Italian fashion forming a pyramid *a yard and a half* round and half a yard high. He piques himself on knowing what a Scotch breakfast is as he went on a tour with the Duke of Montrose last year in the Yacht of the latter, the Coral Queen, which he had at Florence with him. Every evening they have had their carriages for us and we have seen some of the most lovely country I ever saw in my Life.... I was much pleased with the way the 3 young men [Thun, Diller, and probably Foster] who were with us spoke to the country people, and the way the latter answered and told me in the different places we had been that we might do every thing we liked, gave us flowers and chattered away to us in the sweet Veronese dialect and seemed quite as happy in the presence of the Marshall's uniform as if they were Italians. The young [men] say the upper classes are entirely to blame and altogether dissented amongst themselves.

We return to Venice this evening and spend another week. We return here on Saturday and on the following Monday set off en route to Basle and Strasburg and Paris. I don't know how I shall ever leave Italy where I have always been so kindly and indulgently treated. I hope I am not spoiled but grateful and all the people I have known best, have been *the best*. I am very sorry to leave Mdme. Pallavicini; she is very fond of me and she is so unhappy that it is a comfort for her to see me to cheer her sometimes....

Venice, 12th June, 1852

... You will wonder what is keeping us still here after having
told you we should be in Verona as today and, but for the somewhat unfortunate affair which I shall relate, we should have been
there. Today I got all my things spread out in my little room
and began packing up to go away by the 4 o'clock train. Yesterday Ct. Carlo Morosini having brought his sister Ctsse. Venier
to see me, although it poured with rain I had promised to return
her visit, and proceeded to see them and moreover was curious to see the Ménage of a young Venetian Lady descended from
such an illustrious house as they never come into society and
I only made acquaintance with the brother by chance.[1]

Before going I told Mary to stay in the room as every thing
was lying about and I would be in in half an hour. I went and
Mdme Venier received me most kindly and showed me her
atelier, as she is a great artist, and her hair the most splendid
I ever saw and quite fair. They were so sorry to let me go, and
made me write my name in her Almanac and overwhelmed me
with amiabilities and I was home in less than an hour. I began
to pack and took up the case with the Major's [Guthrie] bracelet [his wedding present] in it. I felt it very light; I opened it—it
was gone! I rang for Mary; she knew nothing. All my Jewels
were lying together and all my best things gone—my Serpent—
my Diamond bird [a dove] and heart [a ruby]—John's Diamond
studs and several other things.[2] Whoever took them must

---

[1] Maria Venier, famous in Venice for her beauty and charm, was born in
1823, the daughter of Count Girolamo Morosini and his wife, *née* Adriana
Maria Aurora Bragadin. Her husband was Count Giuseppe Maria Venier
(1818-82). They had two daughters. John wrote on June 13: 'We have just at
the eleventh hour made the acquaintance of a Venetian lady whom I am really
glad to have known—bearing two of the greatest of ancient names—born,
a Morosini—married a Venier: now, Contessa Morosini-Venier and who does
not disgrace her name—domestic—quiet—industrious—fond of her children and her brother—if not of her husband, it must be his fault. She is eight
or nine and twenty—and never goes out usually—but was brought by her
brother to see us as being out of the way people—Effie returned her visit
yesterday—and I today—and it is a great pleasure to me to have been
received by *one* noble Venetian lady whom I could respect.' Her friendship
for Effie grew in correspondence, and in April, 1854, she was writing to her,
'Ma Bonne Effie ... Aimez moi toujours un peu...'

[2] The cameo of Bacchus given to her by Mr Brown was not taken. She

be most experienced, for my money was left, my other bracelets left and a number of trinkets. The Master of the Café and all the house were instantly in the greatest consternation. The Police came and have set their agents to work and I hope something may come of it, but the thing is most mysterious for nobody saw anybody come in or go out, and after I left, Mary locked the door and only opened it for John, who however left it open for ten minutes, not more, before I came in. The Police have desired us to stay till Monday. After I had recovered the disagreeable effect a little I rushed away to my Venier who was astonished to see me again and came this evening with her brother to pass the evening with us. Every one else in Venice thinks us gone, as it will be very disagreeable to say all the adieux over again and yesterday I had such a day of it you haven't an idea.

Sunday Morning [*13th*]—Nothing has been heard of my Jewels yet and I find that my blue enamel ear-rings are missing and also the chain of Pearls you gave me. The Police say that it is a very mysterious affair as it has been so cleverly done and in so short a time, and the master gives his servants an excellent character; and the Master of the Café is so vexed about it that he has given the chief of the Police a number of Napoleons to find out if possible, as he says he has only been here a short time and it will almost ruin him such a thing happening. Another curious thing is that the Countess Anersberg was in these very rooms all the winter and I constantly met her out at Balls and Soirées with Diamonds to the value of many thousands of Pounds, and in many different settings, and they, like us, were perfectly satisfied with the Hotel. We have no suspicion and it could not have been done in the night although the windows were all open as the bureau was always locked and I have a little dog who barks at the least thing.[1] It must have been done

---

wrote to him from London that she was grateful for this as she would never have anything so pretty or so nice, and wore it often and it was admired by everybody.

[1] After she got home, Effie wrote to her mother that this little dog, Zoe, given to her by Count Thun, had fallen out of the window of the Meurice Hotel on their last morning in Paris. It survived and, after some days at a veterinary surgeon's, was brought over to her by Lord Feilding. In *Praeterita* (Vol. III, Ch. II) Ruskin writes several paragraphs about this dog,

between twelve and one yesterday. You may imagine how it deranges our plans and puts everybody about; and I have very little hope of getting them again as the police are so dilatory in their proceedings and I fear it will not make John stay long enough to give them a chance.

We also received a letter yesterday from Sir C. Eastlake saying that although the Trustees were exceedingly obliged to John for all the trouble he had taken, at present they could not give so large a sum of money and could only send him their best thanks for his zeal. I thought they would end by grudging so much money and perhaps another time they may take the opportunity of our being abroad to give John the funds he has asked for.[1]

The other day I asked Mdme. Pallavicini to take me to pay a visit to Gorzkowski, the Governor, as I wished to wish him goodbye and thank him for all the kindness and liberality I have met with during my stay here.[2] He was delighted to see us and said that he should certainly refuse to sign my passport. Falkenhayn also came and did me the great favor to come from Treviso, where he commands in the absence of the Arch Duke Ferdinand, on purpose to bid me goodbye and give me his blessing. He also signed a petition for me for some Italians here, who wished the permission of Government to sew Soldiers' clothes, which he granted. He is so good & kind; I am sure a worthier man does not breathe. I hope you will excuse me writing more as I am very tired with all this excitement....

'a white Spitz, exactly like Carpaccio's dog in the picture of St. Jerome'. He calls it Wisie and claims that it was given to *him* by Count Thun. There is no doubt, however, that it is the same dog, for he also describes how it fell from the window at Meurice's.

[1] John makes no mention of receiving Sir Charles's letter—he was probably too disgusted—but in *Praeterita* he writes that he would probably have got the *Crucifixion* 'but for Mr Edward Cheney's putting a spoke in the wheel for pure spite'. It had been resolved at a meeting on June 7 that the Trustees did not find themselves in a position to ask the government for £12,000 for two pictures, especially as Cheney did not concur with Ruskin in his valuation of the works. These Tintorettos are still in the churches where Ruskin saw them.

[2] Effie sent her father a signed picture of Gorzkowski at the same time as the one of Radetzky with the request that it, too, might be hung in the dining-room at Bowerswell.

[Postmarked Venezia 16 Giugno; probably written 15th]

I hoped to have been able in a few days to have told you of the recovery of my Jewels, but till now nothing has transpired and the affair has assumed a most disagreeable aspect. Having given all our depositions at the Police and undergone severe examinations, Mr Brown & Mr Cheney have advised us to get out of Venice as soon as possible as now the thing is so public & so many interested in the detection that our presence cannot aid them and our staying here might subject us to great unpleasantness. The thing might become so complicated and confused that the Consul might have to take it up against the Austrian authorities and we might have another affair like Mr Mather.[1] The reason of all this is that the suspicions of the Police & the gossip of the town have laid all their doubts upon a gentleman, an *Englishman*, and an Officer serving in the Emperor's own Regiment. The individual in question has been constantly with us for nine months and bears the highest character for bravery & honor amongst his companions, being introduced to me by a General Officer who had known him all through the campaign and presented him to me at Ctse. Pallavicini's. I never thought him particularly bien élevé but John liked his conversation which was always sensible, and for Ladies he was a very correct visitor in conversation, but I did not much like him, but the circumstances of the case leave no doubt on our minds of his guilt although not having any proof we would not say so for the world, but Mr B. & Mr C. are of the same opinion, but it seems so dreadful to suspect a gentleman, a soldier, and a friend of our own that we were some time before we could allow ourselves to harbour the idea.[2]

---

[1] In December, 1851, Erskine Mather, an Englishman of nineteen, alone in Florence with his younger brother, had been struck down by the sword of an Austrian officer while trying to cross the road through a detachment of troops. His head was cut open and he almost bled to death. The affair created a great stir in England.

[2] Foster was, of course, the man in question. John naturally told his father about the robbery, and on the 17th wrote of Foster (without mentioning his name or even that he was in the army): ' ... having in his general character or appearance of character much that I liked—was continually attacking the clergy; never went to church, and in other ways showed a degree of irreligion which I have till now, supposed compatible with an ill

The above two gentlemen are of the opinion that the jewels have been found but that the Military authorities are so interested for the honor of their cloth that they have bought over the *sbirri* [police] who certainly came here the day after the robbery and said to the Master of the Café that they had found the things at a *certain House* and named the Officer as having taken them there. Now the Police retract this story and it proves there is something wrong somewhere as the Officers of any regiment here won't even allow a man to remain amongst [them] who has the slightest suspicion attached to his name; they put him out of the Regiment unless he can justify himself, and if he is wise he puts the affair into his Colonel's hands who will immediately institute a procès against the Police for Defamation. Therefore it is bad in every way—the jewels are made away with and a terrible confusion between the Military and the Police is the only result. If the jewels are not forthcoming the Military are saved and the honor of their army retained, but if the Police have the stones a terrible esclandre will ensue, and the Master of this Hotel has paid the Police a large sum to find out the offender and save the reputation of his house, but you can easily conceive that in a country still in a state of seige the Military are all powerfull and all their interest goes to keep the character of their army high. But in our own minds the following circumstances are not free from suspicion:—three days before the Robbery ——— asked me to show him my jewels, admiring at the same time a brooch I had. I pointed to the Bureau and said, "Oh! they are not worth showing you and besides they are locked up in there and Mary has the Key." He asked when he could come to bid us goodbye. I said, "You may come on Saturday morning at 11 1/2 and I will be packing." He came and stayed half an hour; he bid John goodbye, and then me, but hovered about the room and instead of talking to me took up my bible which was lying on the table amongst all my Jewel boxes and appeared to read. He afterwards asked me what I would advise him to send as a present to a Lady from Venice, and asked if 5 Napoleons would buy one. Knowing him to be poor

---

taught honesty: but which I shall henceforth be apt to think as inconsistent with the character of a man of honour, as of a man of sense.' Foster had told Effie that his father was a rich ironmaster at Stourbridge.

I said, "Oh, you may get a very nice bit of Venice chain for much less," showing him at the same time two bits that I had got for Sophie & Alice. He went away and I went out to Mdme. Venier's. I had not been gone ten minutes when he came back, made Mary unlock the door and said he wanted to write a line to John. He was a quarter of an hour writing 7 lines and Mary got impatient; then he went away and some time after John had the door opened for him and left it open ten minutes. Mary says she heard nobody in the passage during that hour I was away, but I find out that he told two different people that he had not seen us since Friday when he was here twice on Saturday.[1] His conduct since has been quite that of a guilty man; he never has come near us, and when he was told at a Lady's house that we were still here he got perfectly pale and never asked why and never mentioned our names after but said he would call on us next day. He never came. Then John, by Mr B. & Mr C.'s advice, wrote him a note very well expressed saying that not having seen him since Saturday he wished to tell him of the disagreeable incident that detained us here, and that in the list of persons asked him by the Police *his name* had been mentioned as one of the people who had been in our rooms that morning. In answer to that came a long rambling note with two mistakes about his engagements, evidently wishing to avoid seeing us, and this is all that has happened yet. We go this afternoon to Verona leaving every body in confusion and myself the loser of £120.[2] *Keep all this to Yrselves.* I assure you I am perfectly nervous with all this affair. Policemen, Courts and taking one's oath is quite new to me....

Venice, 20th [June]
You will be anxious to hear what we are about and how our jewel business goes on. Every thing is doing I believe that can

---

[1] John adds something to this account. After Foster had gone the second time: 'Mary locks up the room again, and, this time—gives the key to the waiter. About five minutes afterwards, I came in—the waiter took the key from its usual place and let me into the room—Mary came in—and gave me the gentleman's letter, which was to ask me to send him some razors! from England.'

[2] John gave the value of the jewels as about £100.

be done but the result is the same as when I last wrote—no trace of the ornaments and no indications of the Thief. John went to Gorzkowski, the Governor, with Mr Dawkins, the Consul, who received them most kindly and expressed his extreme sorrow at so disagreeable a business and said that as the Regiment, to which the gentleman I mentioned before belonged, had determined to investigate into the affair we must stay a few days and see the result. It can only be yet a few days longer and then we shall leave—first, I fear without any satisfaction as the property seems irrecoverably lost; secondly, money spent in remaining here beyond our time; thirdly, having irritated against us, most unjustly, all the Officers belonging to the Regiment who feel naturally enough the insult attached to their corps but should seek redress from the Police who suspected their companion and not us who never said a word.

Thun [Foster's best friend] himself is probably our personal enemy so that it is all very disagreeable, besides the bad odour it will cast on this House also and every body in it which will half ruin it and we are very sorry for we have never been so well treated in any Hotel. The servants have undergone long examinations and the Police are active, but if the Jewels [are] not destroyed they may appear months after this and then some clue may turn up as to the offender. The Diamonds however I have no hope for as they would instantly be taken from their setting and all clue lost, so you may easily conceive how uncomfortable we are, added to which is the receiving no news from you for five weeks. Now it is no longer your fault as of course you are now believing us far on our way home. John is also naturally anxious about the effect of his detention on his Father and Mother who will be very much disappointed when they learn we are still here.

During all this affair I must say that General Falkenhayn & Mdme. Pallavicini, Mr Brown & Mr Cheney and Mr Dawkins have been exceedingly kind. We dined with Mr B. on the 18th and drank your and Papa's health....[1]

I go every day to Lido and bathe; it is a great refreshment to me and the sight of the sea is always so beautiful and exhilarating. I only wish I had a more interesting companion in my

[1] Their twenty-fifth wedding anniversary.

excursion than Mary who is the dullest and stupidest living creature I ever met and yet good, too, but her stupidity is fatally in the ascendant. When we go out in the boat she sits baking in the burning sun and when I say, "Are you not very hot, Mary?" she says, "Yes! Mum." Then I say, "Why don't you pull the curtain and sit in the shade?" She says she never thought of it. If it had not been for her stupidity I would have still had my Jewels for, after making her lock up the room and telling her to take care of the Key, which I could not myself as we had very little time and John scolded me once before for taking the key out of the house, she ought to have not let it out of her hand for a minute, but I don't say anything to her for it would make her unhappy to be blamed and she is too dull to understand why....[1]

Apart from distress at causing anxiety to his parents and the extra expense at the hotel, John was 'not the least annoyed' by the affair and rather pleased that Effie had been taught 'a lesson about leaving her jewels about, which she used to do very carelessly', and that he had had some experience of Italian police methods. What pleased him most, however, was that the misfortune had shown Mr Cheney to be 'active—kind—and right-minded, in the highest degree'.

Mr Ruskin *was* annoyed, though, and on June 20 was writing to Mrs Gray: 'My own opinion is that if the fair sex were robbed of all their Jewels & finery beyond recovery & clad in plainer attire—it would tend greatly to their advantage.' And in a postscript he added: 'They are both as careless as possible—The loss of the jewels is nothing to the Injury they will have done by their Carelessness throwing suspicion on several parties.'[2]

Venice, 27th June

I am sure you will be wondering very much at our still being detained here but I hope you are not at all anxious for us, for indeed there is no occasion, only you may easily believe that

[1] Perhaps they thought she was too dull to be dishonest for they seem never to have suspected her. She left Effie's service in February, 1854, giving as her reason that life at Herne Hill was too dull and the house too quiet; she wanted to get back to Venice.

[2] From an unpublished letter in Bowerswell Papers.

such a very disagreeable business causes us much painful feeling and an excitement that makes one quite feverish & nervous.
Not a day passes but some variation or change comes out which
keeps alive one's interest or anxiety, and then our continual examinations at the Police which are so strict that they would do
credit to any Spanish Inquisition and where one is kept two or
three hours to answer all the questions one has answered before.
That they are most polite and courteous I cannot deny, and the
same class of people I fancy in England would not be half so civil
I am pursuaded, but you may imagine how I am put to it
sometimes when three or four people question me at once in
Venetian. Sometimes they misunderstand me and I them; then
they send for an Interpreter who speaks English perfectly but
when he begins translating my words, goes all wrong and I have
to stop him & bungle it out by myself.

The fact is that the Military are persuaded, they say, of
———'s innocence and wish to prove it, and send back the
depositions from the Police, who are of a different opinion, to
get further information. I do not see how it can be otherwise.
Until the Procès is finished at the Police, the Military Court
of enquiry will not sit nor give us our Passport. The Governor
of Venice cannot give it, as he has no authority over Regimental
business, each regiment being managed in its own peculiar way.
Gorzkowski goes tonight to Verona to see Radetzky and we shall
know when we are likely to get away, but if our passport is still
refused, the affair must become public, as if they keep us
much longer [something apparently left out here] and if that
were the case I do not know when the business would be
ended. One thing is very sure, that John & myself have acted,
they tell us, with the greatest moderation throughout and
have cast suspicion on no one, but told the truth when required.
We have been most prudently advised and done nothing which
in any way can be blamed or misunderstood.

The unfortunate ——— is not under arrest but confined to his
barracks and I feel much for him knowing his excessive love of
liberty and freedom, and in this very hot weather such restraint
must be most irksome. I assure you I would have thrown my
Jewels ten times over into the sea than that any person should
suffer for me but these things are not in our power & we now

only have the consolation of feeling that we have acted rightly. Another most painful feature in this affair is, I fear, the loss of the friendship of our kind & good hearted Ct. Thun who has been since we came into Italy everything that could be amiable & polite to us which I must often have mentioned to you before. He has quite a romantic & touching friendship for ——— & every moment he can leave the Marshal he comes over here to be with ———. Whilst with him he trys to be cheerful and divert him, & when he goes back to Verona he gives himself up to the most unrestrained grief and cries for hours and feels the thing deeper than anything else that could happen to him in the world, and naturally will not come near or see us which must also hurt him in a way for he was very fond of both John & me and his kindness I can never forget.

It is so delightfully warm now that I feel much stronger and better. It is to me real comfort to plunge into the sea which is quite warm and roll about for 20 minutes and dress myself in the evening in a muslin frock with one petticoat, no stays and a chemise only, and go out in the open boat on the water where is always a little breeze, and the beauty of the Place was never seen to such advantage.

We have Lord & Lady Feilding here to amuse & try to convert us, fresh as they are from the "Holy Father", as they call him, and all the Cardinals and Priests in Rome. They wanted to know us, & Mr Brown & Mr Cheney were too happy to make us known as they are bored with people so full of Holy water and what they call fashionable piety. It is really wonderful to hear them with all their zeal, & very interesting to observe the curious net of error thrown over them. Lady F.[1] is pretty, about my age and looks as if she were dying of consumption, poor thing. She has suffered agonies with sciatica, but declares that a Holy man at Rome whose family have been tillers of the ground since St. Peter & St. Paul and received from them the gift of curing Rheumatic disorders by praying and laying on hands, when she was in dreadful agony the man came and she instantly walked and remained cured for six weeks—but now

---

[1] Daughter of David and Lady Emma Pennant, she had married Viscount Feilding in 1846. They had no children. She died in Naples on May 1, 1853, aged twenty-four.

it returns from time to time. He is remarkably handsome, about 28, and it is to me very odd to hear so elegantly dressed a man with carefully trimmed moustache, Joinville tie,[1] the whitest hands in the world, and small fresh [*sic*] boots—talking about miracles, the gifts of the Spirit, Penance and crucifying the flesh—and now on his way to Strasburg to visit a nun who he says is in direct communion with the Saviour & who, if you recommend anything to her prayers, gets it very often. Sometimes I feel inclined to smile but I must say that he seems perfectly happy & very well aware of what he believes & can argue like any Priest—in fact he talks of nothing else. He says his conversion cost him a dreadful struggle but he was received into the Church at Edinburgh by Dr Gillis[2] whilst she [Lady Feilding] was under Simpson's care. He delights in talking to me, and certainly he could not have a better listener and I let him go on at score as he did last night about the "winking Virgin at Rimini". He is the most affectionate Husband I almost ever saw and I think she requires all his care poor thing. His estrangement from his father Ld. Denbigh makes him probably depend more on her. He told me that it was an awful grief to his Father who is a most devoted Christian, I believe. He has never seen him since and does not allow him to correspond with any of the family but his twin sister, who he says he has no hope of, as she has such a strong independent mind & will not bow to the authority of the Church.[3] But now goodbye....

[1] A cravat with square fringed ends which came into fashion in England in 1844 after the Prince de Joinville's visit to Windsor.

[2] James Gillis (1802-64) founded St Margaret's Convent, Edinburgh, in 1835, and became Vicar-apostolic of Eastern Scotland in 1852.

[3] This twin sister, Mary, never married. In 1857 Lord Feilding married again, Mary, daughter of Robert Berkeley, by whom he had seven children. He succeeded his father as 8th Earl of Denbigh in 1865, and died in 1892 at the age of sixty-nine.

CHALLENGE TO A DUEL

✌

John and Effie at last got away to Verona on Tuesday, June 29, but there an unpleasant incident occurred, described in the following extract from the draft of a letter (undated) from Edward Cheney to Mr Dawkins, the Consul, who was away at Recoaro.[1]

'I suppose Ruskin has written to you, but as it is possible he may not have done so—I hasten to tell you that he was not permitted to leave Verona without receiving a hostile message from M. de Thun. An officer on the part of that gentleman called on him—to ask, 1st why he left Venice, 2ndly if he was ready to deny by writing having any suspicion of Mr Foster's honor & on his not replying satisfactorily to these two questions, to request that he would name the weapons with which he would meet M. de Thun—The manner of the officer was perfectly polite & he acquitted himself of his disagreeable commission with evident reluctance—Ruskin replied, that he sought no man's life & had no intention to risk his own, upon which the officer told him that M. de Thun would consider him as "quite otherwise than a man of honor". This information Ruskin conveys in an open letter to Count Falkenhaim (which he wishes Brown & me to read) not written to him *officially*, but as to a gentleman & a friend. He says farther he neither cherishes resentment towards M. de Thun nor desires to lodge a complaint against him but he wishes his friends to be acquainted with what has passed and to explain his own motives of action. In the letter which he writes to Brown, he concludes by saying he has stayed at Verona later than he intended by Mrs Ruskin having been alarmed & agitated by *hearing* the conversation from her own bed room to which she had retired and not having slept well in consequence—but that he hoped nevertheless to commence his journey in an hour, promising to write from

[1] This unpublished letter is in the possession of Mr Nigel Capel Cure. It is the only account in existence of what happened at Verona.

Bellinzona....[1] I believed M. de Thun had too much feeling & good nature to act in the way he has done towards a man so well meaning as Ruskin & so little used to the sort of encounters proposed to him. If this story should get into the newspapers (which God forbid) it would tell more heavily against the Austrian discipline & Austrian magnanimity than fifty such stories as Mr Mather's. In my opinion it was the bounded duty of the high authorities *here* to protect Ruskin as long as he remained in the Austrian territory & have taken means to cool the zeal of the well meaning but most injudicious friends of Mr Foster—nothing appears to me now to be done but to give all publicity to the fact that Ruskin in his depositions purposed only to detail the circumstances of the robbery & by no means to accuse any one.'

John did not mention the challenge to his father, although he wrote from Verona on the evening of the 29th and several times on the way home. Effie did not mention it either in her next letter but she had plenty to say about it later on. They were now anxious to get home as soon as possible. They hired a carriage at Verona and posted to Basle, stopping only on Sunday at Airolo. As well as resting on Sundays while travelling, Effie had to have her day of 'necessary rest', as John called it, and the best thing that could happen, according to him, was that this day should fall on a Sunday.

> Airolo, Piedmont, 4th July '52
>
> This letter posted at Lucerne will show you that we are a good part of the way home. We are here at a little town on the Italian side of the St. Gotthard which we pass D.V. tomorrow.[2] This being Sunday we take a rest and are none the worse for it as we, by the advice of our friends in Venice, got over the Austrian ground as fast as possible, for what reason I see not as they

[1] John had intended to get off at 6 a.m. on the 30th. His letter to Brown, enclosing the open letter to Falkenhayn, is now in the possession of Mr V. Cavendish-Bentinck. His actual words are: 'Effie is pretty well. She had gone to bed before Count Thun's representative arrived—but hearing us talking, imagined what was the matter—and was a little put off her sleep by it.'

[2] There was a carriage road over the St Gotthard completed in 1832. Even in winter carriages could be taken over the pass on sledges.

had no idea to do us any harm, and if they had kept us back I would have been more than obliged to them as "Les absents ont toujours tort" and our absence gives room for all manner of calumnies which our presence till the trial was over might have disproved. —— is still in confinement in his Barracks and must be until the Regiment is decided, which must take several weeks yet. It is to me a great proof of the fine order and discipline of the Austrian Army, the incapability of their belief in a comrade's dishonesty, and as far as I have seen any thing in our own army and theirs I should say that the young men in the Army of Italy were as perfect in their behaviour as it was possible to be, and although this —— is our country-man, they have taken him as if he had been an Austrian.

On arriving at Verona on Tuesday Evening I found George's long and very nice letter, the first for six weeks, but the information it contained of Albert's having Scarlet fever added not a little to my other troubles. I shall be very anxious until I have other letters from you but in one of Mr Ruskins' of three weeks later date, he mentions the fact of the children's having been ill but says they are all better. I fear only from this that the others may have taken it but trust all are going well and that I shall find letters from you or Mr Ruskin at Lucerne and Basle. After leaving Verona we reached Como, passing Berg-amo & Brescia, and since Como we passed Bellinzona, the most beautiful small fortified town I ever saw....

I feel the change of air from Venice exceedingly. The hot sultry air was to me perfectly delicious and here I feel shiver-ing and wretched with severe toothache. The air is too exciting, and the relaxing sea air of Venice made me feel better than I have been for years. All the rest, John & the Servants, are de-lighted with the change, & George was quite delighted, being violently republican, to get out of Austria, and when he got over the frontier waved a forbidden hat which he had on and said, "Now I can call my nose my own." I said, "& your hat too."[1]

You may write now to Denmark Hill for I fancy we shall be there as soon as you can answer this. We go to Basle, Strasburg,

[1] After the 1848 revolt in Sicily, the wearing of the Calabrian hat, with feath-ers and a buckle in front, was prohibited by the Austrian authorities.

Paris and Boulogne, which, with Railway, will not take long.[1]
I have seen few Travellers' names in the Books this year and
the Innkeepers complain everywhere that since the Revolution
things have not again returned to what they were before....

I must conclude as I have to write to Venice. Mr Cheney has
also left now and gone home by Vienna. Nothing could exceed
his goodnature in this business of ours and the respect I have
for his great probity and knowledge of the world and what
ought to be said & done. Although John and myself wished
to do every thing that was right, also the Consul & Mr Brown,
Mr Cheney advised us all, and without him we should I think
have committed some bêtise or other....

Airolo, 4th July '52

My dear Mr Brown
I suppose now that I am out of the Austrian Dominions I may
write you a few lines. I have been vainly looking for an opportunity to do so since we passed the frontier, for before that I
had no time, and remembering besides that you only wished
to hear from me after that we had gained Switzerland, although
still hearing Italian spoken I consider I yet greet you in Italy,
which perhaps may make my letter more acceptable knowing
that you love it more than other lands, and this little corner
amongst the mountains is no disgrace to the rest. We are passing our Sunday quietly here purposing to pass the St. Gotthard
tomorrow and reach Lucerne on Tuesday. The carriage we
hired at the "Due Torri " answers extremely well, and being
light and strongly put together, we have as yet been quite
satisfied that we decided for it instead of coming by Diligence.[2] You must excuse my writing you so stupid a note but you
remember I did not walk great distances at Venice and today I
went up with John to see a certain waterfall which looked tempt-

---

[1] At Fluelen they put the carriage on the steamer for Lucerne, and from
Lucerne posted to Basle. There they sent back the carriage and took the railroad to Strasbourg.

[2] The carriage would have cost more than even the coupé in the diligence,
i.e. the front part, designed like a post-chaise to hold three people, which,
by paying extra, they could have reserved for themselves. The charges for
posting were very high in Switzerland; on the other hand, by diligence, they
would have had to pay excess baggage.

ing from our window below. To get to it I had more scrambling than I could have believed myself capable of, and you would have laughed heartily, as we did, if you had seen us both lose our balance on a steep ascent of smooth turf and roll over and over until some bushes stopped us....

John was so happy to get amongst his Alps again and it was quite a pleasure to see him enjoying himself so much—but then he begun drawing comparisons between what he calls the vice and misery of Venice and the liberty of the Mountains and asked me if I did not think that this was the right sort of Life. I said I supposed it was, and for him doubtless it was much better, but to tell you the truth, the snow makes me shiver and I feel the change excessively from Venice....

I am afraid you will now be feeling Mr Cheney's absence very much but you are sure to see him very soon again. He said to me that he would return to see you and I don't think England will hold him very long. He is so good and perfect in every way that I think you are favoured in having had such a friend so many years. I never ceased admiring both he & you in this late affair of ours and without you both I am sure I do not know what we should have done. We very likely might have committed some bêtise which would have kept us in Venice till now and weeks longer. I am wondering much whether any thing has happened since we left or if you kept or sent the letter to Genrl. Falkenhayn. You would not be surprised at Ct. Thun's conduct. John did not say in the letter another rather strong expression which he made use of, through his representative, that he thought John's conduct "tres peu honorable" and that it must be actuated by some "basse vengeance" &c. I am very sorry for Ct. Thun. I am sure he will be very unhappy and fret himself into a fever. If necessary he will spend his last sou to maintain or save his friend. I never knew any one so generous or so unselfish. His heart is greater than his Judgement but that is rare and I hope he will not change.[1]

---

[1] Count Thun became an Imperial Chamberlain. From 1864 to 1867 he commanded an Austrian volunteer corps in Mexico. He was later a Privy Councillor and Commander General for the Tyrol in Innsbruck. In 1877 he married a grand-daughter of Eugène de Beauharnais. He had two children. Many of his descendants are still living in the Tyrol. Ruskin, in his only

When you see my kind friends at St. Servolo, be so good as
to say how sorry I was not to bid them goodbye and say that
if ever we can be of the slightest use to them we shall be so glad
and grateful if they will use us....[1]

My love to Joan and I hope to see her in your pretty house
and your Brown man [Bastian?] again. Indeed I trust you
will be very comfortable in it for long and not find the winter
cold.[2] I shall remember whenever I get home to send you
some "Calme" for yr. stairs, and the "Nightside of Nature".[3]
If you want anything else, please just to hint it to me, for
although I may be in London, I never forget Venice and
everything is before me just as if I were there; I am always
thinking about it. God bless you and make you happy there.

Your very affecte. and obliged
Effie R.

Hotel Meurice, Saturday, July 10th

Dearest Mama

I have had three kind notes from you this morning and on the
whole I feel less anxious about the children than I was. I think
the fever seems to be taking its course and I trust the three invalids are going on well and with care will soon gain what they
have lost, and I trust that you with so much hard work in this
very hot weather (for Paris is hotter than any place we have yet
been at) will not have any bad effects from your attention to the
children. I have destroyed yr. letters as Mr Ruskin seems afraid
of them—why I know not for I have no fear of infection in any
way and only wish that I could have been with you to help you.

---

passage about him in *Praeterita*, states wrongly that he 'fell at Solferino'. He
did take part in that battle in 1859 and might have been killed if the grenade splinter which hit him had not glanced off the metal part of a satchel
he was carrying.

[1] As well as chloroform and snuff, Effie sent reports of Hanwell Asylum
to the Fate Bene Fratelli.

[2] Brown had just moved into the Ca' Grimani della Vida on the Grand
Canal, opposite the Ca' Pesaro. This was his last home in Venice. He died
there on August 25, 1883, and is buried in the Protestant cemetery on San
Michele. The banner of St Mark's with the winged lion, given by the
Municipality, was wrapped round his body in his coffin.

[3] By Catherine Crowe (1800?-76), published 1848. It was about legends
and ghost stories. She wrote several novels and books on the supernatural.

As it is, when you are all well again and my house affairs a little in order, I shall try and come down and I don't think they will refuse me as I shall be very anxious to see you all again. Paris seems very quiet and very clean. I bought you a pretty white bonnet today and the Milliners tell me that they have never held such a gay season. Their light-heartedness is astonishing; they never seem as if any thing could make them serious. I bought you a bonnet because I am sure of the woman's taste and it is always useful. I see nothing else that tempted me. I took one for myself and some *boots* as I was actually shoeless— that is all I have.

You will be surprised to hear that I am here by myself having left John behind at Strasburg, the reason being that we have been travelling off and on nearly all the way from Venice with the Feildings and at Strasburg Ld. F. heard such wonderful accounts from the Bishop of the *Soeur Alphonse*, the "Estatica" who I mentioned before, who sees visions and prophercys, that Lord F., who I think is very anxious to convert us, and has told me more stories about Miracles than I ever read before in my Life, about bleeding roses, blushing stones, Appearances, visions and the like, and finally brought us an invitation from the Bishop of Strasburg to dine with him and see this woman whom he was to send for, for the purpose, from the Country at Niederbrunn where she lives with an order of nuns which she has founded, both there and also in Strasburg, for educating the poor and visiting the sick in their own houses. I told them that I would not remain although I should have liked it much as the woman seemed to be remarkable; every body knows about her there and if it is a trick it is a very cleverly got up one. I advised John if he wanted to stay to send me on with the servants and luggage as I thought I could not travel all the way to Paris without stopping, but you will be, I think, astonished to hear how strong I am. I left yesterday at eleven o'clock, had Diligence to Nancy [95 miles] till 7, then came through all night by Railway and arrived this morning at 4.[1] I got to the Hotel

---

[1] The railway from Paris to Strasbourg had only just been completed as far as Nancy—indeed John was still uncertain whether it went further than Bar le Duc. The journey took Effie 27 hours, whereas the diligence from Strasbourg to Paris had taken 16 1/2.

at six, threw myself on a bed and dozed for three hours, then had cold bath and breakfast; I then drove out to buy some things and am only returned but not at all tired. I called on the different French people [the Domecqs] but all are in the country.

This woman at Strasburg foretold the Revolution so exactly that since then all she predicts is signed by the clergy and transmitted to the Archbishop of Paris. Last year she had a vision that foretold all the President's doings and also that Heaven was soon to end these continued strifes and France would be happy for a short time under an old man who would bring back the Bourbon line in his person. They asked her if it was not the Ct. de Chambord and some others but she said it was an old man and none of these. As they had never heard of any old man, they applied to the Legitimists who said there was indeed an old man whom many believe to be the Dauphin (I have heard of him before also) but said that he was so obstinate and went so seldom out that he never would be prevailed on to meet her. However he was asked and consented. He met her as if by accident and whenever she saw him she cried out in German— "That is the man". She called out to him instantly to speak to her and he was so affected that he begged to be *confirmed* which he had never been in his Life, and has seen her several times and she has written for him, they say, a wonderful book on the way he is to Govern France. She also predicts a speedy death to this Pope who she says will be killed,[1] but his successor will be the best Pope that has ever been yet, and that the Church now gaining so many converts will be in great glory under him. She thinks, but is not sure, that the Emperor of Russia will have great power given him and will shortly unite the Greek to the Latin Church and will be received by rebaptism on the banks of the Rhine. John was very anxious to see, as you may believe, how they managed such an affair and I shall be interested to hear what he says. Ld. and Lady Feilding seem to think England in a most flourishing state and told me of ever so many convents and places I had never before heard of.

We have letters from Venice and Mr Brown seems most anxious that John should write an account for private circulation of the whole affair so that if it should become public John

[1] Pius IX lived another twenty-six years.

may take the Initiative, and I think they are right as I believe that the moment F. gets his Liberty he will bring it out in some way or other and denounce John as a coward for refusing to Fight at Verona and also refusing to give Ct. Thun or his representative any farther explanations.[1] All our friends say that in any case it was no fighting matter and never could have been, altogether a police affair. If John had told Radetzky, these officers would have been put under arrest, as the Governor at Venice and Falkenhayn both said nothing could exceed the delicacy of our conduct, and told the Officers whoever entered our house or spoke to us in any way would be arrested. The Chiefs of the Army did all they could, but it showed us completely that little was even in Radetzky's power as they are afraid of the army who has done every thing for Austria and they had even trouble in procuring our passport. Mr Brown & Mr Cheney are sorry that we did not apply to Radetzky for an escort to conduct us out of the Territory, but I always hope the thing will not come out, but if it does some queer stories will appear from Florence where at Lady Walpole's,[2] and other houses who receive these same people, Jewels disappeared. When I first knew F. he had just come from there—he showed letters to the Consul clearly proving his origin as a gentleman and he had no want of money about him.

Hoping to hear on my arrival in London on Tuesday D.V. that you are all better, believe me

Ever Yrs
Effie

It is uncertain whether John saw the 'Estatica' at Strasbourg. His last letter was written from there on the 9th when he said he hoped to see her at the Bishop's palace that evening, but it was one of those *either* to night or to morrow morning' invitations and tomorrow morning would be too late as he had to leave early for Paris. (If he

---

[1] Unless there is a letter missing, which does not seem to be the case, this is Effie's first mention to her mother of the challenge. The Grays must have been mystified and could have obtained no information from Mr Ruskin.

[2] The wife of the Earl of Oxford's eldest son, whom she had married in 1841. In 1850 Lord Walpole had eloped with Lady Lincoln, wife of the Duke of Newcastle's heir.

wrote from Paris, where they spent a day and a half, the letter has not survived.) He was 'highly curious' about her, chiefly because he had been puzzled for a long time about the cessation of miracles in the Protestant Church. He wrote that from the evidence of their existence in the present Church of Rome which Lord Feilding had laid before him, it seemed to him that only two hypotheses were possible: 'One, that Satan is working powerfully therein at present: the other, more charitable and I trust more rational—that when really good and faithful people are bred up in a church which *expects* miracles—God will not refuse such answers to their prayers—and that we Protestants have them not because we don't expect, and don't ask for them. I cannot bring myself to accept the third hypothesis—of supposing that all men who bear witness to such things to be liars.'

In a letter to Rawdon Brown of July 22, 1852, from Herne Hill, Effie tells of the Feildings' efforts to convert them in Paris: 'The Feildings followed us the whole way home & are now in town. I am sure they gave themselves a great deal of trouble for we were always before them and they were always coming after us and stopping where we stopped &, in short, spared no pains to convert us. We arrived in Paris before them and they had previously told us if we spent a Sunday there to go to "Notre Dame des Victoires" & we would find the most wonderful assemblage of the Parisian poor and indeed all classes, for John had complained of the bad attendance of men in the French Churches. We went, never thinking of them, when in the middle of the service I found myself kneeling side by side with Ld F & *she* behind and the Abbé calling on all the congregation to pray for the conversion of John & myself who, they said, were already united to the true Church in heart. When I got out I told Lord F I should be glad to have half an hour's talk with him, which we had at tea beside the other two who listened. He began by saying that if I would only take from him a miraculous medal of the Virgin blessed by the Pope & recite an Ave Maria per day that I would soon be converted. Although I thought he uttered some horrible blasphemies I kept my temper which was diffi- cult, refused his medal and told him in a few words what I believe to be our only hope for salvation. He was so horrified by my senti- ments that he plainly told me that I was an Arian, a Lutheran, a pupil of that evil spirit Knox and on the high road to the bottomless pit.

Since then we have never mentioned the subject but he writes long letters to John and would evidently do anything to get him.'

Effie and John got home on Tuesday, July 13, and went to Denmark Hill for a few days before moving into their new house at Herne Hill close by. Mr Ruskin, Effie reported to Rawdon Brown, was dreadfully angry about the challenge at Verona and hurt at the idea of John having to justify his conduct in anything.[1] She was quite frightened by the vehemence of his indignation and grief. John and his mother were both indifferent to any number of duels, whereas Effie thought the father's feelings very natural and was sorry for him. He was angry with her too for bringing home the dog Count Thun had given her. Nevertheless he gave her a diamond pin he never wore, and Mrs Ruskin an enamel bracelet and brooch, as some compensation for the loss of her jewels.

They were so afraid of the story of the theft getting about that Effie begged her mother and George not to speak of it, and was relieved to hear from Mr Cheney, who had stayed in Vienna on his way home, that no word of it had reached that city. Mr Dawkins also wrote that it was no longer talked about in Venice and that those of Count Thun's friends who knew of his conduct at Verona blamed him. All the same, on Mr Brown's advice, John put down on paper a full account of the circumstances lest he should ever again be called upon to justify himself.

Just as they were hoping that the whole affair had blown over, the *Morning Chronicle* of July 21 came out with the story; other papers copied it, giving names and details supplied from Italy and wrongly reporting that it was John who had accused Foster, the implication being that he had done so out of jealousy.

By the end of July the story was in six journals and going the rounds of the clubs and dinner parties. Mr Ruskin imagined that already the young couple were being slighted in society and did not hesitate to point out to Mr Gray that malicious tongues might well say that the lady had been visiting the barracks and merely dropped her jewels there. He insisted that John should write a letter to *The Times* giving the facts of the case and stating that *he* had never accused anyone, it was entirely the doing of the police and the

[1] Presumably Mr Ruskin did not know about the challenge until John told him after they got home.

people of the hotel who naturally wished to divert suspicions from themselves. The letter appeared on Monday, August 2, 1852.

Although John had never actually accused Foster, he and Effie were never in any doubt as to his guilt. Indeed, Effie had written on July 18 that he could never be whitewashed in the eyes of those who knew all the circumstances, and John wrote to Mr Gray on August 8 that the affair had taught him never to presume on his own impressions of character. Eventually Foster was acquitted and was not even obliged to leave his regiment.

It was not until March of the following year, 1853, that Foster was heard of again, when, on the 4th, Effie recounted to Mr Brown that 'A gentleman named Gibson called on John before breakfast. John said the purpose was evidently to insult him and say disagreeable things. John showed him the narrative which (thanks to your wisdom) he has drawn out. Mr G was quite astonished and said it was perfectly contrary to the statement F. had made to him. John said nevertheless it was true & that he was glad he had at last heard from F. for he had wondered for some time that none of his relations or friends had communicated with him but that now his having given his friend so false a statement looked very ill, and he begged the gentleman would take steps to ascertain the truth of the matter. Mr G, John said, looked perfectly astounded. F. had been filling him with all sorts of calumnies of me—so he said to John that he had never known F. in England & knew none of his family or anything about them. He had served with F. abroad a year & a half but that he begged to retract the message he had brought and said that he would rather be shot thru than act in the affair if he found F's statement to be false. John made him tell him everything F. had to say which shows him to be more wicked than I could have imagined.'

Two days later John himself was writing to Brown to tell him of the sequel to Mr Gibson's visit. According to Gibson, Foster was asserting that John's 'motive in the whole affair was jealousy', but after hearing John's side of the story he 'went away in a very crest-fallen manner'. That same evening, however, a letter came from him which John copied out for Mr Brown:

'I am desired by Mr F. to communicate to you that his sentiments as read to you by me this morning, are still and will continue unchanged. As to the reports on which I spoke so strongly this morning, as Mr Foster is not their originator, he does not wish to assert them

or enter into any discussion respecting them, and is about immediately to join his regiment at Venice. I have therefore to close any
further communication with you on this or any other topic.'

John continued: 'I wrote an instant account of the whole to Mr
Cheney [in London]—who advised me to trouble myself no more
about the matter. But I am not well pleased at the idea of this
rascal proclaiming to his brother officers that he *had not proceeded
in the affair in mercy to Mrs Ruskin's reputation*. Effie was at once so
kind and so prudent in all her intercourse with these Austrian
gentlemen that I did not believe it possible they could allow any
scandalous reports to go abroad respecting *her*, whatever views
they might be disposed to take of *my* conduct.... Effie thinks
Mme Pallavicini must have got some ideas into *her* head from her
countrymen—as she has behaved rudely of late.'[1]

The breach with Mme Pallavicini was evidently lasting because
Effie never mentions her again, whereas she often sent messages to
Mme Nerly, Lady Sorell and Mme Venier in her letters to Rawdon
Brown.

Four months afterwards she had further proof of Foster's mendacity.
She told Mr Brown that Foster was totally unknown to the Fosters
of Stourbridge: 'Lord Glenelg inquired of a gentleman who knew
every branch of the family as well as his own.' Before concluding that
Foster was guilty we must take into consideration one circumstance
which came to light eleven months later. On June 12 1854, Mme Nerly
told Effie in a letter from Venice that a family staying at the 'Restaurant Français' had been robbed of 90 Napoleons. The maitre d'hôtel
had been put in prison but was later released having all along
protested his innocence.

Effie and John both hated their small, ugly, red brick house at
Herne Hill. Mr Snell, according to Effie, had done it up and furnished it as cheaply and vulgarly as possible and put half the money
in his own pocket. If only Mr Ruskin, she complained to Rawdon
Brown, had given *John* the money what things they might have
bought in Venice, especially at Mr Cheney's sale. John was far more
enraged than Effie (she was at least delighted with her 'wee garden'
at the back), and declared he had never before felt ashamed to ask

[1] From an unpublished letter in the possession of Mr Victor Cavendish-
Bentinck.

his friends to visit him and that it was only fit for a clerk to live in. He refused to move into it at first and Effie had to pacify and persuade him. What *she* minded more than the house itself was that at first they had no servants except George and Mary and had to dine every evening at Denmark Hill with the Ruskins; moreover John spent all his days there in his old study, and as they had no carriage she was only 'let in' to London on Wednesdays when the old people lent her theirs. All London, anyway, looked hideous and smoky after Venice she said; it rained half the day and cleared up into a fog the other half.

It would be eight months before Effie was writing to her mother from this same ugly little house: 'These last few days I have been sitting to Millais from immediately after breakfast to dinner, thru all the afternoon till dark.'

There a new chapter in her life begins.

BOOKS CONSULTED

Apart from newspapers, guide-books, directories and other reference books covering the period of Effie's letters, and the Library Edition of the *Works of Ruskin*, the following books have been particularly helpful:

Connell, Brian: *Regina v. Palmerston* (Evans, 1962)
Falk, Bernard: *Old "Q's" Daughter* (Hutchinson, 1937)
Flagg, Edmund: *Venice* (Sampson Low, 1853)
Le Grand Canal (Ongania, Venice, 1887)
The Greville Memoirs
Guest, Ivor: *Fanny Cherito* (Phoenix House, 1950)
Howe, Bea: *Lady with Green Fingers* (Country Life, 1961)
Levinson, André: *Marie Taglioni* (Felix Alcan, Paris, 1929)
Lorenzetti, Giulio: *Venice and its Lagoons* (Rome, 1961)
Maurois, Simone: *Miss Howard and the Emperor* (Collins, 1957)
Payot, Paul: *Au Royaume du Mont-Blanc* (1950)
Pope-Hennessy, James: *Monckton Milnes, The Years of Promise* (Constable, 1949)
Postgate, Raymond: *The Story of a Year, 1848* (Cape, 1955)
Sprigge, Sylvia: *The Lagoon of Venice* (Max Parish, 1961)
Thrupp, G. A.: *The History of Coaches* (Kirby and Endean, 1877)
Thurn and Taxis, Princess Marie of: *Memoirs of a Princess* (Hogarth Press, 1959)
Trevelyan, G. M.: *Manin and the Venetian Revolution of 1848* (Longmans, Green, 1923)
Viljoen, Helen Gill: *Ruskin's Scottish Heritage* (University of Illinois Press, 1956)

LIST OF ILLUSTRATIONS

❧

Frontispiece: Effie Ruskin's letter of December 28, 1851 *Reproduced by courtesy of the Trustees of the Pierpont Morgan Library*

Paulizza's balloon for bombarding Venice *Contemporary Italian engraving*

Effie's first letter after leaving Bowerswell *Reproduced by courtesy of the Trustees of the Pierpont Morgan Library*

PLATES

1. Effie from the portrait in chalks by G. F. Watts, exhibited in the Royal Academy, 1851 *Reproduced by courtesy of the National Trust, Wightwick Manor, Wolverhampton*

2. Effie in 1860 *Marble bust by J. E. Boehm*

3. Effie in 1851 *Drawing by G. F. Watts*

4. First photograph of Effie taken in London by daguerrotype in 1851 *Reproduced by courtesy of Sir Ralph Millais*

5. John Ruskin in 1853, from a drawing by J. E. Millais *Reproduced by courtesy of the Educational Trust Ltd, Ruskin Galleries, Bembridge School*

6. John James Ruskin in 1848, from a painting by George Richmond, given by Mr. Ruskin to his son as a wedding present *Reproduced by courtesy of the Educational Trust Ltd, Ruskin Galleries, Bembridge School*

7. The only known picture of Mrs J. J. Ruskin, from a portrait by James Northcote painted in 1825, now at Brantwood *Reproduced by courtesy of the Educational Trust, Brantwood, Coniston*

8. The Verona-Venice train, carrying a private carriage, crossing the post road at Mestre *Contemporary Italian engraving*

9. The first train arrives in Venice at the new station, in 1846 *Contemporary Italian engraving*

10. Adam and Eve on the corner of the Doge's Palace *daguerrotype from Ruskin's collection, probably taken by his manservant Crawley under Ruskin's supervision*

11. The Danieli Hotel in Effie's time *Lithographed from a drawing by G. Pividor*

12. The hall of the Danieli Hotel, towards the end of the nineteenth century *Contemporary photograph*

13. The Casa Wetzlar in 1851, now the Gritti Palace Hotel *Contemporary engraving*

14. 1848: in St Mark's Square *Contemporary print*

15. The bombardment of Venice in 1849, showing Paulizza's explosive-carrying balloons *Contemporary Italian engraving*

16. The bombardment of Venice in 1849, seen from Mestre *Contemporary Austrian gouache*

17. The Grand Duke Constantine in 1850 *From the Almanach de Gotha, 1850*

18. The Grand Duchess Constantine in 1850 *From the Almanach de Gotha, 1850*

19. The Fenice Theatre during a performance in 1851 *Reproduced from a watercolour by courtesy of Prince Clary Aldringen*

20. The scene of the Emperor's arrival in Venice as described by Effie in February 1852 *Drawn and lithographed by Marco Moro*

21. The Emperor Franz Josef in 1849 *From the Almanach de Gotha, 1850*

22. Field Marshal Radetzky in 1849 *From the Almanach de Gotha, 1850*

INDEX

❧

Acland, Dr Henry and Mrs, 24, 29
Adelaide, Queen, 88
Adelaide, Queen of Sardinia, 226-7, 236
Ainsworth, Miss, 5
Airolo, 332-6
Albert, Archduke, 219-21, 224, 252
Albert, Prince, 61-2, 67, 198
Amazon, S.S., 246-7
Andersen, Hans, 101, 110
Angoulême, Duchesse d', 196, 203, 210-11
Ann (Strachan), Ruskin's nurse, 214, 315
Aosta, 182-3
Arco, Countess d', 305-6
Arsenal, the, 16, 104, 112, 298; murder at, 87-8
Aspre, Count d', 227
Austrian society, 141, 204, 211, 220, 223, 234, 245, 253-4, 294-5, 299
Avonbank School, 4, 5, 17

Balmat, Gideon, 49; daughter, 48
Barbarigo della Terrazza, Palazzo, 134
Barbaro, Palazzo, 237
Barras, Father, 51, 183*n*
Bastian (Mr Brown's gondolier), 217; son, 298
Beatrix d'Este (Infanta), 78*n*, 195-7, 203, 280, 284
Becker, Mr, 135, 144
Bellini, Gentile and Giovanni, 66, 72, 165
Bembo, Cardinal, 54, 113
Bembo, Count and Countess, 113
Beppo (Effie's gondolier), 186 *et passim*; on religion, 218, 230-1
Berchtold, Count and Countess, 142
Berry, Duchesse de, 88, 196, 203, 248, 269-70, 280*n*, 302, 309; Effie visits, 283, 287, 314; daughters, 269, 309; secret marriage, 269*n*
Bersaglio, Venice, 309
Béthune, Comte de, 27, 145, 159-62, 301
Béthune, Comtesse de (*née* Caroline Domecq), 27-8, 145, 159-64, 167, 301; Ruskin's suggested marriage with, 159
Blair Athol, 20-1, 31
Blumenthal, Carlo, 85-6, 89, 93-4, 100, 121, 144, 153-4
Bonneville, 46, 179
Bordeaux, Duc de, *see* Chambord
Borgia, Lucrezia, 54, 113
Borromeo, S. Carlo, 52
Borromeo, Count, 52

Boswell, Jane, 31, 82
Botanical Gardens, Venice, 93, 155
Boulogne, 43, 165-7, 175, 334
Bowerswell, 4, 5, 9, 10, 21, 24, 31, 263, 318*n*; Effie at, 5, 9, 29, 30, 170; Ruskin at, 13-14, 19, 39, 170
Bowerswell Papers, 18*n*, 22*n*, 28*n*, 30*n*, 33, 35*n*, 59*n*, 148*n*, 175, 318*n*, 327*n*
Brown, Horatio, 246
Brown, Rawdon, 89 *et passim*; Ruskins meet, 90-3; his house, 107, 120, 155, 185, 326; in London, 174; ups and downs in relationship with Effie, 224-5, 230, 235, 266, 295, 301; letters to E., 114, 123, 174; gives E. brooch, 155, 320*n*; death, 336*n*
Brown, Rev Walter, 85*n*
Businello, Palazzo, 91*n*, 120, 185
Buzzolla, Antonio, 144*n*
Byron, Lord, 118, 137

Café Français, Venice, 312, 321, 343
Cameron, Col., 299, 300*n*
Campo di Marte, Venice, 135
Carlo (Ruskin's gondolier), 74, 77, 82, 86, 88, 96, 104, 186, 250; brother, 125
Carlos, Don, 55, 78*n*, 86, 273
Cavalchina, *see under* Fenice
Cavalli (Franchetti), Palazzo, 237*n*, 288
Cerito, Fanny, 161
Chabrillan, Comtesse de (*née* Cécile Domecq), 159, 162-3, 167-8
Chambord, Comte de, 55, 144, 196, 203, 248, 280*n*, 290, 294, 338; appearance, 120; Effie visits, 287, 289
Chambord, Comtesse de, 120*n*, 203*n*, 267, 284*n*; her soirées, 289, 301
Chamonix, 14, 16, 32, 35, 38, 46-9, 64, 179-82
Champagnole, 35, 45
Charlemont, Countess of, 169, 171
Charles X, 55, 196*n*, 203, 229
Charles Albert, King of Sardinia, 16, 30, 52, 60, 226-7
Charles, Archduke, 220
Charles Ferdinand, Archduke, 252, 257-8, 284*n*
Charles Louis, Archduke, 298*n*
Cheney, Edward, 108 *et passim*; opinion of Ruskin, 225; his letter about challenge, 331-2; the Ruskins stay with, 170, 173
Chioggia, 106, 283*n*
Chloroform, 126*n*

Cockburn, Lord, 17
Constantine, Grand Duchess; appearance, 215, 221, 232, 238, 248, 253, 273, 285; on Grand Canal, 300; her Christmas, 243-4; stares after Effie, 305; mentioned, 219, 222, 270, 299
Constantine, Grand Duke; appearance, 215, 221, 238, 270, 285; mentioned, 219, 221-2, 232, 237, 244, 248, 268, 282, 299, 300
Cooke, E. W., 222
Correr Museum, 63, 121n, 215n
Couttet, Joseph, 47, 49n, 50-1, 180-1
Couttet, Judith, 48, 181
Crawley, Frederick, 315n
Crossmount, 9, 10n

Danieli, Hotel, 63, 65, 74-5, 78-9, 95, 97, 174, 190n, 193-4, 199; the Ruskins' rooms in, 63, 90n
Danieli, Mme, 150, 153
Danieli, M., 78, 153
Davy, Lady, 59, 71, 80, 169, 303n, 304
Dawkins, Mr and Mrs Clinton, 197-198 et passim; Ruskins dine with, 237-8; give balls, 240-1, 267
Denbigh, Earl of, 302, 330
Denmark Hill, 6 et passim; Ruskin debates whether to settle at, 261-3; inconvenience of, 303
Dent, Miss, 212, 276, 280, 293; talks to Count Wrbna, 290
de Salis, Countess, 171, 182
Dickens, Charles, 172, 273n; Mr Winkle, 146
Dijon, 31, 37, 45
Diller, Baron, 257-8 et passim; fights duel over Effie, 275-6
Doge's Palace, 65, 72-3, 77, 97, 114; Ruskin works at, 69; orders casts of, 240, 250, 292, 296; Effie in gallery of, 239, 266, 295
Domecq, Adèle Clotilde (Baroness Duquesne), 6, 10, 27, 159, 163-6
Domecq girls, 6, 27, 145, 158, 160
Domecq, John Peter, 145, 159
Domecq, Peter, 6, 159
Domenico (valet-de-place), 74, 77, 81, 86, 144, 146
Donizetti, Gaetano, 106, 116
d'Oro, Ca., 72, 121n
Ducal Palace, see Doge's Palace
Due Torri Hotel, 55, 58, 153n, 256, 334
Dufferin, Helen, Lady, 204
Dufferin, Lord, 201, 204-5
Duquesne, Baron, 159, 164, 166, 168
Duquesne, Baroness, see Domecq, Adèle
Eastlake, Sir Charles, 170, 303-4, 316-17, 322
Eastlake, Lady, 170, 246-7
Edinburgh, 10, 17, 29, 31
Elgin, Countess of, 165
Elizabeth, Archduchess, 284
Esterhazy, Countess, 194 et passim; her soirée poudrée, 274, 278-9
Esterhazy, Princess Paul, 257
Examples of Architecture of Venice, 250n, 307-8

Falkenhayn, Count, 209 et passim; Ruskin's open letter to, 331, 335
Farquharson, Mrs James, 9n, 42
Fate Bene Fratelli, 108-10, 125, 138, 237, 336n
Fawkes, Francis, 173, 243
Feilding, Viscount, 302, 321n, 329-330, 337, 340-1
Feilding, Viscountess, 329-30, 337, 340
Fenice Theatre, 86, 99, 122, 150n, 242, 272n; Effie at, 139, 144, 238, 253; Cavalchina at, 136, 139-40, 271, 274, 276, 280; Grand Duchess at, 253; sociability at, 238-9; illuminated, 193, 300
Ferdinand, Archduke, 124, 322
Ferdinand, Don, 273
Ferrari, Count, 152, 156
Festitics, Count, 212 et passim; appearance and character, 223, 294; displeased with Effie, 235-236, 277, 279; last visit to E., 317-18
Flagg, Edmund, 64n, 72n, 139n, 198n, 246, 306n
Florence, 39, 43, 59, 80, 85, 103, 292, 294, 314, 319, 339
Florian's Café, 65n
Folkestone, 14, 23-4, 30, 43, 167
Ford, Clare, 170, 175
Ford, Richard, 169-70, 198, 235n
Foster, Mr, 226, 241, 252, 256, 259, 268, 276, 319; dines with Effie, 272; lunches with E., 313; Ruskin's opinion of, 292, 323n; suspected of theft, 323 et seq.
Franz Josef, Emperor of Austria, 60-1, 105, 150, 186, 190, 193, 197, 209, 244, 280-2, 294-5; appearance, 188-9, 282; in storm, 283; in love, 284
Furnivall, F. G., 23, 175

Gaglignani's Messenger, 200
Gannal, Jean-Nicholas, 282
Gardner, Mrs William, 9, 22
Gavazzi, Allessandro, 220
Geneva, 31, 36, 45-6, 179, 184
George (John Hobbs), 15 et passim; plays violin, 218; wishes to leave, 314-15; copies Ruskin's MS., 315n
German Church, Venice, 147, 198, 224, 229, 237
Gibbs, F. W., 198-200
Gifford, Earl of, 201, 204n
Giordani, G., 293, 296
Giorgione, 66, 72, 74, 212
Giovanelli, Prince, 122-3
Giovanelli, Prince Joseph, 122-3, 309
Giustiniani, Count, 134
Glenelg, Lord, 189, 192, 309, 343
Goitres, 47, 50, 183
Gorzkowski, General, 106n, 204, 215 et passim; compliments Effie, 264; his picture, 322n
Grant, Dr, 11n, 29
Gray, Albert, 155n, 170, 333
Gray, Alice, 32, 46, 69, 76, 79, 163, 216, 303, 325
Gray, Everett, 155n
Gray, George, Senior, 4-7, 83, 130; financial difficulties, 14, 17-21, 26, 29; business better, 104; letters to Mr Ruskin, 26, 33, 67, 288, 296

Gray, George,Junior, 5, 43, 74, 116, 124, 136, 245, 249, 333, 341; ill- feeling with old Ruskins over, 25-6; Ruskin's generosity to, 26; his jealousy, 130, 133; gossips about Effie, 175; sends Bowerswell's letters to E.'s daughter, 175, 318n; in London, 169, 173

Gray, John, 46, 144, 216, 298

Gray, Melville, 46, 54-5, 144

Gray, Robert, 29, 30

Gray, Sophia, 4, 5, 10, 13, 27; birthday, 155; her good sense and discretion, 68, 156, 274; letter to Mr Ruskin, 67; letters to Mrs Ruskin, 19-20, 31

Gray, Sophie, 46, 69, 76, 79, 135, 163, 166, 216, 240, 325

Greek Church, Venice, 95

Grimani della Vida, Ca', 336n

Gritti hotel, 127n, 185

Guerrieri, Count, 235, 252

Hawkins, Capt. and Mrs, 314

Haynau, Field-Marshal, 121n, 208

Herne Hill (No. 28), 4, 5, 159-60, 288, 303

Herne Hill (No. 30), 288-9, 296, 302-3, 311, 314, 327n, 340-1, 343-4

Hertford, Marquess of, 142

Hohenloe, Princess, 194, 197, 280, 305; her dress, 267, 273, 278, 291

Holland House, 215n, 225

Holland, Lady, 215

Holland, Lord, 108n, 225, 244n, 270n, 280n

Holzammer, Lt., 131-2, 135, 144, 148

Hope, James, 8

Howard, Harriet, 141

Imperial Palace, see under Venice

Isabella II, 55, 253n, 280n

Jablonowski, Prince Felix, 298-9

Jablonowska, Princess, 218-19 et passim

Jameson, Andrew, 10, 17, 245; death of wife, 29

Jameson, Eliza, 69, 79, 163

Jameson, Melville, 26, 202; death of wife, 27, 59n

Jephson, Dr, 10

Jewish Cemetery, Lido, 68-9, 290

Joanna (Mr Brown's housekeeper), 123-4, 295, 296n, 336

Jones, Mrs David, 164

Jones Loyd, Sarah (Lady Wantage), 200-1

Juan, Don, 78n, 86, 195, 273n

Keith, Capt., dances polka with Effie, 300

Ker, Charlotte, 40 et passim; praises Ruskin, 76; apparently forgotten by R., 131n; anonymous letter about, 67; never marries, 134n

Ker, Robert, 40, 101

Ker, Mrs Robert, 71, 101

King of the Golden River, The, 5, 131n

Kinnaird, Lord, 142

Kintore, Lord and Lady, 314

Kirkmichael, Dr, 59, 78

Knights of Malta, Hall of, Venice, 269

Kossuth, Louis, 135, 198, 200, 208- 209, 212, 220

Lansdowne, Marquess of, 22, 303-4

Leeching, 109, 111-212, 116, 123-4, 126, 128, 130, 132

Leonardo da Vinci, 54

Leoncini, Piazzetta dei, 126n

Levis, Duchesse de, 301

Lido, 68-9, 92, 143-4, 194, 290, 306; picnic at, 308, 310; bathing at, 317, 326-7

Liechtenstein, Prince, 233

Lockhart, Charlotte, 7, 8, 11, 12, 14, 249

Lockhart, J. G., 11, 12, 14

Loredan, Palazzo, 78n, 86n

Loudon, Jane and daughter, 199, 200

Louis Napoleon, 25, 141, 164, 166, 226, 229

Louis Philippe, 16, 165

Louvre, the, 42n, 165

Lucchesi-Palli, Count, 269

Macdonald, William, 9, 42, 254, 266, 284; wife, 254

Madonna della Salute, 74

Maison, Comte and Comtesse, 159, 161, 165

Malghera, Fort, 39, 63, 97, 132n, 133

Malvern, 174, 206

Manfrini, Palazzo, 134

Manin, Daniele, 16, 39, 70

Manners, Lord and Lady John, 199

Manning, Frederick and Maria, 76, 89

Marianna, the, 283n, 290, 295

Marlay, Brinsley, 199, 200

Marmont, Marshal, 120, 193, 203- 204, 209, 228-9; admires Effie, 212, 254, 288; wounded arm, 234-5, 244, 248, 254; visiting card, 244; death, 282-3; in coffin, 302 ; funeral, 306

Martigny, 49, 50

Mary (Effie's maid), 175 et passim; leaves, 327n

Marzari, Signor, 121-2, 144, 309n

Mather, Erskine, 323, 332

Maximilian, Archduke, 294, 298n

Maywood, Augusta, 116-17, 145, 161

Mazzini, Giuseppi, 220, 270n

Mecklenburg-Schwerin, Prince and Princess of, 79, 80

Melina (Effie's maid), 101-2, 157, 169n, 172, 228, 240, 275

Mendelssohn, Felix, 242

Mestre, 39, 64, 66, 132n

Metternich, Prince, 16, 135n

Meurice Hotel, Paris, 38, 45, 158, 179, 321n, 336

Meyendorff, Baron, 276, 279

Meyendorff, Baroness, 211, 214-15

Michael, Grand Duke, 285, 290-1, 300, 305

Milan, 51-5, 64, 184-5

Military Balls, 126-8, 130-1, 136, 256-259, 269, 272, 274-6

Millais, John Everett, 3, 23, 38, 91n, 155n, 172, 175, 240n, 344

Millais, Mary, 160, 172n

Milman, Dean and Mrs, 189

Minischalchi, Count and Countess, 112-13, 152, 235, 252, 257, 275

Mitford, Mary Russell, 24

Mocenigo, Count, 118*n*, 122; visiting card, 148

Mocenigo, Countess, 98, 117-20; visiting card, 148*n*

Mocenigo, Lurietta, Countess, 98, 118-19, 128, 153, 229, 316; visiting card, 148*n*

Modena, Duke of, 78*n*, 120*n*, 196*n*, 299, 300

Modern Painters, 6, 29, 39, 101, 261

Moneta Patriottica, 70

Mont Blanc, ascent of, 181

Montanvert, 179, 181

Montemolin, Comte de, 55, 78*n*, 86, 155

Montléart, Princesse de, 226-7

Moore, Rev Daniel, 179, 181-2

Morosini, Count, 320

Munro, H. A. J., 263

Murano, 79, 83, 192, 206

Murchison, Sir Roderick, 200

Murray, John, 80, 89

Murray's *Hand-Book for France*, 43-4

Murray's *Hand-Book for Northern Italy*, 51*n*, 64, 73, 78*n*, 89, 134

Murray's *Hand-Book for Switzerland, Savoy and Piedmont*, 45*n*, 50*n*, 183*n*

Nani (cook), 186, 204, 217-18, 239- 241, 313*n*; Effie dissatisfied with, 295-6; menus, 190, 221, 296; son, 217, 241; daughter, 240

Napoleon I, 54*n*, 120, 153*n*, 159, 165*n*, 220*n*, 228*n*, 229*n*, 256, 282*n*; tomb of, 166

Napoleon III, *see* Louis Napoleon

Nerly, Frederigo, 92, 117, 137, 293-4

Nerly, Fritz, 92, 128, 222

Nerly, Mme, 92, 117, 128, 148, 222, 343

Newton, Charles, 179-81, 183-4, 247, 265

Nicholas, Grand Duke, 285, 290-1, 300, 305

Normanby, Marchioness of, 166-7

Normandy, tour of, 25-7, 30

Notes on the Construction of Sheepfolds, 172

Nugent, Count Albert, 224 *et passim*; appearance, 234; wounded, 233*n*; dances polka with Effie, 233

Nugent, Count Laval, 204, 208-9, 233, 291, 313

Offenbach, Jacques, 162

Order of Release, The ; book, 31*n*, 156*n*; picture, 23

Orsini, Countess, 211

Otway, Lady, 53, 55, 101-2

Overstone, Lord, 200

Oxford, 6, 10, 24, 29, 34

Palladio, Andrea, 114, 152, 221

Pallavicini, Count, 204*n*, 212, 227-8, 236, 280-1

Pallavicini, Countess, 204, 208-9 *et passim*; death of aunt, 226-7

Pallavicini, Marchesa, 279

Palmerston, Viscount, 90, 198, 203, 212

Paris, 42-3, 45, 83, 158-68, 175, 179, 319, 334, 336-9

Park Street (No. 31), 23, 25, 28-9, 41, 157, 169-75, 190*n*

Parma, Duke of, 253, 280

Parry, Mr and Mrs Gambier, 205

Paulizza, Lt., 94-5 *et passim*; appearance, character and accomplishments, 97, 105, 110-12, 124, 130, 133, 136, 148, 158; devotion to Effie, 124-5, 133, 143, 149, 151, 158; E. asks favour of, 125; letters to E., 116, 123, 151, 158, 185; offers to put leeches on E., 111-12, 130; says good-bye, 153-5; illness, 158; death, 185, 191, 196, 205-6; mother, 112, 154, 191, 205-6

Peel, Sir Robert, 3rd Bt., 180

Pepé, General, 39, 133*n*

Perth, 4 *et passim*

Piazza di San Marco; band plays in, 65, 73-4, 95, 128, 191, 233; Effie looks on to, 188, 239, 313, 315, 317; E. walks in, 65, 95, 120, 224, 248, 293; Emperor in, 188, 282; English in, 291-2; flooded, 194, 210; Grand Duchess in, 232, 248; illuminated 193; masking in, 269, 271; parade in, 232-3; Ruskins take rooms in, 302, 308, 312; serenade in, 233; mentioned, 16, 39, 72, 174, 211*n*

Pierpont Morgan Library, 318*n*

Pisani, Palazzo, 92, 148

Pividor, Giovanni, 101

Police House, Venice, 86

Postage, 49

Praeterita, 15*n*, 46*n*, 47*n*, 63, 117*n*, 131*n*, 159-60, 321*n*, 322*n*, 336*n*

Pritchard, Mr and Mrs John, 170, 179, 181-2

Prosdocimo, Padre, 109-11, 113-14, 116-117, 123, 125-6, 128, 130, 150

Prout, Samuel, 297

Purvis, Dr, 74-5

Quadri's café, 65*n*, 312

Rachel, 192, 214

Radetzky, Countess, 61, 245, 257, 275

Radetzky, Field-Marshal, 52-3 *et passim*; Effie sees, 56, 155, 233; E. hopes to meet, 92-3, 98, 150, 158, 164; E. meets, 257-8, 275; admires E., 264, 268; courtesy to E., 281; sends E. his picture, 318; his balls at Verona, 256-9, 268, 274-6

Reischach, Baron, 209 *et passim*; admires Effie, 272, 289; as Knight of Malta, 223-4

Reuss, Prince of, 273, 279

Richardson, Jessie, 4, 83*n*; daughter, 10

Richardson, Mary (Miss Bolding), 13, 31-2, 254*n*

Richardson, Dr, 29, 32, 83*n*

Richmond, George, 28, 172

Richmond, Thomas, 28, 172, 199*n*

Rossim, G. A., 238

Roys, Comtesse des (*née* Elise Domecq), 159-62, 166

Rumhor, Baron, 92*n*, 293

Ruskin, Euphemia Chalmers (1828- 1897); appearance, 22-3, 76-7, 111, 135-6, 200, 220, 225, 240, 264, 275*n*, 278*n*, 303; character and manners, 5, 33, 35, 67-8, 71, 99, 149, 175, 221; destroys mother's letters, 73, 213, 251, 303; dances, 5, 23, 124, 131, 134-136, 138, 233, 237*n*, 241, 267, 272, 275-

6, 300; entertains, 172, 222, 272; gossiped about, 31, 42, 175, 251; learns and speaks languages, 6, 58, 68, 71, 85, 94-5, 101, 110, 128, 221, 255; at opera, 52, 85, 106, 116-17, 144, 150, 161, 238-9; plays chess, 82-3, 106, 124, and piano, 5, 73, 189, 191, 242-3; presentation at Court, 80, 169, 172, 267n; rows gondola, 76, 224; tries to keep warm, 58, 64, 73, 76, 83, 87, 96, 100

Effie Ruskin's relationships:
with John Ruskin, 8, 9, 13-15, 17, 19-21, 30-9, 60, 99, 149, 156, 251, 264, 296-7; letters to, 15-16; love for and happiness with, 22, 149, 156; praises, 58, 76, 149; reads to, 255; secrecy on leaving, 149n; understands perfectly, 99; walks with, 48-9, 58, 65, 171, 248, 334-5; wants children, 32, 170
with John's parents, 10-13, 19, 22, 24, 26, 28-9, 41, 67, 99, 174, 213, 249, 296-7; comments on, 7-9, 26, 41, 156, 202, 213, 249-51, 263-6, 296-8, 303, 305, 341; letters to Mr Ruskin, 74, 131, 254n;
with own family, 33, 67, 202, 214; letters to father, 20-1, 26, 45-6, 51, 83, 104, 203, 249, 303; letters to George, 46, 50, 68, 109, 140, 152, 182, 190, 203, 291
Letters to Rawdon Brown, 115, 123n, 136n, 163n, 169-71, 173, 334-6, 340-2

Ruskin Galleries, The, 10n, 19, 44n, 176

Ruskin, John (1819-1900); appearance, 23, 284-5, 316; buys antiques, 317, and bonnet, 42; defence at time of annulment, 3, 15, 19, 20-1, 34n; dislikes babies, 171, 254; extravagance, 249-51, 296-7; has no friends, 266; health, 6, 10, 21, 24-5, 32, 59n, 213, 246, 265, 274; looks for houses in Venice, 68, 76, 78; miserable in society, 14-15, 22, 39, 85, 146, 171, 173, 222n, 229, 238, 255, 260; at opera, 52, 75, 117, 150, 161; partial to pretty French girls, 228; plays ball, 84; pleased and amused, 46, 54, 136, 140, 143-4, 146-7, 310, 333, 335; rails against society, 146, 266, 335; on religion, 217n, 243, 307, 340; spoils servants, 187, 315; sufferings in love, 4, 6, 10; takes daguerrotypes, 146; unworldliness, 60, 136n, 229, 236; at work, 8, 54, 58, 69, 72, 75, 77, 85-86, 99, 103, 145-6, 150, 173, 190-2, 242-3, 245, 260, 317-18
his relationships:
with Effie; admires and takes pride in, 22, 128, 134, 149, 150, 166n, 240, 254, 261, 275n, 278n; angry with, 296; criticises, 34, 35-7, 251, 262; devoid of jealousy, 75; fears for her happiness, 13-14, 288, 311; glad she should amuse herself, 58-60, 71, 74-75, 85, 92, 99, 134; kindness to, 58-9, 76, 99, 134, 149, 164n, 264; love for and happiness with, 6, 7, 14, 16-17, 22, 30, 32, 134, 156, 171, 249, 262; letters to, 9, 14-16, 24-5, 30-2, 35-8, 39, 75n, 94n; refuses to consult, 264; requires wife to take care of herself, 99, 133; satisfied with her conduct, 134, 251, 343
with his parents, 6, 7, 10-13, 175, 202, 213, 250-1, 262, 264, 305, 341; letters to father, 10, 44, 63, 66, 145-6, 147n, 176, 183n, 184n, 186n, 187, 190, 197, 199n, 202n, 209n, 212n, 213, 216-17, 217n, 221,

222n, 225, 237n, 251, 259n, 260n, 261-2, 263n, 265n, 272n, 273n, 275n, 278n, 283n, 285n, 287-8, 293, 307n, 308n, 310-12, 318-19, 320n, 325n, 332, 340
Letters to Mr Gray, 17, 22, 28, 33-4, 191, 342; to Mrs Gray, 10, 13-14, 22, 59n, 171

Ruskin, John James (1785-1864), 4 *et passim*; account books, 25n, 27n, 169n, 174n, 288n; health, 24, 41, 87, 156; looks for houses, 261, 264; pride, 6, 14, 22, 174, 250, 288-9, 341; letters to John, 10-13, 39, 44, 65n, 74n, 80, 80n, 87, 87n, 131n, 139n, 145, 159, 176, 186-7, 190n, 200n, 213, 235n, 245n, 247n, 259n, 263, 265, 273n, 274, 275n, 287, 303n, 315n, 333; criticises Effie, 10, 11, 19, 33, 65n, 67, 174, 187, 202, 249, 263, 275n, 289, 296; disappointed in E., 32-3, 249; praises E., 27-8, 169, 174; gives presents to E., 27, 169n, 174, 341; letter to E., 71; letters to Mr Gray, 7, 17-19, 26-8, 30, 32-3, 67, 169, 249, 288-9, 341; to Mrs Gray, 67-8, 327

Ruskin, John Thomas, 4, 9

Ruskin, Margaret (1781-1871), 4 *et passim*; hatred of Perth, 7, 9, 19; diet sheet, 213; fusses over John, 24-5, 265n; letters to J., 13, 14, 265-266; praises Effie, 8, 13; refuses to live with E., 262; scolds E., 28; Newton's opinion of, 265

Rutherford, Grace, 99, 102, 128

Ruthven, Lady, 165, 192

S. Ambrogio, 54
S. Arianna, island of, 206
S. Benedetto Theatre, 86n, 150, 192n
S. Clemente, island of, 209
St Giorgio Maggiore, 89, 106, 114, 115n
SS. Giovanni e Paolo, 122
S. Giuliano, Fort, 93n, 132-3, 136
S. Lazzaro, island of, 137
S. Marco, *see* St Mark's
S. Martin, 74
S. Michele, cemetery of, 309, 336n
S. Rocco, Scuola di, 73
S. Servolo, island of, 108, 110n, 125, 336
St Bernard, Hospice of Grand, 52n, 182-4
St Leon, Arthur, 161
St Mark's Church, 65, 313; Ruskin works in, 77, 150; Effie in, 84-5, 95, 97, 104, 106, 150-1, 230, 236-7; Emperor in, 188; cleaner, 186, 210; illuminated, 102
St Mark's Library, 91, 93, 307
St Mark's Square, *see* Piazza
St Martin, 46-7, 180
Salisbury, 24-5, 34, 203n
Salute, *see* Madonna della
Samoilow, Countess, 56-7
Scaligeri family, 55, 58
Schwarzenberg, Prince Charles, 226, 227n
Schwarzenberg, Prince Felix, 292, 294
Scott, Dr, 59
Scott, Sir Francis, 201
Scott, Sir Walter, 7, 12, 234n
Selvatico, Marchese, 139, 141

Seven Lamps of Architecture, The, 24, 28-9, 71, 77, 85*n*, 86, 87*n*, 186

Severn, Mrs Arthur (Joan Agnew), 247*n*, 294

Simplon Pass, 46, 49, 51, 183*n*

Simpson, Dr (Sir James), 31, 32, 38-9, 59, 64, 109, 170, 330

Sismondi, J. C. L., 38

Smith, Albert, 181-2

Snell, Mr, 288, 343

Soeur Alphonse, 330, 337-8

Sophie, Archduchess, 61, 294, 298, 300

Sorell, Lady, 189, 192 *et passim*

Soult, Marshal, 228-9

Sternberg, General, 257-8, 279, 292

Stewart, Sir Houston, 174

Stones of Venice, The, 75, 85, 86*n*, 89*n*, 115*n*, 173, 176, 192*n*, 246, 256*n*, 261; advertised, 85; published, 172; not selling, 250; Index to, 72*n*, 73*n*, 115*n*

Strachan, Sir Richard and Lady, 142*n*

Strasbourg, 308*n*, 319, 330, 333, 337-9

Strozzi, Marchesa, 227, 291, 299

Strzelecki, Count, 200-1

Stuart, Lady, of Wortley, 175, 318*n*

Stuart Wortley, Hon. Clare, 32*n*, 82*n*, 172*n*

Taglioni, Marie, 46, 72, 117, 120-1, 128, 131, 138-9, 141, 144-5, 155, 268; son, 120, 128, 144-5; daughter, 120, 139, 144, 158*n*

Thalberg, Sigismund, 117, 127

Thackeray, W. M., 145, 172

Thomson, Joanna, 5

Thun, Count, 219 *et passim*; challenges Ruskin to duel, 331; subsequent career, 335*n*

Tiepolo, G. B., 237*n*

Times, The, 76*n*, 88, 89*n*, 235*n*; Ruskin's letters to, 284, 342

Tintoretto, 72-3, 316; Ruskin buys, 293-4, 297; R. wants to buy for nation, 303, 316*n*, 322*n*

Titian, 66

Torcello, 146-7

Trapani, Count and Countess, 253

Trieste, Marine College at, 235-6, 277*n*

Troubetzkoi, Prince, 120-1 *et passim*; makes love to Effie, 137; calls on E. in London, 157-8; marriage, 139*n*; subsequent career, 158*n*; bad character, 204

Turner, J. M. W., 8, 88, 105, 139, 169, 173, 211*n*, 247, 251, 263; Ruskin becomes his executor, 242; leaves R. nothing, 297

Tuscany, Grand Duke of, 214, 253

Ürmenyi, Baron, 131, 135-6, 139

Valentine, Mr, 71, 83, 85-6, 89

Vendramin Calergi, Palazzo, 88*n*

Venetian life and people, 66, 69, 70, 74-5, 81-2, 89, 96, 100, 102, 122, 140-1, 218, 293, 307

Venice, 14 *et passim*; Effie asks to be taken to, 39, 85*n*; E.'s love for, 170, 173, 310, 333, 336; at night, 218; birds in, 268; wells in, 245-6; railway bridge, 63-4, 66, 93, 255; Imperial Palace, 215, 232-3, 269-70, 281; Patriarchs, 84-5, 210

Venier, Countess, 320-1, 343

Verona, 16 *et passim*; Ruskins at, 55-62, 152-7, 185-6, 252, 255-60, 274-6, 318-19, 331-2

Veronese, Paul, 72, 293

Vevey, 32, 102, 182, 184

Vicenza, 66, 145, 152, 212, 221, 223, 228, 235, 277, 318

Victor Emmanuel II, 30, 227*n*

Victoria, Queen, 61-2, 169

Wales, Prince of, 67, 182, 198, 199*n*

Walpole, Lady, 339

Warburton, Mr and Mrs Eliot, 246

Watts, G. F., 172, 191

Watts Russell, Michael, 205, 209, 217, 307; children, 217, 230, 293

Wayancoff, Mlle, 268-70, 285, 300- 301, 305

Wellington, Duke of, 8, 164*n*, 189*n*, 193

Wellington, 2nd Duke of, 235*n*

Westminster, Marchioness of, 157, 169, 204*n*

Wetzlar, Baroness, 117*n*, 127 *et passim*; gives balls, 138-9, 299-300

Wetzlar, Casa, 126, 127*n*; Ruskins take rooms in, 174; description of rooms, 185, 188, 193, 207-8; fire-grate in, 186, 216-17, 223; kitchen of, 217-18; party in kitchen, 241

Whewell, Dr, 173

Wimpffen, Count Alphonse, 57-8, 60-2, 71, 91-2, 95-6, 104, 107, 137, 152, 156-7

Wimpffen, Count Emile, 137, 156-7

Wimpffen, Count François, 57*n*, 58, 60, 96, 98, 125, 209, 283, 298

Wimpffen, Count Victor, 57-8, 60

Wimpffen, Countess, 58, 95-6, 98, 189

Wladimir, Russian steamer, 222, 231-232, 300

Wrbna, Count, 219 *et passim*; appearance, 228, 233, 258; buys glass from Effie, 243; offended by E., 267-8, 270, 277, 279, 285-6, 290

Zichy, Countess, 135, 138

Zöe (Effie's dog), 321*n*, 341